高 橋 和 希

PROCRASTINATION...IS THERE SOMETHING I CAN DO
ABOUT IT? I PLAY AS MUCH AS TIME PERMITS. I
SLEEP. I GO OUT DRINKING. I EAT. THEN SLEEP
AGAIN. AND WHEN IT GETS TO THE LAST MINUTE, I
THINK "WHY DIDN'T I START WORKING SOONER? WHY
DIDN'T I THINK OF IDEAS?" BUT WHEN I SOMEHOW
MANAGE TO FINISH MY WORK, I DO THE SAME THING
OVER AND OVER AGAIN. DEADLINES ARE WONDERFUL!
-KAZUKI TAKAHASHI, 2001

Artist/author Kazuki Takahashi first tried to break into
the manga business in 1982, but success eluded him
until **Yu-Gi-Oh!** debuted in the Japanese **Weekly
Shonen Jump** magazine in 1996. **Yu-Gi-Oh!**'s themes
of friendship and fighting, together with Takahashi's
weird and wonderful art, soon became enormously
successful, spawning a real-world card game, video
games, and two anime series. A lifelong gamer,
Takahashi enjoys Shogi (Japanese chess), Mahjong,
card games, and tabletop RPGs, among other games.

YU-GI-OH!: DUELIST VOL. 20
The SHONEN JUMP Manga Edition

STORY AND ART BY
KAZUKI TAKAHASHI

Translation & English Adaptation/Joe Yamazaki
Touch-up Art & Lettering/Eric Erbes
Design/Andrea Rice
Editor/Jason Thompson

Managing Editor/Frances E. Wall
Editorial Director/Elizabeth Kawasaki
Vice President & Editor in Chief/Yumi Hoashi
Sr. Director of Acquisitions/Rika Inouye
Sr. VP of Marketing/Liza Coppola
Exec. VP of Sales & Marketing/John Easum
Publisher/Hyoe Narita

In the original Japanese edition, YU-GI-OH!, YU-GI-OH!: DUELIST and YU-GI-OH!: MILLENNIUM WORLD are known collectively as YU-GI-OH!. The English YU-GI-OH!: DUELIST was originally volumes 8-31 of the Japanese YU-GI-OH!.

Printed in the U.S.A.

Published by VIZ Media, LLC
P.O. Box 77010
San Francisco, CA 94107

SHONEN JUMP Manga Edition
10 9 8 7 6 5 4 3 2 1
First printing, April 2007

www.viz.com

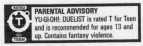

PARENTAL ADVISORY
YU-GI-OH!: DUELIST is rated T for Teen and is recommended for ages 13 and up. Contains fantasy violence.

THE WORLD'S MOST POPULAR MANGA

www.shonenjump.com

SHONEN JUMP MANGA

Vol. 20

EVIL VS. EVIL

STORY AND ART BY
KAZUKI TAKAHASHI

THE STORY SO FAR...

YUGI MUTOU/ YU-GI-OH

When 10th grader Yugi solved the Millennium Puzzle, another spirit took up residence in his body...Yu-Gi-Oh, the King of Games, a dark avenger who challenges evildoers to "Shadow Games" of life and death!

YUGI FACES DEADLY ENEMIES!

Using his gaming skills, Yugi fights ruthless adversaries like Maximillion Pegasus, multimillionaire creator of the collectible card game "Duel Monsters," and Ryo Bakura, whose friendly personality turns evil when he is possessed by the spirit of the Millennium Ring. But Yugi's greatest rival is Seto Kaiba, the world's second-greatest gamer—and the ruthless teenage president of Kaiba Corporation. At first, Kaiba and Yugi are bitter enemies, but after fighting against a common adversary—Pegasus—they come to respect one another. But for all his powers, there is one thing Yu-Gi-Oh cannot do: remember who he is and where he came from.

HIROTO HONDA

ANZU MAZAKI

KATSUYA JONOUCHI

MARIK

ISHIZU ISHTAR

SETO KAIBA

THE TABLET OF THE PHARAOH'S MEMORIES

Then one day, when an Egyptian museum exhibit comes to Japan, Yugi sees an ancient carving of himself as an Egyptian pharaoh! The curator of the exhibit, Ishizu Ishtar, explains that there are seven Millennium Items, which were made to fit into a stone tablet in a hidden shrine in Egypt. According to the legend, when the seven Items are brought together, the pharaoh will regain his memories of his past life.

THE EGYPTIAN GOD CARDS

But Ishizu has a message for Kaiba as well. Ishizu needs Kaiba's help to win back two of three Egyptian God Cards—the rarest cards on Earth—from the clutches of the "Rare Hunters," a criminal syndicate led by the evil Marik, Ishizu's brother. In order to draw out the thieves, Kaiba announces "Battle City," an enormous "Duel Monsters" tournament. As the tournament rages, Yugi, Kaiba and Marik struggle for possession of the God Cards, ending up with one apiece. The other surviving semi-finalist is Yugi's friend Jonouchi. But now the stakes are higher, because the bloodshed has awakened Marik's split personality, a megalomaniacal sadist who sends his opponents to horrible deaths. And although Bakura lost in the last round, he's still scheming to get back into the game...

Yu-Gi-Oh! Duelist

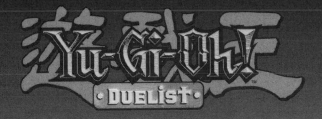

Vol. 20

CONTENTS

DUEL 174: DUEL IN THE DARK!

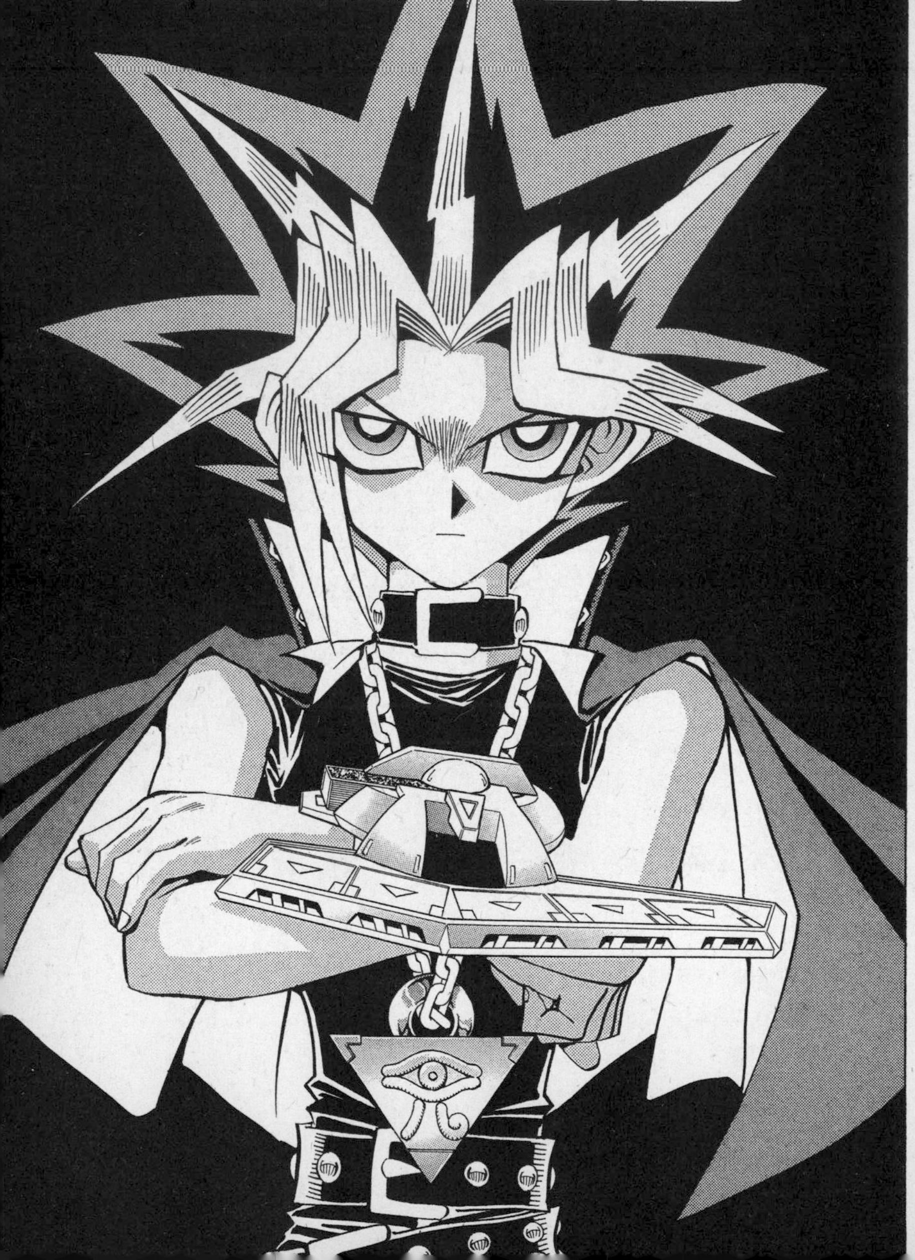

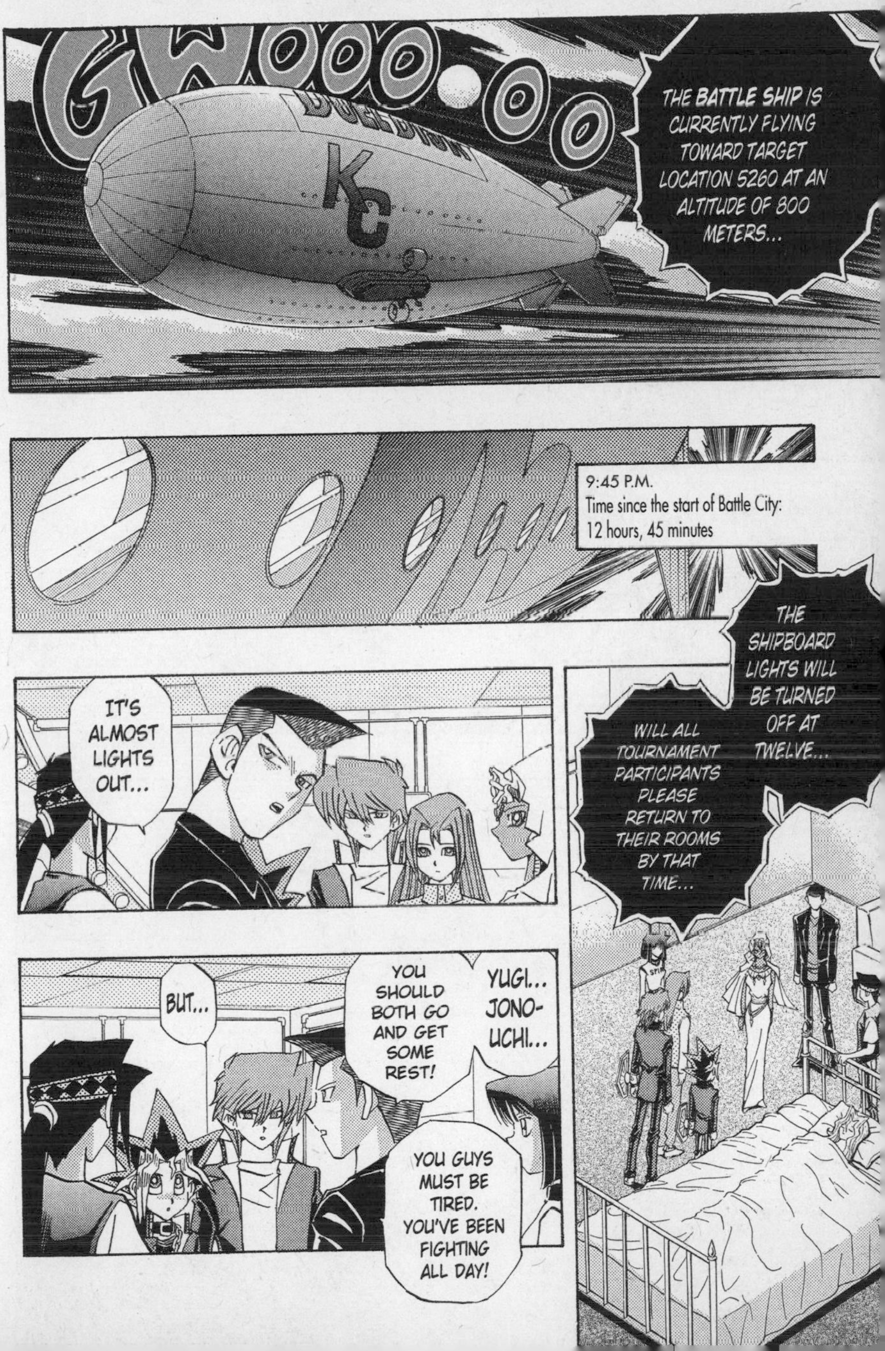
GWOOO...OO
THE BATTLE SHIP IS CURRENTLY FLYING TOWARD TARGET LOCATION 5260 AT AN ALTITUDE OF 800 METERS...
9:45 P.M.
Time since the start of Battle City:
12 hours, 45 minutes
THE SHIPBOARD LIGHTS WILL BE TURNED OFF AT TWELVE...
WILL ALL TOURNAMENT PARTICIPANTS PLEASE RETURN TO THEIR ROOMS BY THAT TIME...
IT'S ALMOST LIGHTS OUT...
YUGI... JONO-UCHI...
YOU SHOULD BOTH GO AND GET SOME REST!
BUT...
YOU GUYS MUST BE TIRED. YOU'VE BEEN FIGHTING ALL DAY!

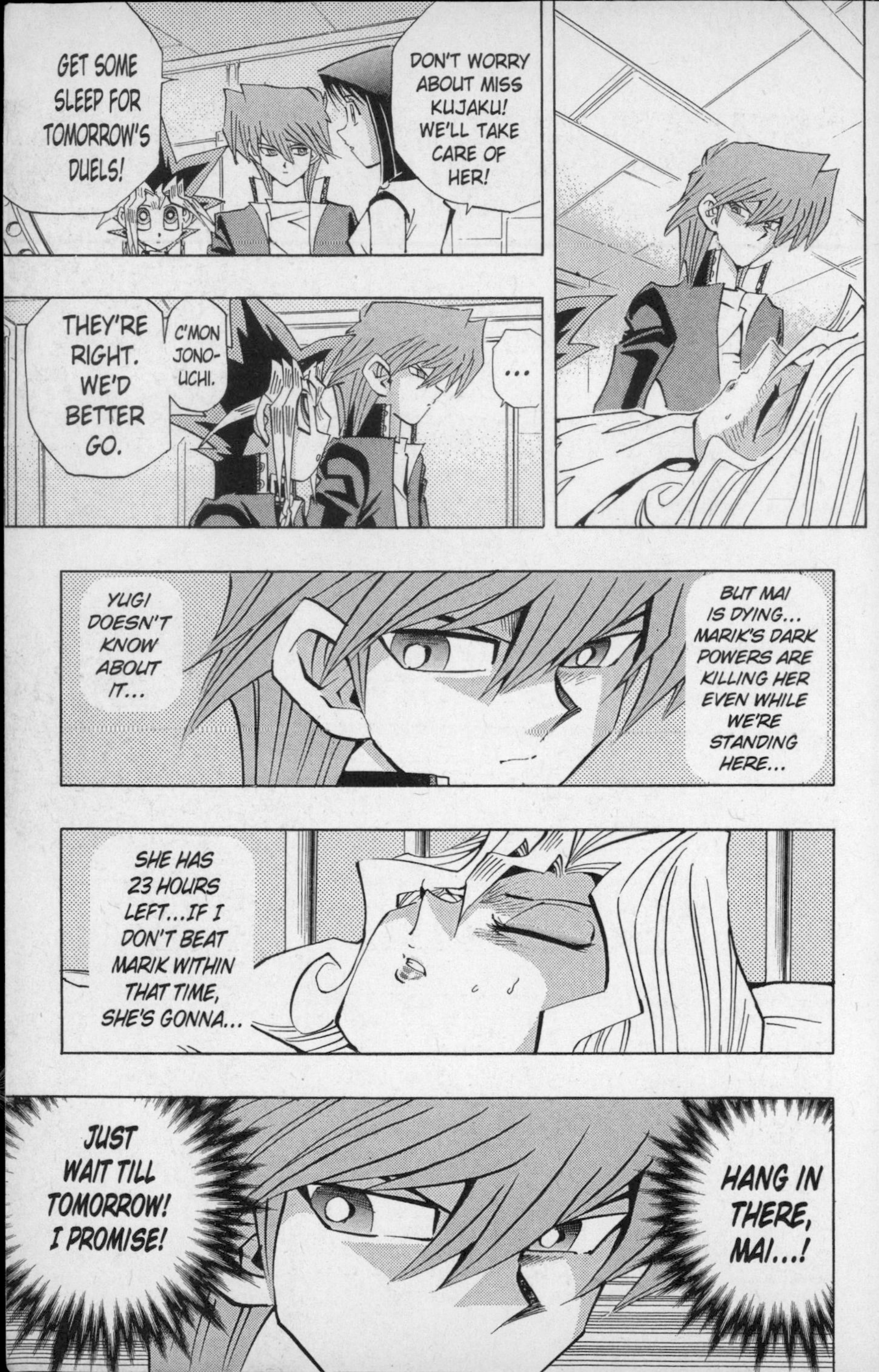
DON'T WORRY ABOUT MISS KUJAKU! WE'LL TAKE CARE OF HER!
GET SOME SLEEP FOR TOMORROW'S DUELS!
...
C'MON JONOUCHI.
THEY'RE RIGHT. WE'D BETTER GO.
BUT MAI IS DYING... MARIK'S DARK POWERS ARE KILLING HER EVEN WHILE WE'RE STANDING HERE...
YUGI DOESN'T KNOW ABOUT IT...
SHE HAS 23 HOURS LEFT...IF I DON'T BEAT MARIK WITHIN THAT TIME, SHE'S GONNA...
HANG IN THERE, MAI...!
JUST WAIT TILL TOMORROW! I PROMISE!

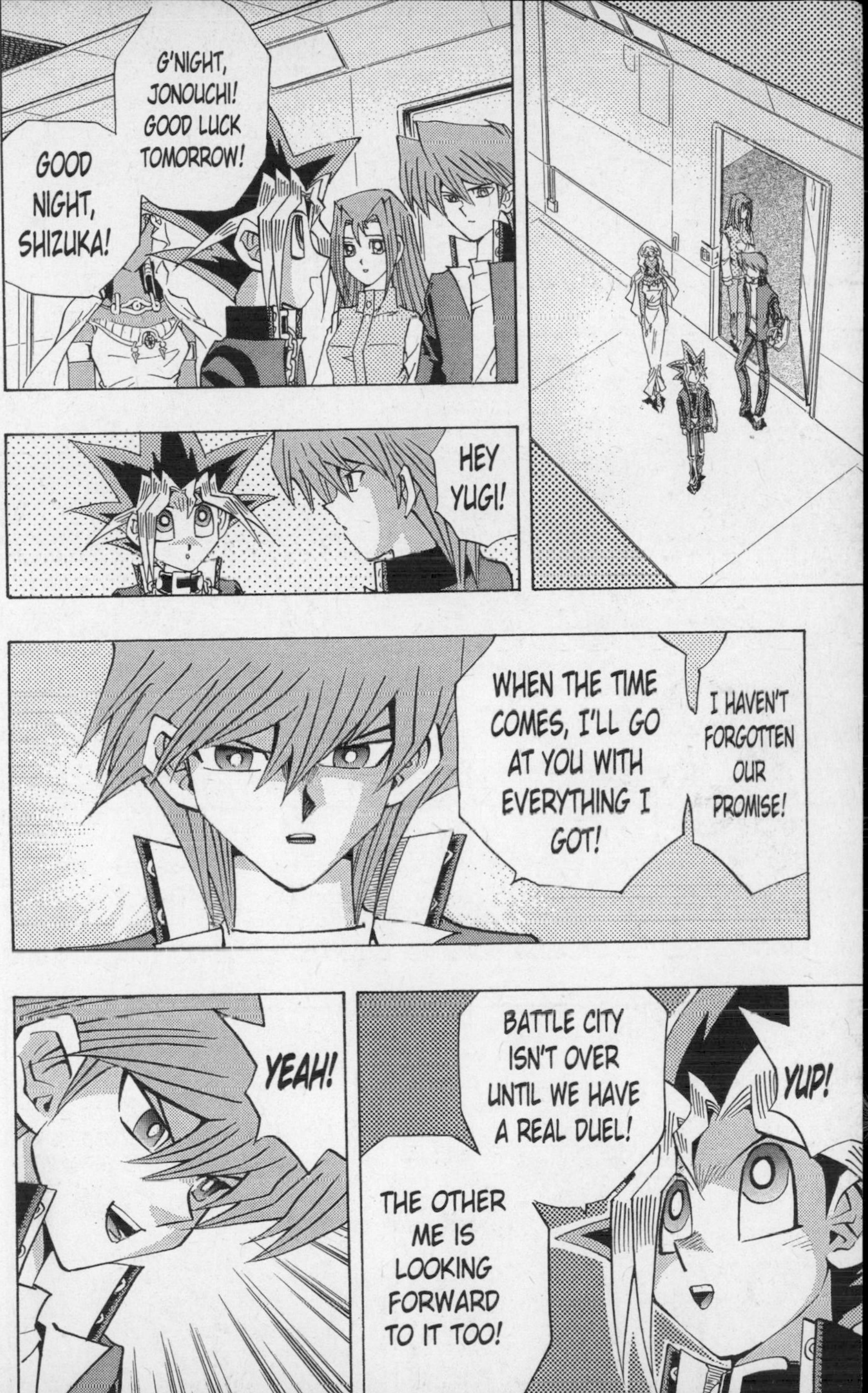

G'NIGHT, JONOUCHI! GOOD LUCK TOMORROW!
GOOD NIGHT, SHIZUKA!
HEY YUGI!
I HAVEN'T FORGOTTEN OUR PROMISE!
WHEN THE TIME COMES, I'LL GO AT YOU WITH EVERYTHING I GOT!
YUP!
BATTLE CITY ISN'T OVER UNTIL WE HAVE A REAL DUEL!
THE OTHER ME IS LOOKING FORWARD TO IT TOO!
YEAH!

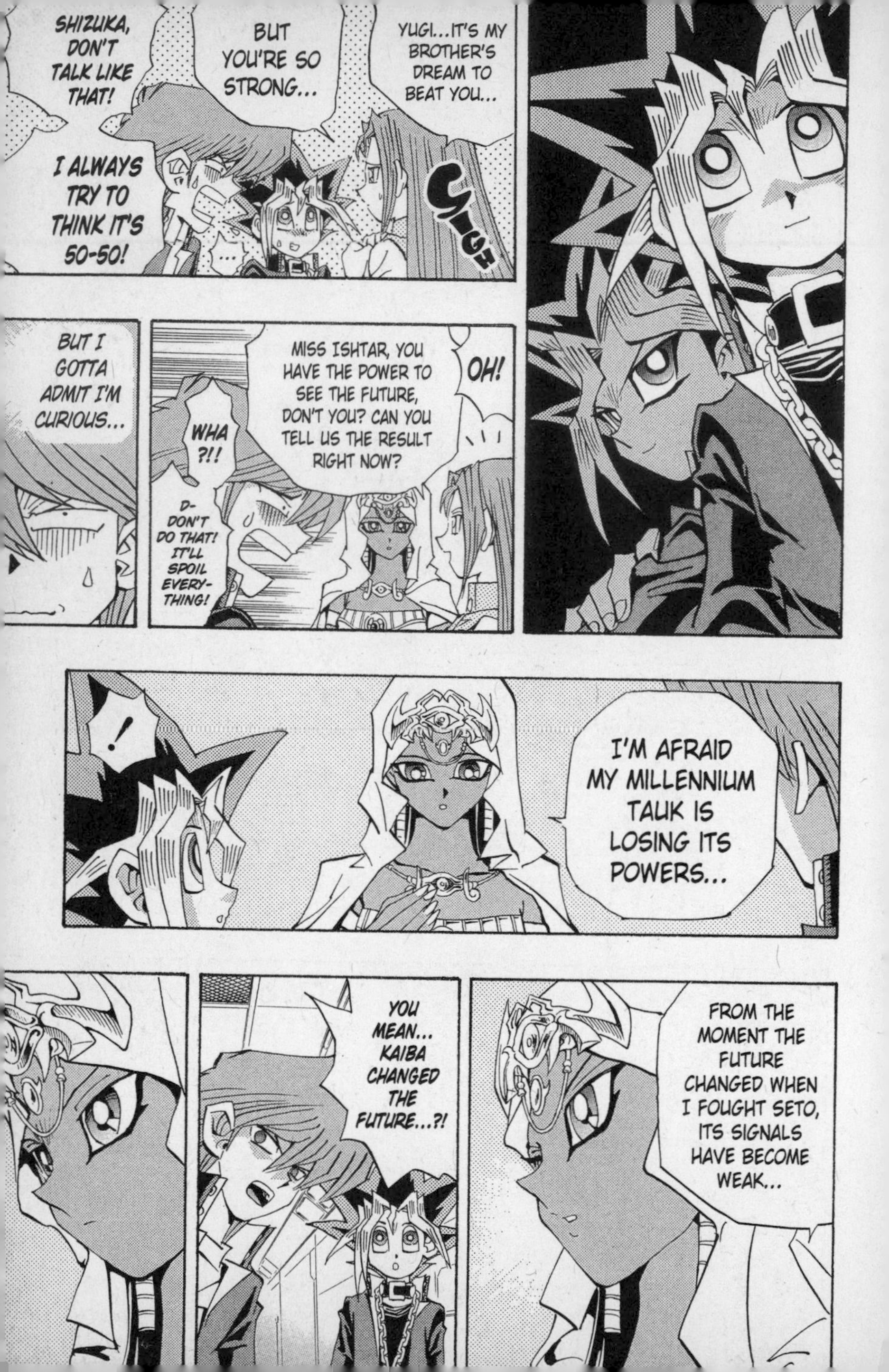
YUGI...IT'S MY BROTHER'S DREAM TO BEAT YOU...
SIGH
BUT YOU'RE SO STRONG...
SHIZUKA, DON'T TALK LIKE THAT!
I ALWAYS TRY TO THINK IT'S 50-50!
...
OH!
MISS ISHTAR, YOU HAVE THE POWER TO SEE THE FUTURE, DON'T YOU? CAN YOU TELL US THE RESULT RIGHT NOW?
WHA?!!
D-DON'T DO THAT! IT'LL SPOIL EVERYTHING!
BUT I GOTTA ADMIT I'M CURIOUS...
I'M AFRAID MY MILLENNIUM TAUK IS LOSING ITS POWERS...
!
FROM THE MOMENT THE FUTURE CHANGED WHEN I FOUGHT SETO, ITS SIGNALS HAVE BECOME WEAK...
YOU MEAN... KAIBA CHANGED THE FUTURE...?!

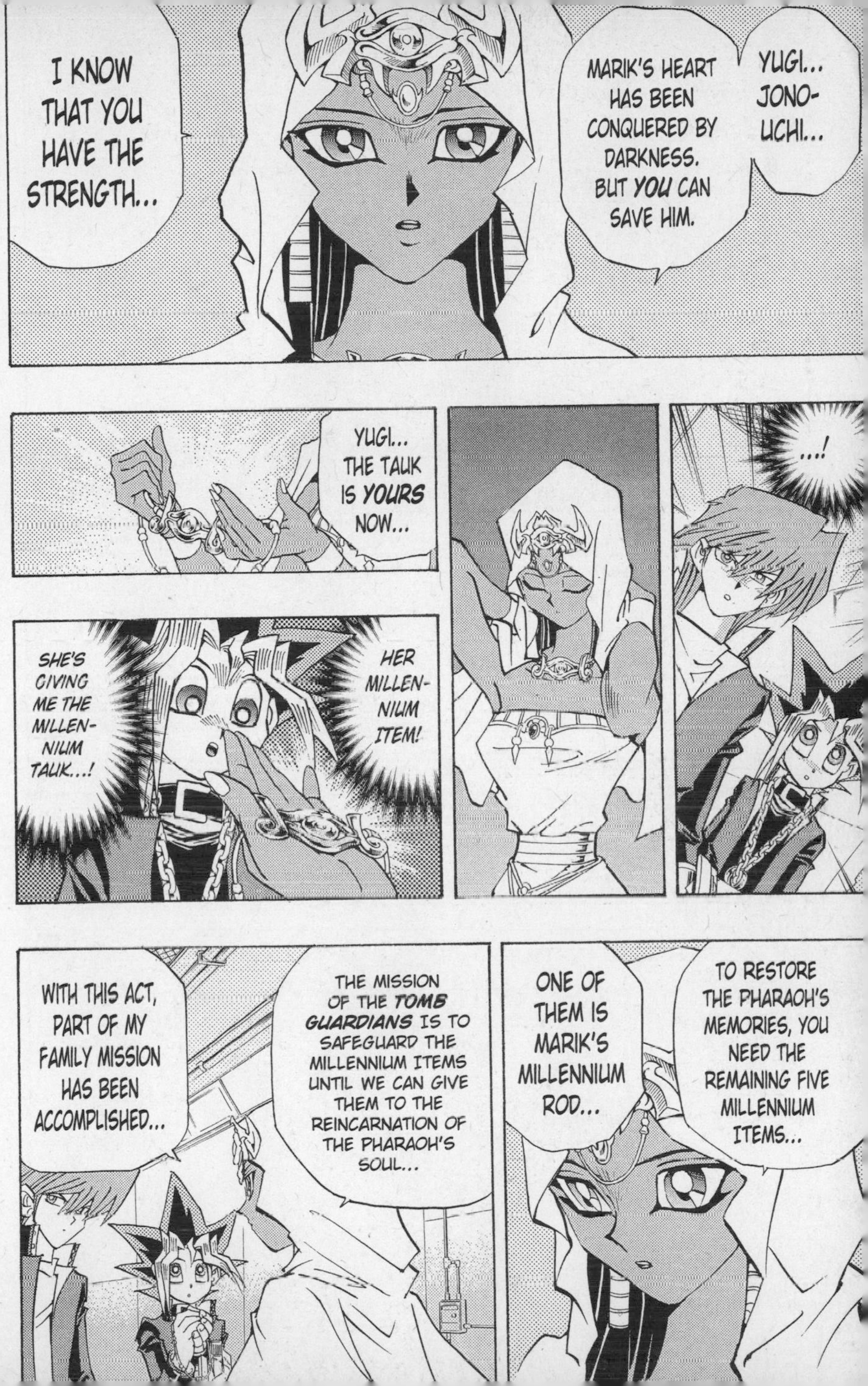
YUGI... JONO-UCHI...
MARIK'S HEART HAS BEEN CONQUERED BY DARKNESS. BUT *YOU* CAN SAVE HIM.
I KNOW THAT YOU HAVE THE STRENGTH...
...!
YUGI... THE TAUK IS *YOURS* NOW...
HER MILLENNIUM ITEM!
SHE'S GIVING ME THE MILLENNIUM TAUK...!
TO RESTORE THE PHARAOH'S MEMORIES, YOU NEED THE REMAINING FIVE MILLENNIUM ITEMS...
ONE OF THEM IS MARIK'S MILLENNIUM ROD...
THE MISSION OF THE ***TOMB GUARDIANS*** IS TO SAFEGUARD THE MILLENNIUM ITEMS UNTIL WE CAN GIVE THEM TO THE REINCARNATION OF THE PHARAOH'S SOUL...
WITH THIS ACT, PART OF MY FAMILY MISSION HAS BEEN ACCOMPLISHED...

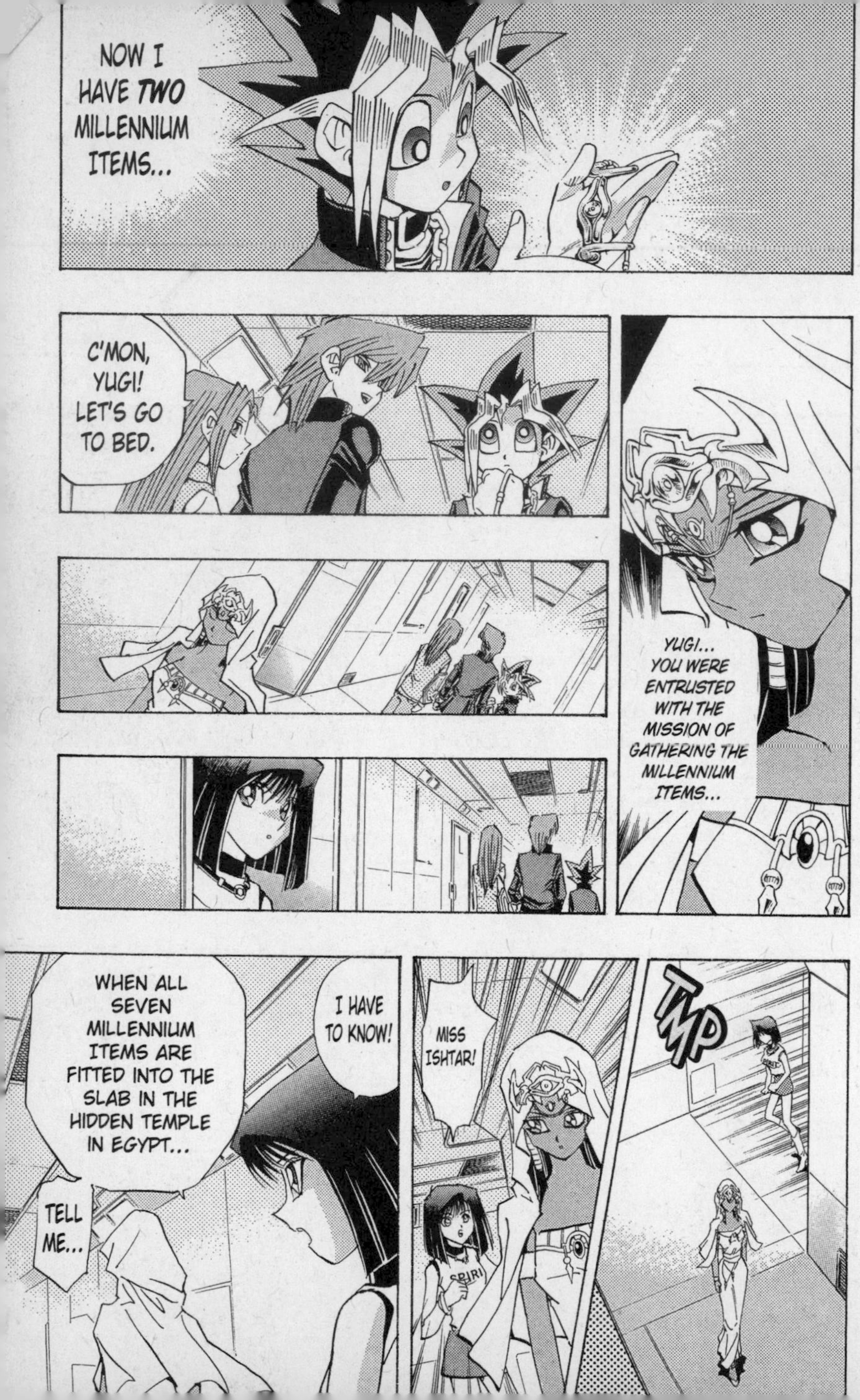
NOW I HAVE *TWO* MILLENNIUM ITEMS...
YUGI... YOU WERE ENTRUSTED WITH THE MISSION OF GATHERING THE MILLENNIUM ITEMS...
C'MON, YUGI! LET'S GO TO BED.
TMP
MISS ISHTAR!
I HAVE TO KNOW!
WHEN ALL SEVEN MILLENNIUM ITEMS ARE FITTED INTO THE SLAB IN THE HIDDEN TEMPLE IN EGYPT...
TELL ME...

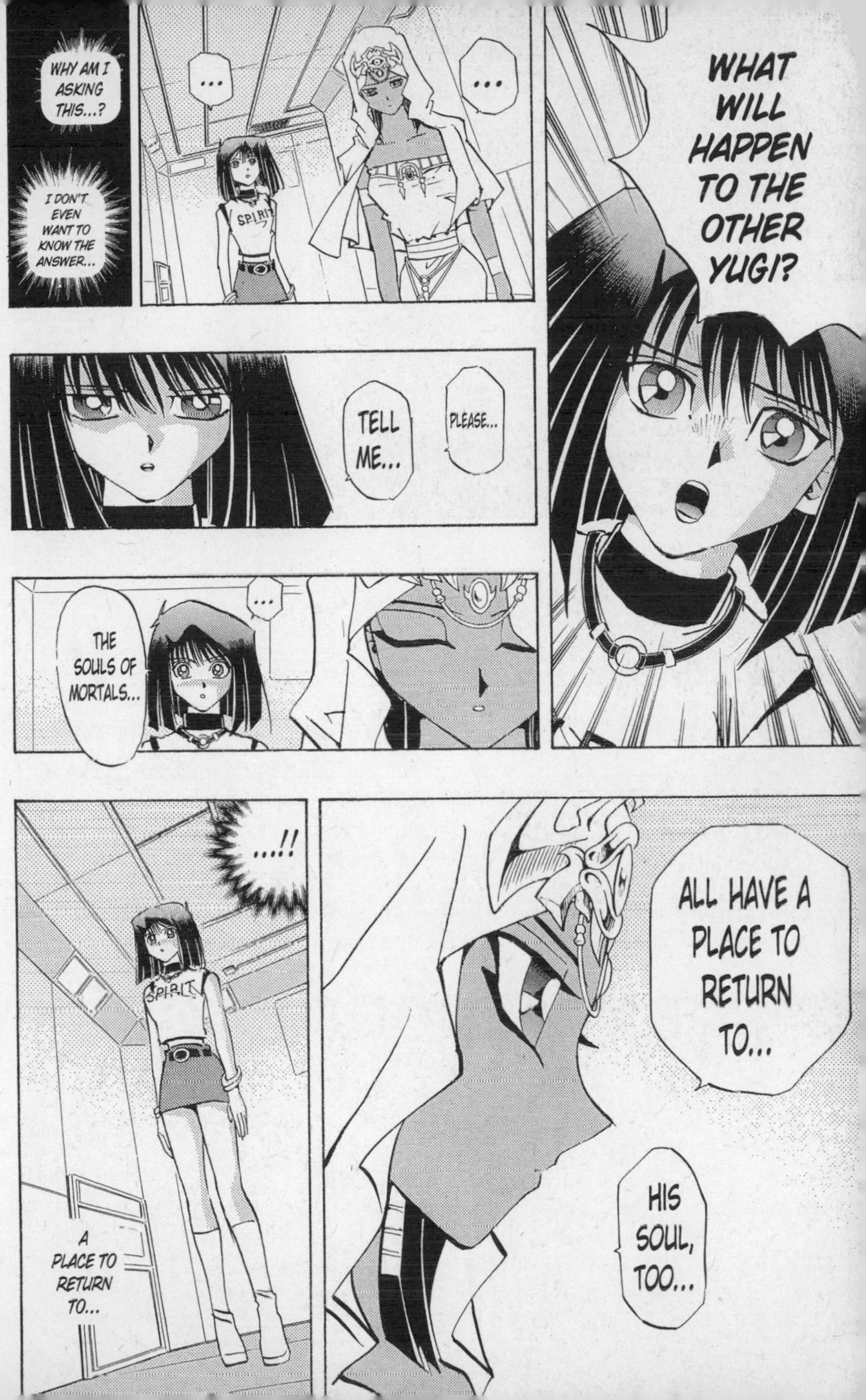
WHAT WILL HAPPEN TO THE OTHER YUGI?
...
...
WHY AM I ASKING THIS...?
I DON'T EVEN WANT TO KNOW THE ANSWER...
PLEASE...
TELL ME...
...
THE SOULS OF MORTALS...
ALL HAVE A PLACE TO RETURN TO...
HIS SOUL, TOO...
...!!
A PLACE TO RETURN TO...

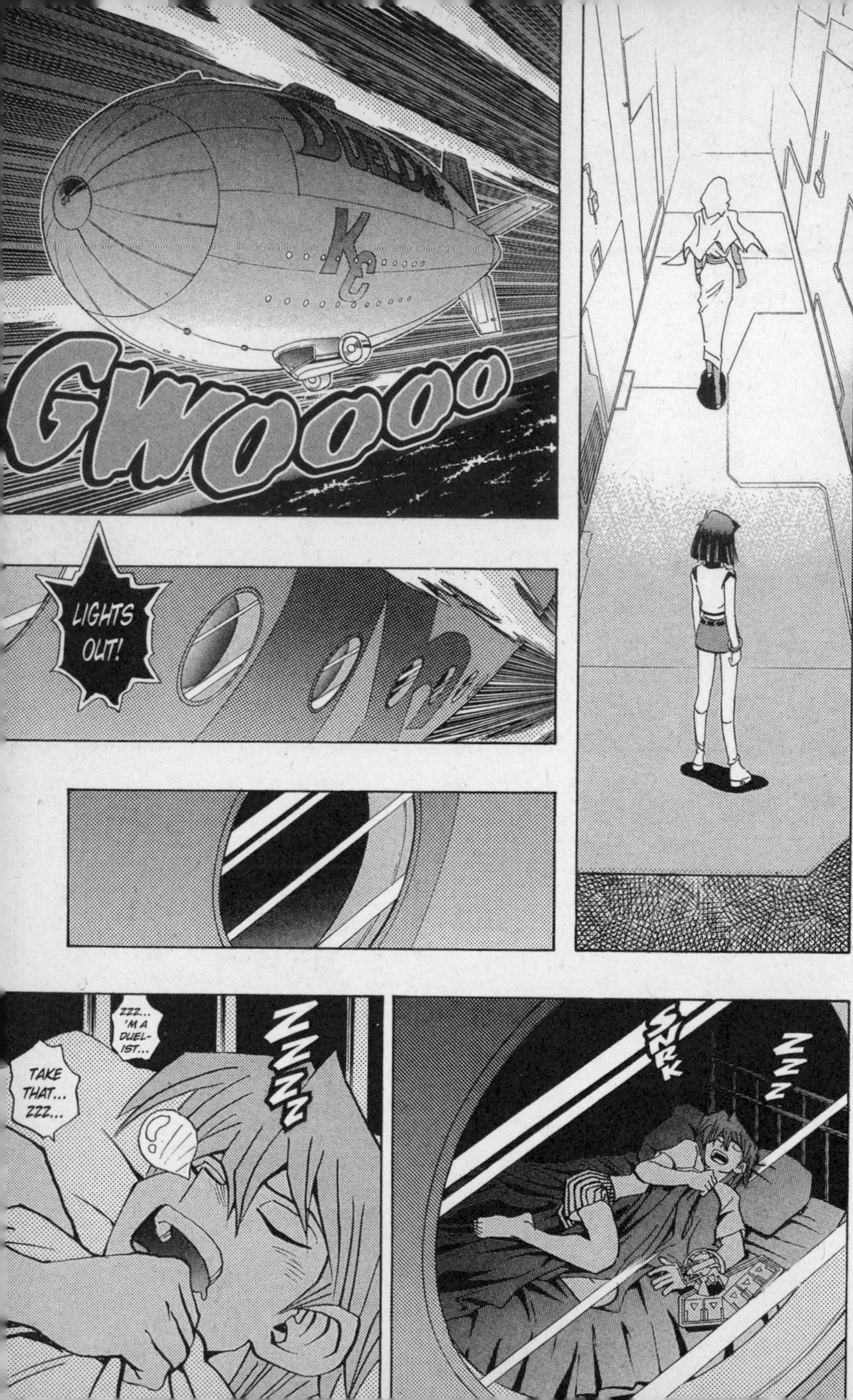
GWOOOO
LIGHTS OUT!
SNRK
ZZZ
ZZZ... 'M A DUEL-IST...
TAKE THAT... ZZZ...
ZZZZ

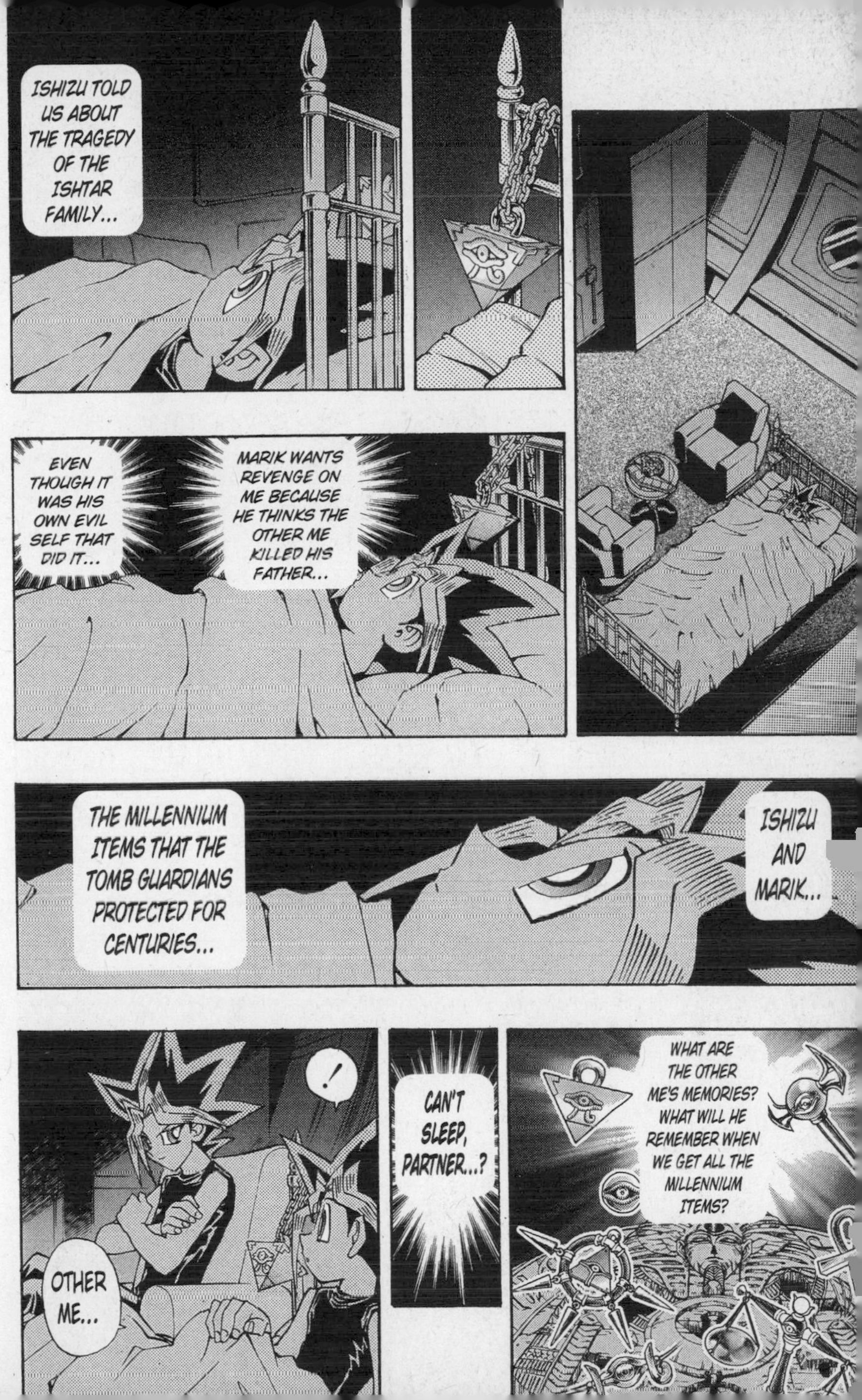
ISHIZU TOLD US ABOUT THE TRAGEDY OF THE ISHTAR FAMILY...
MARIK WANTS REVENGE ON ME BECAUSE HE THINKS THE OTHER ME KILLED HIS FATHER...
EVEN THOUGH IT WAS HIS OWN EVIL SELF THAT DID IT...
ISHIZU AND MARIK...
THE MILLENNIUM ITEMS THAT THE TOMB GUARDIANS PROTECTED FOR CENTURIES...
WHAT ARE THE OTHER ME'S MEMORIES? WHAT WILL HE REMEMBER WHEN WE GET ALL THE MILLENNIUM ITEMS?
CAN'T SLEEP, PARTNER...?
!
OTHER ME...

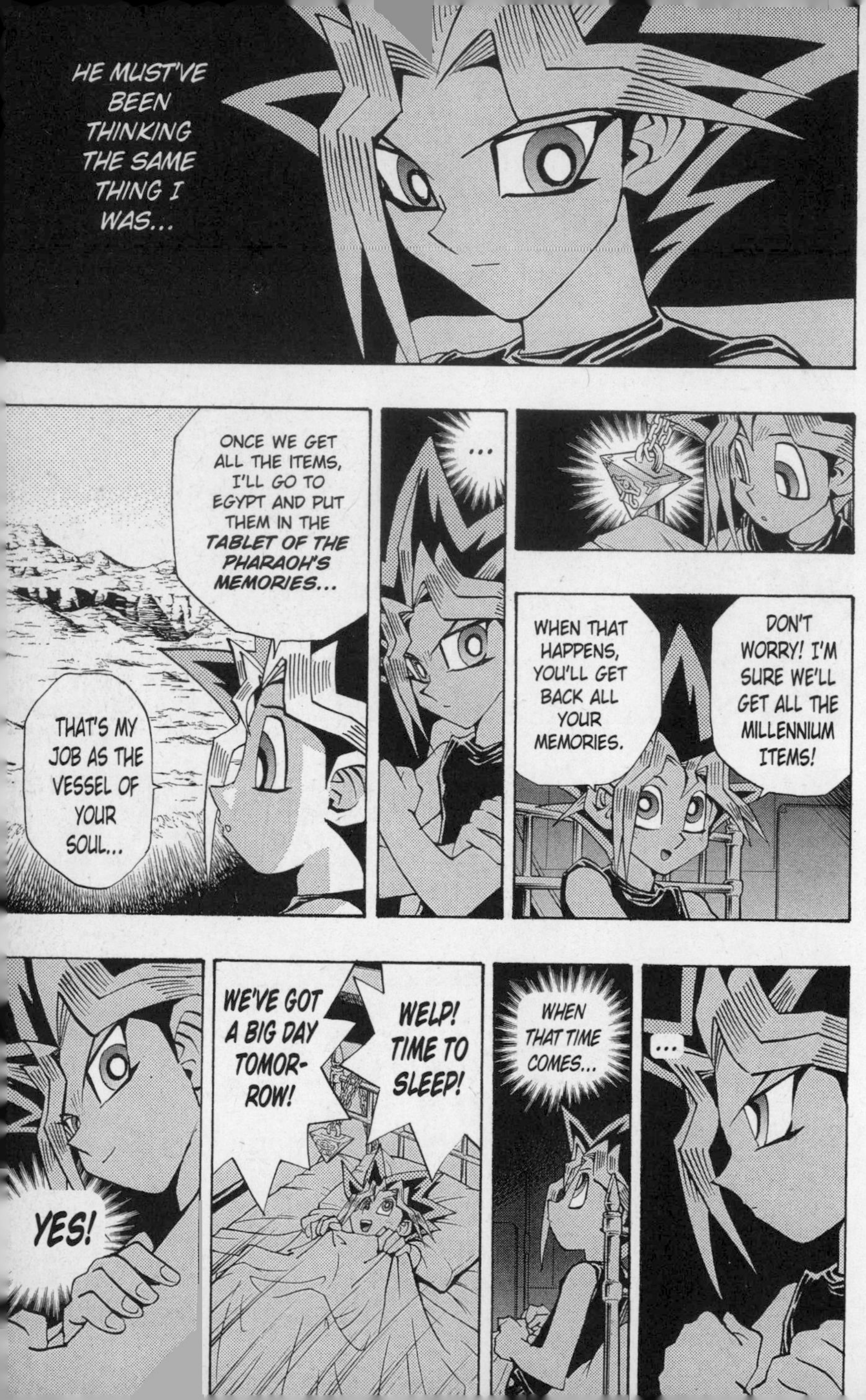
HE MUST'VE BEEN THINKING THE SAME THING I WAS...
DON'T WORRY! I'M SURE WE'LL GET ALL THE MILLENNIUM ITEMS!
WHEN THAT HAPPENS, YOU'LL GET BACK ALL YOUR MEMORIES.
...
ONCE WE GET ALL THE ITEMS, I'LL GO TO EGYPT AND PUT THEM IN THE *TABLET OF THE PHARAOH'S MEMORIES...*
THAT'S MY JOB AS THE VESSEL OF YOUR SOUL...
...
WHEN THAT TIME COMES...
WELP! TIME TO SLEEP!
WE'VE GOT A BIG DAY TOMOR-ROW!
YES!

UNLESS I BEAT THE EVIL MIND WITHIN MARIK, I'LL NEVER BE ABLE TO TRAVEL THE PATH I HAVE TO GO...

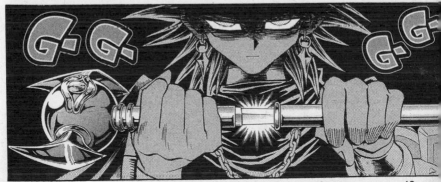

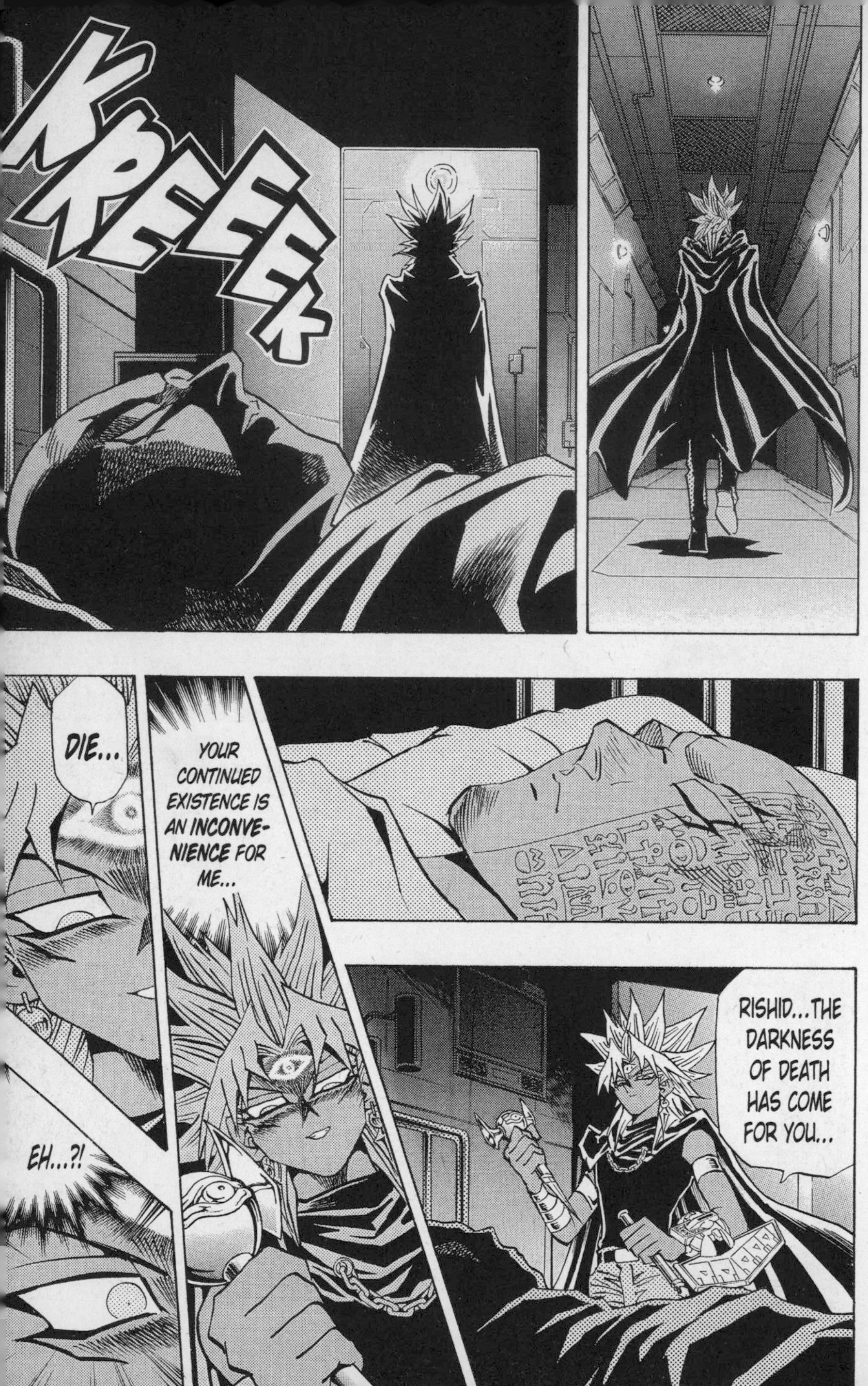
KREEEK
RISHID...THE DARKNESS OF DEATH HAS COME FOR YOU...
YOUR CONTINUED EXISTENCE IS AN INCONVE-NIENCE FOR ME...
DIE...
EH...?!

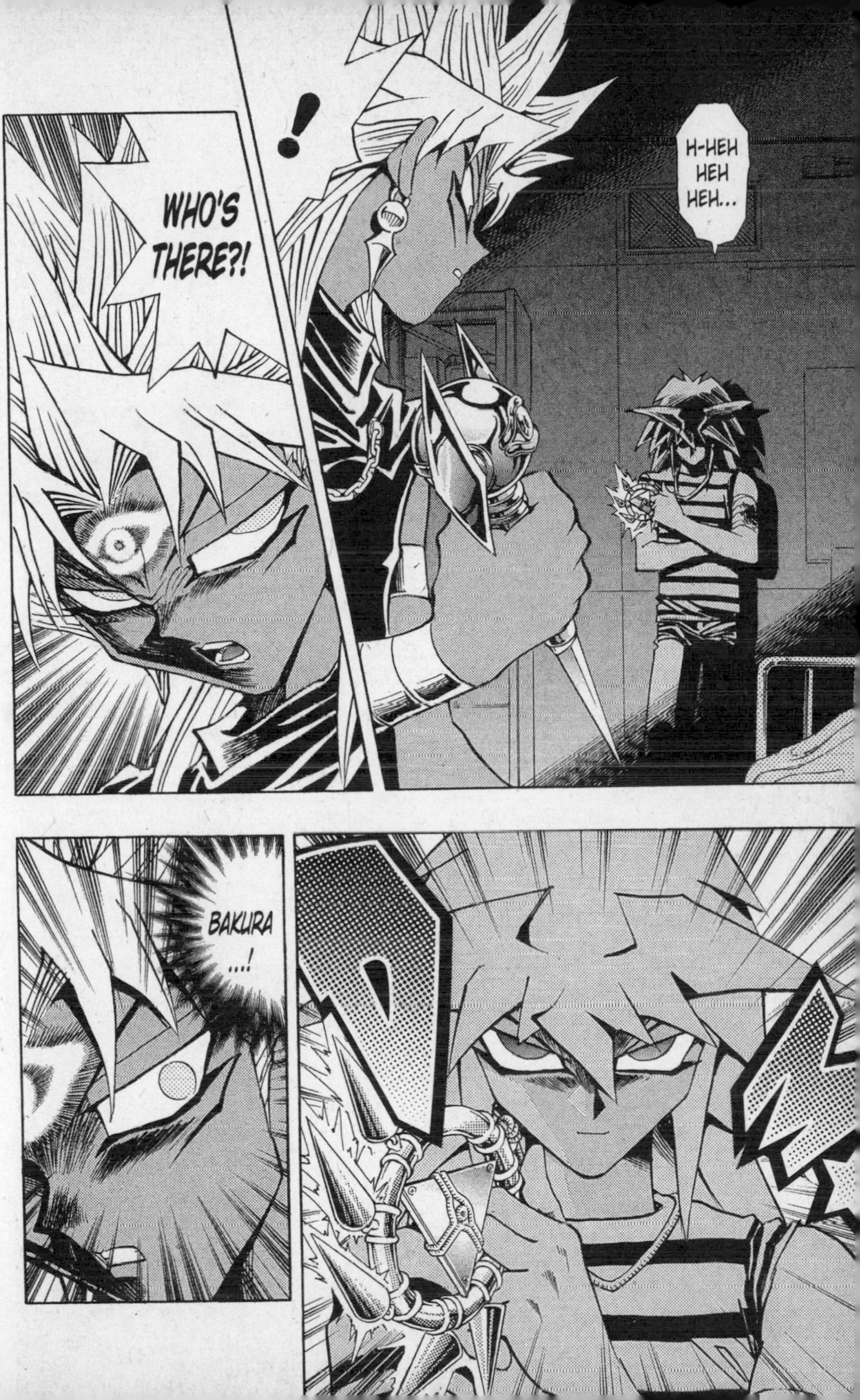
H-HEH HEH HEH...
!
WHO'S THERE?!
BAKURA ...!

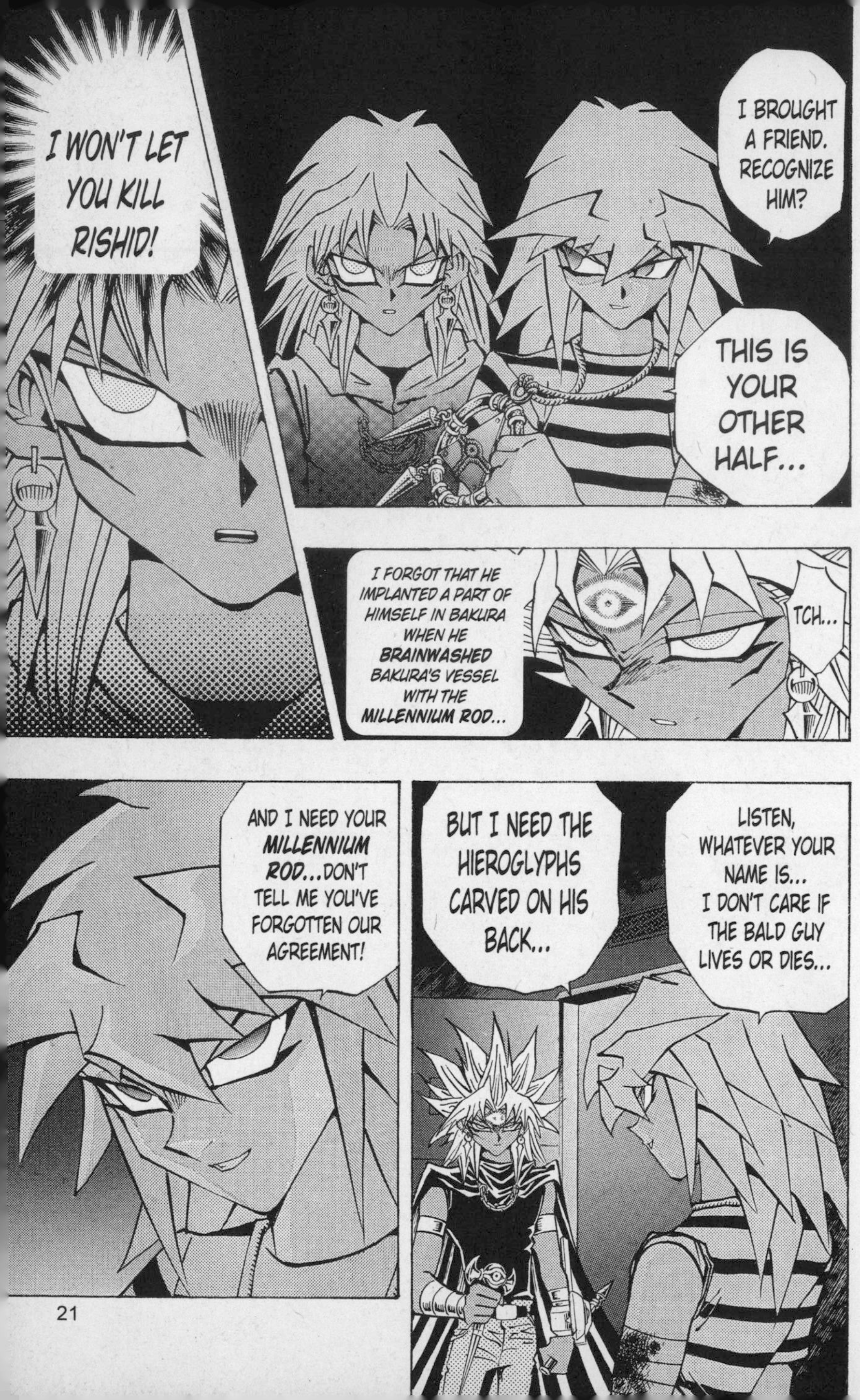
I BROUGHT A FRIEND. RECOGNIZE HIM?
THIS IS YOUR OTHER HALF...
TCH...
I FORGOT THAT HE IMPLANTED A PART OF HIMSELF IN BAKURA WHEN HE BRAINWASHED BAKURA'S VESSEL WITH THE MILLENNIUM ROD...
I WON'T LET YOU KILL RISHID!
LISTEN, WHATEVER YOUR NAME IS... I DON'T CARE IF THE BALD GUY LIVES OR DIES...
BUT I NEED THE HIEROGLYPHS CARVED ON HIS BACK...
AND I NEED YOUR MILLENNIUM ROD...DON'T TELL ME YOU'VE FORGOTTEN OUR AGREEMENT!

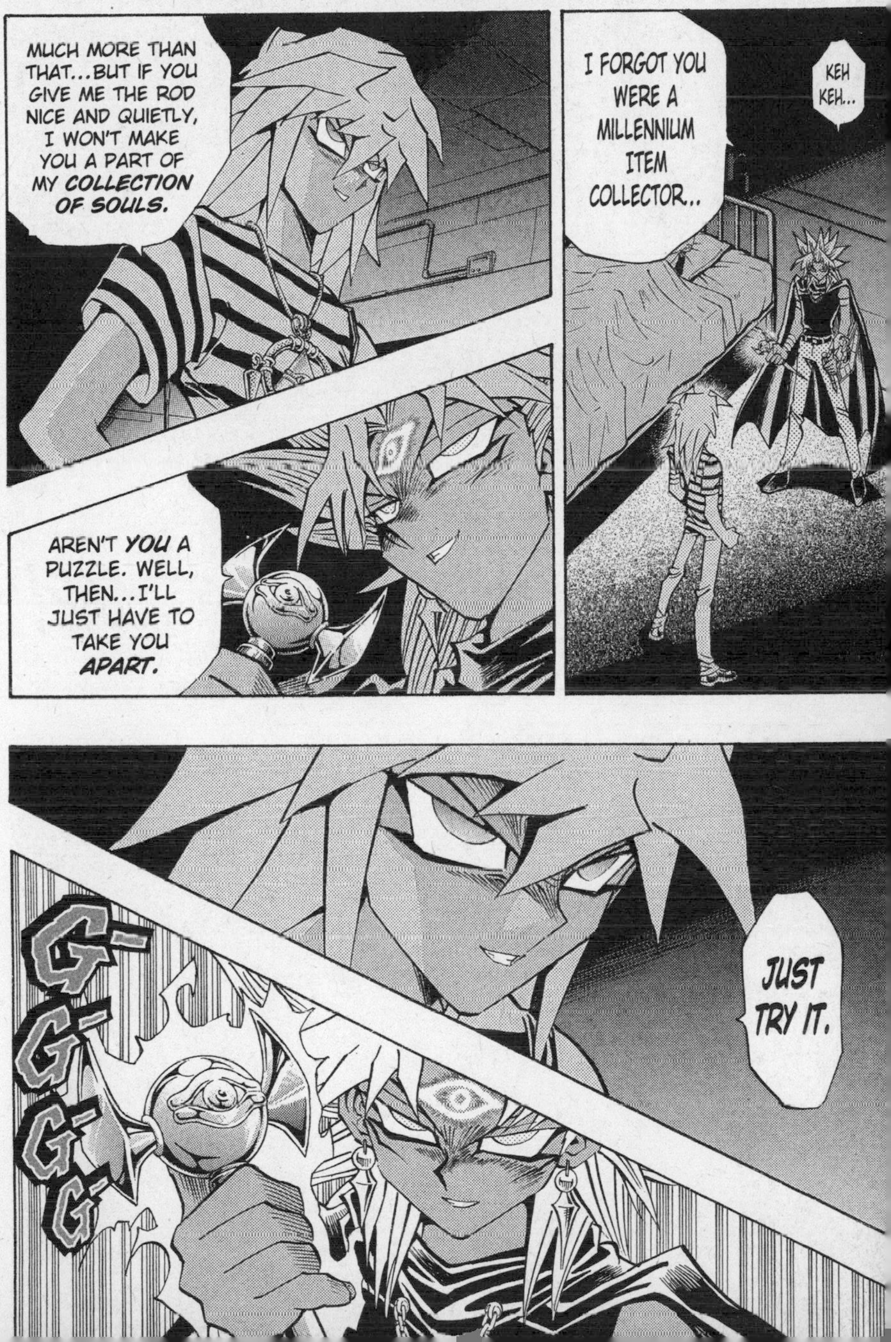
KEH KEH...
I FORGOT YOU WERE A MILLENNIUM ITEM COLLECTOR...
MUCH MORE THAN THAT...BUT IF YOU GIVE ME THE ROD NICE AND QUIETLY, I WON'T MAKE YOU A PART OF MY COLLECTION OF SOULS.
AREN'T YOU A PUZZLE. WELL, THEN...I'LL JUST HAVE TO TAKE YOU APART.
JUST TRY IT.
G-G-G-G-

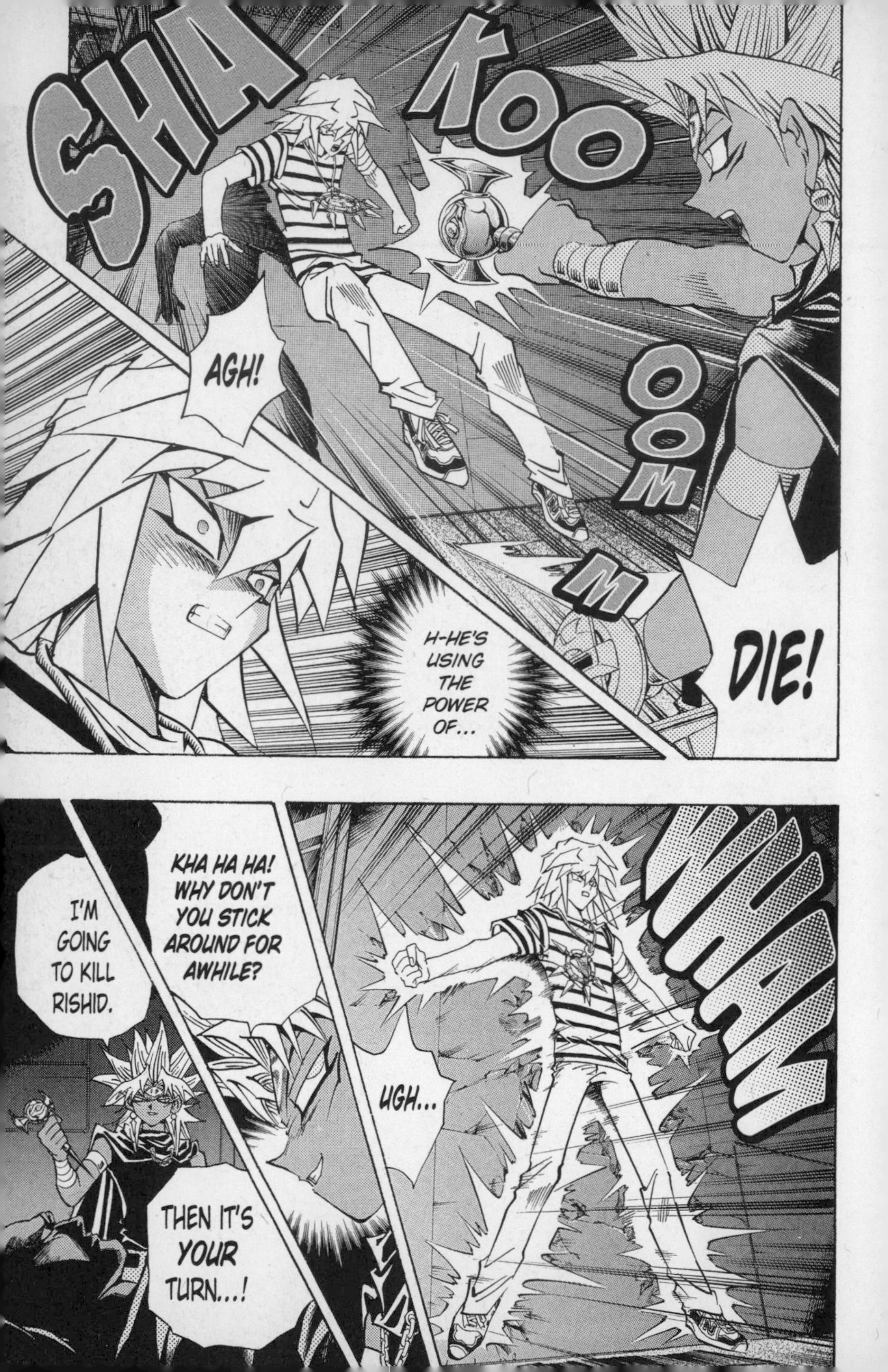
SHA
KOO
OOOM
M
DIE!
AGH!
H-HE'S USING THE POWER OF...
UGH...
KHA HA HA! WHY DON'T YOU STICK AROUND FOR AWHILE?
THEN IT'S YOUR TURN...!
I'M GOING TO KILL RISHID.

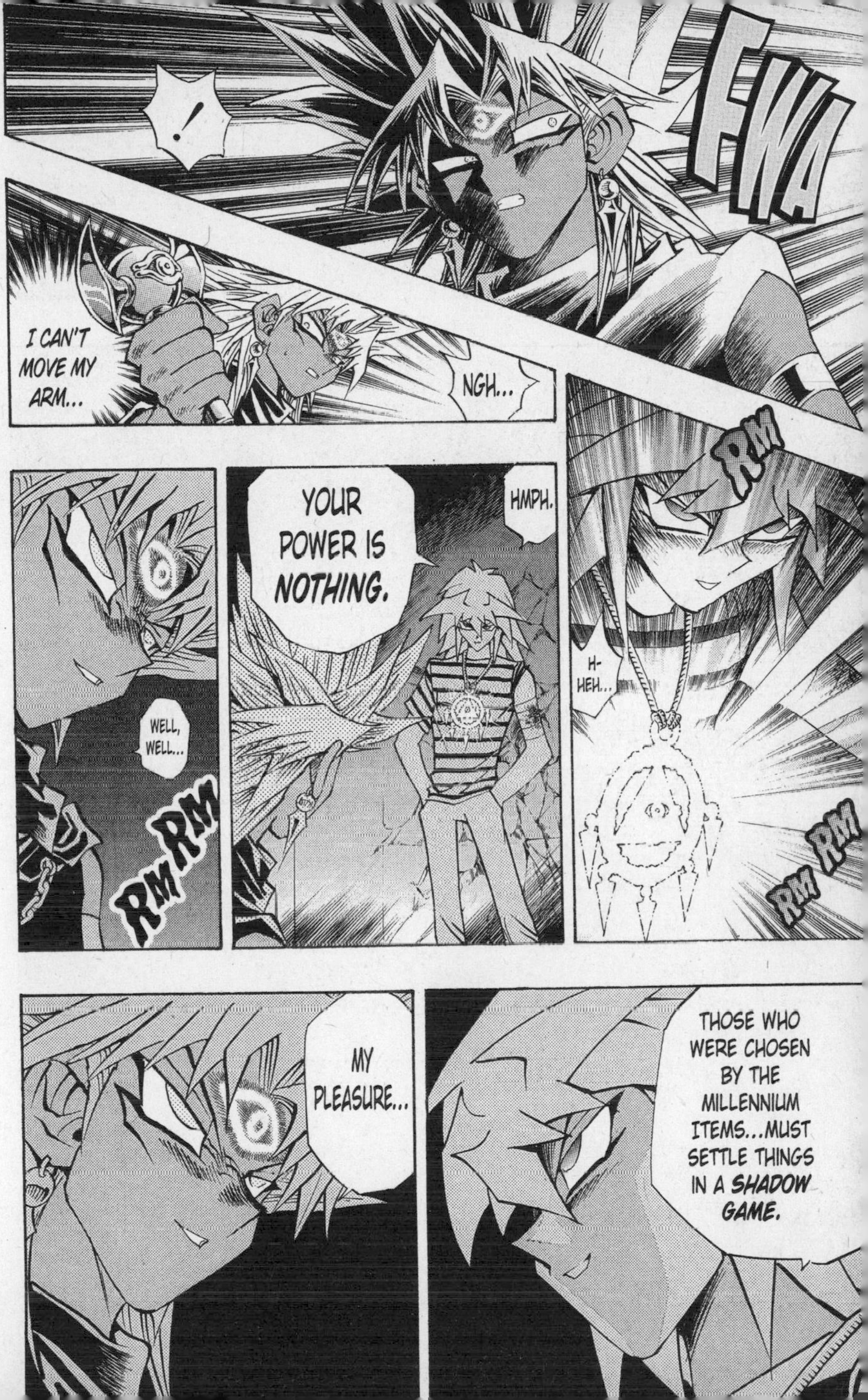
FWA
!
NGH...
I CAN'T MOVE MY ARM...
RM
H-HEH...
RM RM
HMPH.
YOUR POWER IS *NOTHING.*
WELL, WELL...
RM RM RM
THOSE WHO WERE CHOSEN BY THE MILLENNIUM ITEMS...MUST SETTLE THINGS IN A *SHADOW GAME.*
MY PLEASURE...

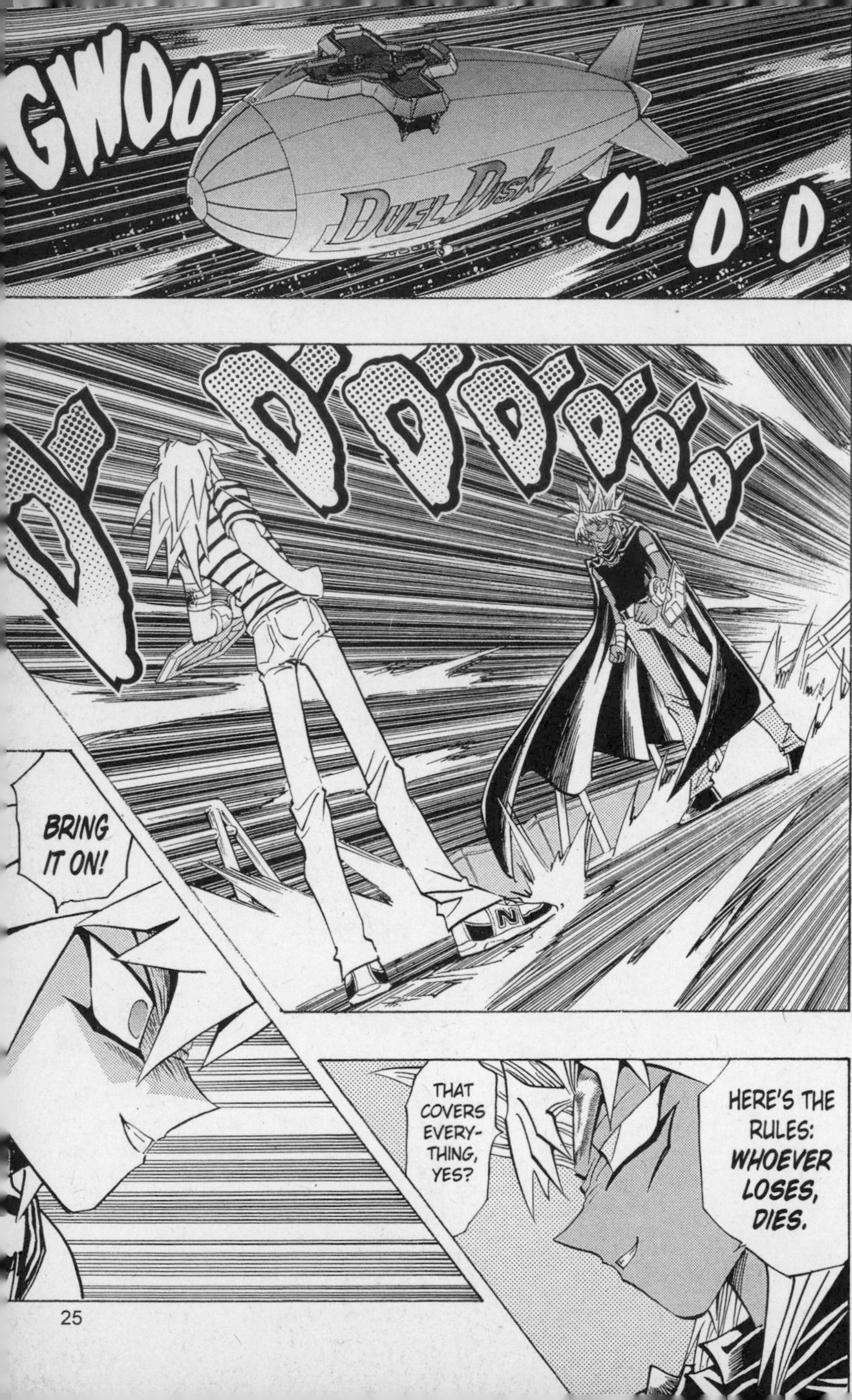
GWOO
OOO
HERE'S THE RULES: WHOEVER LOSES, DIES.
THAT COVERS EVERY-THING, YES?
BRING IT ON!

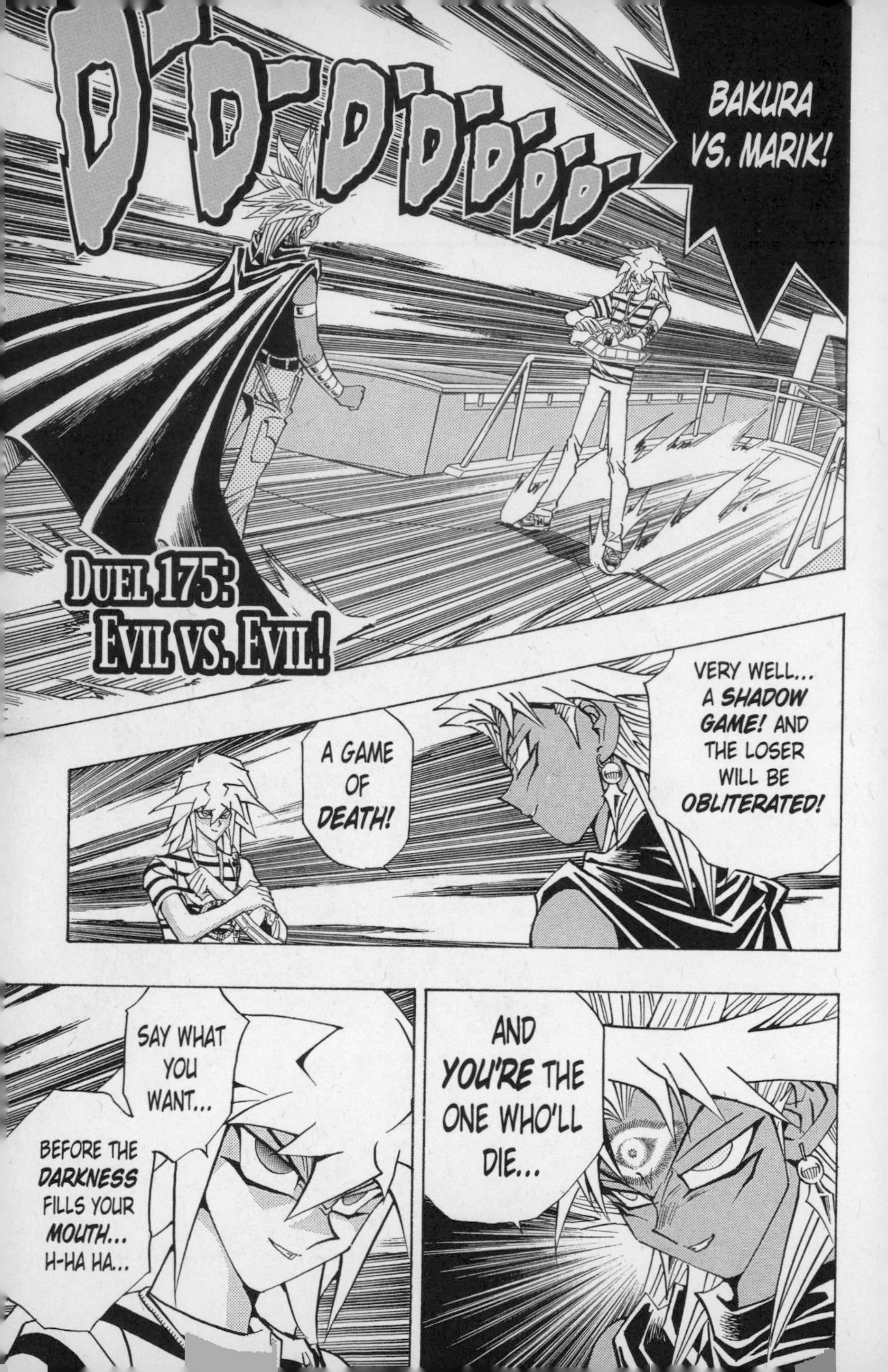
BAKURA VS. MARIK!
D-D-D-D-D-D-D-D-
DUEL 175: EVIL VS. EVIL!
VERY WELL... A SHADOW GAME! AND THE LOSER WILL BE OBLITERATED!
A GAME OF DEATH!
AND YOU'RE THE ONE WHO'LL DIE...
SAY WHAT YOU WANT...
BEFORE THE DARKNESS FILLS YOUR MOUTH... H-HA HA...

Duel 175: Evil vs. Evil!

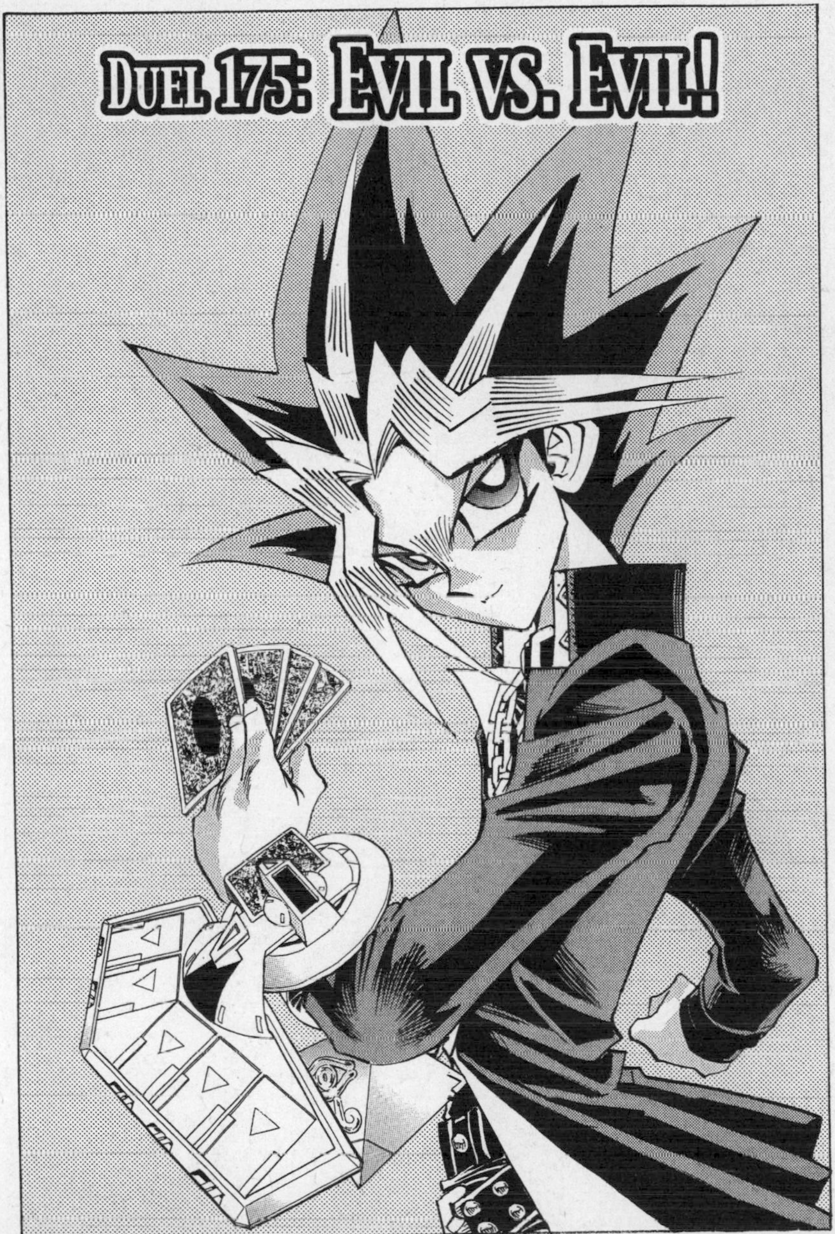

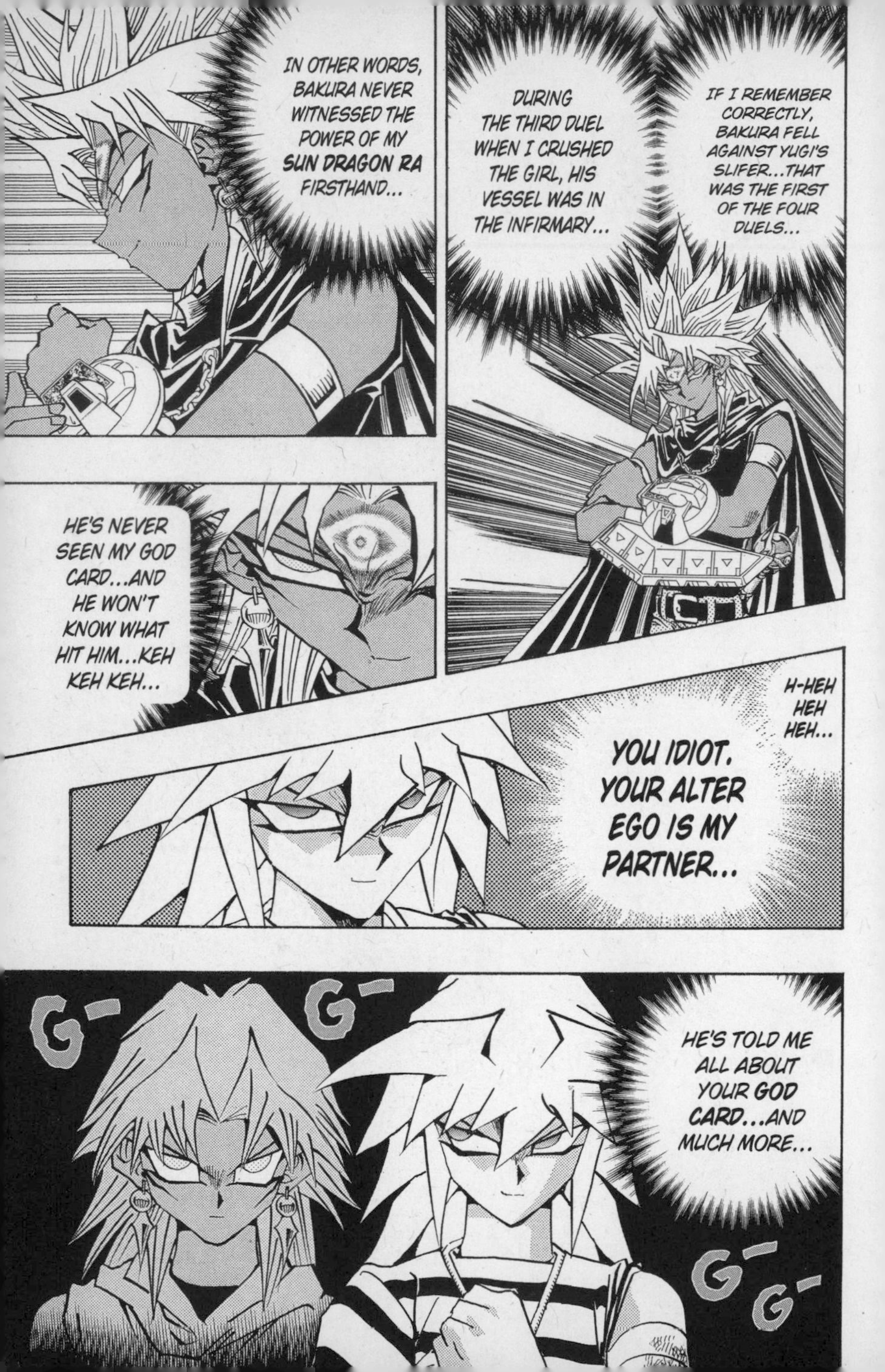

IF I REMEMBER CORRECTLY, BAKURA FELL AGAINST YUGI'S SLIFER...THAT WAS THE FIRST OF THE FOUR DUELS...
DURING THE THIRD DUEL WHEN I CRUSHED THE GIRL, HIS VESSEL WAS IN THE INFIRMARY...
IN OTHER WORDS, BAKURA NEVER WITNESSED THE POWER OF MY SUN DRAGON RA FIRSTHAND...
HE'S NEVER SEEN MY GOD CARD...AND HE WON'T KNOW WHAT HIT HIM...KEH KEH KEH...
H-HEH HEH HEH...
YOU IDIOT. YOUR ALTER EGO IS MY PARTNER...
HE'S TOLD ME ALL ABOUT YOUR GOD CARD...AND MUCH MORE...
G-
G-
G-
G-

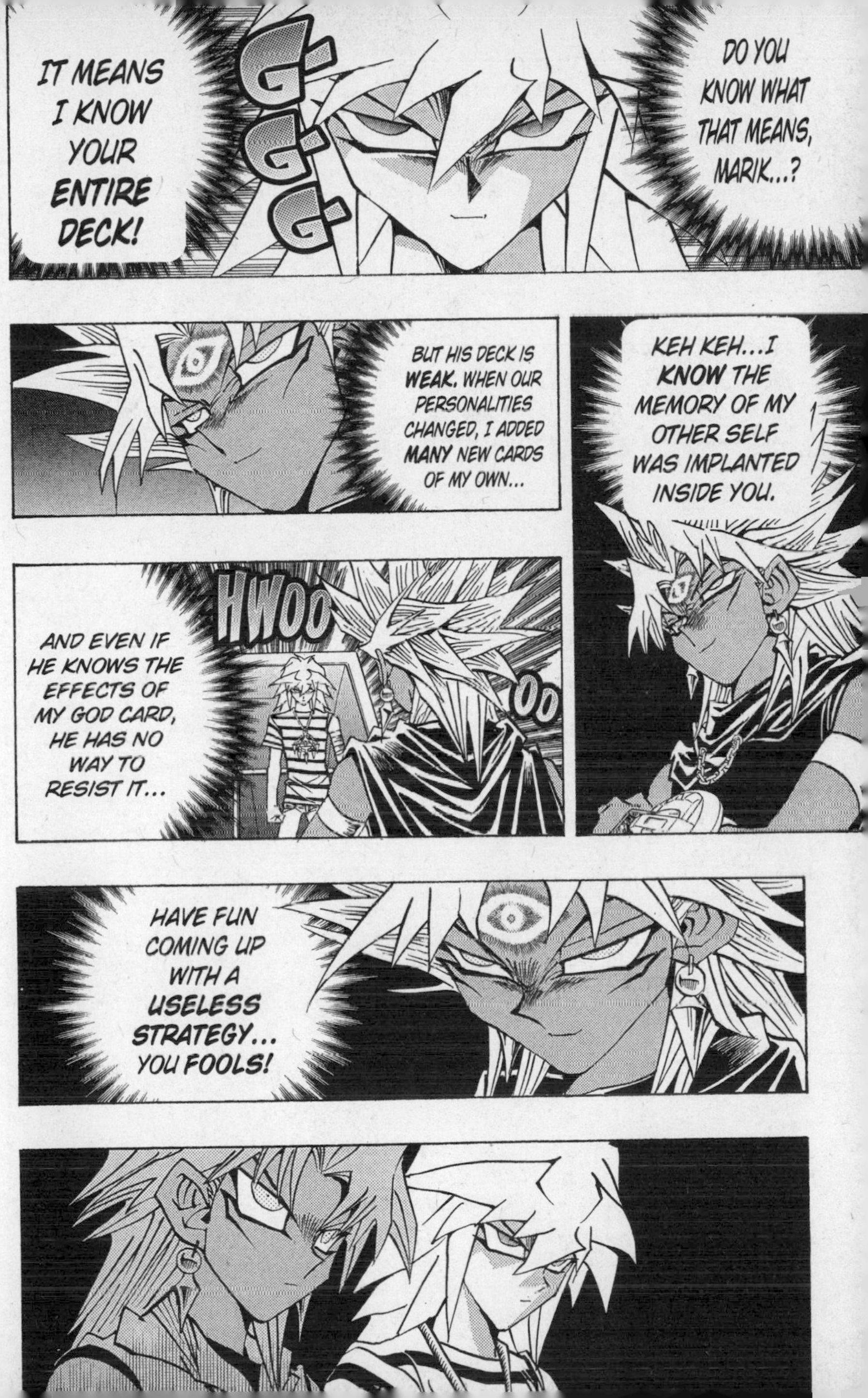
DO YOU KNOW WHAT THAT MEANS, MARIK...?
GGG
IT MEANS I KNOW YOUR ENTIRE DECK!
KEH KEH...I KNOW THE MEMORY OF MY OTHER SELF WAS IMPLANTED INSIDE YOU.
BUT HIS DECK IS WEAK. WHEN OUR PERSONALITIES CHANGED, I ADDED MANY NEW CARDS OF MY OWN...
HWOOOO
AND EVEN IF HE KNOWS THE EFFECTS OF MY GOD CARD, HE HAS NO WAY TO RESIST IT...
HAVE FUN COMING UP WITH A USELESS STRATEGY... YOU FOOLS!

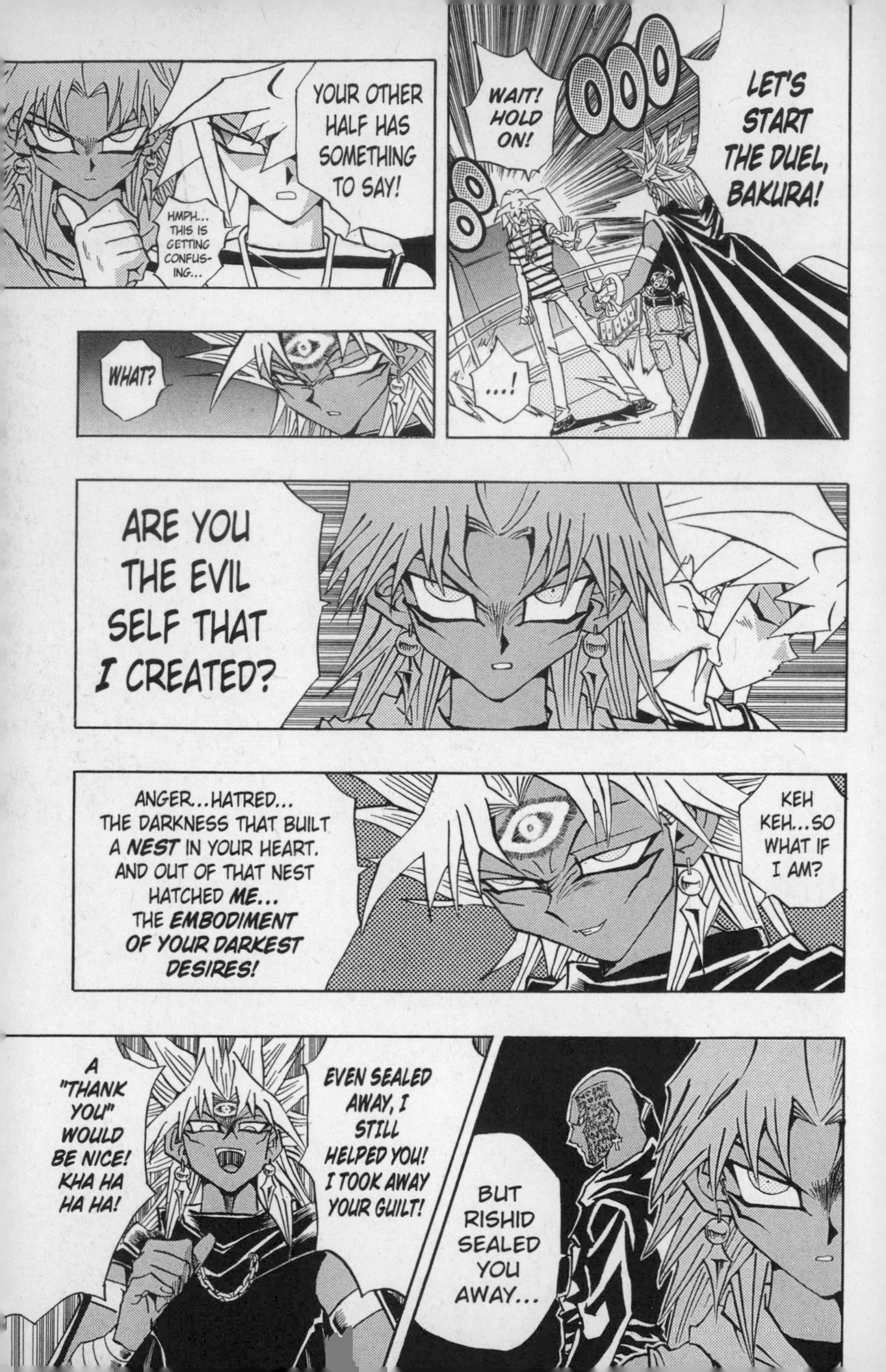
LET'S START THE DUEL, BAKURA!
WAIT! HOLD ON!
...!
YOUR OTHER HALF HAS SOMETHING TO SAY!
HMPH... THIS IS GETTING CONFUS-ING...
WHAT?
ARE YOU THE EVIL SELF THAT I CREATED?
KEH KEH...SO WHAT IF I AM?
ANGER...HATRED... THE DARKNESS THAT BUILT A NEST IN YOUR HEART. AND OUT OF THAT NEST HATCHED ME... THE EMBODIMENT OF YOUR DARKEST DESIRES!
BUT RISHID SEALED YOU AWAY...
EVEN SEALED AWAY, I STILL HELPED YOU! I TOOK AWAY YOUR GUILT!
A "THANK YOU" WOULD BE NICE! KHA HA HA HA!

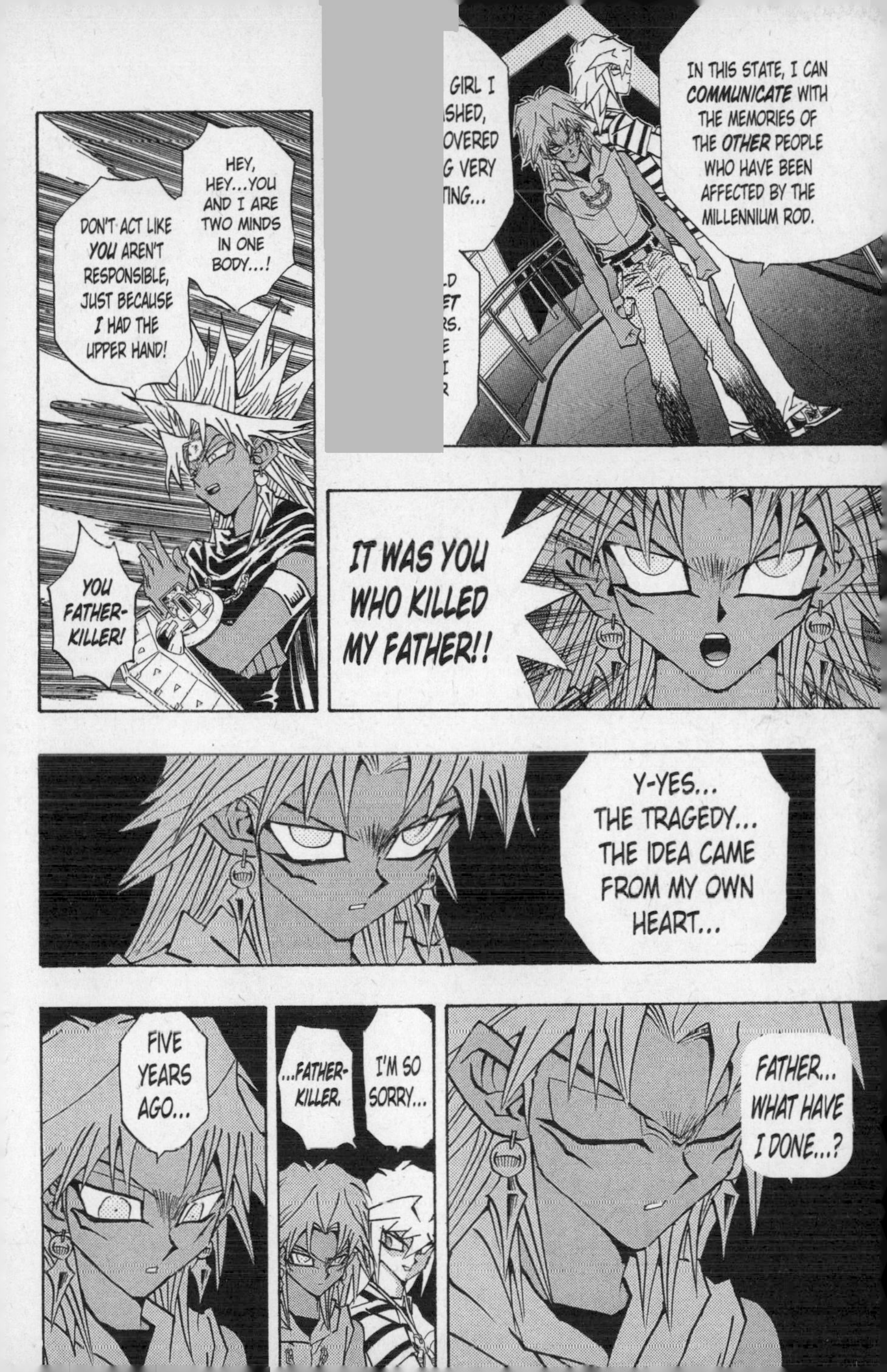
IN THIS STATE, I CAN COMMUNICATE WITH THE MEMORIES OF THE OTHER PEOPLE WHO HAVE BEEN AFFECTED BY THE MILLENNIUM ROD.
IT WAS YOU WHO KILLED MY FATHER!!
HEY, HEY...YOU AND I ARE TWO MINDS IN ONE BODY...!
DON'T ACT LIKE YOU AREN'T RESPONSIBLE, JUST BECAUSE I HAD THE UPPER HAND!
YOU FATHER-KILLER!
Y-YES... THE TRAGEDY... THE IDEA CAME FROM MY OWN HEART...
FATHER... WHAT HAVE I DONE...?
I'M SO SORRY...
...FATHER-KILLER.
FIVE YEARS AGO...

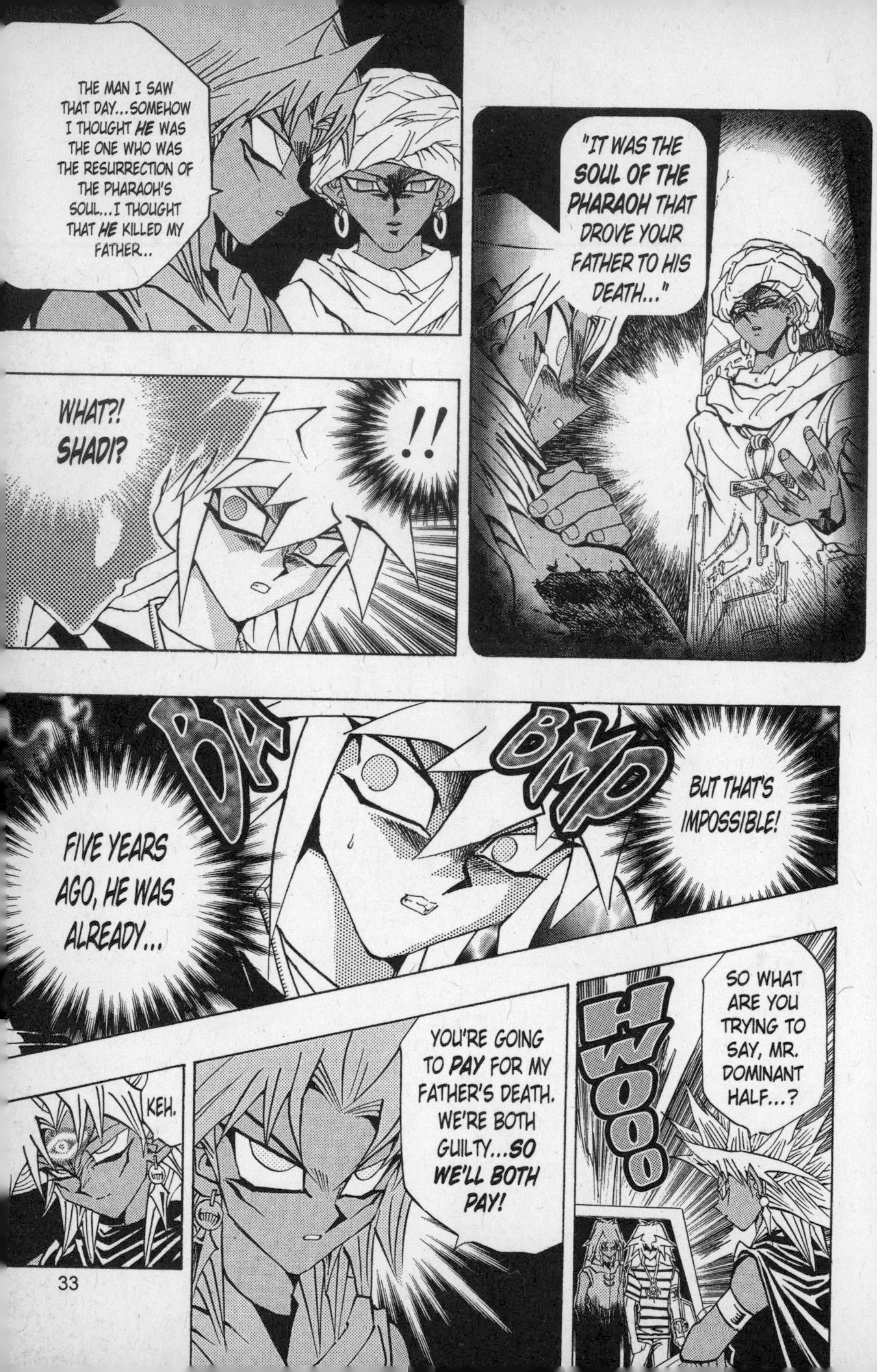
"IT WAS THE SOUL OF THE PHARAOH THAT DROVE YOUR FATHER TO HIS DEATH..."
THE MAN I SAW THAT DAY...SOMEHOW I THOUGHT HE WAS THE ONE WHO WAS THE RESURRECTION OF THE PHARAOH'S SOUL...I THOUGHT THAT HE KILLED MY FATHER..
!!
WHAT?! SHADI?
BA BMP
BUT THAT'S IMPOSSIBLE!
FIVE YEARS AGO, HE WAS ALREADY...
SO WHAT ARE YOU TRYING TO SAY, MR. DOMINANT HALF...?
HWOOO
YOU'RE GOING TO PAY FOR MY FATHER'S DEATH. WE'RE BOTH GUILTY...SO WE'LL BOTH PAY!
KEH.

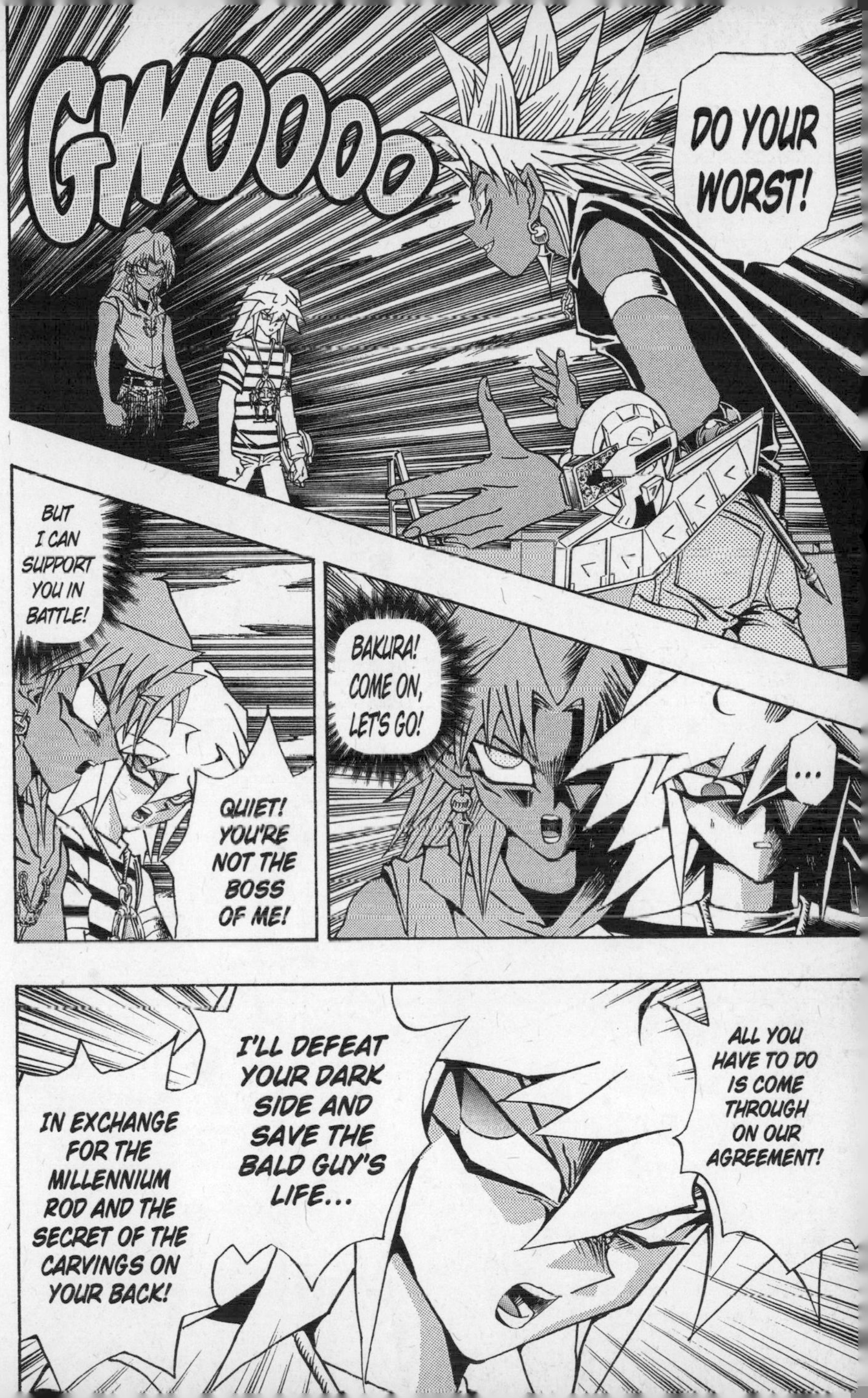
DO YOUR WORST!
GWOOOO
BAKURA! COME ON, LET'S GO!
...
BUT I CAN SUPPORT YOU IN BATTLE!
QUIET! YOU'RE NOT THE BOSS OF ME!
ALL YOU HAVE TO DO IS COME THROUGH ON OUR AGREEMENT!
I'LL DEFEAT YOUR DARK SIDE AND SAVE THE BALD GUY'S LIFE...
IN EXCHANGE FOR THE MILLENNIUM ROD AND THE SECRET OF THE CARVINGS ON YOUR BACK!

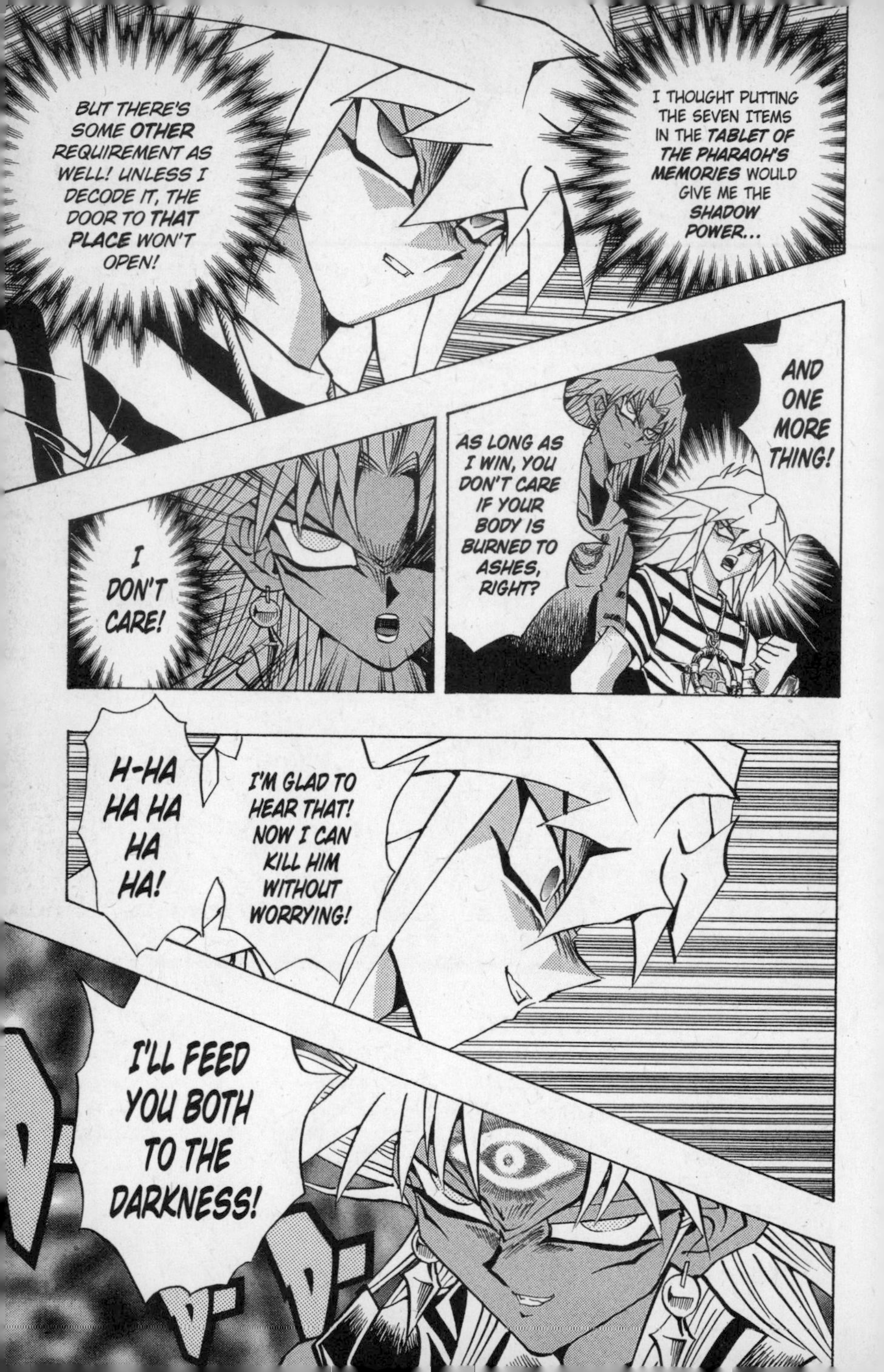
I THOUGHT PUTTING THE SEVEN ITEMS IN THE TABLET OF THE PHARAOH'S MEMORIES WOULD GIVE ME THE SHADOW POWER...
BUT THERE'S SOME OTHER REQUIREMENT AS WELL! UNLESS I DECODE IT, THE DOOR TO THAT PLACE WON'T OPEN!
AND ONE MORE THING!
AS LONG AS I WIN, YOU DON'T CARE IF YOUR BODY IS BURNED TO ASHES, RIGHT?
I DON'T CARE!
I'M GLAD TO HEAR THAT! NOW I CAN KILL HIM WITHOUT WORRYING!
H-HA HA HA HA HA!
I'LL FEED YOU BOTH TO THE DARKNESS!

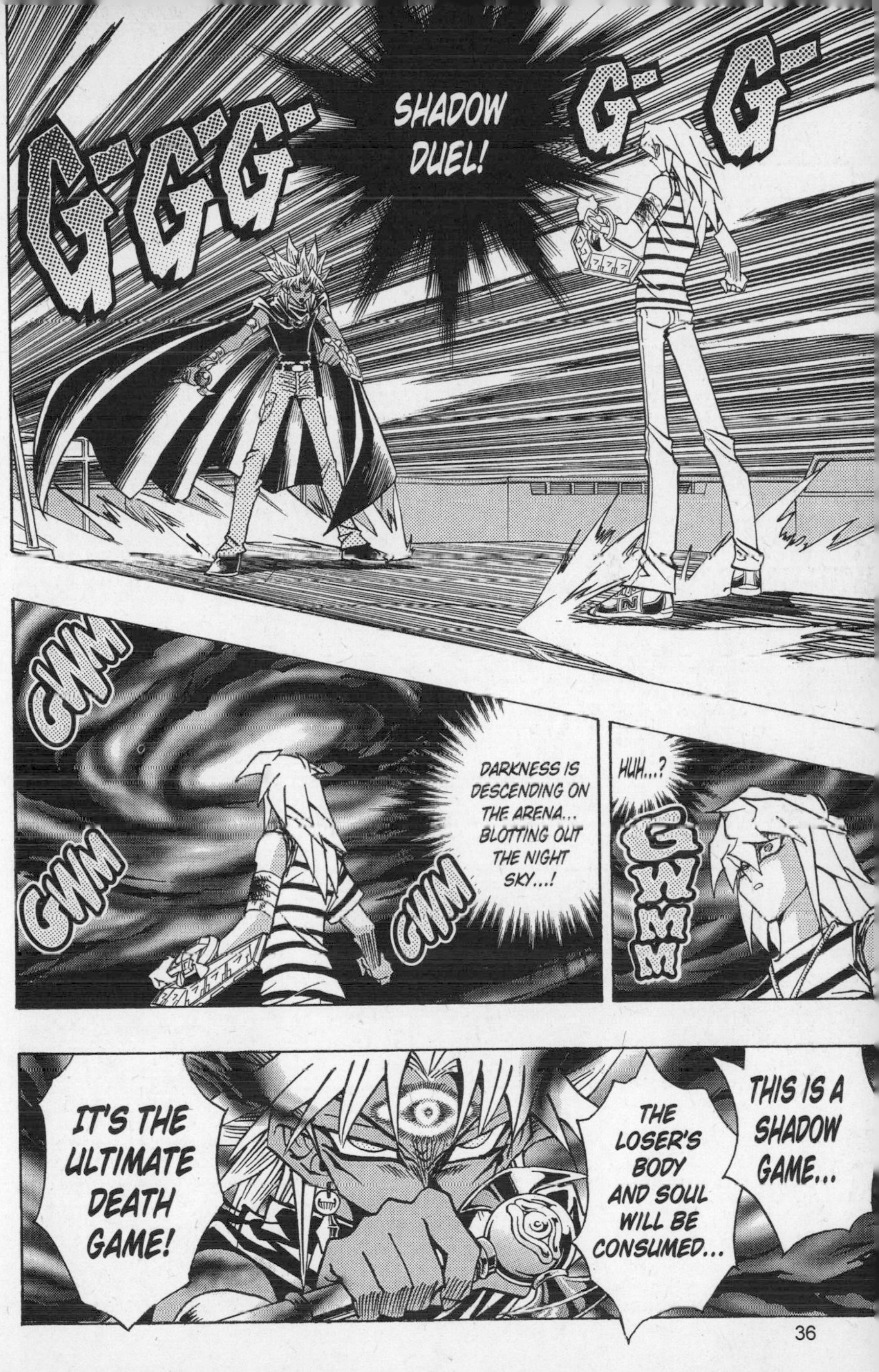
G- G-
SHADOW DUEL!
GGG-
HUH...?
GWMM
DARKNESS IS DESCENDING ON THE ARENA... BLOTTING OUT THE NIGHT SKY...!
GWM
GWM
GWM
THIS IS A SHADOW GAME...
THE LOSER'S BODY AND SOUL WILL BE CONSUMED...
IT'S THE ULTIMATE DEATH GAME!

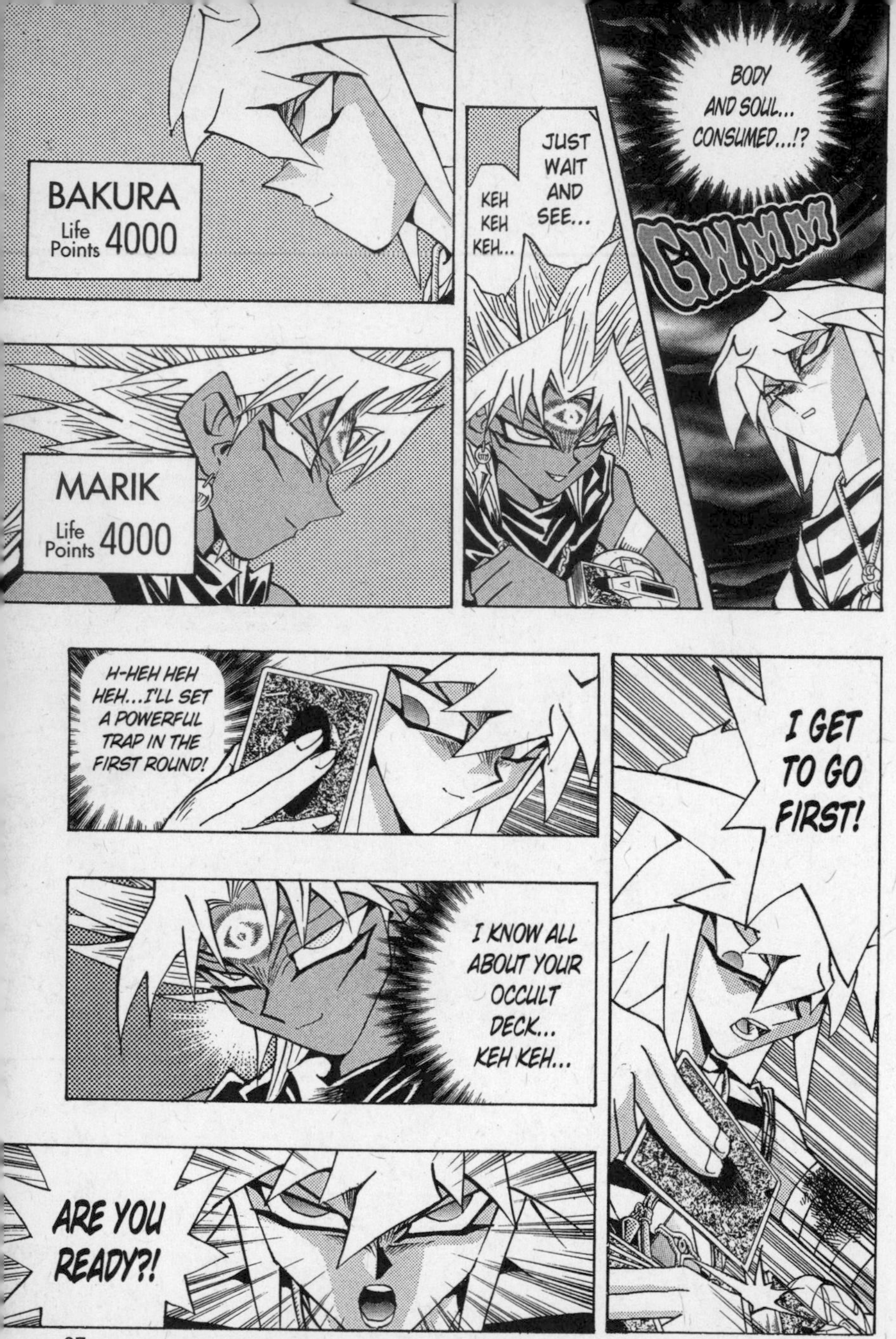
BODY AND SOUL... CONSUMED...!?
GWMM
JUST WAIT AND SEE...
KEH KEH KEH...
BAKURA
Life Points 4000
MARIK
Life Points 4000
I GET TO GO FIRST!
H-HEH HEH HEH...I'LL SET A POWERFUL TRAP IN THE FIRST ROUND!
I KNOW ALL ABOUT YOUR OCCULT DECK... KEH KEH...
ARE YOU READY?!

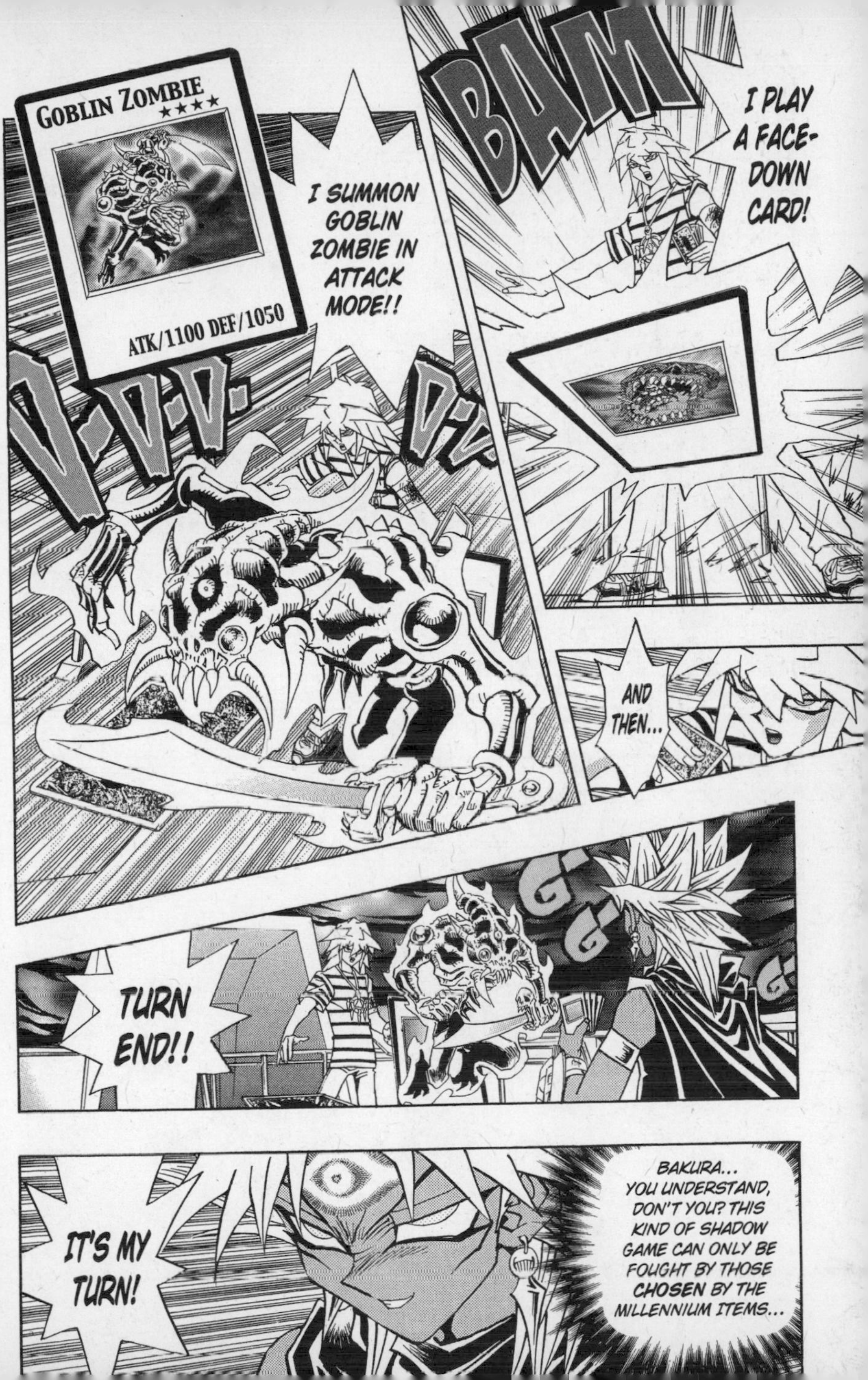
BAM
I PLAY A FACE-DOWN CARD!
AND THEN...
GOBLIN ZOMBIE
ATK/1100 DEF/1050
I SUMMON GOBLIN ZOMBIE IN ATTACK MODE!!
D-D-D-
G G
TURN END!!
BAKURA... YOU UNDERSTAND, DON'T YOU? THIS KIND OF SHADOW GAME CAN ONLY BE FOUGHT BY THOSE CHOSEN BY THE MILLENNIUM ITEMS...
IT'S MY TURN!

READ THIS WAY

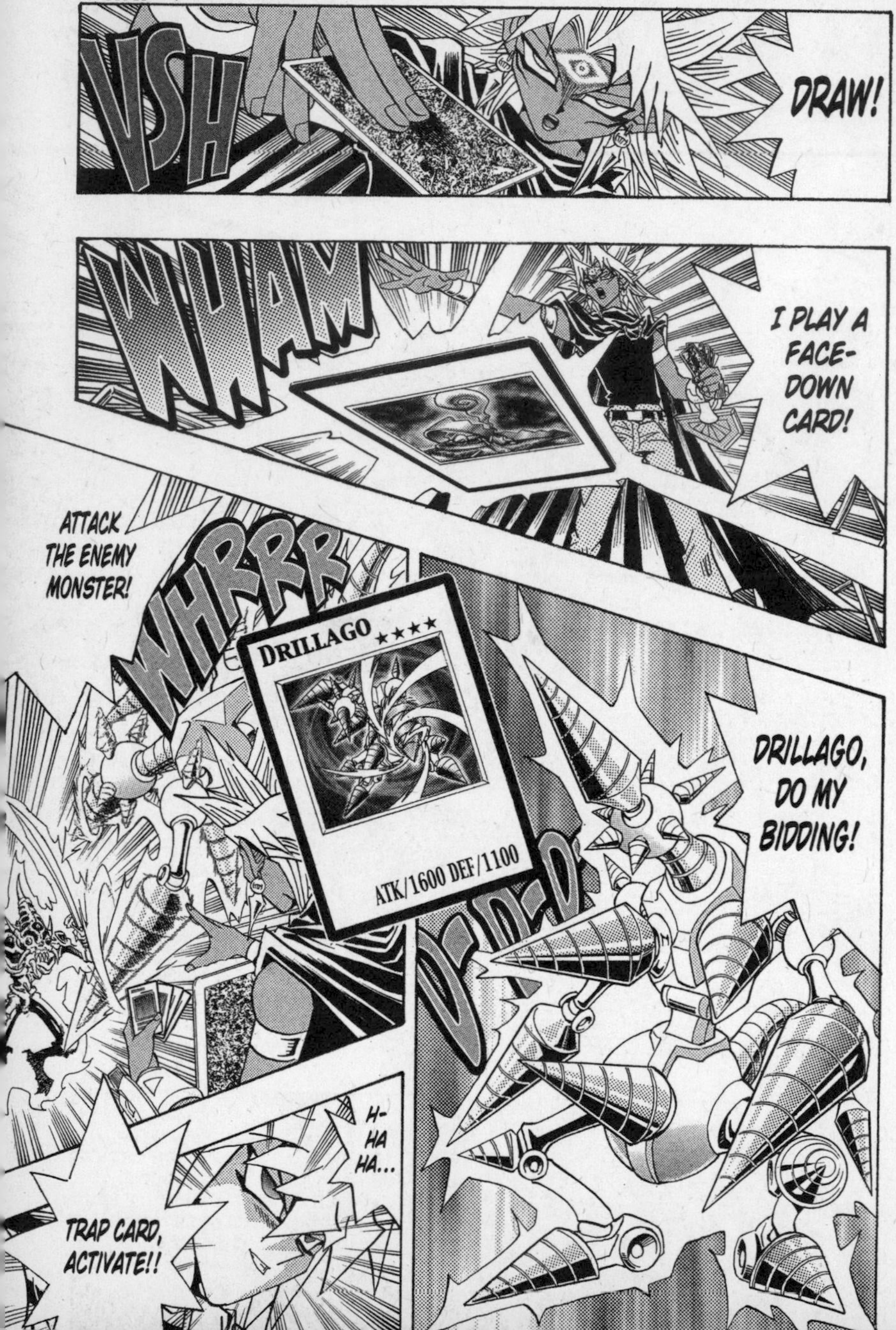
DRAW!
VSH
I PLAY A FACE-DOWN CARD!
WHAM
DRILLAGO, DO MY BIDDING!
DRILLAGO ★★★★
ATK/1600 DEF/1100
D-D-D
ATTACK THE ENEMY MONSTER!
WHRRR
H-HA HA...
TRAP CARD, ACTIVATE!!

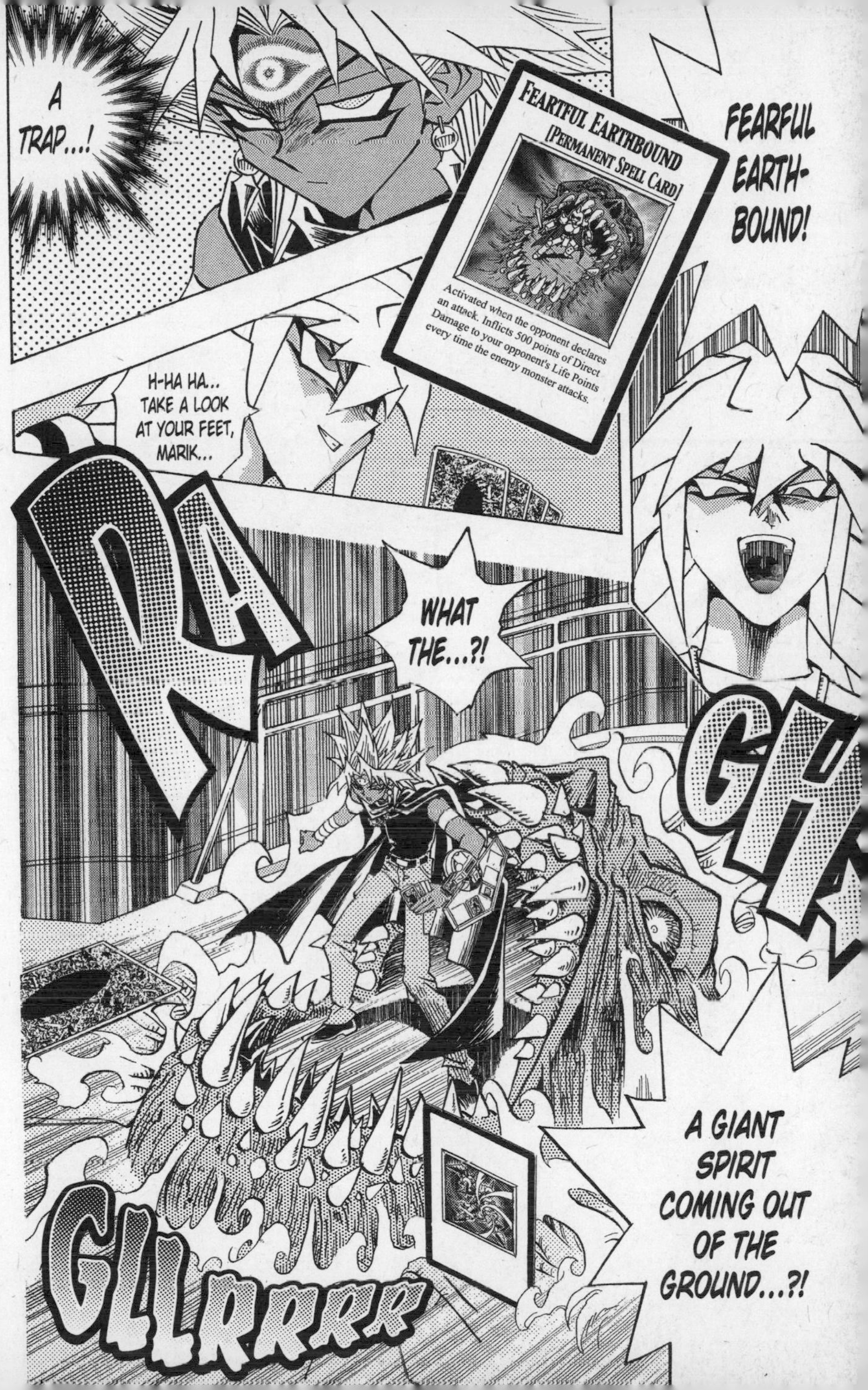
FEARFUL EARTH-BOUND!
FEARFUL EARTHBOUND
[PERMANENT SPELL CARD]
Activated when the opponent declares an attack. Inflicts 500 points of Direct Damage to your opponent's Life Points every time the enemy monster attacks.
A TRAP...!
H-HA HA... TAKE A LOOK AT YOUR FEET, MARIK...
GH
WHAT THE...?!
DA
A GIANT SPIRIT COMING OUT OF THE GROUND...?!
GLLRRRR

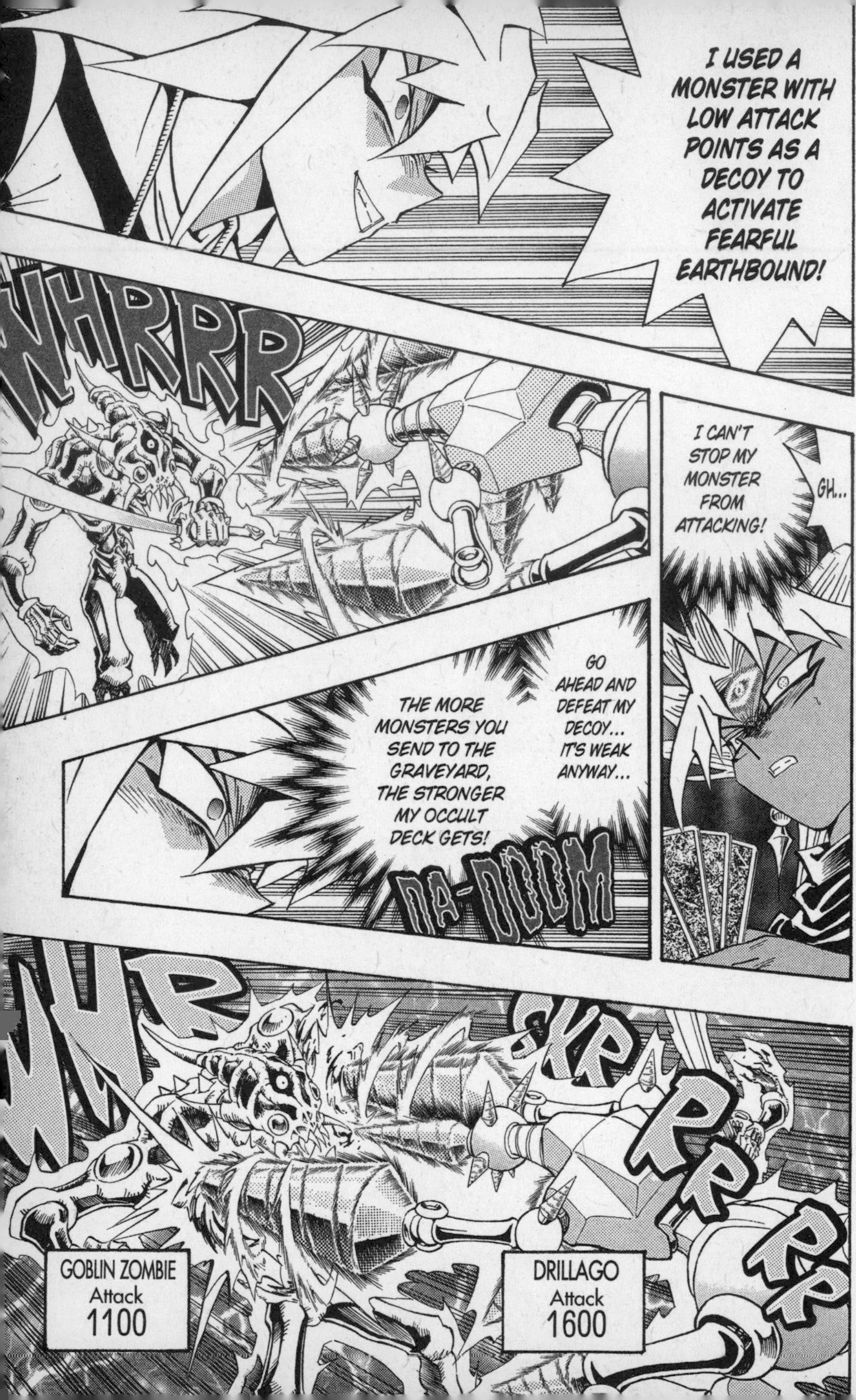
I USED A MONSTER WITH LOW ATTACK POINTS AS A DECOY TO ACTIVATE FEARFUL EARTHBOUND!
WHRRR
I CAN'T STOP MY MONSTER FROM ATTACKING!
GH...
GO AHEAD AND DEFEAT MY DECOY... IT'S WEAK ANYWAY...
THE MORE MONSTERS YOU SEND TO THE GRAVEYARD, THE STRONGER MY OCCULT DECK GETS!
NA-DOOM
SKRRRRR
WHR
DRILLAGO
Attack
1600
GOBLIN ZOMBIE
Attack
1100

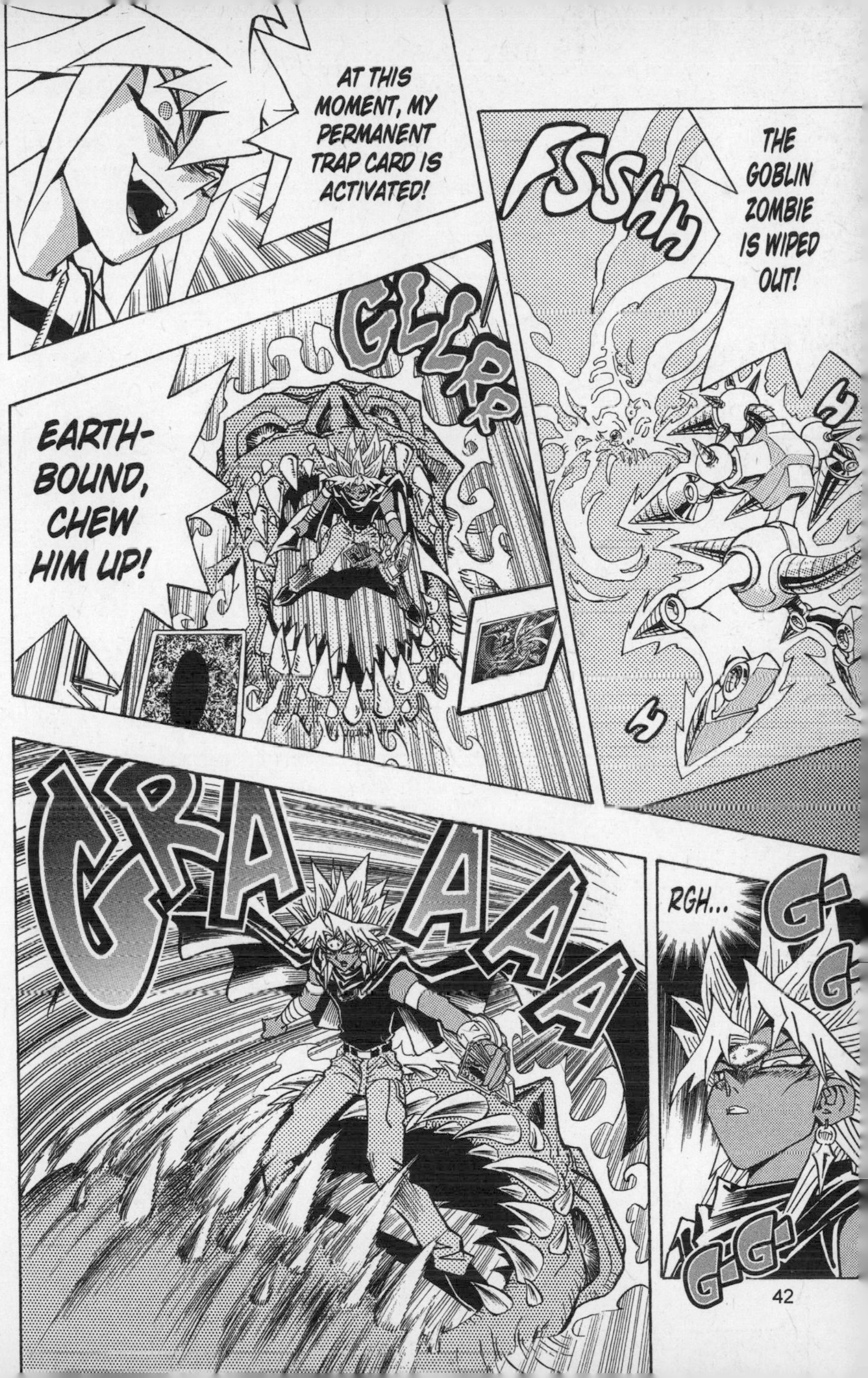
FSSHH
THE GOBLIN ZOMBIE IS WIPED OUT!
H
H
AT THIS MOMENT, MY PERMANENT TRAP CARD IS ACTIVATED!
GLLRR
EARTH-BOUND, CHEW HIM UP!
RGH...
G-G-
G-G-
CRAAAAA

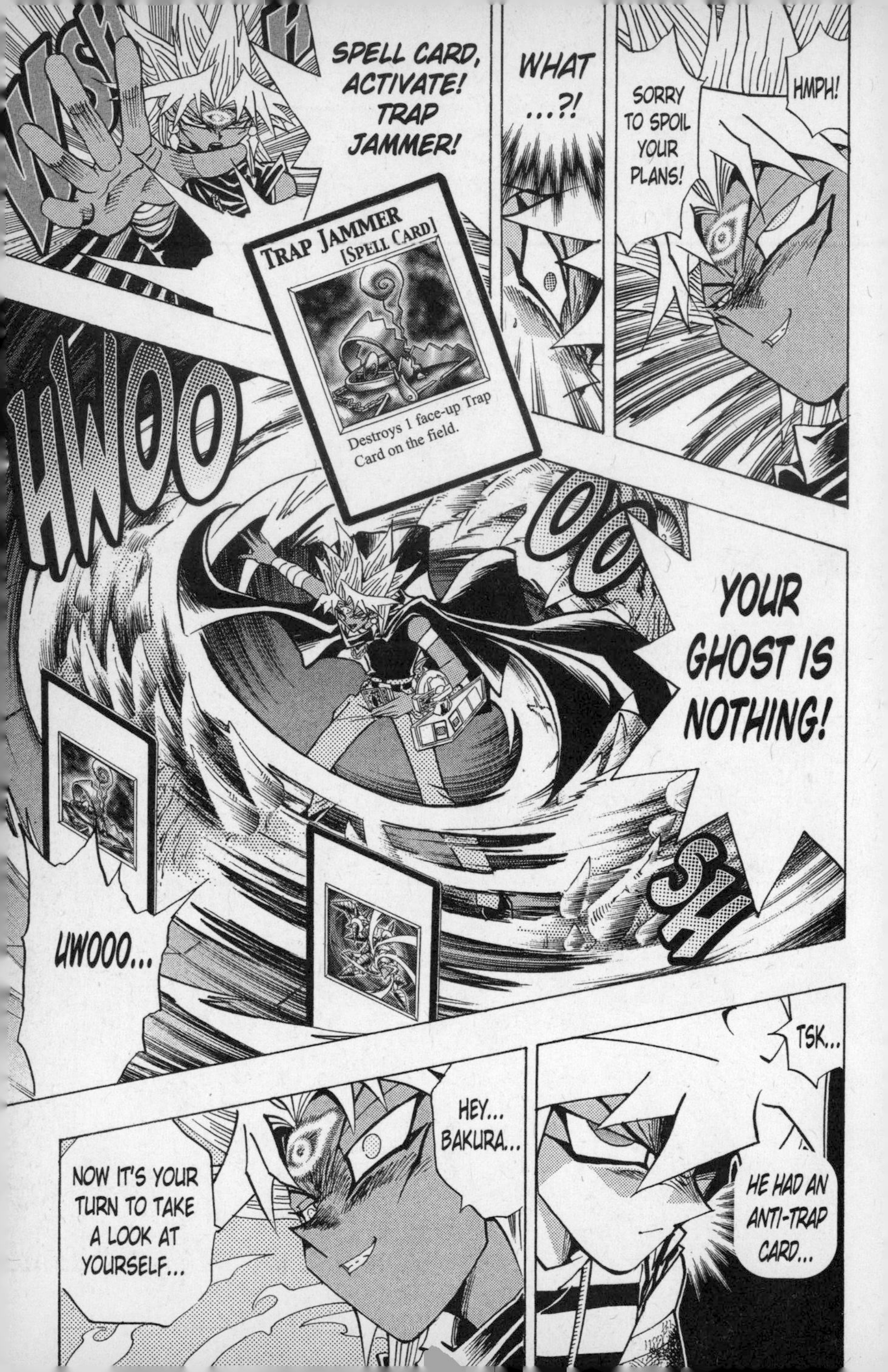
HMPH!
SORRY TO SPOIL YOUR PLANS!
WHAT ...?!
SPELL CARD, ACTIVATE! TRAP JAMMER!
TRAP JAMMER
[SPELL CARD]
Destroys 1 face-up Trap Card on the field.
HWOO
OOO
YOUR GHOST IS NOTHING!
SH
UWOOO...
TSK...
HE HAD AN ANTI-TRAP CARD...
HEY... BAKURA...
NOW IT'S YOUR TURN TO TAKE A LOOK AT YOURSELF...

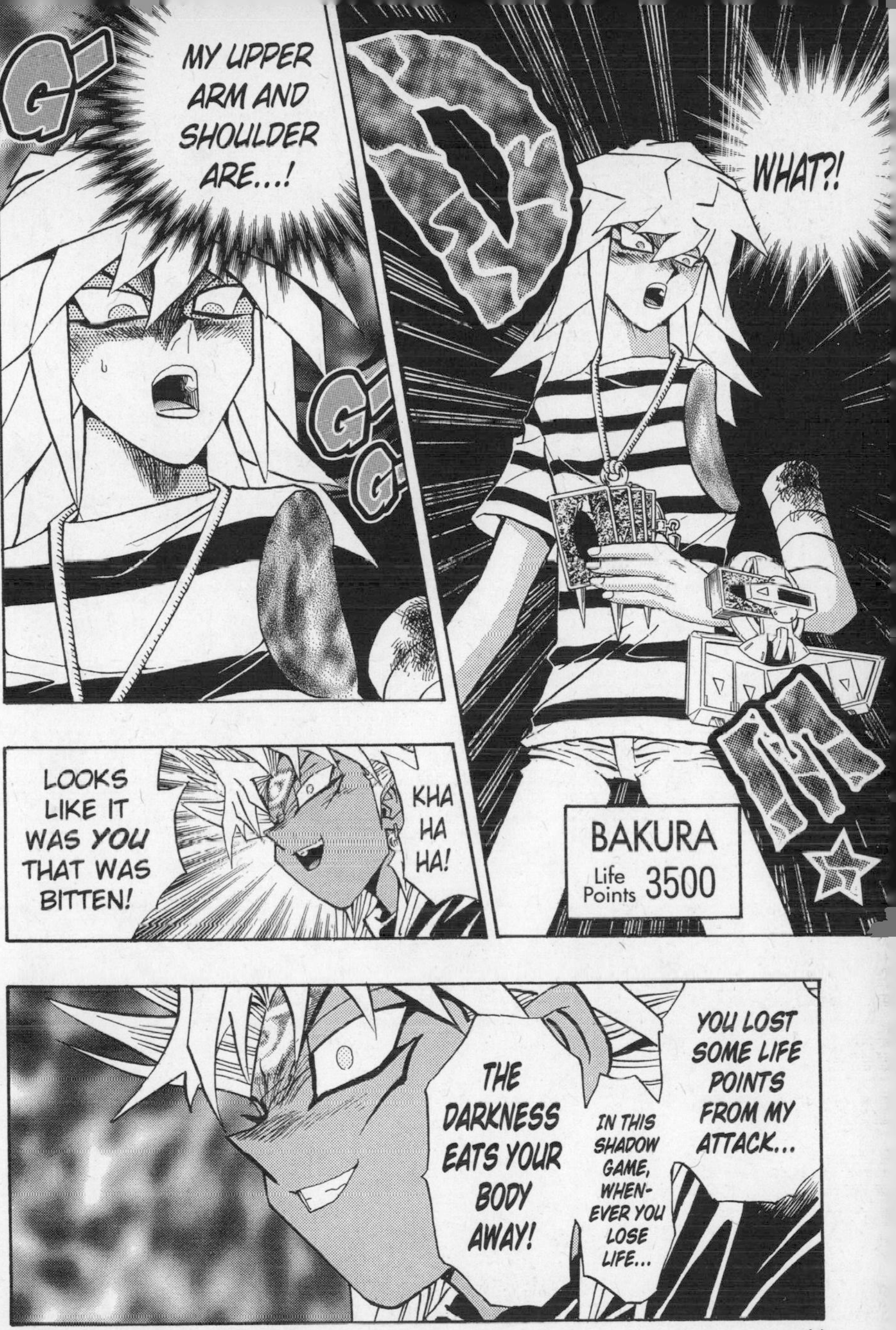
WHAT?!
BAKURA
Life Points 3500
G
MY UPPER ARM AND SHOULDER ARE...!
G G
KHA HA HA!
LOOKS LIKE IT WAS *YOU* THAT WAS BITTEN!
YOU LOST SOME LIFE POINTS FROM MY ATTACK...
IN THIS SHADOW GAME, WHENEVER YOU LOSE LIFE...
THE DARKNESS EATS YOUR BODY AWAY!

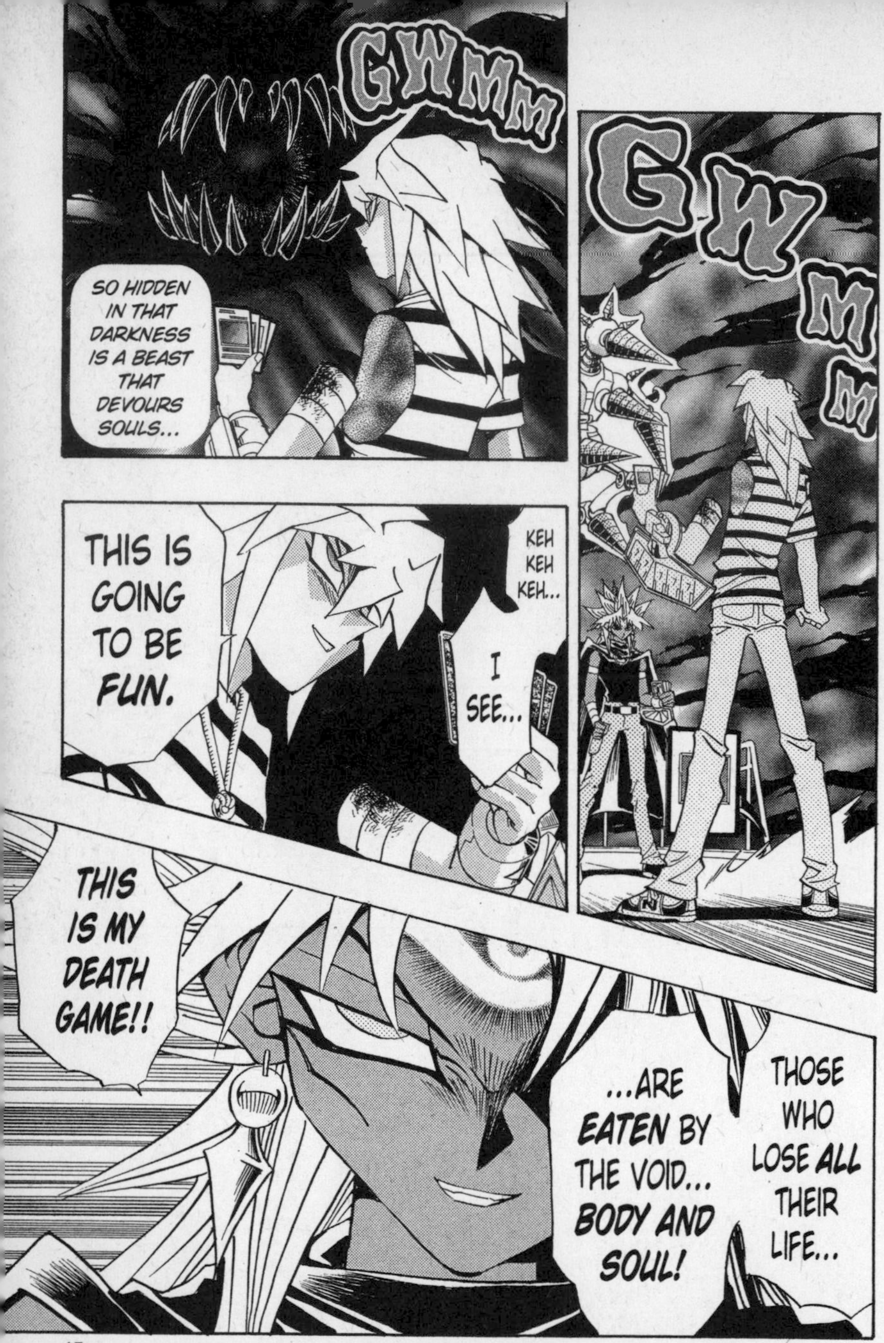
GWMMM
GWMM
SO HIDDEN IN THAT DARKNESS IS A BEAST THAT DEVOURS SOULS...
KEH KEH KEH...
I SEE...
THIS IS GOING TO BE FUN.
THOSE WHO LOSE ALL THEIR LIFE...
...ARE EATEN BY THE VOID... BODY AND SOUL!
THIS IS MY DEATH GAME!!

Duel 176: The Crumbling Darkness

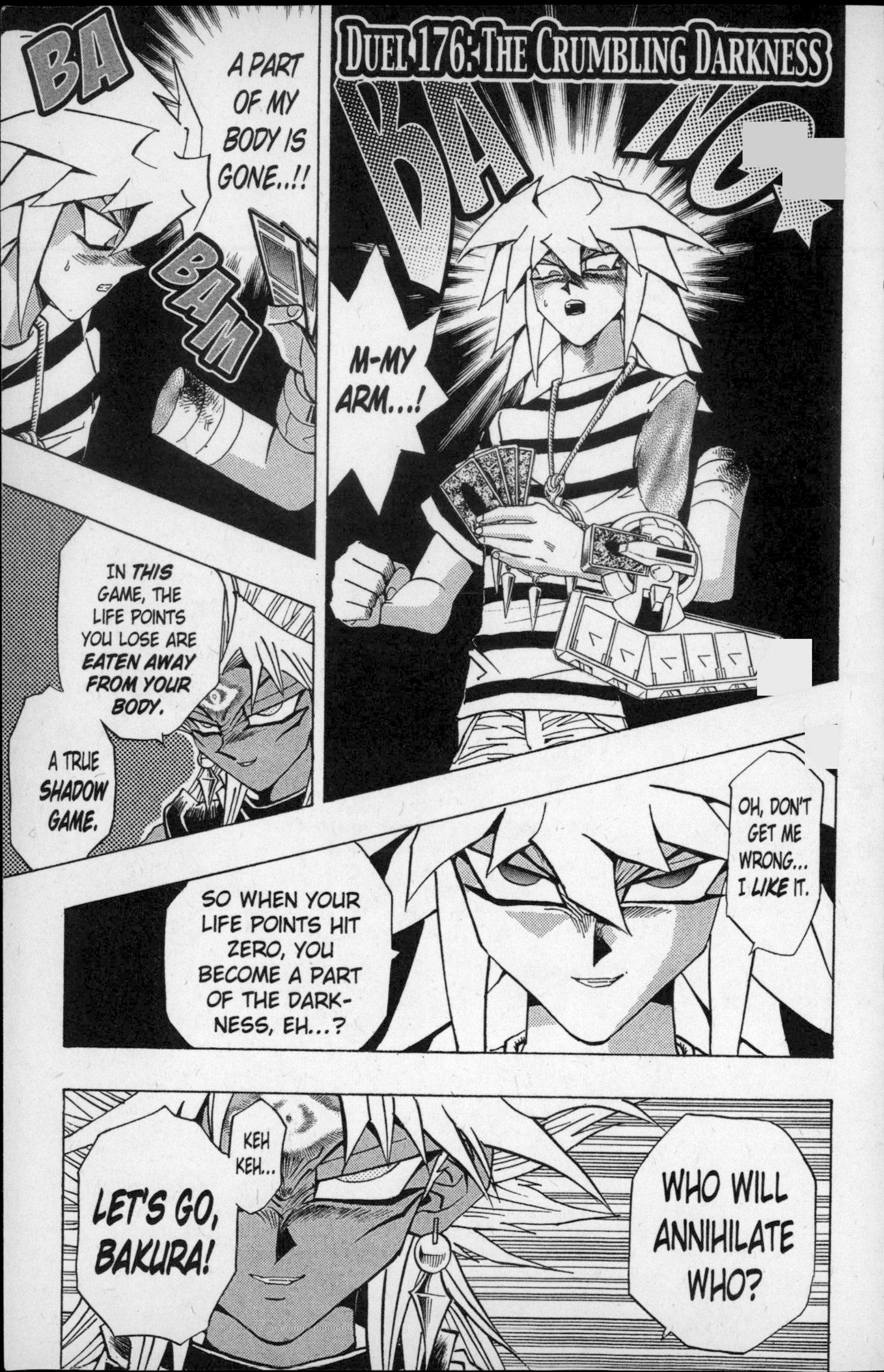
BANG
M-MY ARM...!
BA
A PART OF MY BODY IS GONE...!!
BAM
IN THIS GAME, THE LIFE POINTS YOU LOSE ARE EATEN AWAY FROM YOUR BODY.
A TRUE SHADOW GAME.
OH, DON'T GET ME WRONG... I LIKE IT.
SO WHEN YOUR LIFE POINTS HIT ZERO, YOU BECOME A PART OF THE DARK-NESS, EH...?
WHO WILL ANNIHILATE WHO?
KEH KEH...
LET'S GO, BAKURA!

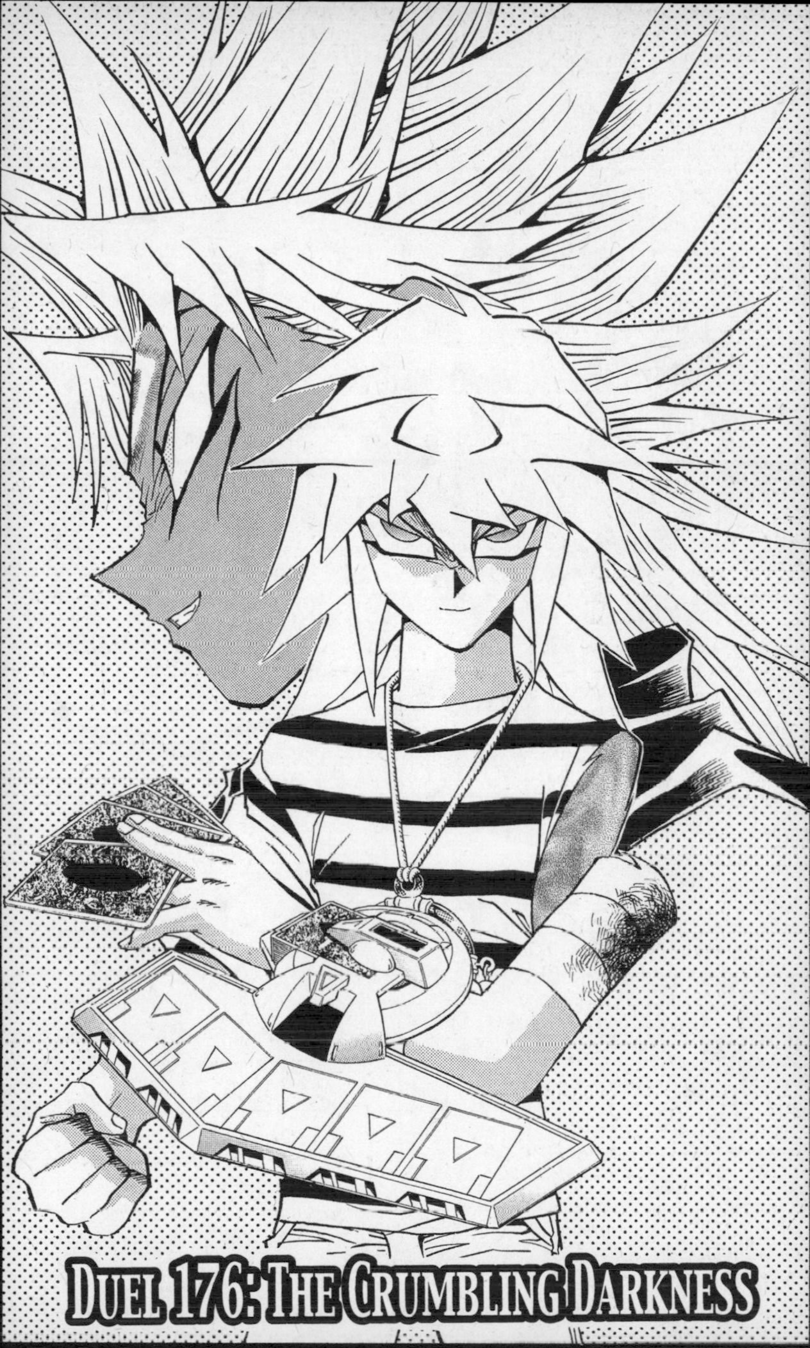

Duel 176: The Crumbling Darkness

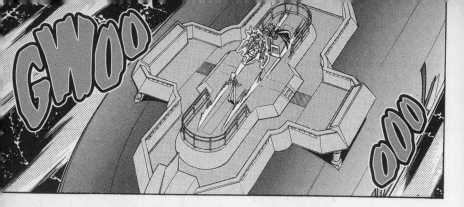

IT'S YOUR TURN...

MARIK
Life Points 4000

BAKURA
Life Points 3500

DRAW CARD!!

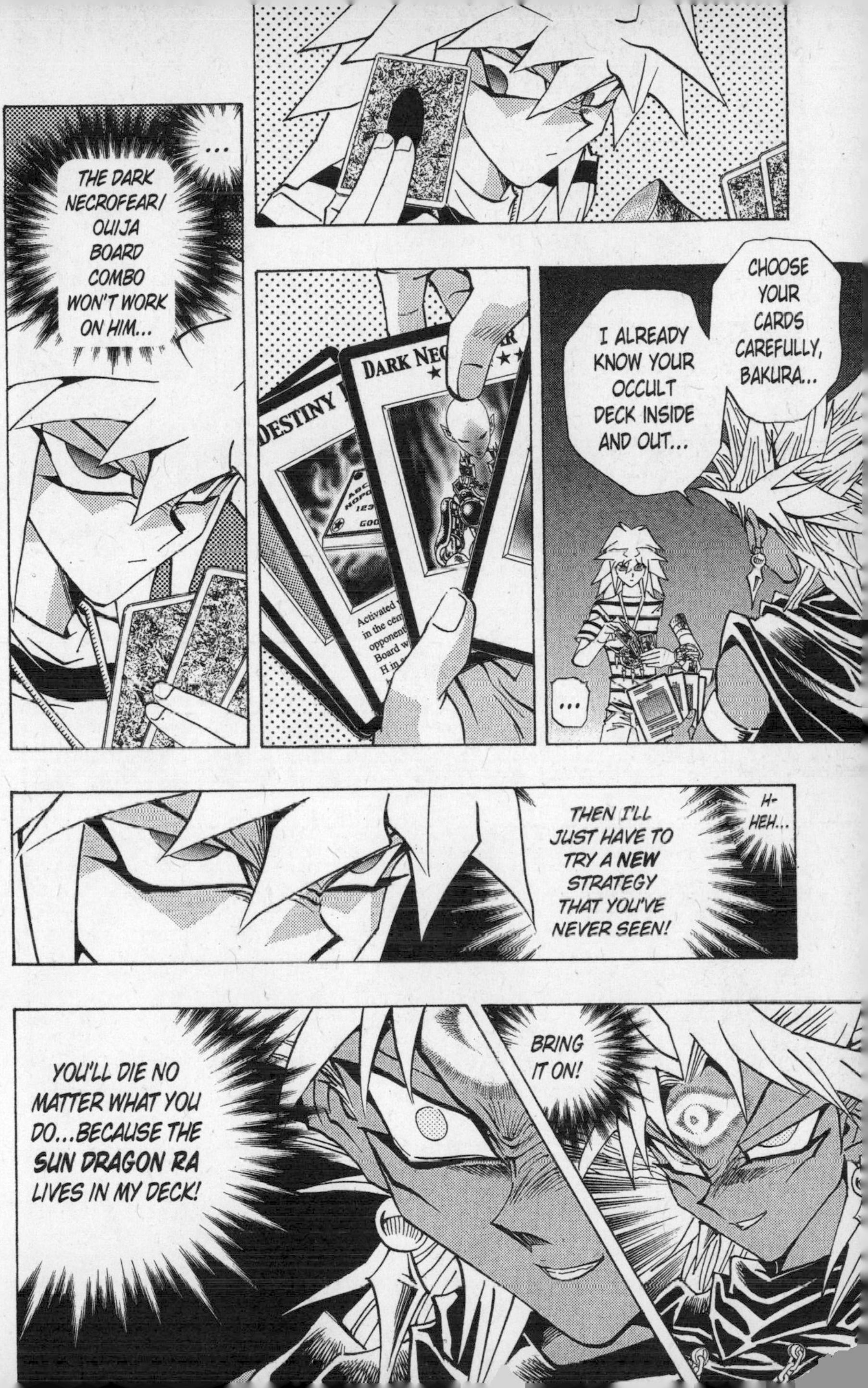
CHOOSE YOUR CARDS CAREFULLY, BAKURA...
I ALREADY KNOW YOUR OCCULT DECK INSIDE AND OUT...
...
...
THE DARK NECROFEAR/OUIJA BOARD COMBO WON'T WORK ON HIM...
H-HEH...
THEN I'LL JUST HAVE TO TRY A **NEW** STRATEGY THAT YOU'VE NEVER SEEN!
BRING IT ON!
YOU'LL DIE NO MATTER WHAT YOU DO...BECAUSE THE **SUN DRAGON RA** LIVES IN MY DECK!

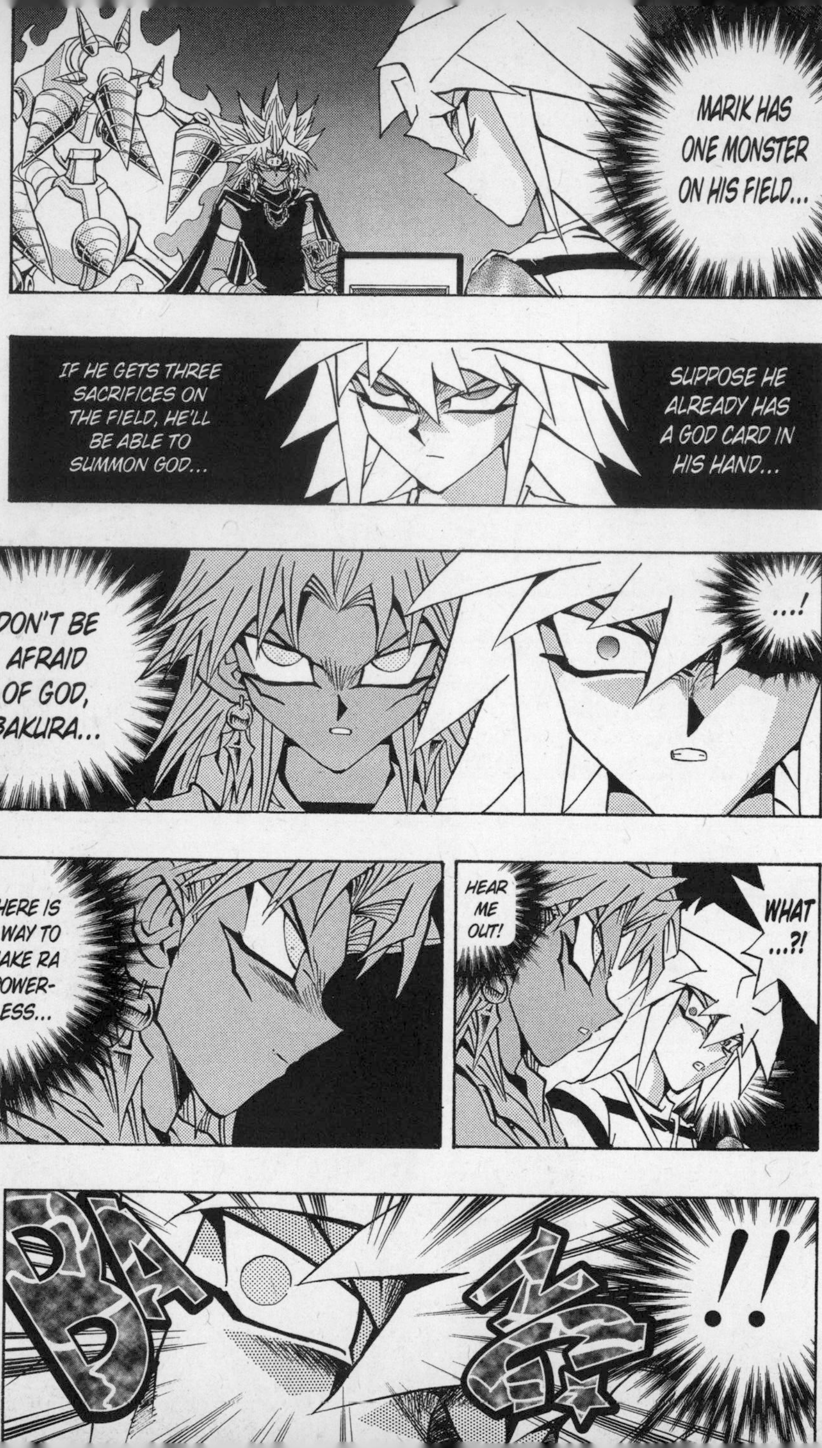
MARIK HAS ONE MONSTER ON HIS FIELD...
SUPPOSE HE ALREADY HAS A GOD CARD IN HIS HAND...
IF HE GETS THREE SACRIFICES ON THE FIELD, HE'LL BE ABLE TO SUMMON GOD...
...!
DON'T BE AFRAID OF GOD, BAKURA...
WHAT ...?!
HEAR ME OUT!
THERE IS A WAY TO MAKE RA POWER-LESS...
BADANG
!!

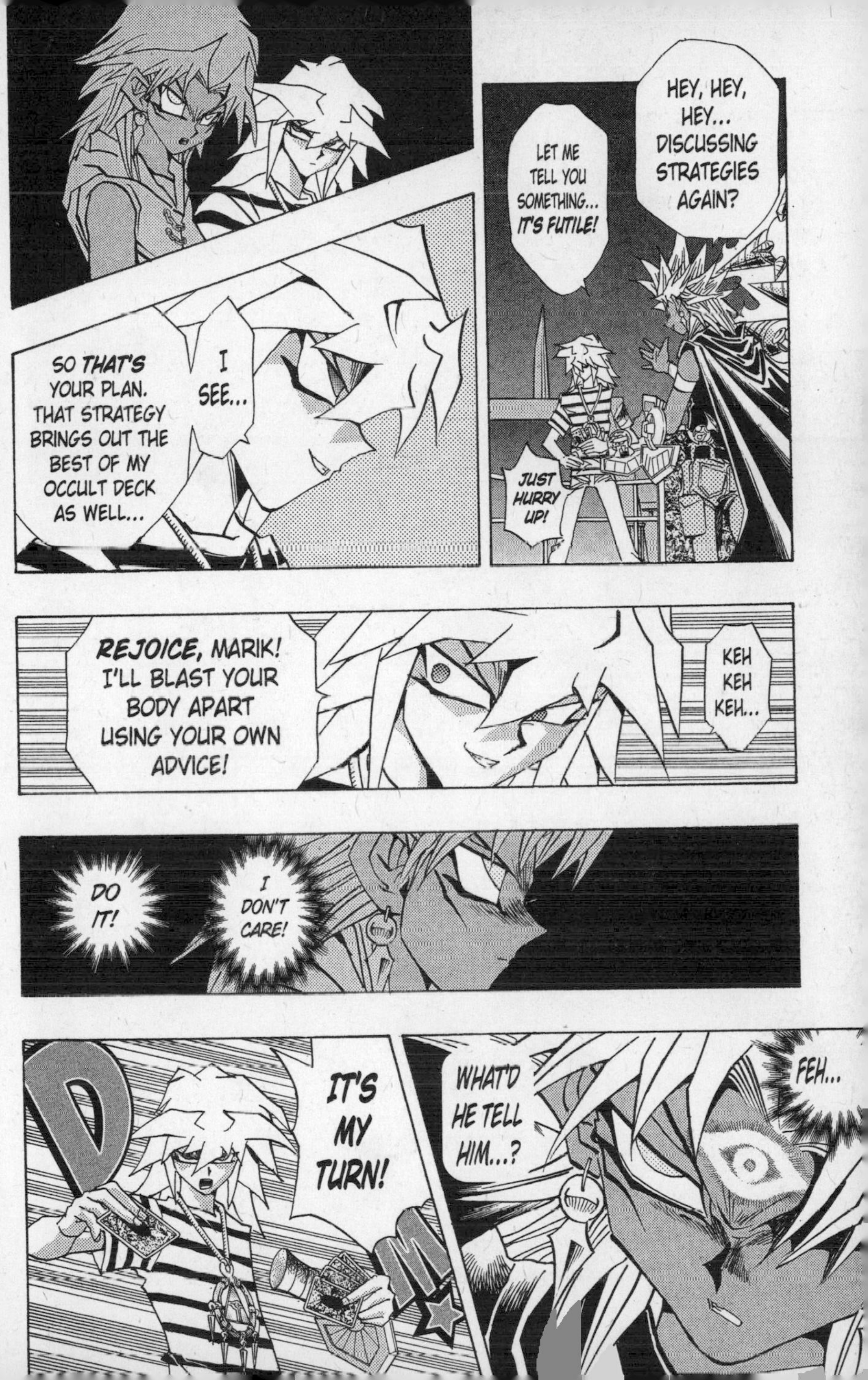
HEY, HEY, HEY... DISCUSSING STRATEGIES AGAIN?
LET ME TELL YOU SOMETHING... IT'S FUTILE!
JUST HURRY UP!
I SEE...
SO THAT'S YOUR PLAN. THAT STRATEGY BRINGS OUT THE BEST OF MY OCCULT DECK AS WELL...
KEH KEH KEH...
REJOICE, MARIK! I'LL BLAST YOUR BODY APART USING YOUR OWN ADVICE!
I DON'T CARE!
DO IT!
FEH...
WHAT'D HE TELL HIM...?
IT'S MY TURN!

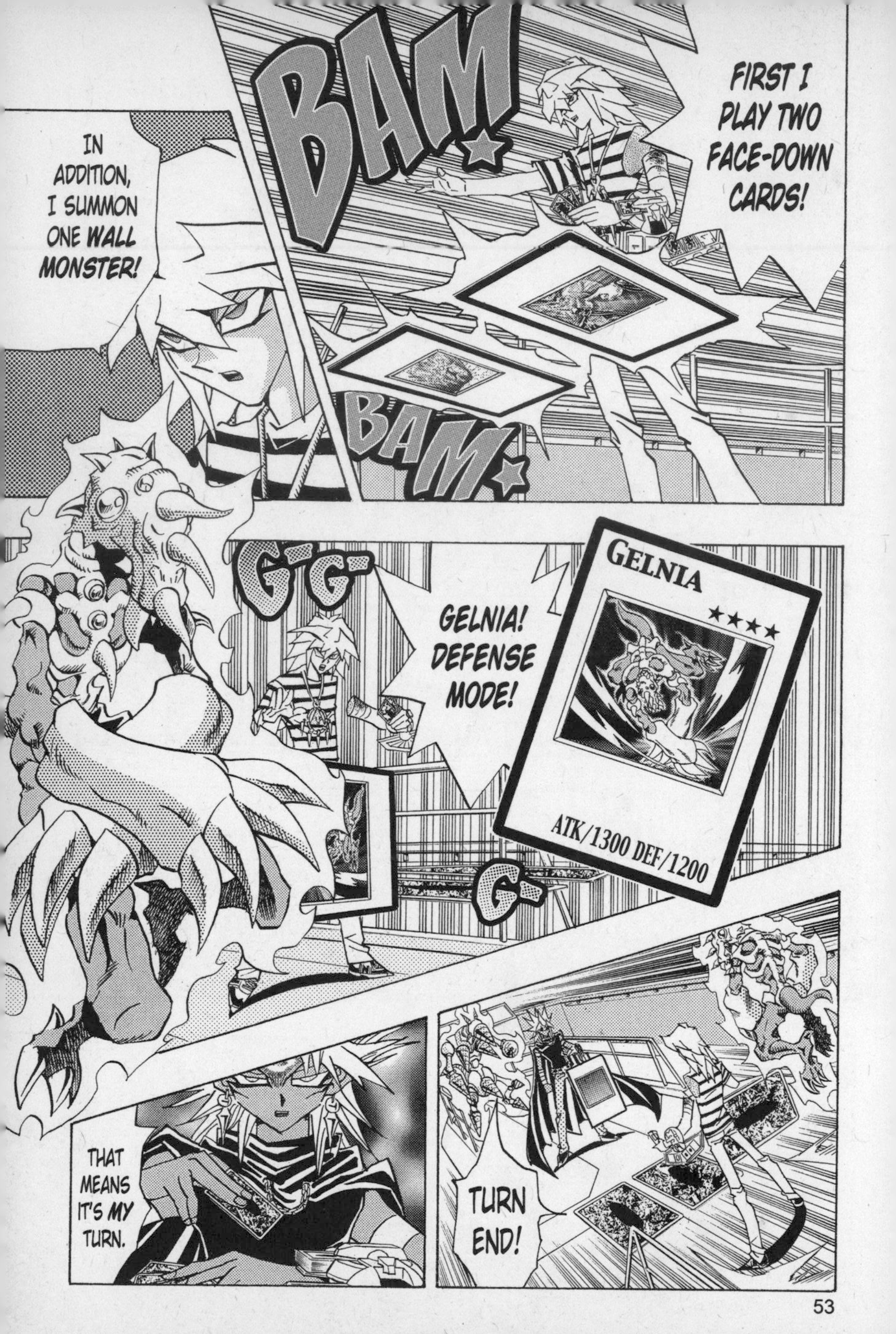
BAM
FIRST I PLAY TWO FACE-DOWN CARDS!
BAM
IN ADDITION, I SUMMON ONE WALL MONSTER!
G-G-
GELNIA! DEFENSE MODE!
GELNIA
ATK/1300 DEF/1200
G-
TURN END!
THAT MEANS IT'S MY TURN.

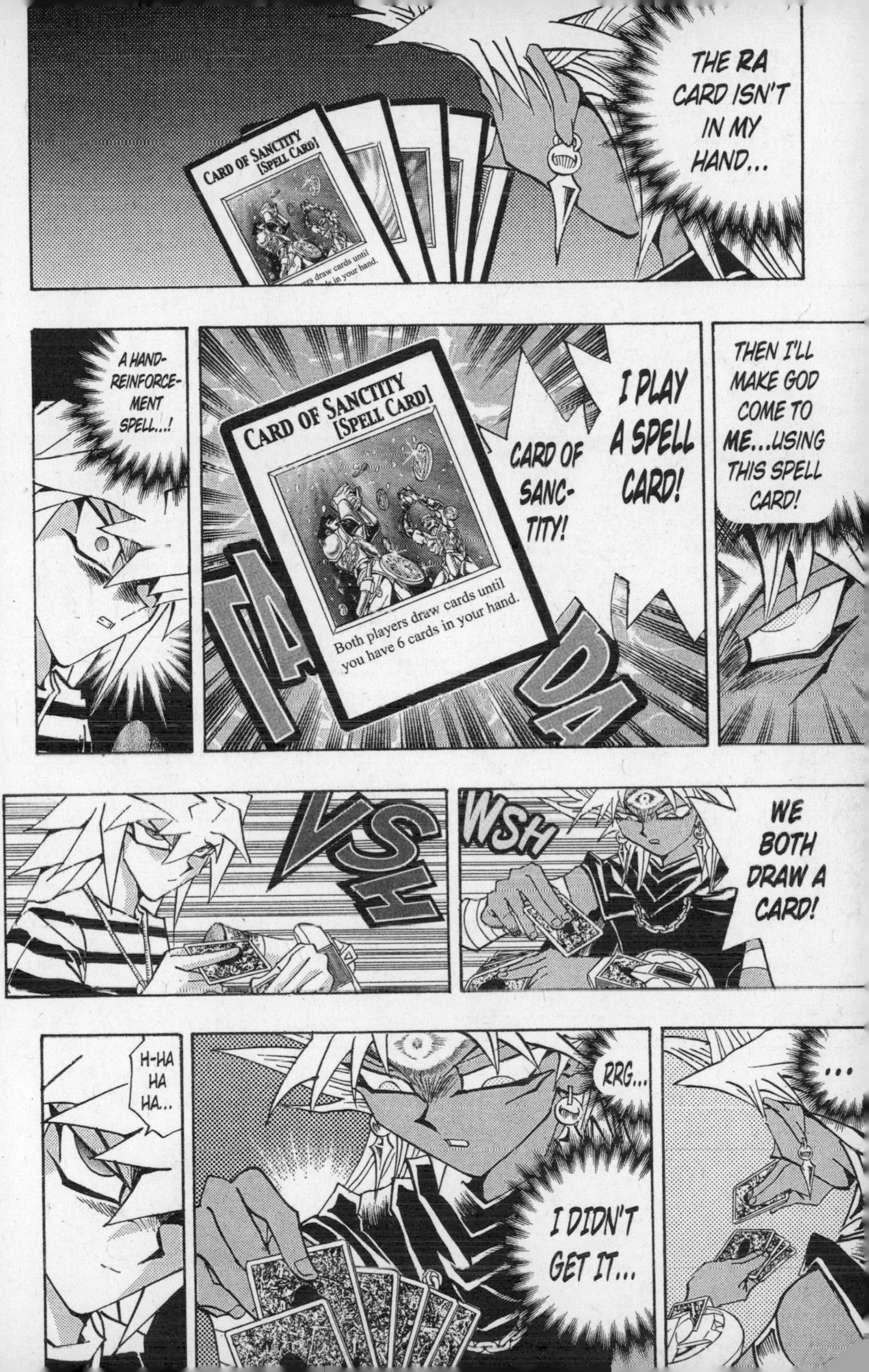
THE RA CARD ISN'T IN MY HAND...
CARD OF SANCTITY [SPELL CARD]
THEN I'LL MAKE GOD COME TO ME...USING THIS SPELL CARD!
I PLAY A SPELL CARD!
CARD OF SANC-TITY!
CARD OF SANCTITY [SPELL CARD]
Both players draw cards until you have 6 cards in your hand.
TA
DA
A HAND-REINFORCEMENT SPELL...!
WSH
WE BOTH DRAW A CARD!
VSH
...
RRG...
I DIDN'T GET IT...
H-HA HA HA...

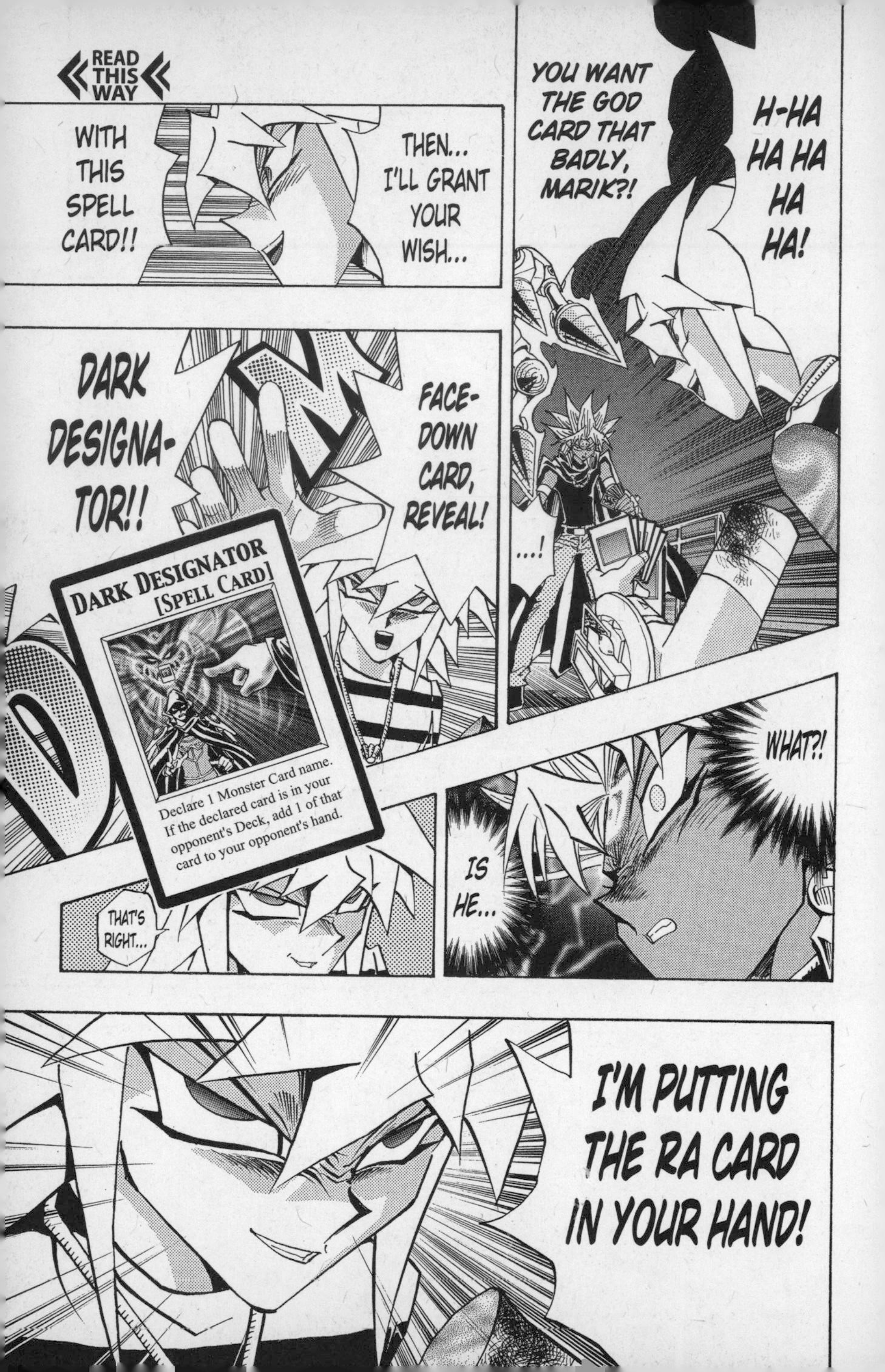
READ THIS WAY
H-HA HA HA HA HA!
YOU WANT THE GOD CARD THAT BADLY, MARIK?!
...!
THEN... I'LL GRANT YOUR WISH...
WITH THIS SPELL CARD!!
FACE-DOWN CARD, REVEAL!
DARK DESIGNA-TOR!!
DARK DESIGNATOR [SPELL CARD]
Declare 1 Monster Card name. If the declared card is in your opponent's Deck, add 1 of that card to your opponent's hand.
WHAT?!
IS HE...
THAT'S RIGHT...
I'M PUTTING THE RA CARD IN YOUR HAND!

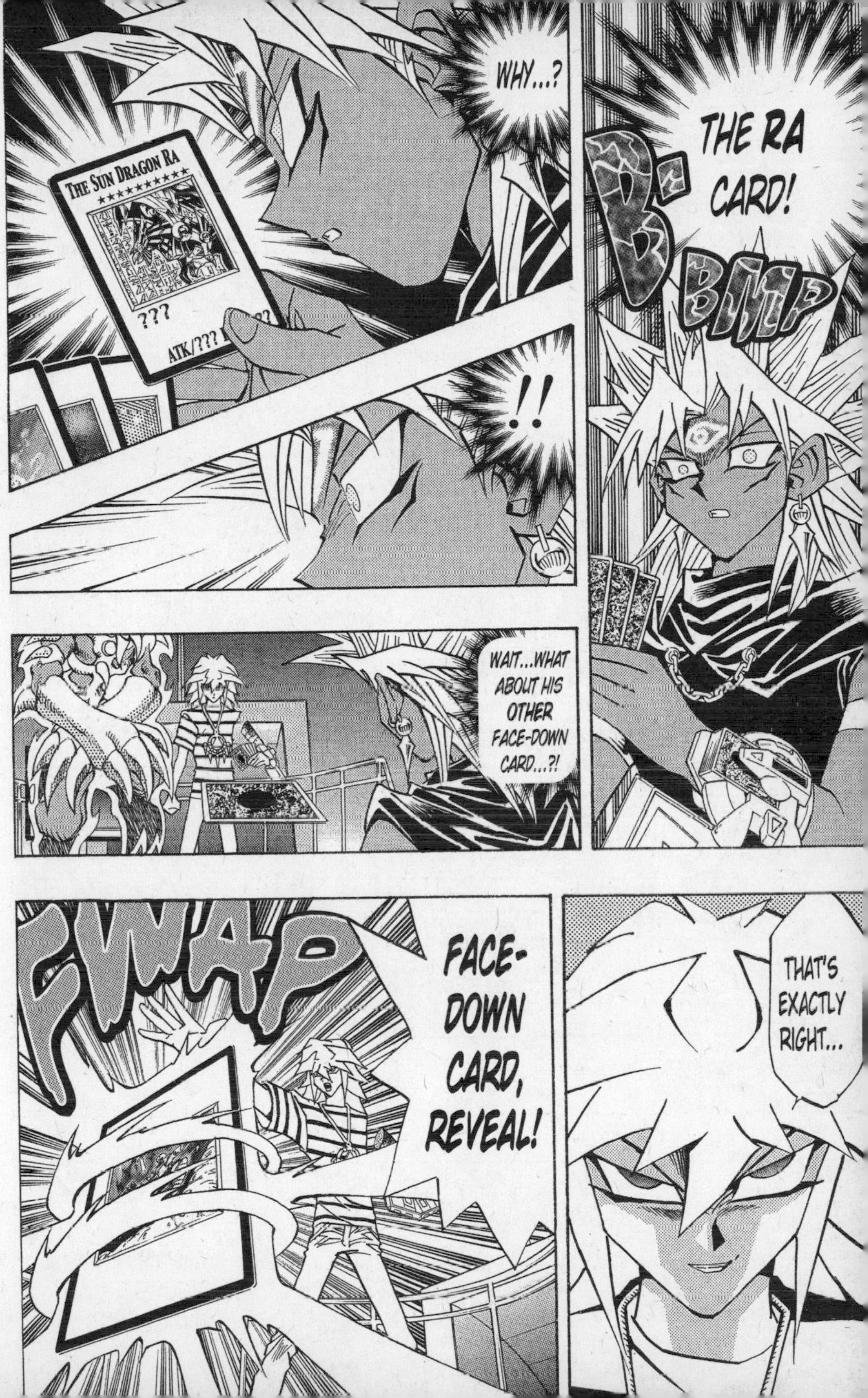
THE RA CARD!
B-BMP
WHY...?
THE SUN DRAGON RA
???
ATK/???
!!
WAIT...WHAT ABOUT HIS OTHER FACE-DOWN CARD...?!
THAT'S EXACTLY RIGHT...
FWAP
FACE-DOWN CARD, REVEAL!

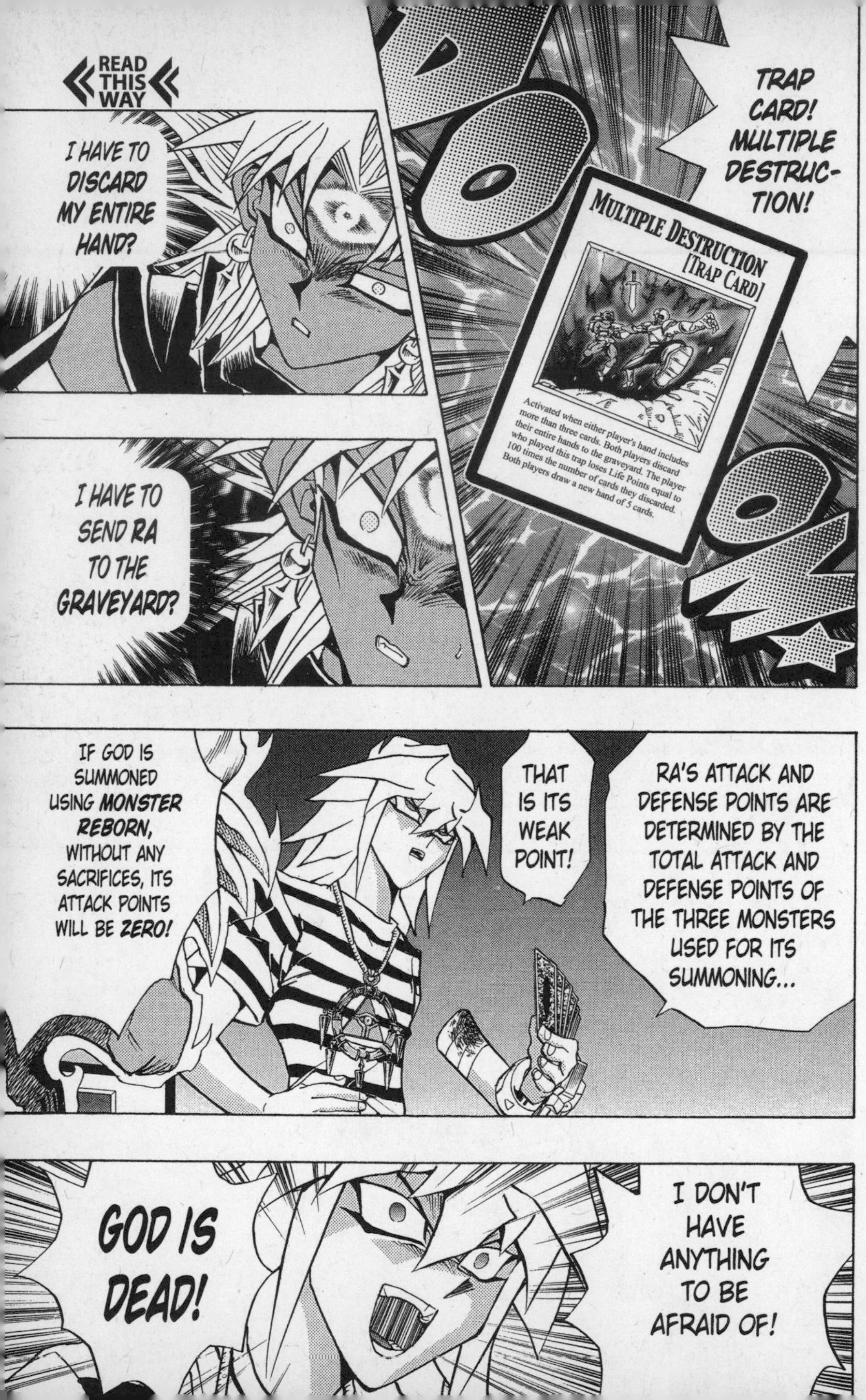
READ THIS WAY
TRAP CARD! MULTIPLE DESTRUCTION!
MULTIPLE DESTRUCTION
[TRAP CARD]
Activated when either player's hand includes more than three cards. Both players discard their entire hands to the graveyard. The player who played this trap loses Life Points equal to 100 times the number of cards they discarded. Both players draw a new hand of 5 cards.
I HAVE TO DISCARD MY ENTIRE HAND?
I HAVE TO SEND RA TO THE GRAVEYARD?
RA'S ATTACK AND DEFENSE POINTS ARE DETERMINED BY THE TOTAL ATTACK AND DEFENSE POINTS OF THE THREE MONSTERS USED FOR ITS SUMMONING...
THAT IS ITS WEAK POINT!
IF GOD IS SUMMONED USING MONSTER REBORN, WITHOUT ANY SACRIFICES, ITS ATTACK POINTS WILL BE ZERO!
I DON'T HAVE ANYTHING TO BE AFRAID OF!
GOD IS DEAD!

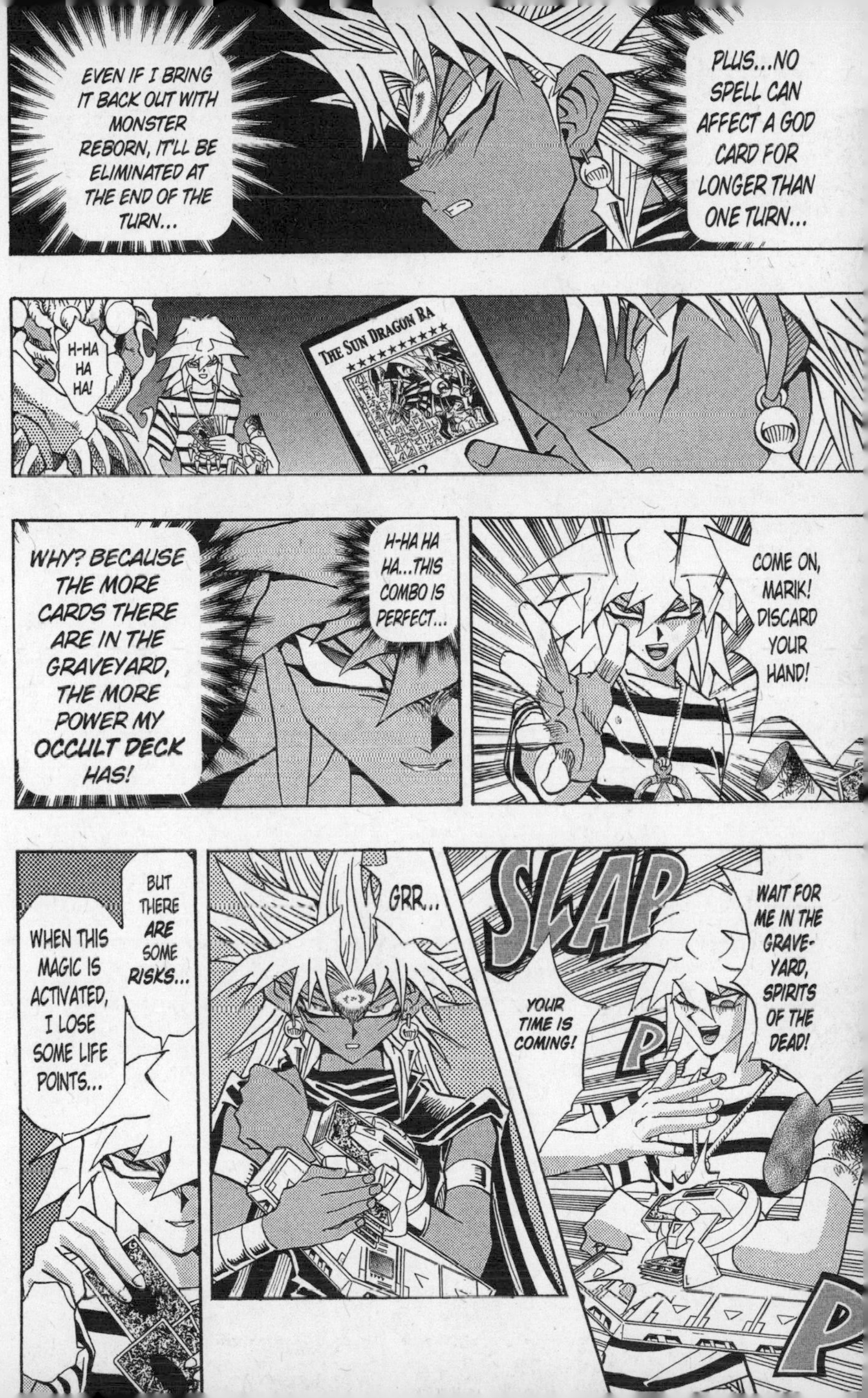
PLUS...NO SPELL CAN AFFECT A GOD CARD FOR LONGER THAN ONE TURN...
EVEN IF I BRING IT BACK OUT WITH MONSTER REBORN, IT'LL BE ELIMINATED AT THE END OF THE TURN...
THE SUN DRAGON RA
H-HA HA HA!
COME ON, MARIK! DISCARD YOUR HAND!
H-HA HA HA...THIS COMBO IS PERFECT...
WHY? BECAUSE THE MORE CARDS THERE ARE IN THE GRAVEYARD, THE MORE POWER MY OCCULT DECK HAS!
SLAP
WAIT FOR ME IN THE GRAVE-YARD, SPIRITS OF THE DEAD!
YOUR TIME IS COMING!
P
P
GRR...
BUT THERE ARE SOME RISKS...
WHEN THIS MAGIC IS ACTIVATED, I LOSE SOME LIFE POINTS...

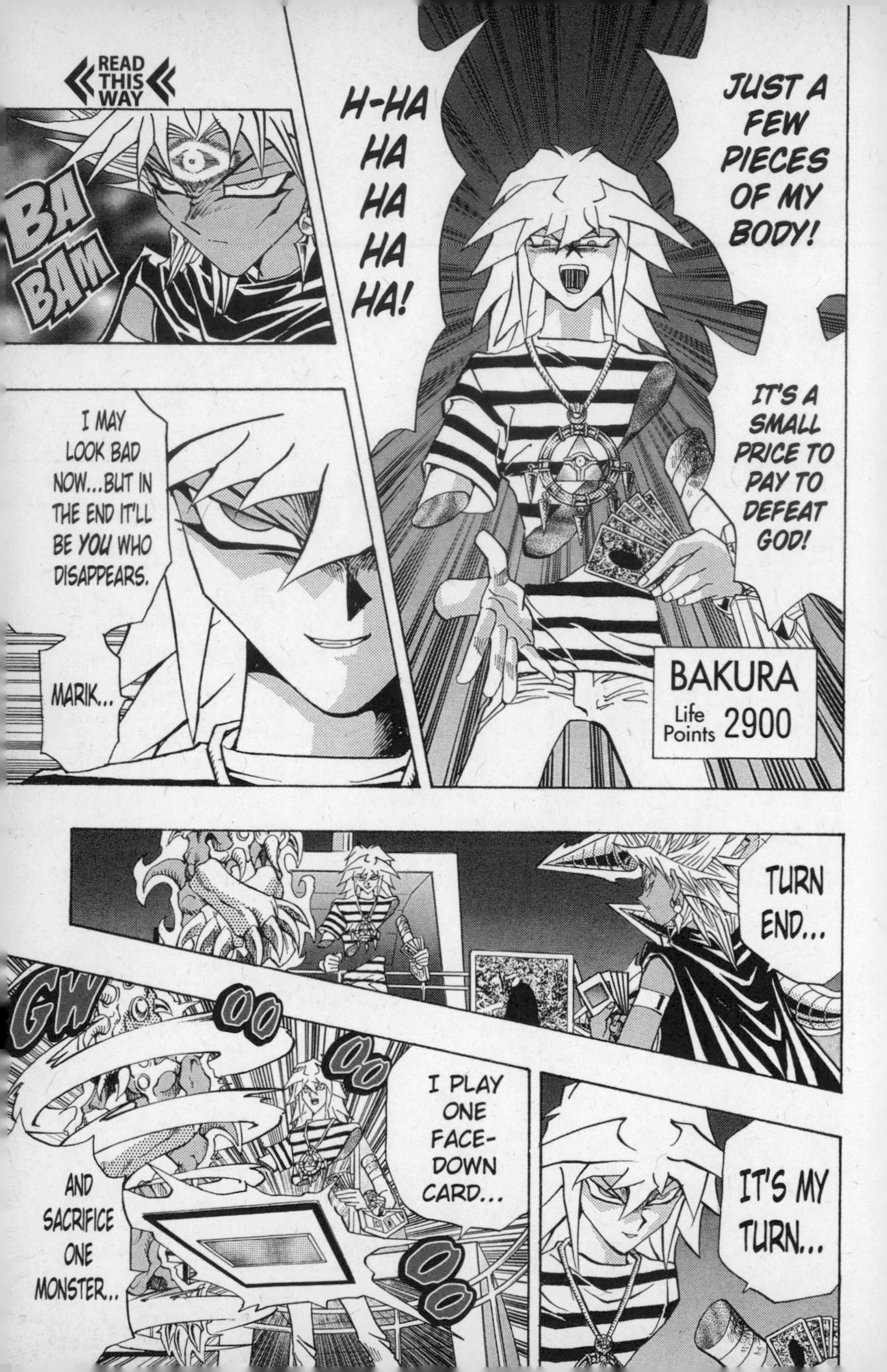
READ THIS WAY
JUST A FEW PIECES OF MY BODY!
H-HA HA HA HA HA!
IT'S A SMALL PRICE TO PAY TO DEFEAT GOD!
BAKURA Life Points 2900
BA BAM
I MAY LOOK BAD NOW...BUT IN THE END IT'LL BE YOU WHO DISAPPEARS.
MARIK...
TURN END...
IT'S MY TURN...
I PLAY ONE FACE-DOWN CARD...
GWOOOO
AND SACRIFICE ONE MONSTER...

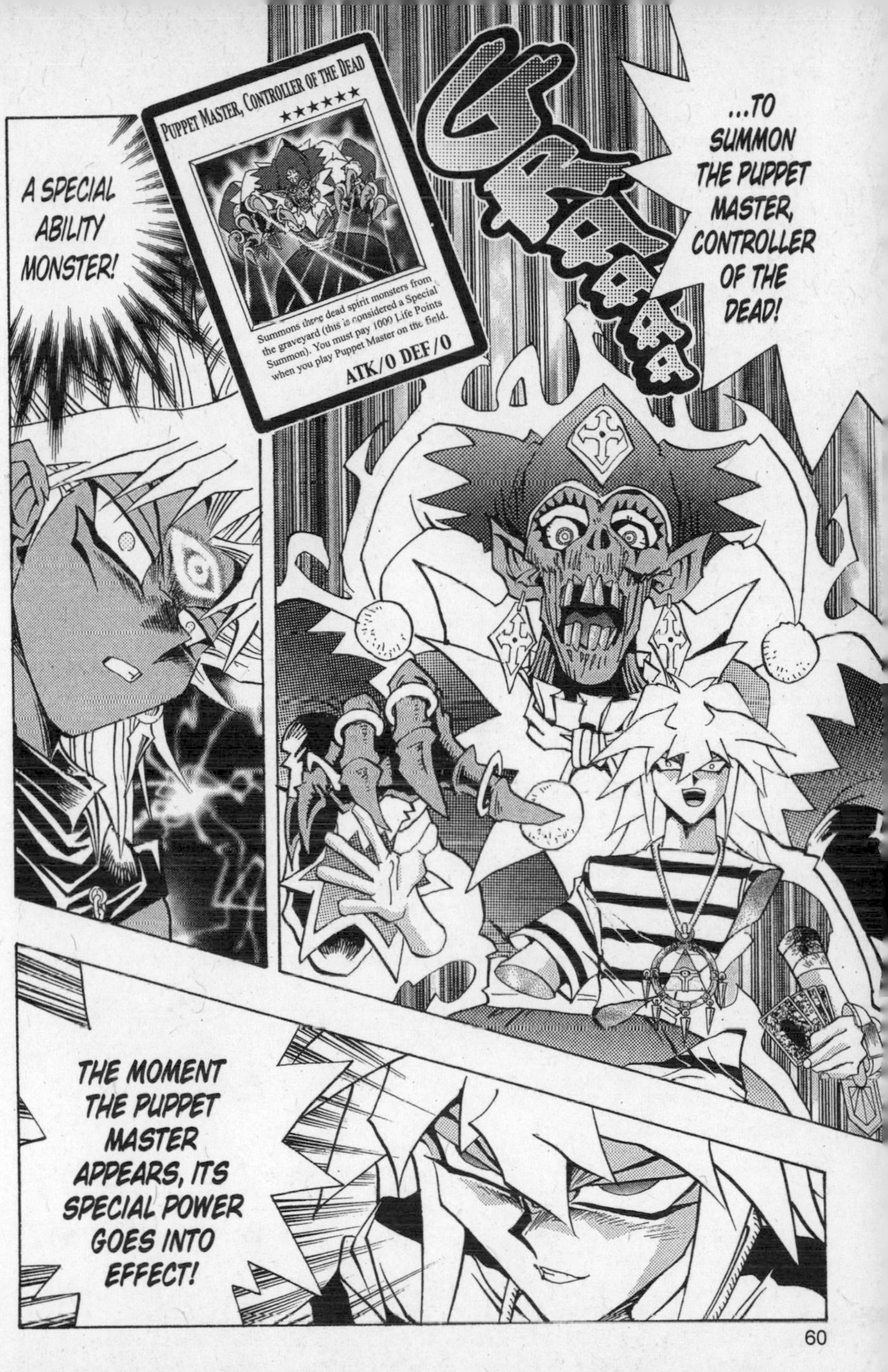
...TO SUMMON THE PUPPET MASTER, CONTROLLER OF THE DEAD!
PUPPET MASTER, CONTROLLER OF THE DEAD
Summons three dead spirit monsters from the graveyard (this is considered a Special Summon). You must pay 1000 Life Points when you play Puppet Master on the field.
ATK/0 DEF/0
A SPECIAL ABILITY MONSTER!
THE MOMENT THE PUPPET MASTER APPEARS, ITS SPECIAL POWER GOES INTO EFFECT!

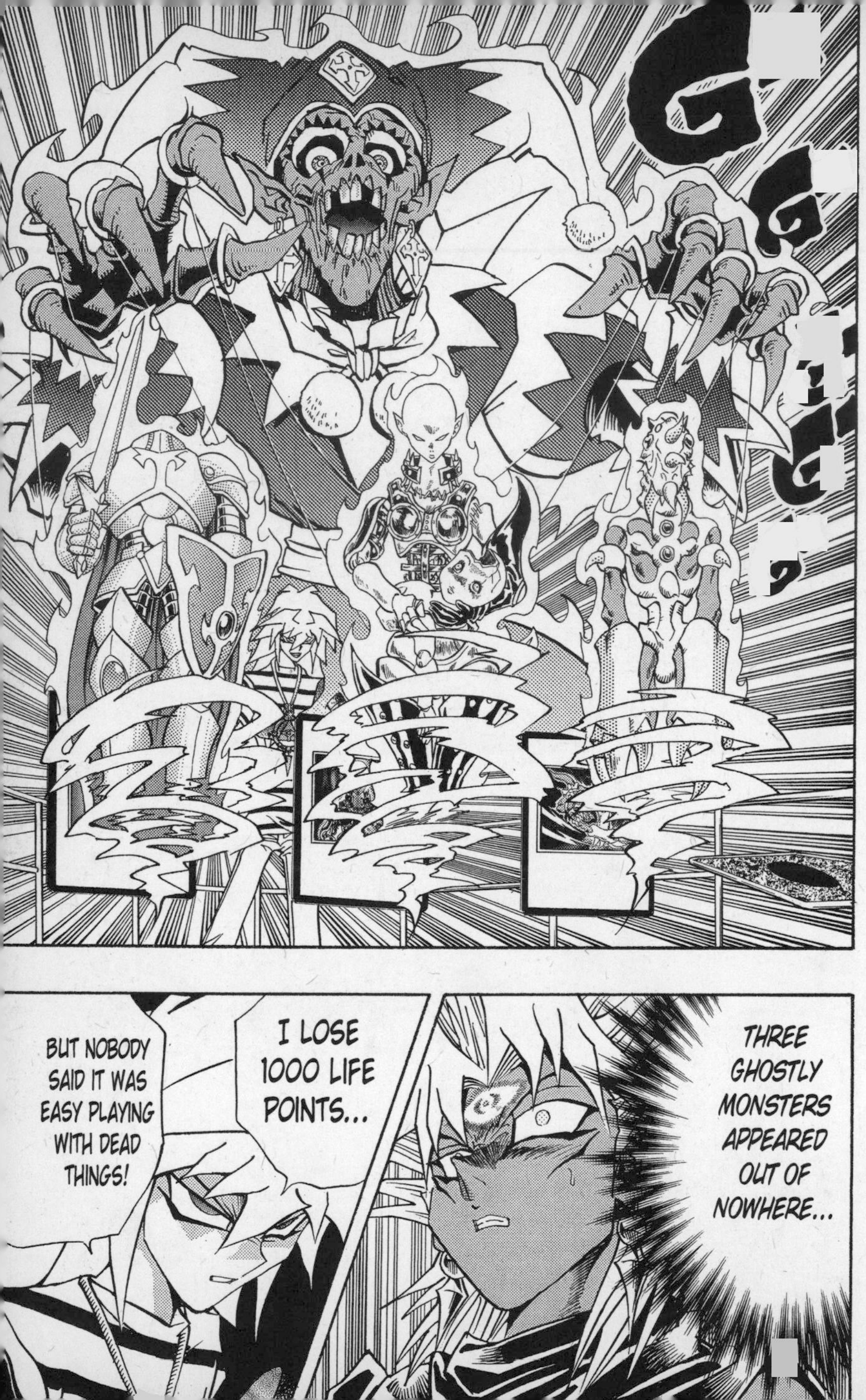
THREE GHOSTLY MONSTERS APPEARED OUT OF NOWHERE...
I LOSE 1000 LIFE POINTS...
BUT NOBODY SAID IT WAS EASY PLAYING WITH DEAD THINGS!

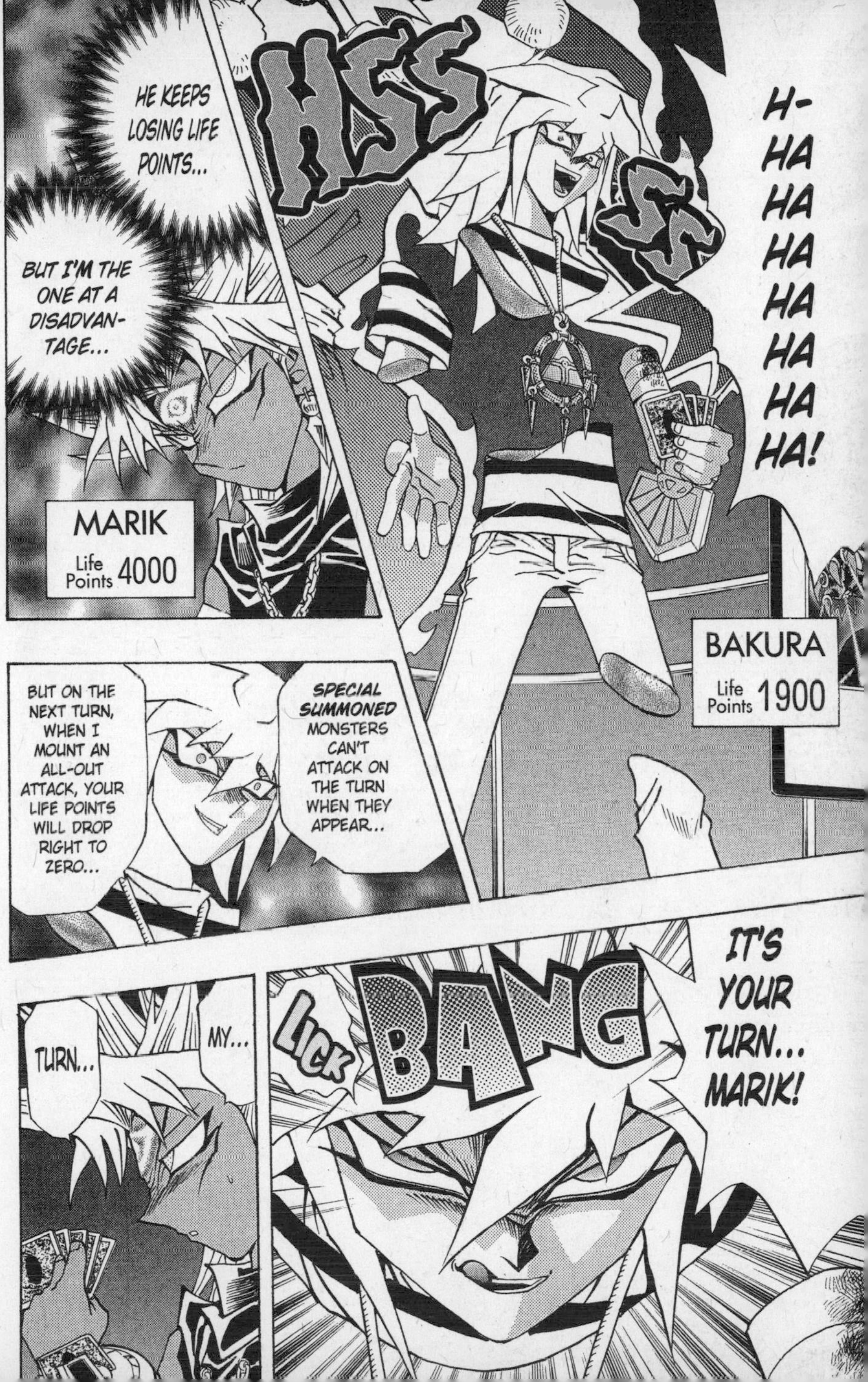

HSS
SS
H-HA HA HA HA HA HA HA!
BAKURA
Life Points 1900
HE KEEPS LOSING LIFE POINTS...
BUT I'M THE ONE AT A DISADVANTAGE...
MARIK
Life Points 4000
SPECIAL SUMMONED MONSTERS CAN'T ATTACK ON THE TURN WHEN THEY APPEAR...
BUT ON THE NEXT TURN, WHEN I MOUNT AN ALL-OUT ATTACK, YOUR LIFE POINTS WILL DROP RIGHT TO ZERO...
IT'S YOUR TURN... MARIK!
LICK
BANG
MY...
TURN...

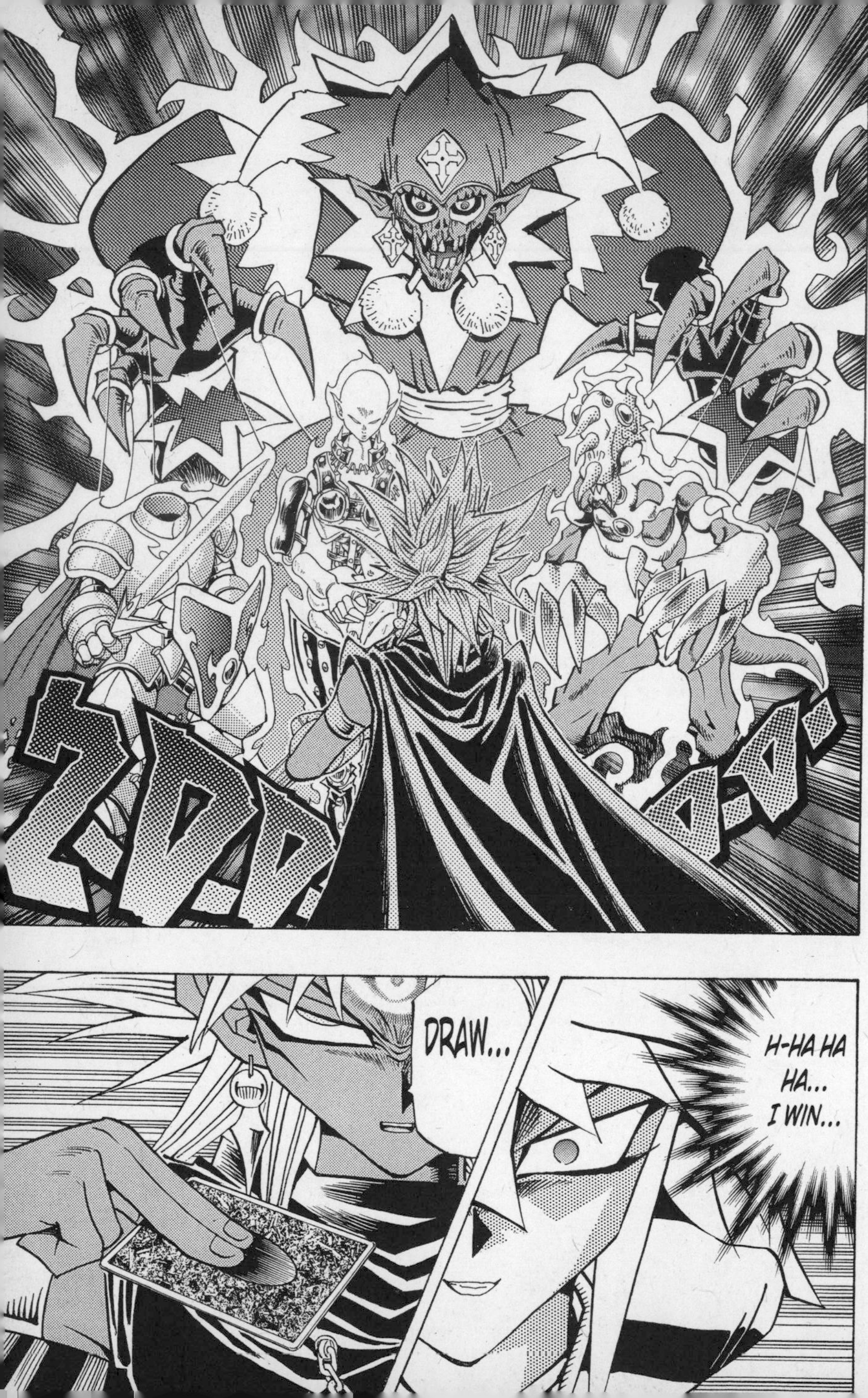
H-HA HA HA... I WIN...
DRAW...

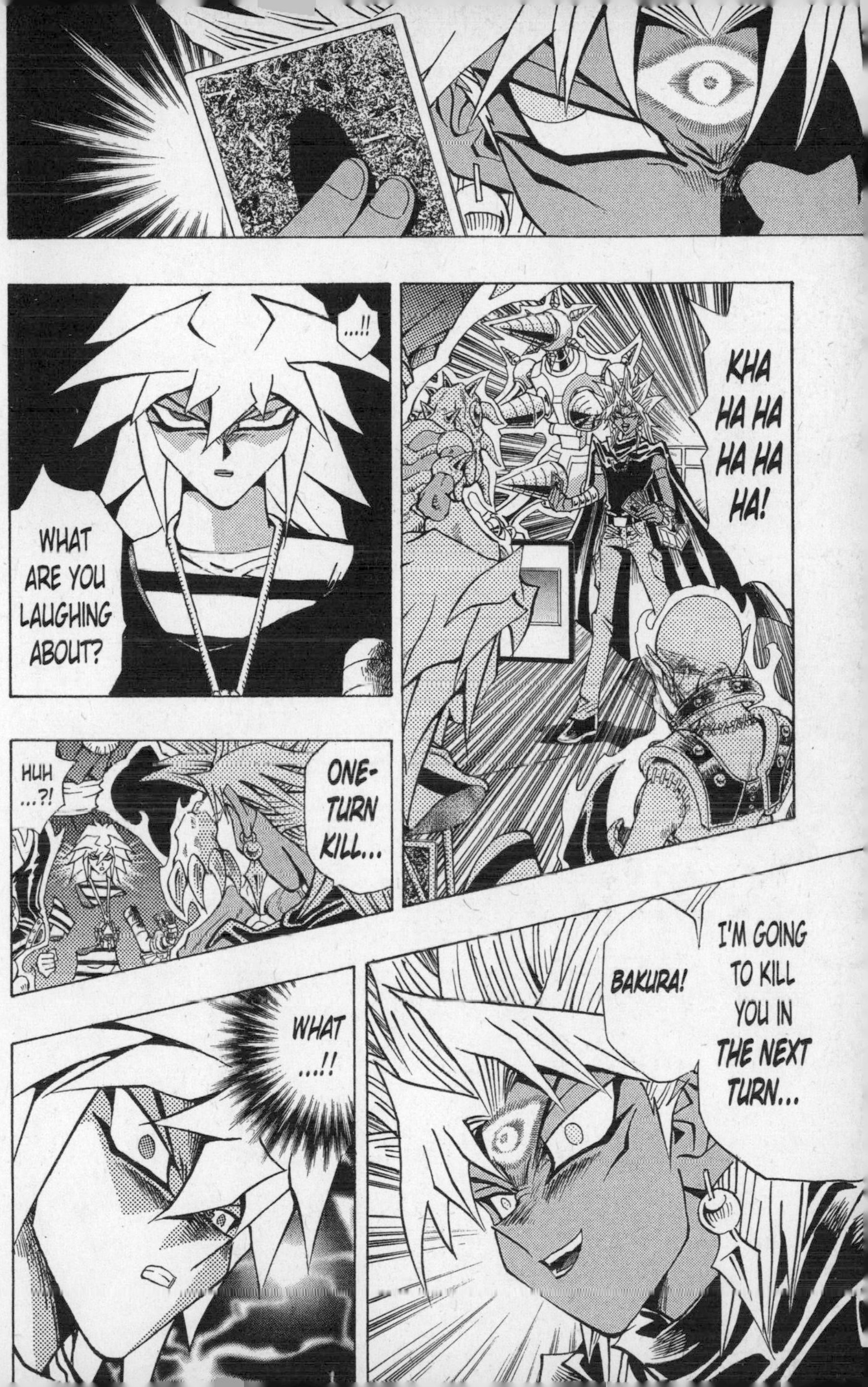
KHA HA HA HA HA HA!
...!!
WHAT ARE YOU LAUGHING ABOUT?
ONE-TURN KILL...
HUH ...?!
I'M GOING TO KILL YOU IN THE NEXT TURN...
BAKURA!
WHAT ...!!

READ THIS WAY

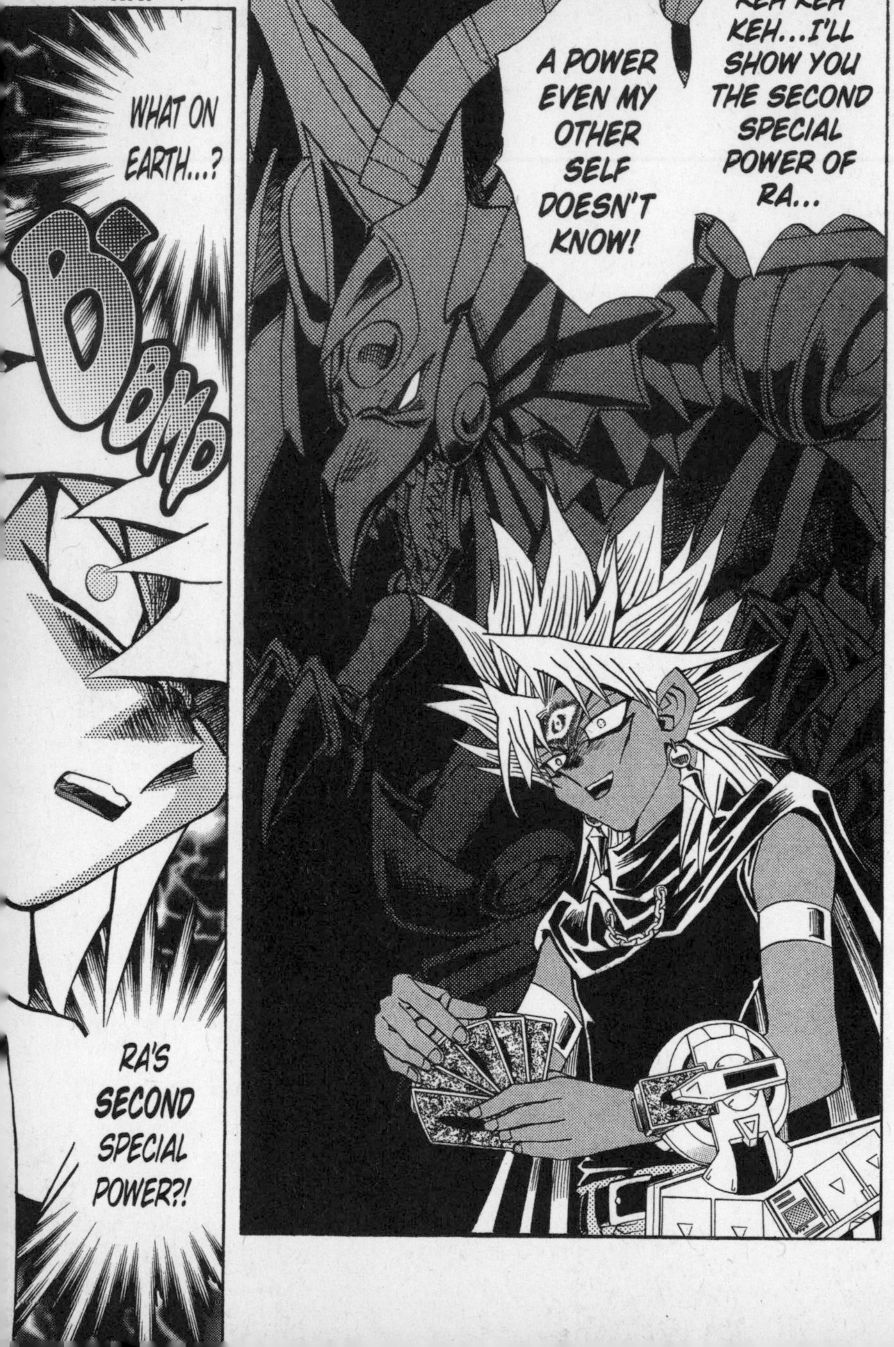
KEH KEH KEH...I'LL SHOW YOU THE SECOND SPECIAL POWER OF RA...
A POWER EVEN MY OTHER SELF DOESN'T KNOW!
WHAT ON EARTH...?
RA'S SECOND SPECIAL POWER?!

Duel 177: The Dark God is Born!

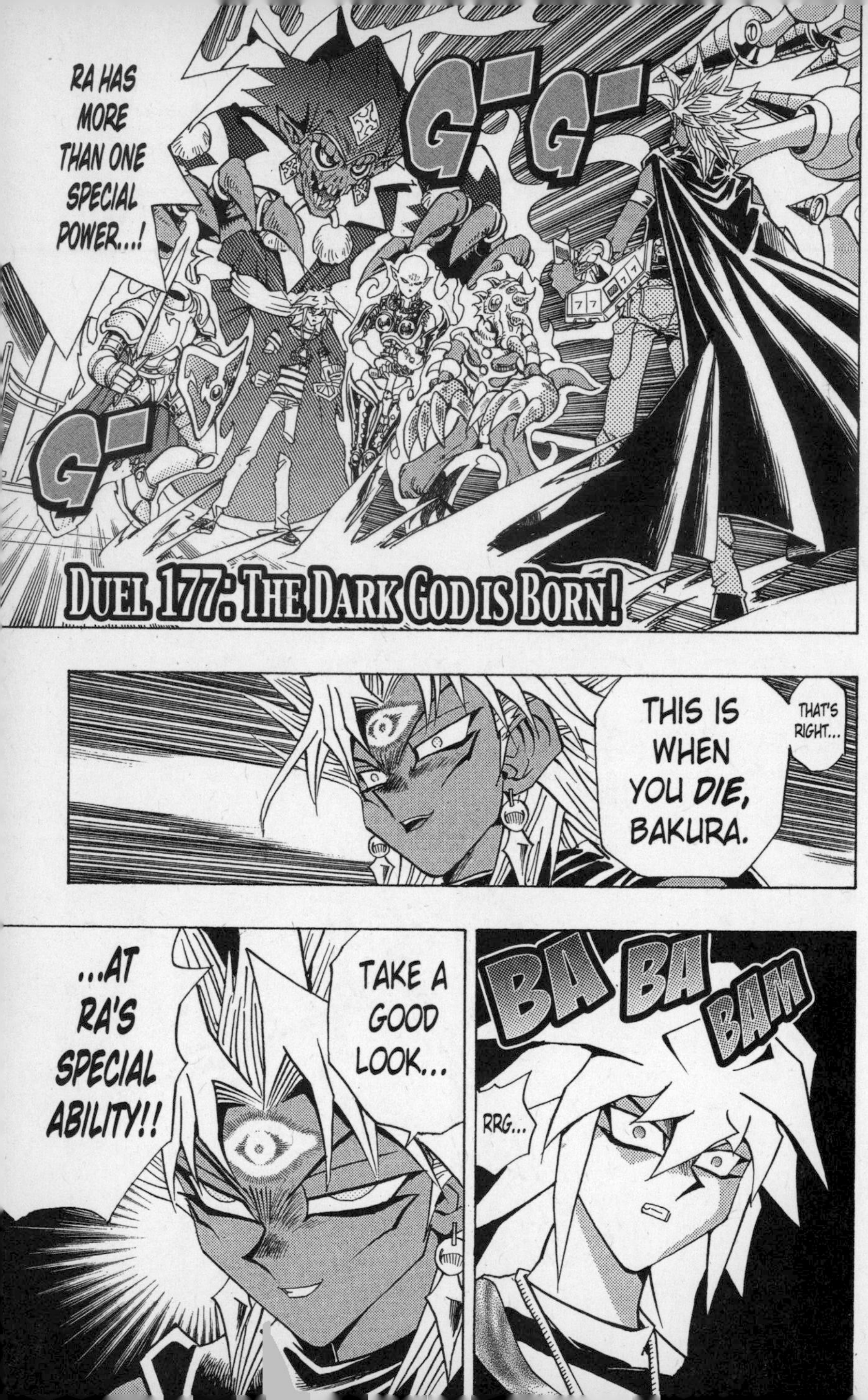

G G
RA HAS MORE THAN ONE SPECIAL POWER...!
G
THAT'S RIGHT...
THIS IS WHEN YOU DIE, BAKURA.
BA BA BAM
RRG...
TAKE A GOOD LOOK...
...AT RA'S SPECIAL ABILITY!!

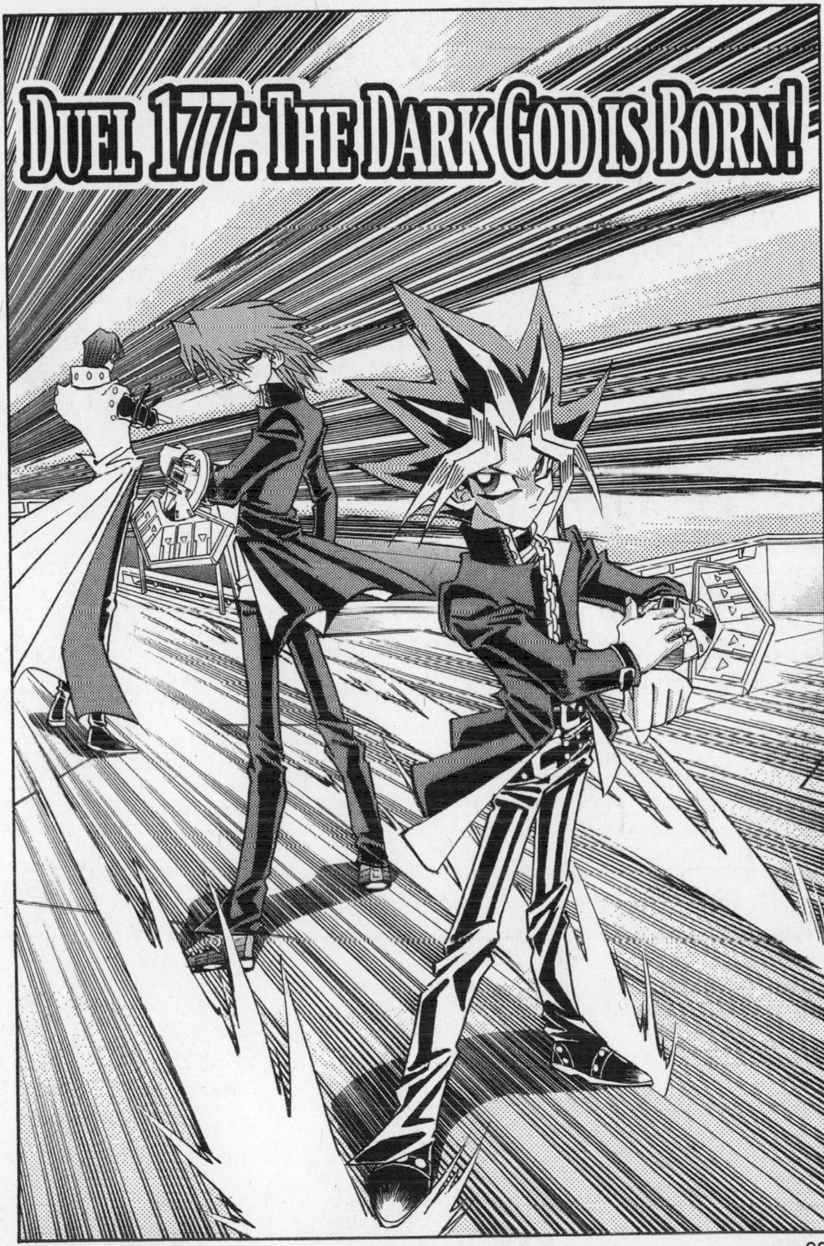
DUEL 177: THE DARK GOD IS BORN!

READ THIS WAY

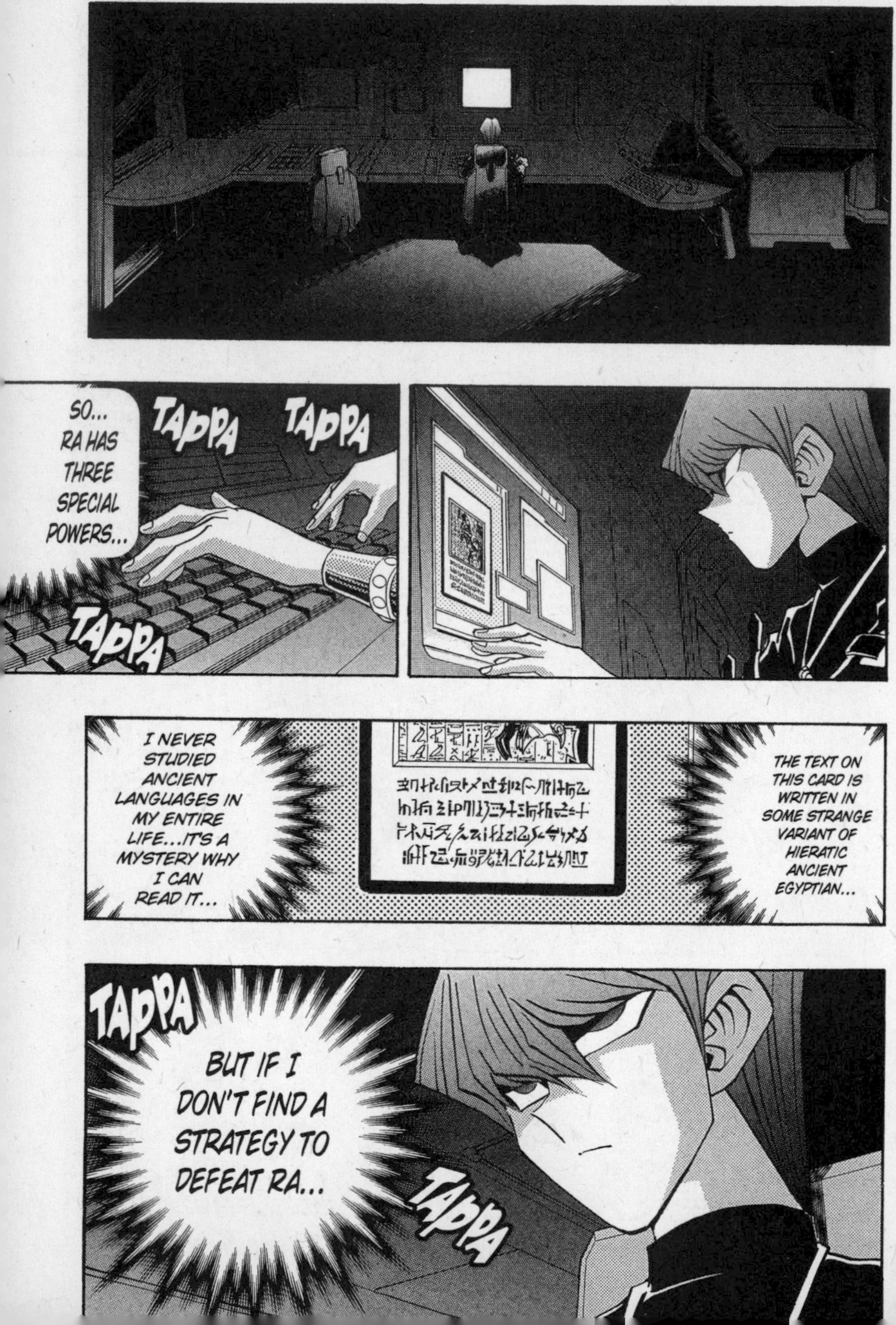
SO... RA HAS THREE SPECIAL POWERS...
TAPPA
TAPPA
TAPPA
THE TEXT ON THIS CARD IS WRITTEN IN SOME STRANGE VARIANT OF HIERATIC ANCIENT EGYPTIAN...
I NEVER STUDIED ANCIENT LANGUAGES IN MY ENTIRE LIFE...IT'S A MYSTERY WHY I CAN READ IT...
TAPPA
BUT IF I DON'T FIND A STRATEGY TO DEFEAT RA...
TAPPA

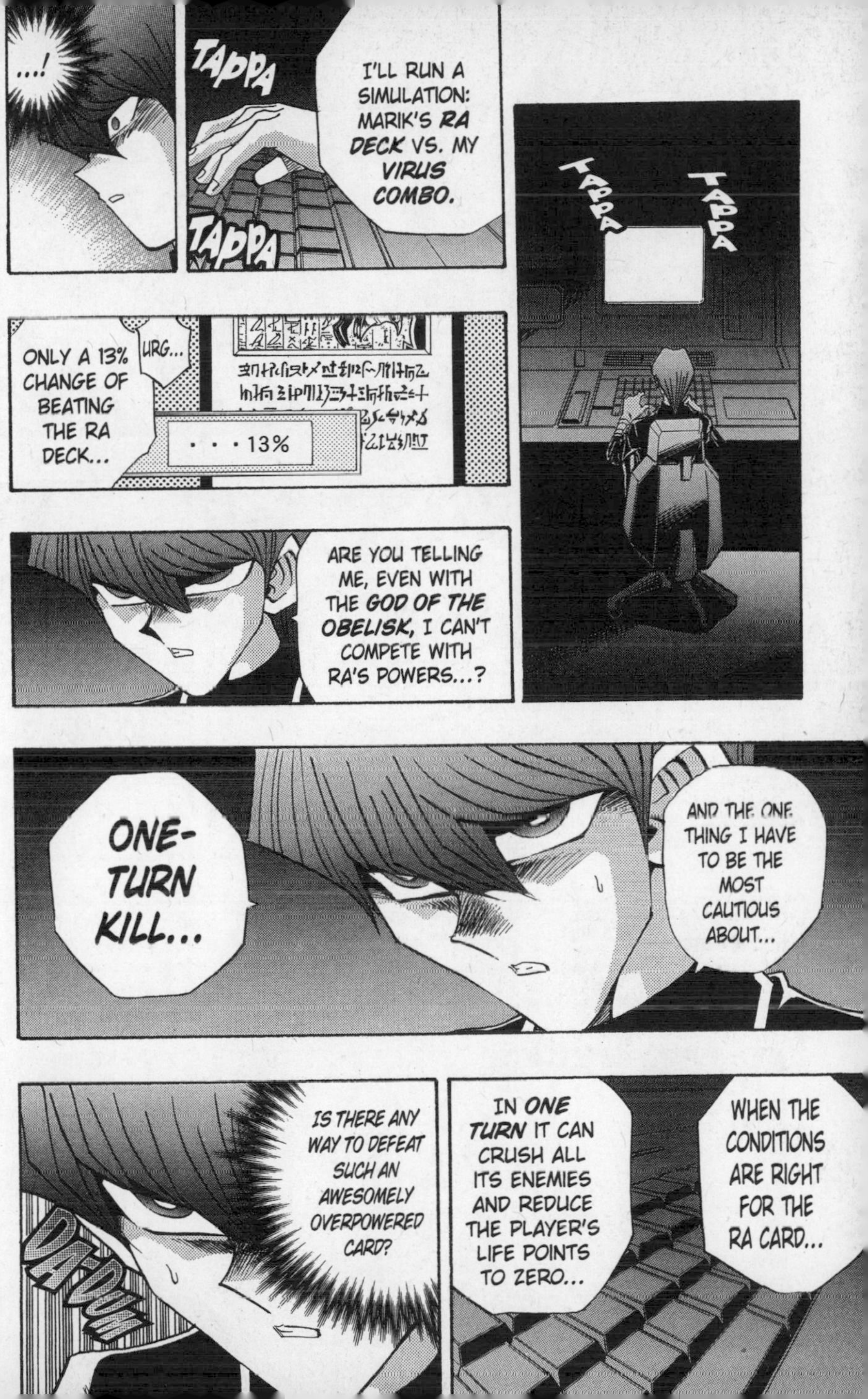
TAPPA
I'LL RUN A SIMULATION: MARIK'S RA DECK VS. MY VIRUS COMBO.
TAPPA
...!
TAPPA
TAPPA
• • • 13%
URG...
ONLY A 13% CHANGE OF BEATING THE RA DECK...
ARE YOU TELLING ME, EVEN WITH THE GOD OF THE OBELISK, I CAN'T COMPETE WITH RA'S POWERS...?
AND THE ONE THING I HAVE TO BE THE MOST CAUTIOUS ABOUT...
ONE-TURN KILL...
WHEN THE CONDITIONS ARE RIGHT FOR THE RA CARD...
IN ONE TURN IT CAN CRUSH ALL ITS ENEMIES AND REDUCE THE PLAYER'S LIFE POINTS TO ZERO...
IS THERE ANY WAY TO DEFEAT SUCH AN AWESOMELY OVERPOWERED CARD?

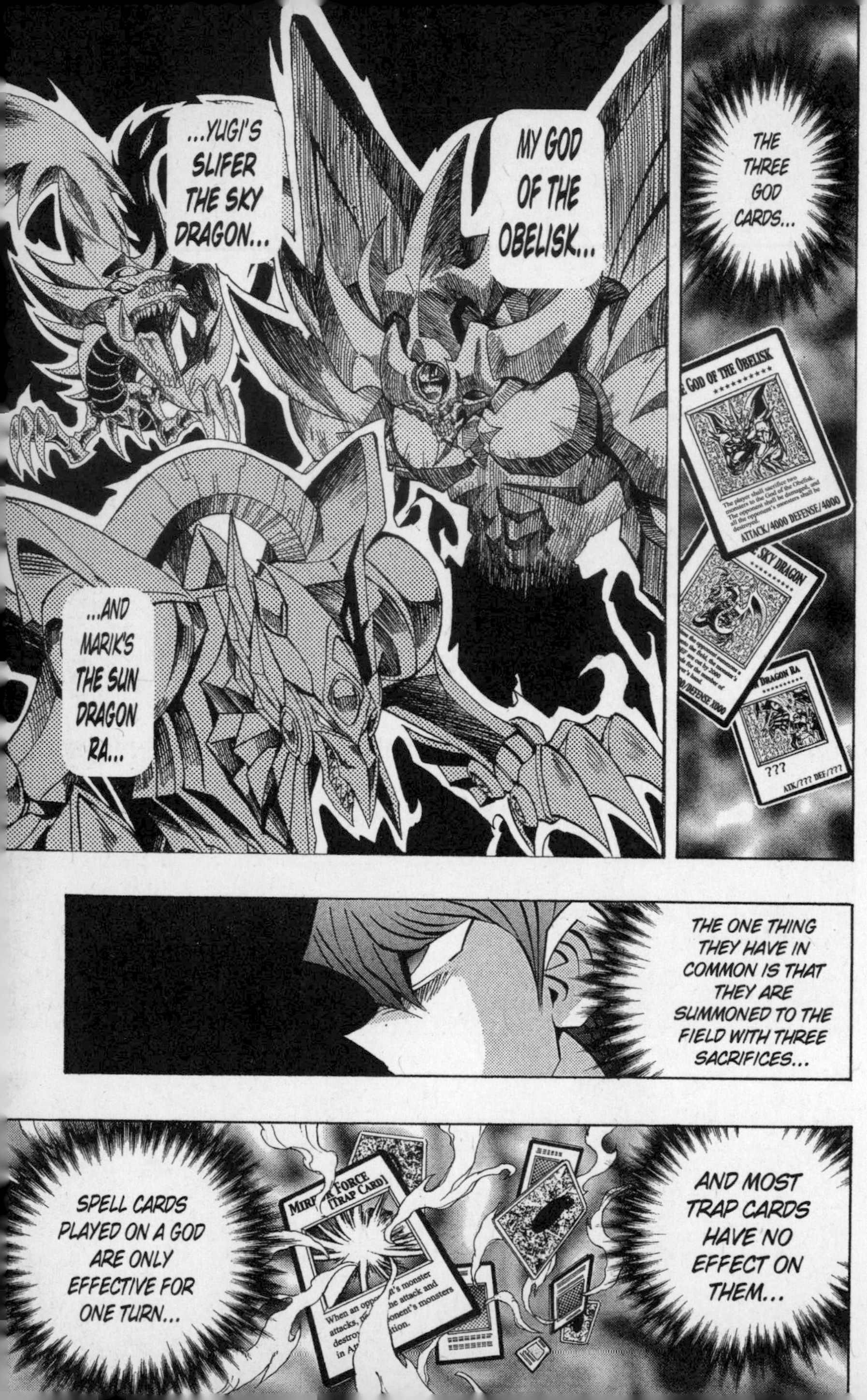
THE THREE GOD CARDS...
MY GOD OF THE OBELISK...
...YUGI'S SLIFER THE SKY DRAGON...
...AND MARIK'S THE SUN DRAGON RA...
ATTACK/4000 DEFENSE/4000
???
ATK/??? DEF/???
THE ONE THING THEY HAVE IN COMMON IS THAT THEY ARE SUMMONED TO THE FIELD WITH THREE SACRIFICES...
AND MOST TRAP CARDS HAVE NO EFFECT ON THEM...
SPELL CARDS PLAYED ON A GOD ARE ONLY EFFECTIVE FOR ONE TURN...

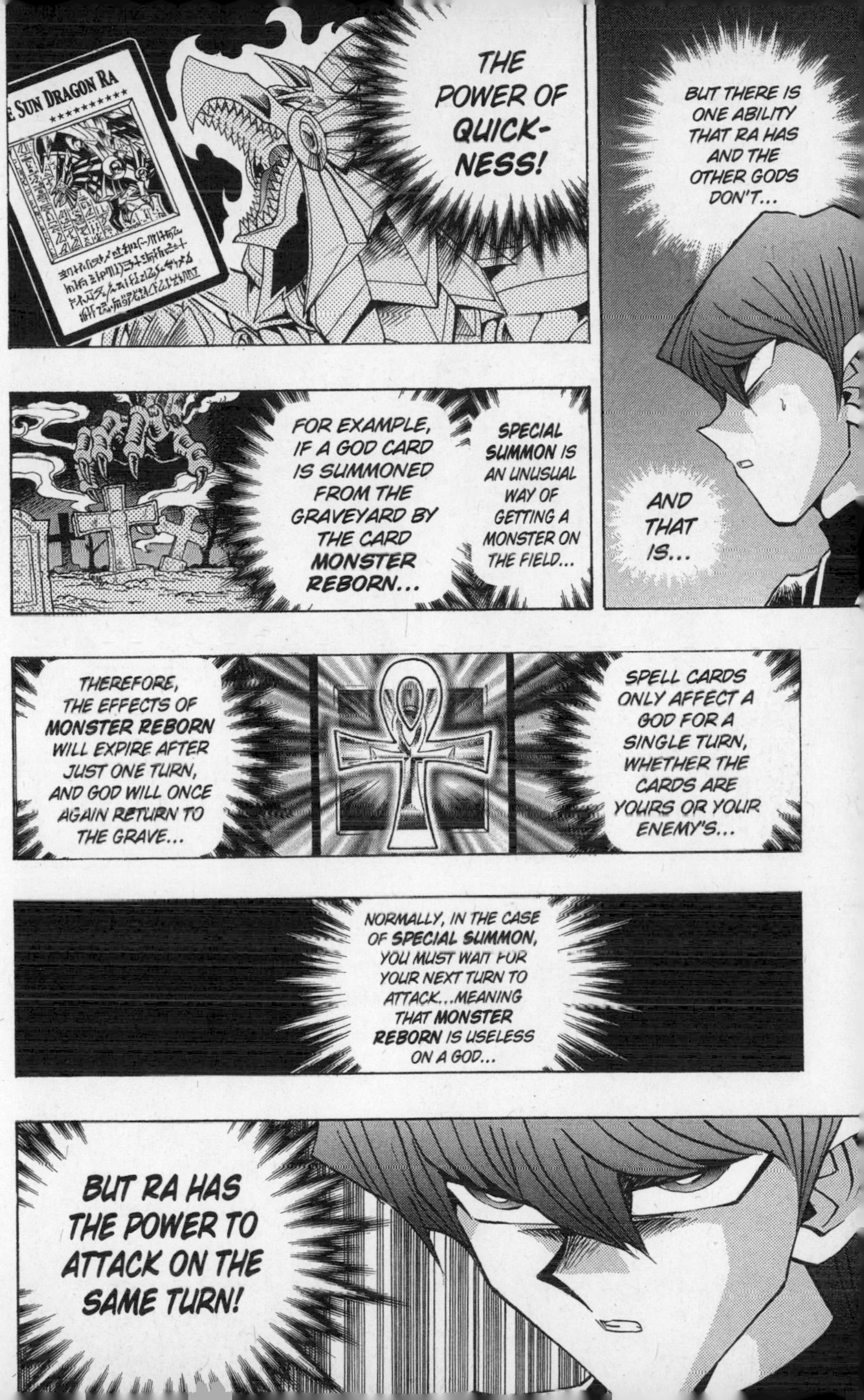
BUT THERE IS ONE ABILITY THAT RA HAS AND THE OTHER GODS DON'T...
AND THAT IS...
SUN DRAGON RA
THE POWER OF QUICK-NESS!
SPECIAL SUMMON IS AN UNUSUAL WAY OF GETTING A MONSTER ON THE FIELD...
FOR EXAMPLE, IF A GOD CARD IS SUMMONED FROM THE GRAVEYARD BY THE CARD MONSTER REBORN...
SPELL CARDS ONLY AFFECT A GOD FOR A SINGLE TURN, WHETHER THE CARDS ARE YOURS OR YOUR ENEMY'S...
THEREFORE, THE EFFECTS OF MONSTER REBORN WILL EXPIRE AFTER JUST ONE TURN, AND GOD WILL ONCE AGAIN RETURN TO THE GRAVE...
NORMALLY, IN THE CASE OF SPECIAL SUMMON, YOU MUST WAIT FOR YOUR NEXT TURN TO ATTACK...MEANING THAT MONSTER REBORN IS USELESS ON A GOD...
BUT RA HAS THE POWER TO ATTACK ON THE SAME TURN!

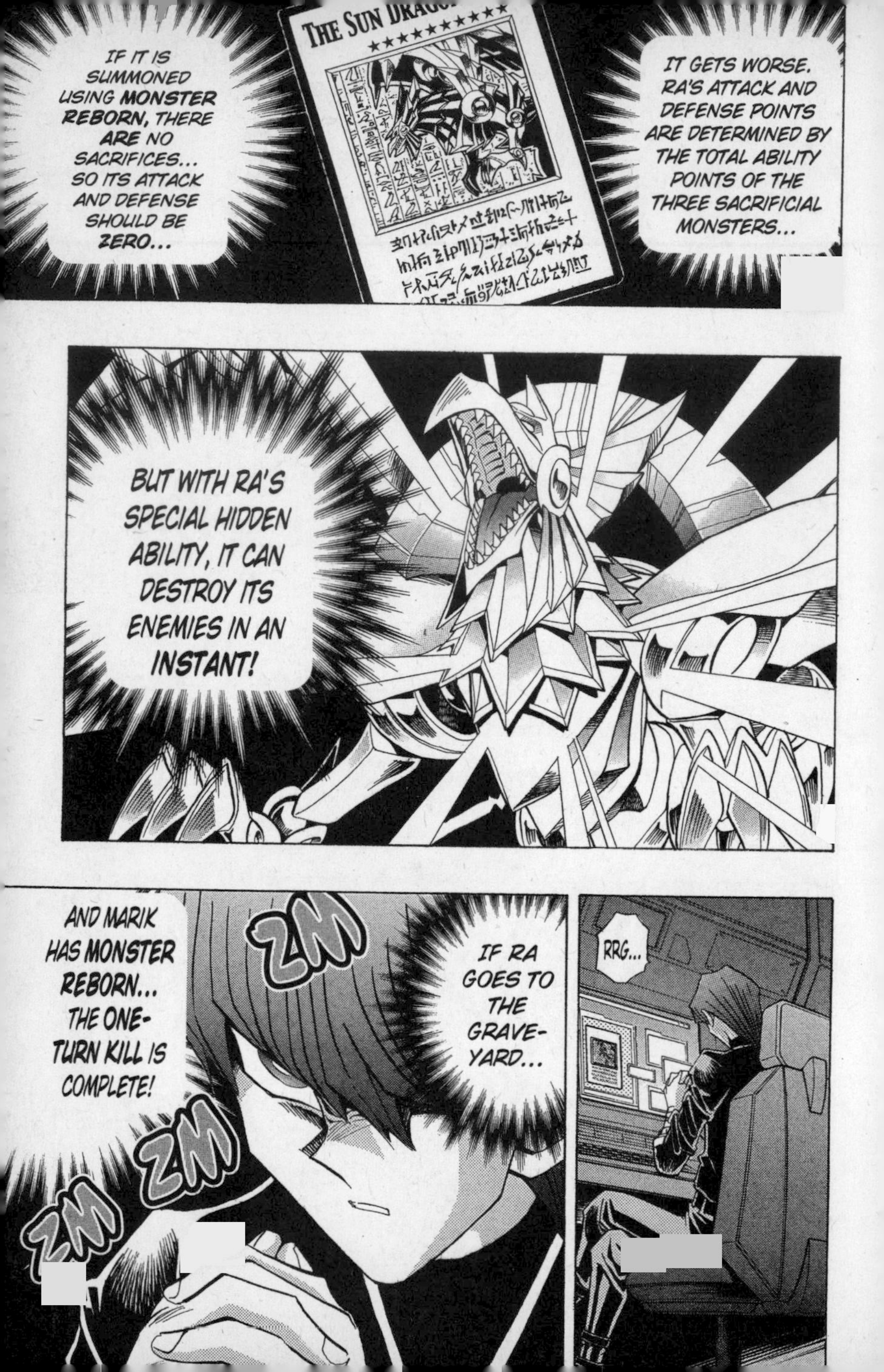
IT GETS WORSE. RA'S ATTACK AND DEFENSE POINTS ARE DETERMINED BY THE TOTAL ABILITY POINTS OF THE THREE SACRIFICIAL MONSTERS...
IF IT IS SUMMONED USING MONSTER REBORN, THERE ARE NO SACRIFICES... SO ITS ATTACK AND DEFENSE SHOULD BE ZERO...
BUT WITH RA'S SPECIAL HIDDEN ABILITY, IT CAN DESTROY ITS ENEMIES IN AN INSTANT!
RRG...
IF RA GOES TO THE GRAVE-YARD...
AND MARIK HAS MONSTER REBORN... THE ONE-TURN KILL IS COMPLETE!
ZM
ZM
ZM

READ THIS WAY

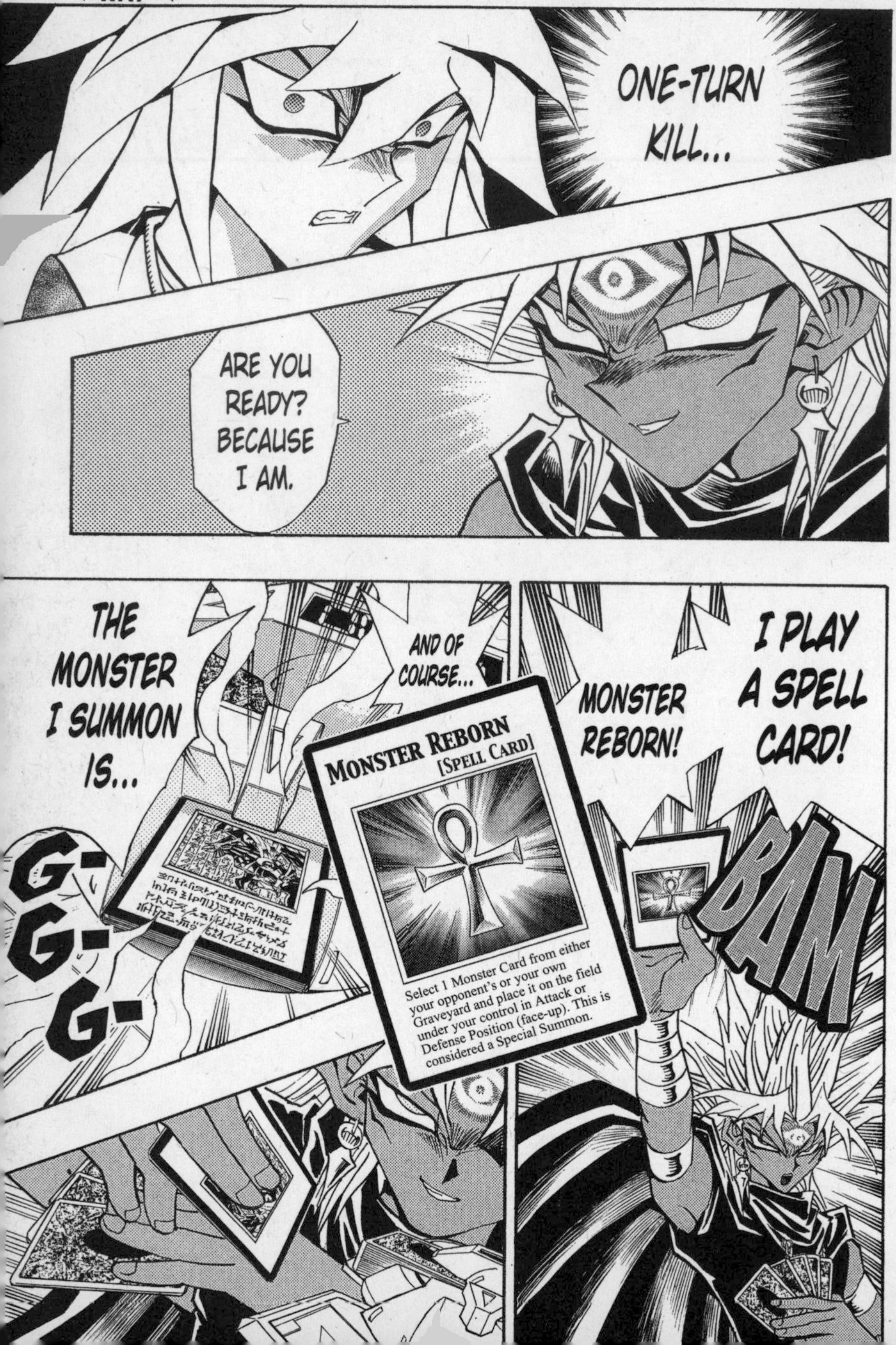
ONE-TURN KILL...
ARE YOU READY? BECAUSE I AM.
I PLAY A SPELL CARD!
MONSTER REBORN!
BAM
MONSTER REBORN
[SPELL CARD]
Select 1 Monster Card from either your opponent's or your own Graveyard and place it on the field under your control in Attack or Defense Position (face-up). This is considered a Special Summon.
AND OF COURSE...
THE MONSTER I SUMMON IS...
G-G-G-

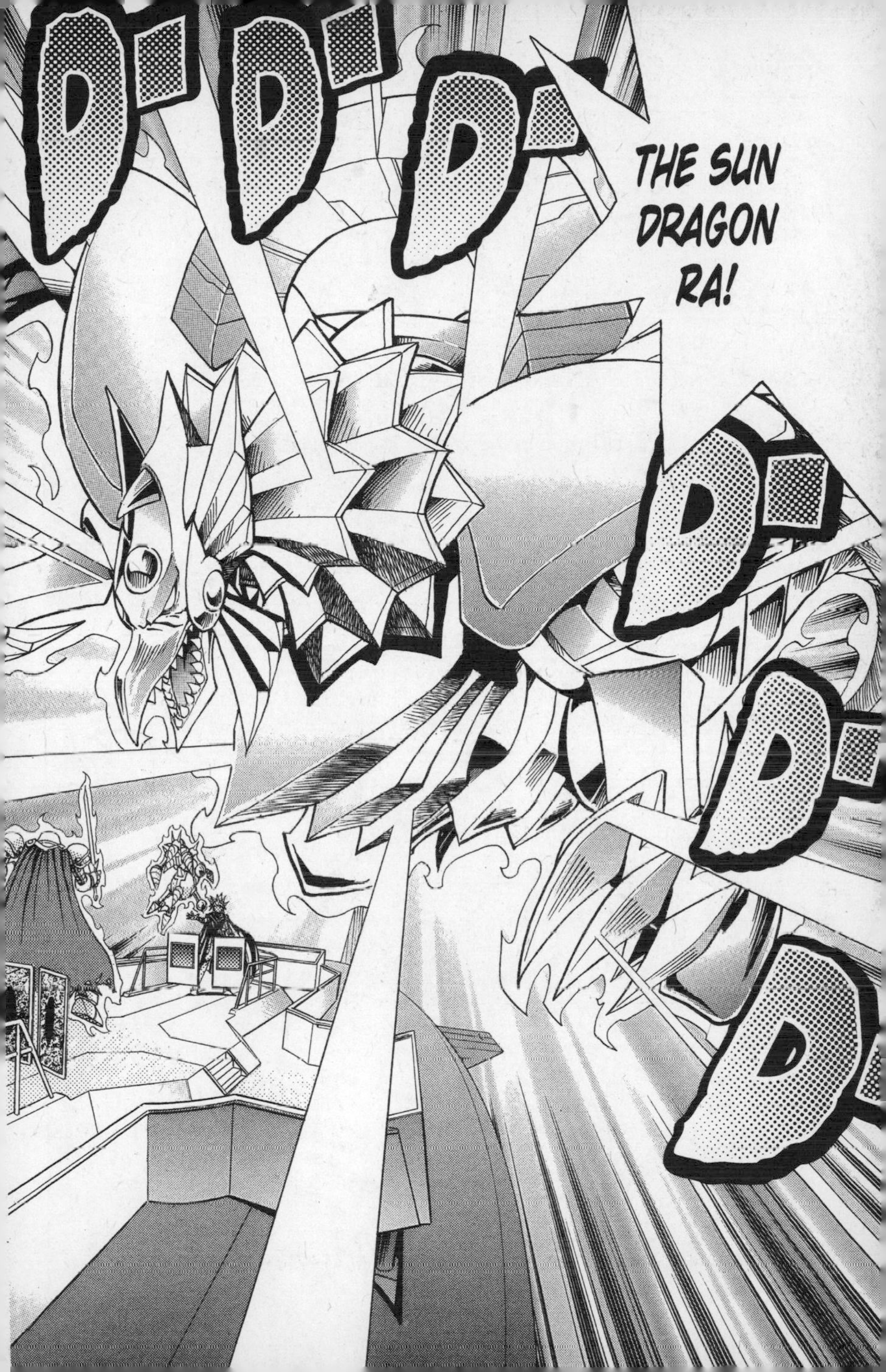
THE SUN DRAGON RA!
D D D
D D D

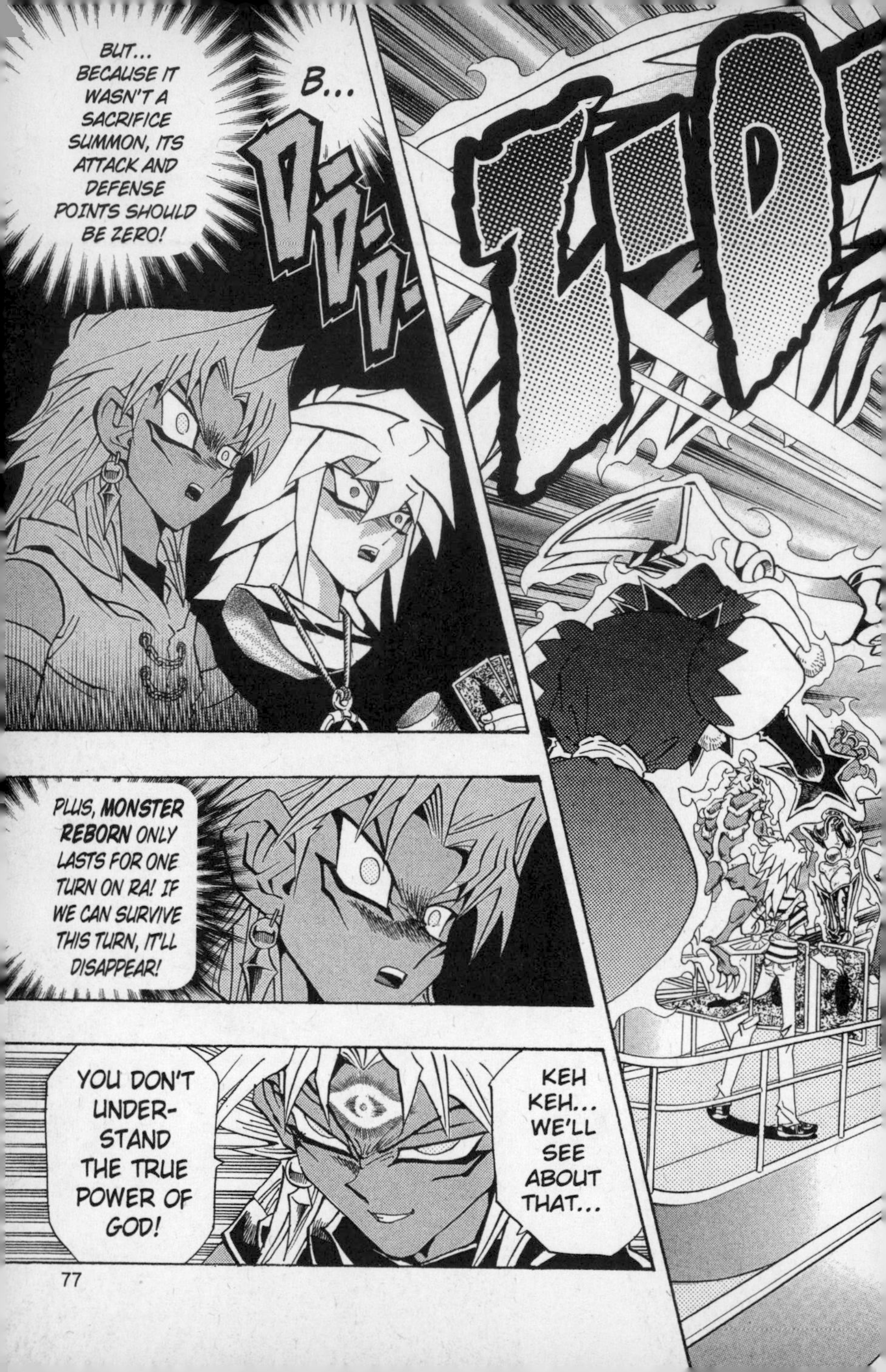
B...
D-D-D-
BUT... BECAUSE IT WASN'T A SACRIFICE SUMMON, ITS ATTACK AND DEFENSE POINTS SHOULD BE ZERO!
PLUS, MONSTER REBORN ONLY LASTS FOR ONE TURN ON RA! IF WE CAN SURVIVE THIS TURN, IT'LL DISAPPEAR!
KEH KEH... WE'LL SEE ABOUT THAT...
YOU DON'T UNDER-STAND THE TRUE POWER OF GOD!

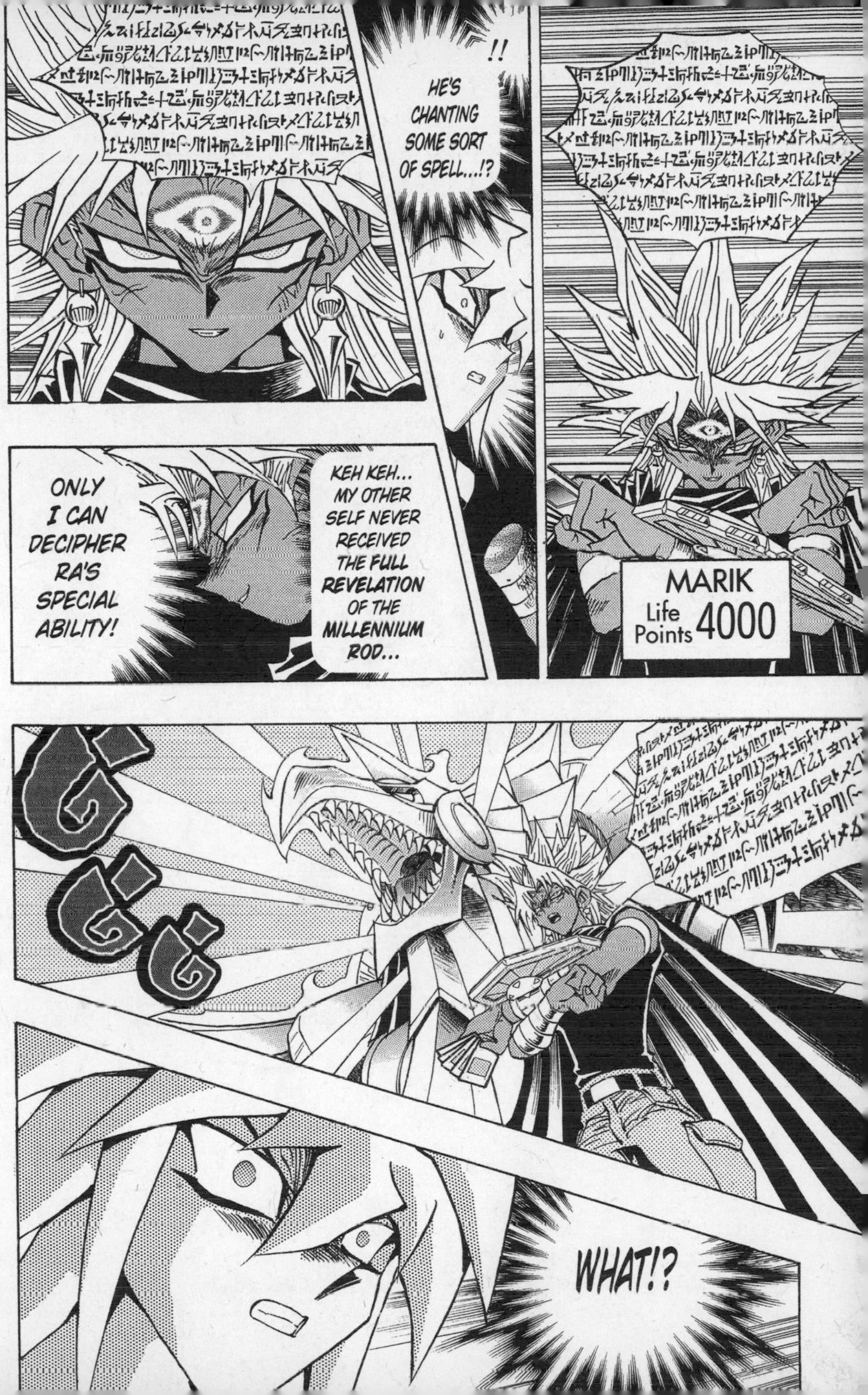
MARIK
Life Points 4000
!!
HE'S CHANTING SOME SORT OF SPELL...!?
KEH KEH... MY OTHER SELF NEVER RECEIVED THE FULL REVELATION OF THE MILLENNIUM ROD...
ONLY I CAN DECIPHER RA'S SPECIAL ABILITY!
GGG
WHAT!?

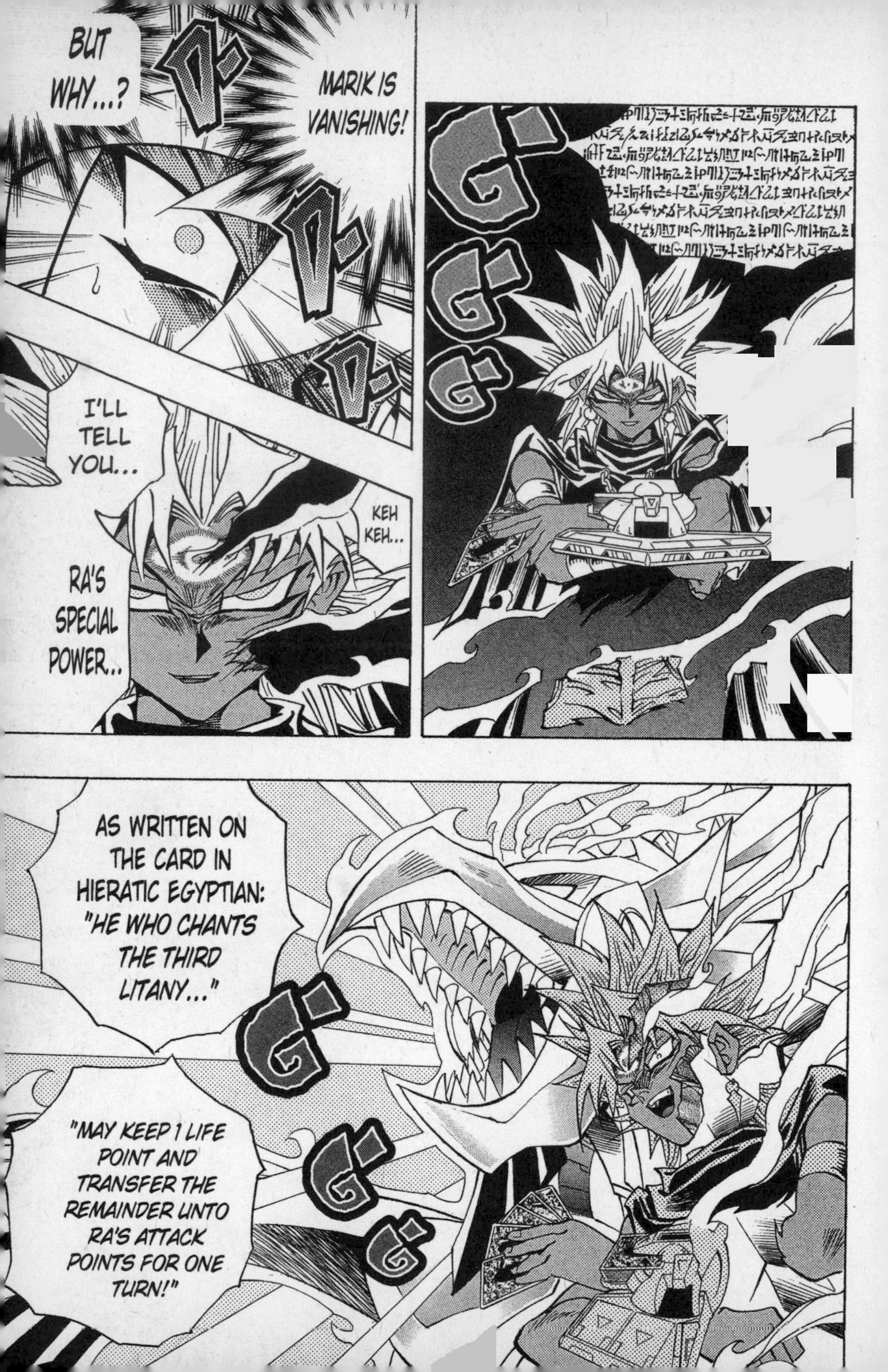
MARIK IS VANISHING!
BUT WHY...?
KEH KEH...
I'LL TELL YOU...
RA'S SPECIAL POWER...
AS WRITTEN ON THE CARD IN HIERATIC EGYPTIAN: "HE WHO CHANTS THE THIRD LITANY..."
"MAY KEEP 1 LIFE POINT AND TRANSFER THE REMAINDER UNTO RA'S ATTACK POINTS FOR ONE TURN!"

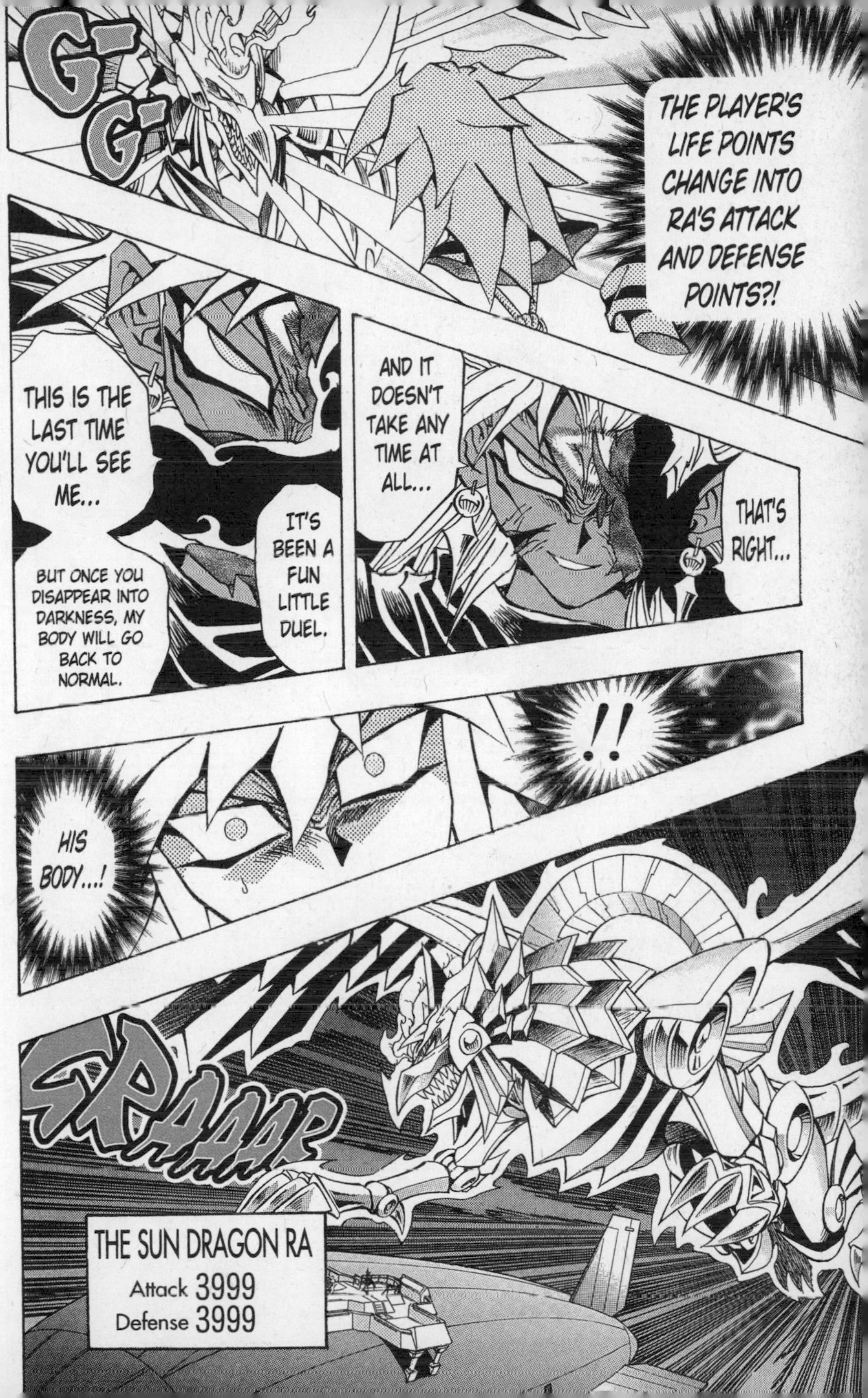
THE PLAYER'S LIFE POINTS CHANGE INTO RA'S ATTACK AND DEFENSE POINTS?!
G-G-
THAT'S RIGHT...
AND IT DOESN'T TAKE ANY TIME AT ALL...
IT'S BEEN A FUN LITTLE DUEL.
THIS IS THE LAST TIME YOU'LL SEE ME...
BUT ONCE YOU DISAPPEAR INTO DARKNESS, MY BODY WILL GO BACK TO NORMAL.
!!
HIS BODY...!
GPAAAR
THE SUN DRAGON RA
Attack 3999
Defense 3999

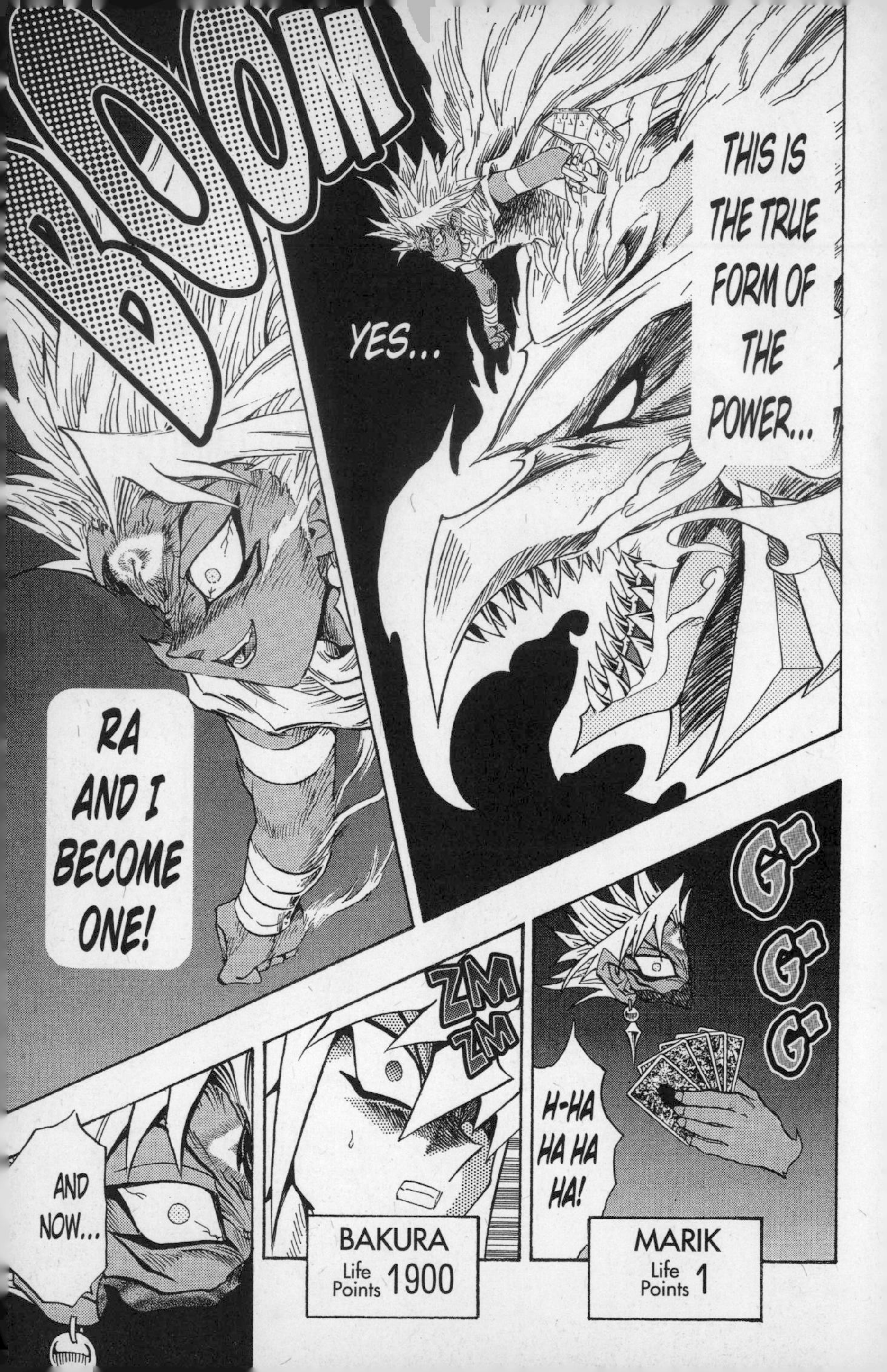
THIS IS THE TRUE FORM OF THE POWER...
YES...
BOOM!
RA AND I BECOME ONE!
G- G- G-
H-HA HA HA HA!
MARIK Life Points 1
ZM ZM
BAKURA Life Points 1900
AND NOW...

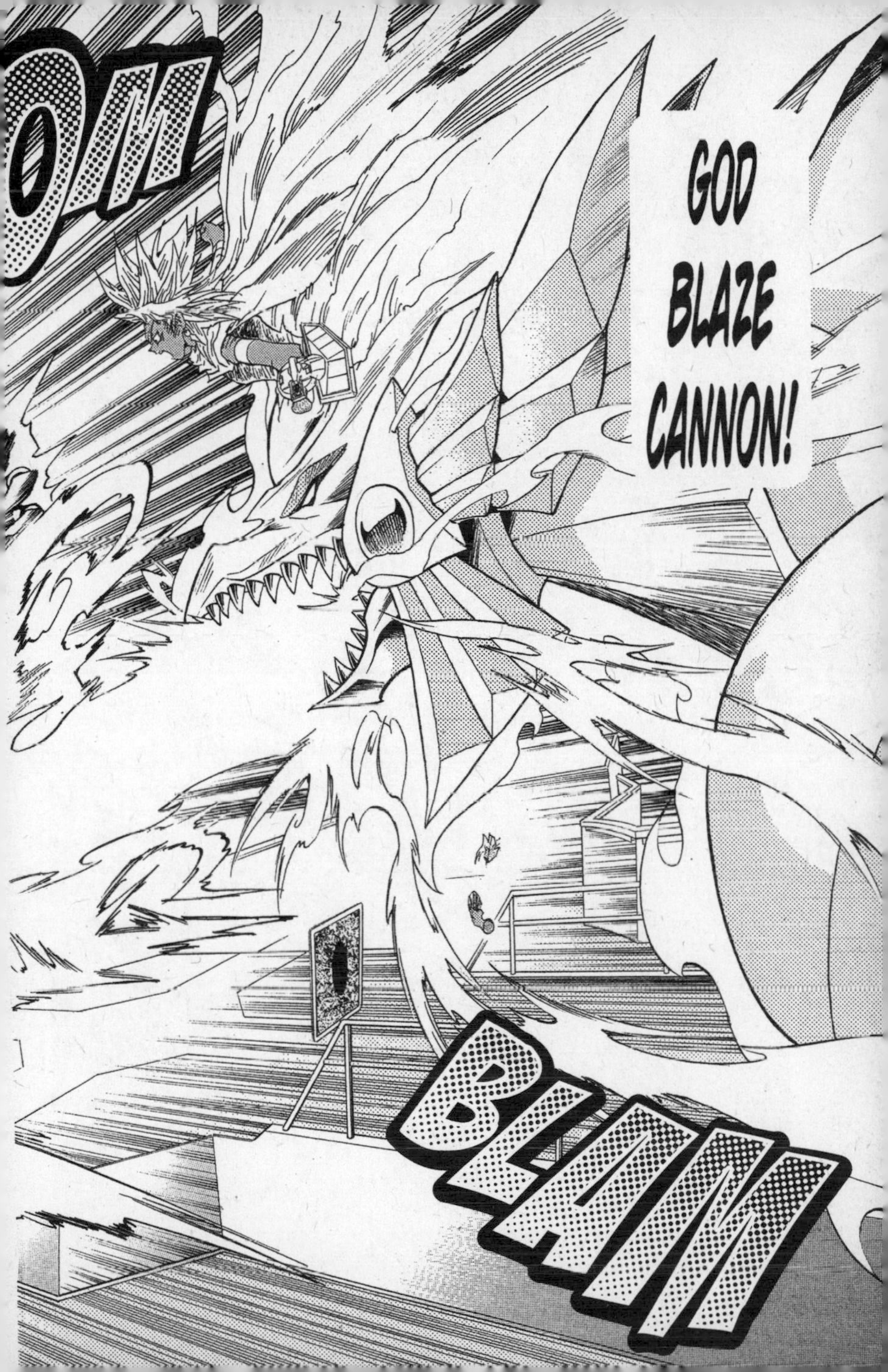
OM
GOD BLAZE CANNON!
BLAM

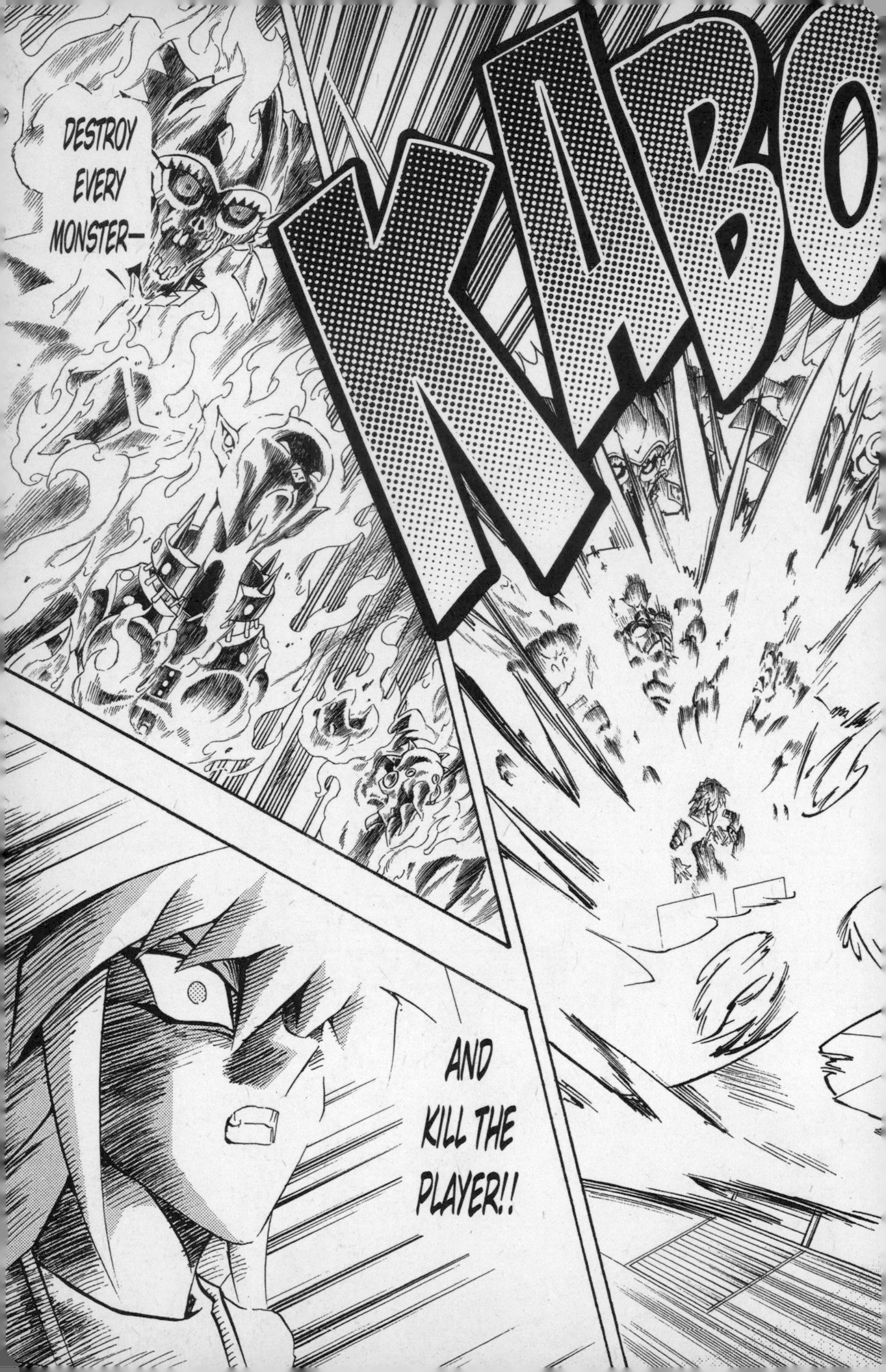
DESTROY EVERY MONSTER—
AND KILL THE PLAYER!!

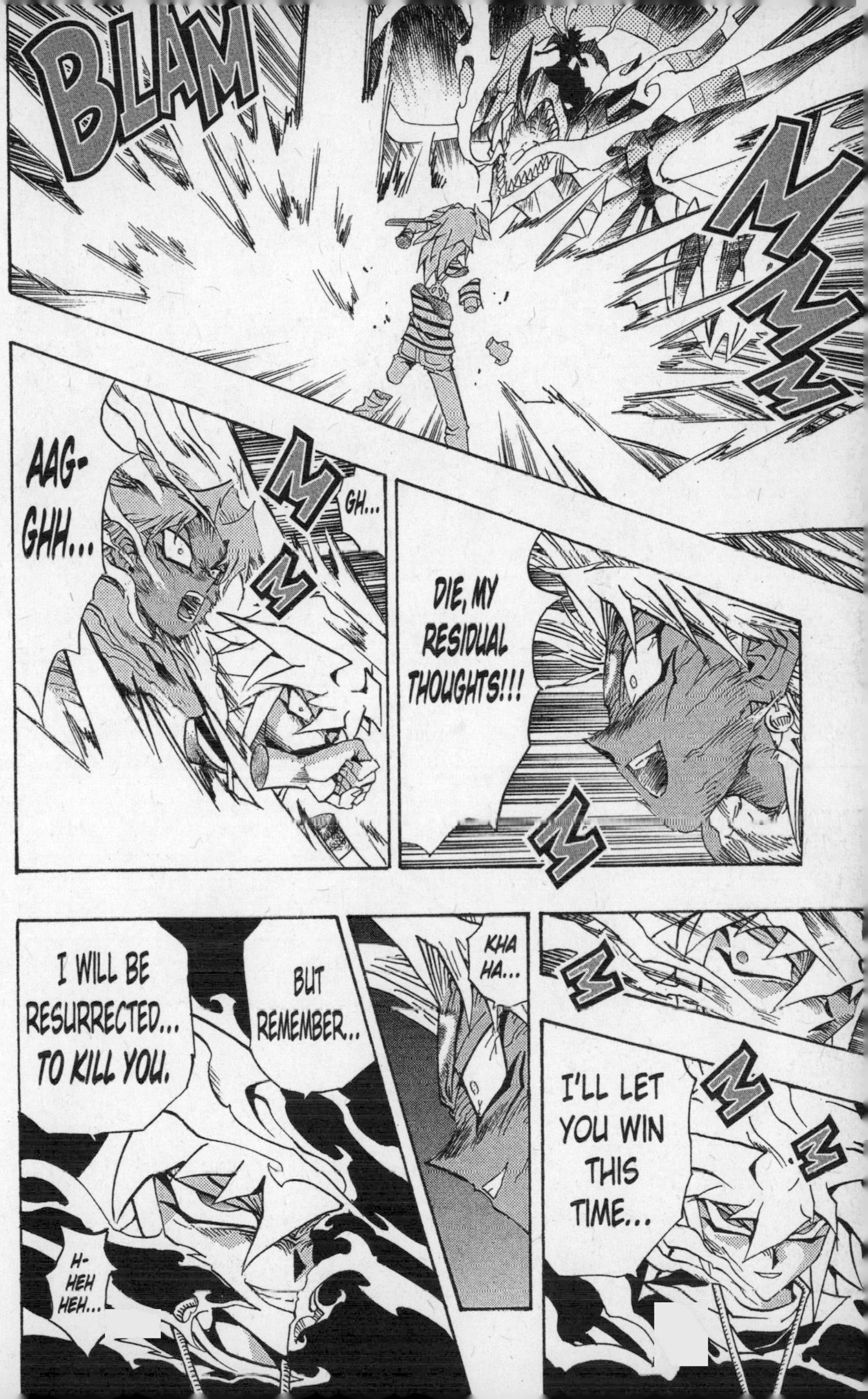
BLAM
MMMM
DIE, MY RESIDUAL THOUGHTS!!!
M
MM
GH...
AAG-GHH...
M
MM
I'LL LET YOU WIN THIS TIME...
KHA HA...
BUT REMEMBER...
I WILL BE RESURRECTED... TO KILL YOU.
H-HEH HEH...

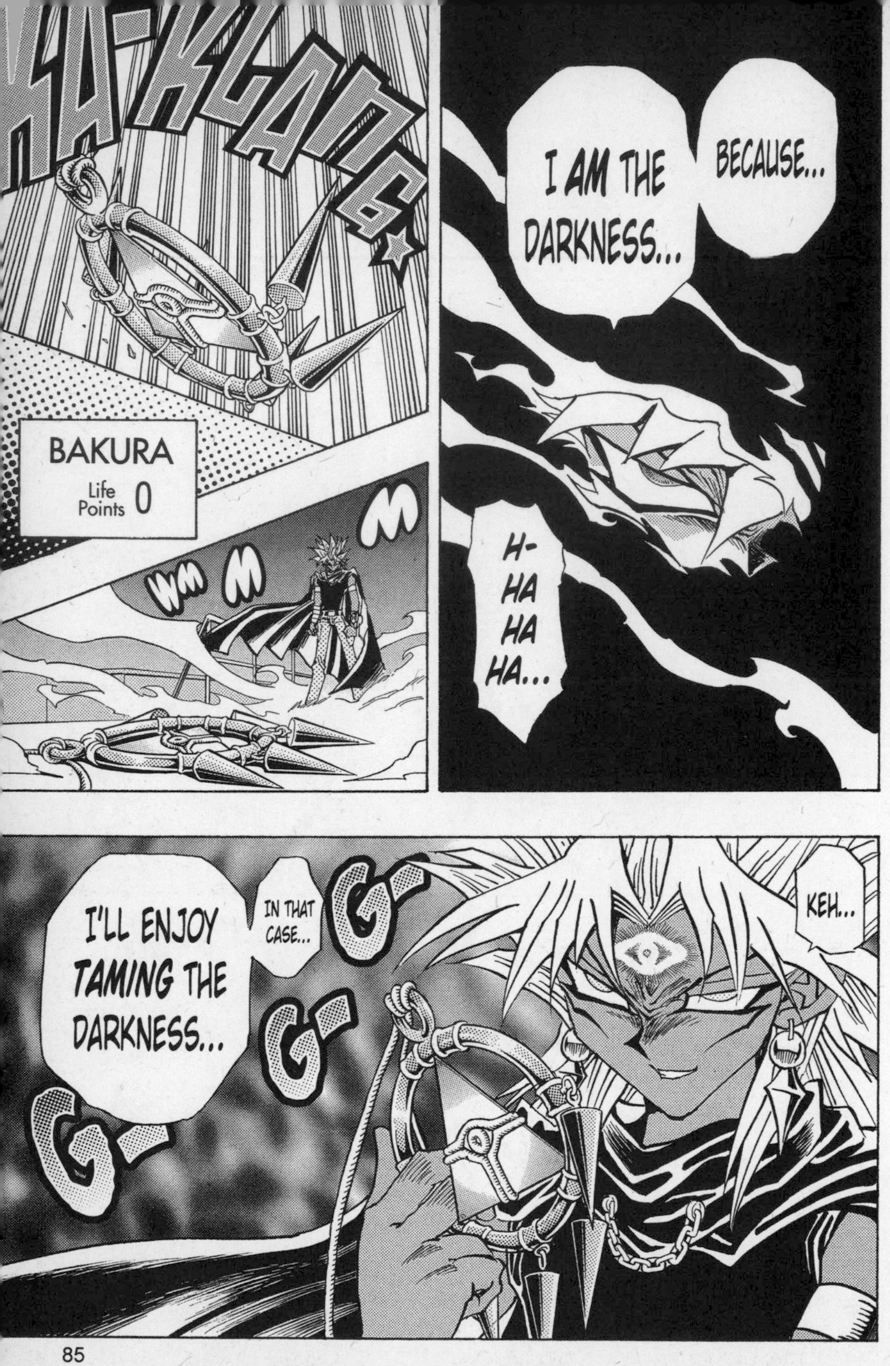
BECAUSE...
I AM THE DARKNESS...
H-HA HA HA...
KA-KLANG
BAKURA
Life Points 0
M
M
WM
KEH...
IN THAT CASE...
I'LL ENJOY TAMING THE DARKNESS...
G-
G-
G-

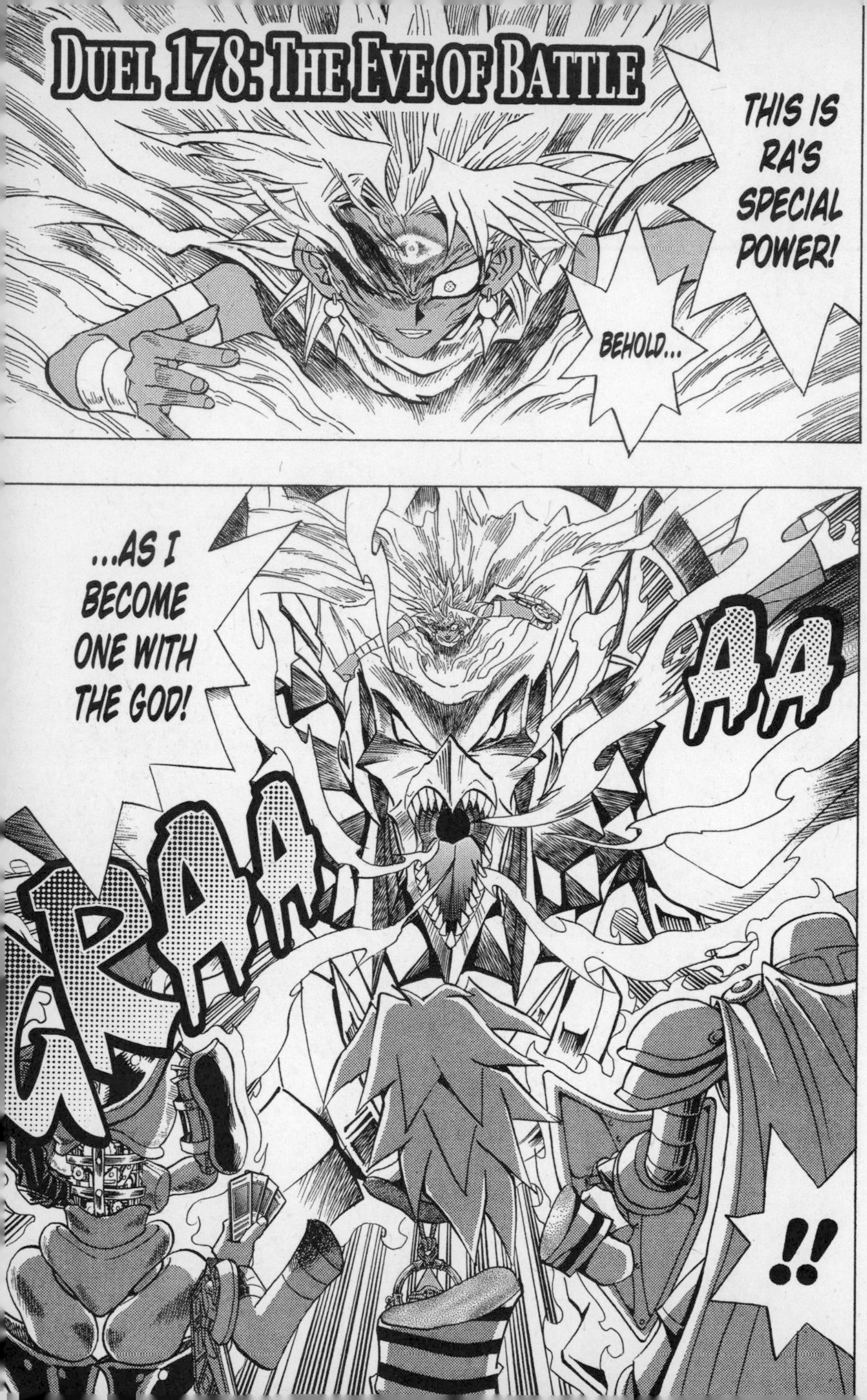
DUEL 178: THE EVE OF BATTLE
THIS IS RA'S SPECIAL POWER!
BEHOLD...
...AS I BECOME ONE WITH THE GOD!
RAA...AA
!!

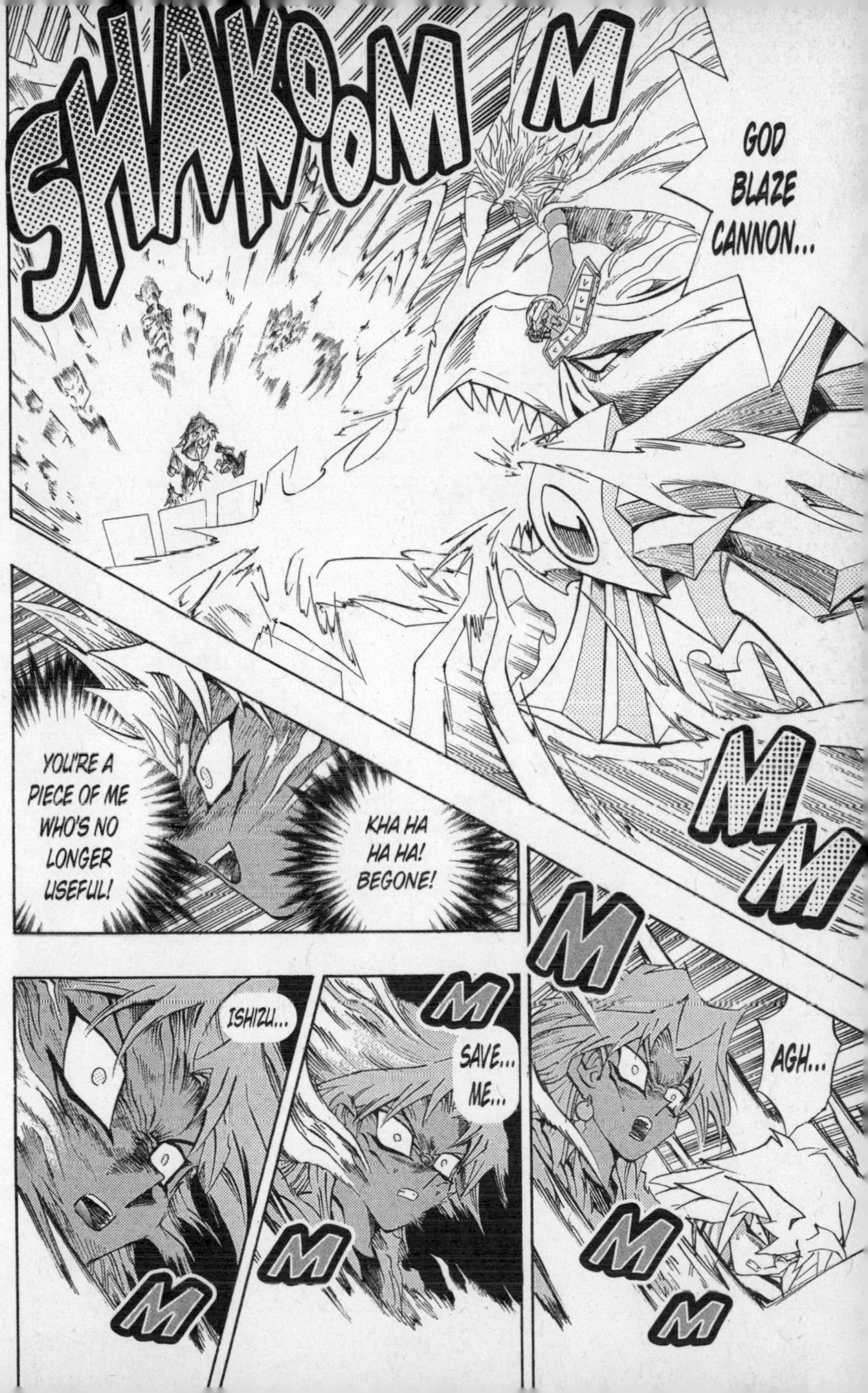
GOD BLAZE CANNON...
M
SHAKOOM
MMM
KHA HA HA HA! BEGONE!
YOU'RE A PIECE OF ME WHO'S NO LONGER USEFUL!
M
AGH...
MM
M
SAVE... ME...
M
ISHIZU...
M

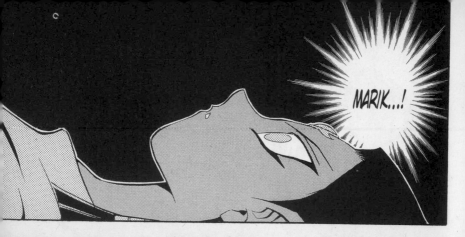

MARIK...!

SPIRIT

!!

...

KREEK

SPIRIT

ANZU...

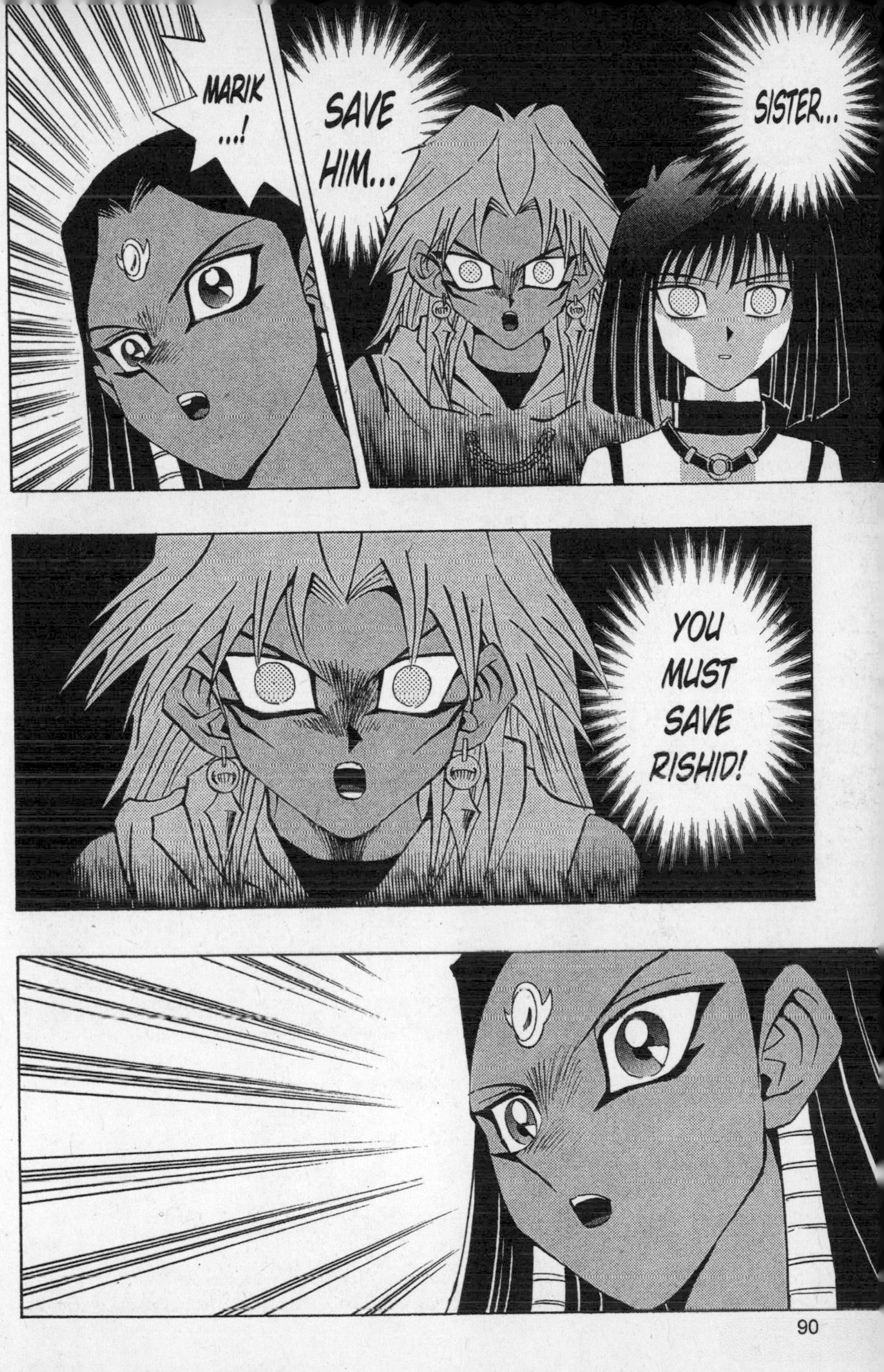
SISTER...
SAVE HIM...
MARIK ...!
YOU MUST SAVE RISHID!

READ THIS WAY

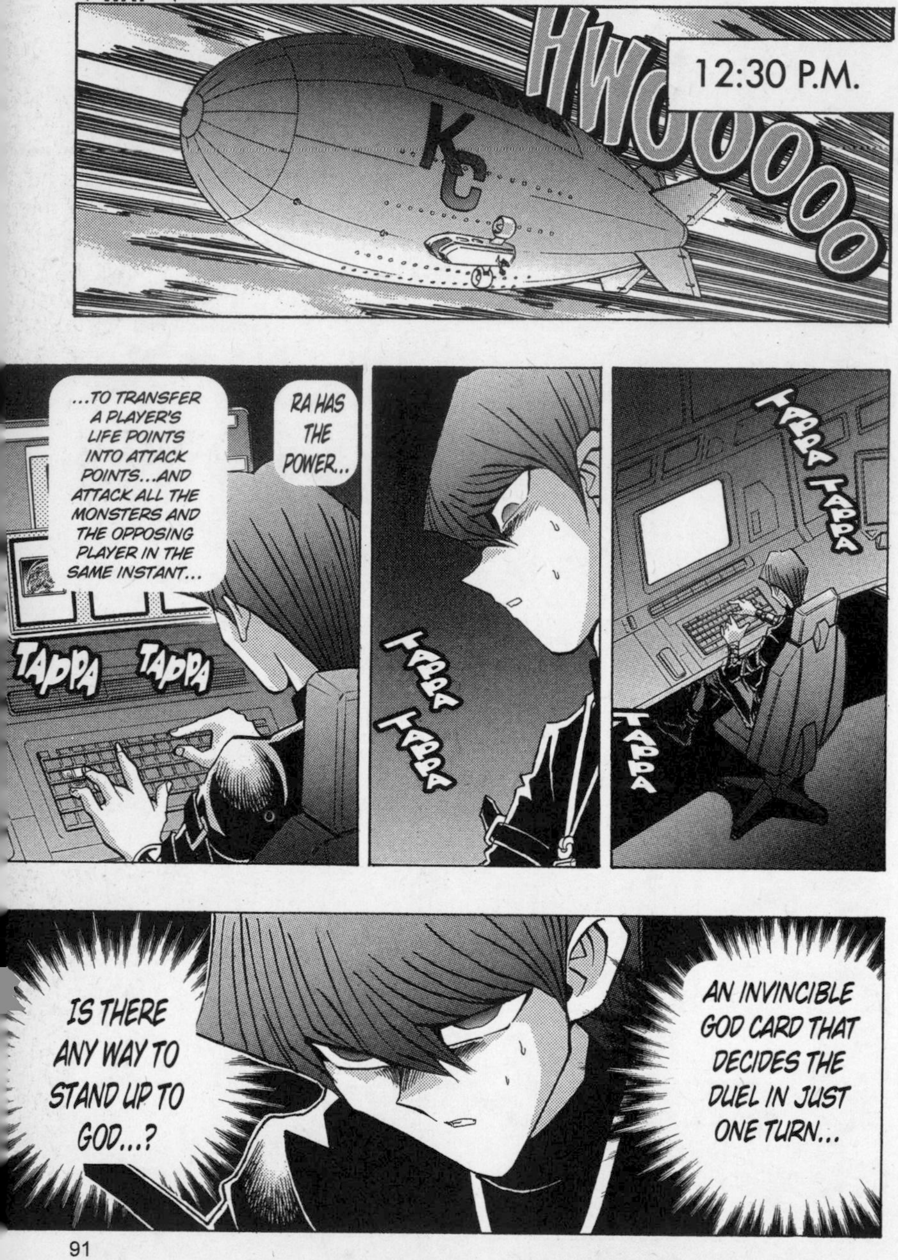

12:30 P.M.
HWOOOOOO
TAPPA TAPPA
TAPPA
TAPPA
TAPPA
RA HAS THE POWER...
...TO TRANSFER A PLAYER'S LIFE POINTS INTO ATTACK POINTS...AND ATTACK ALL THE MONSTERS AND THE OPPOSING PLAYER IN THE SAME INSTANT...
TAPPA
TAPPA
AN INVINCIBLE GOD CARD THAT DECIDES THE DUEL IN JUST ONE TURN...
IS THERE ANY WAY TO STAND UP TO GOD...?

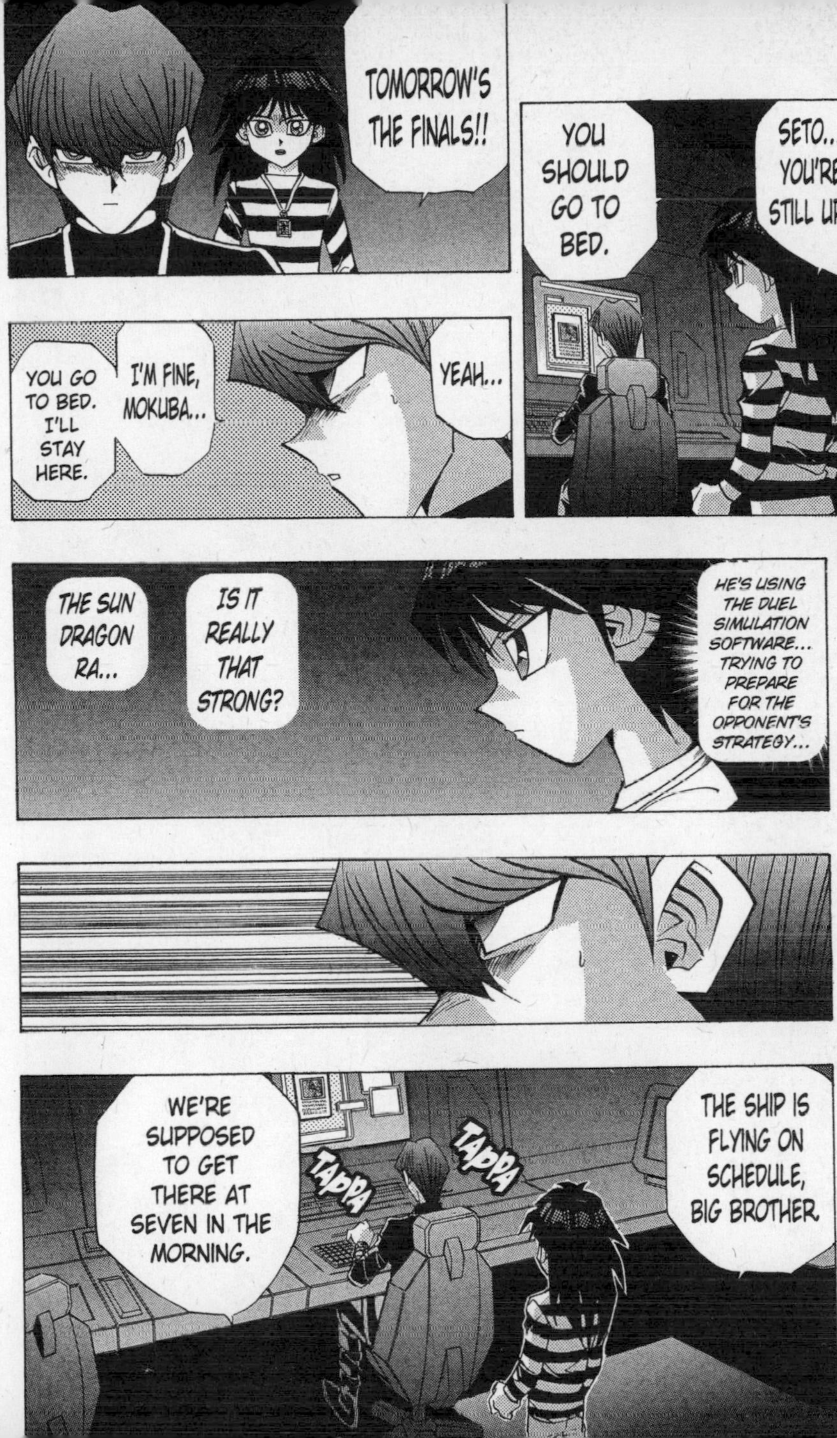
SETO... YOU'RE STILL UP?
YOU SHOULD GO TO BED.
TOMORROW'S THE FINALS!!
YEAH...
I'M FINE, MOKUBA...
YOU GO TO BED. I'LL STAY HERE.
HE'S USING THE DUEL SIMULATION SOFTWARE... TRYING TO PREPARE FOR THE OPPONENT'S STRATEGY...
IS IT REALLY THAT STRONG?
THE SUN DRAGON RA...
THE SHIP IS FLYING ON SCHEDULE, BIG BROTHER.
TAPPA
TAPPA
WE'RE SUPPOSED TO GET THERE AT SEVEN IN THE MORNING.

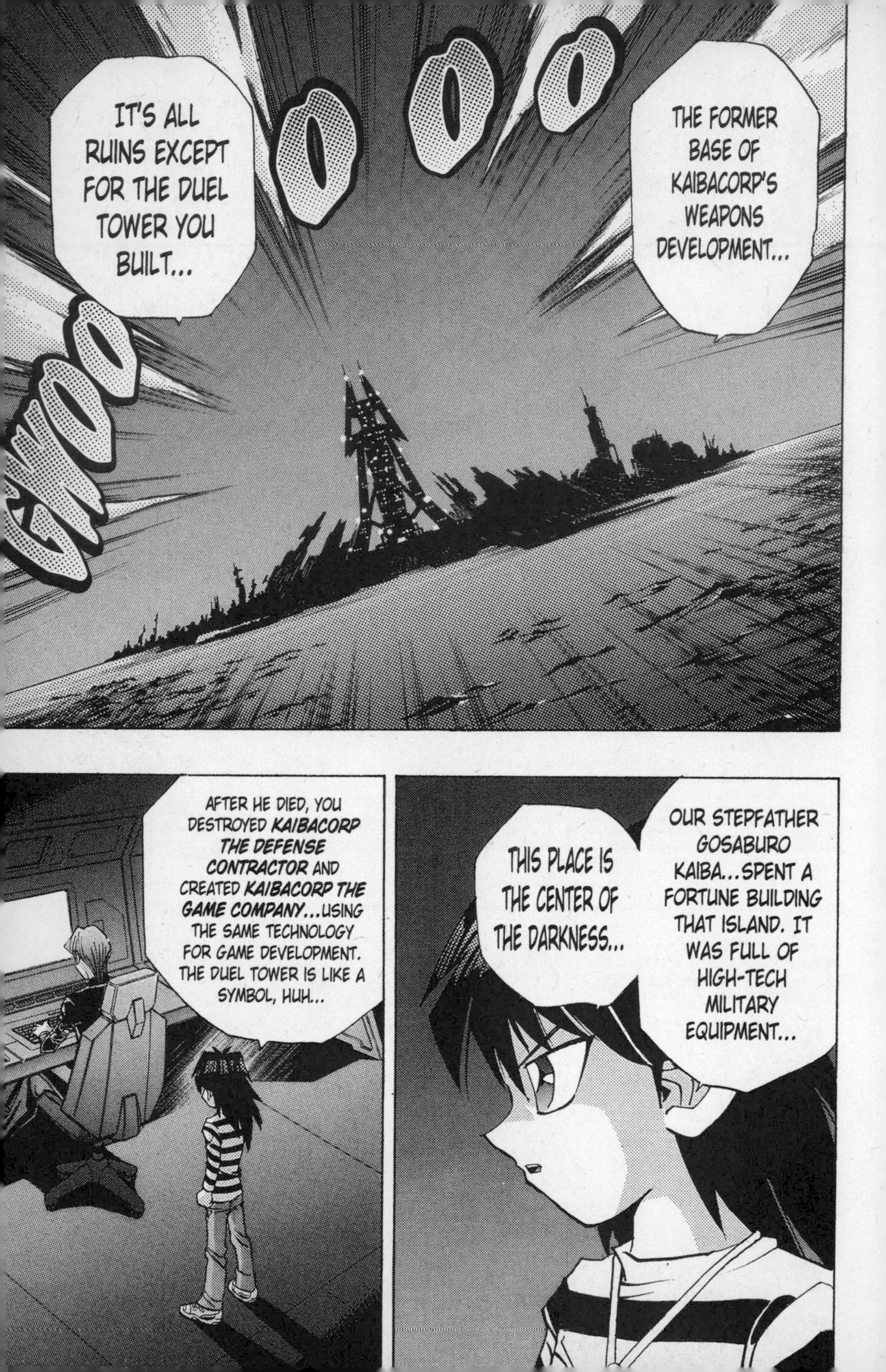
THE FORMER BASE OF KAIBACORP'S WEAPONS DEVELOPMENT...
IT'S ALL RUINS EXCEPT FOR THE DUEL TOWER YOU BUILT...
OUR STEPFATHER GOSABURO KAIBA...SPENT A FORTUNE BUILDING THAT ISLAND. IT WAS FULL OF HIGH-TECH MILITARY EQUIPMENT...
THIS PLACE IS THE CENTER OF THE DARKNESS...
AFTER HE DIED, YOU DESTROYED KAIBACORP THE DEFENSE CONTRACTOR AND CREATED KAIBACORP THE GAME COMPANY...USING THE SAME TECHNOLOGY FOR GAME DEVELOPMENT. THE DUEL TOWER IS LIKE A SYMBOL, HUH...

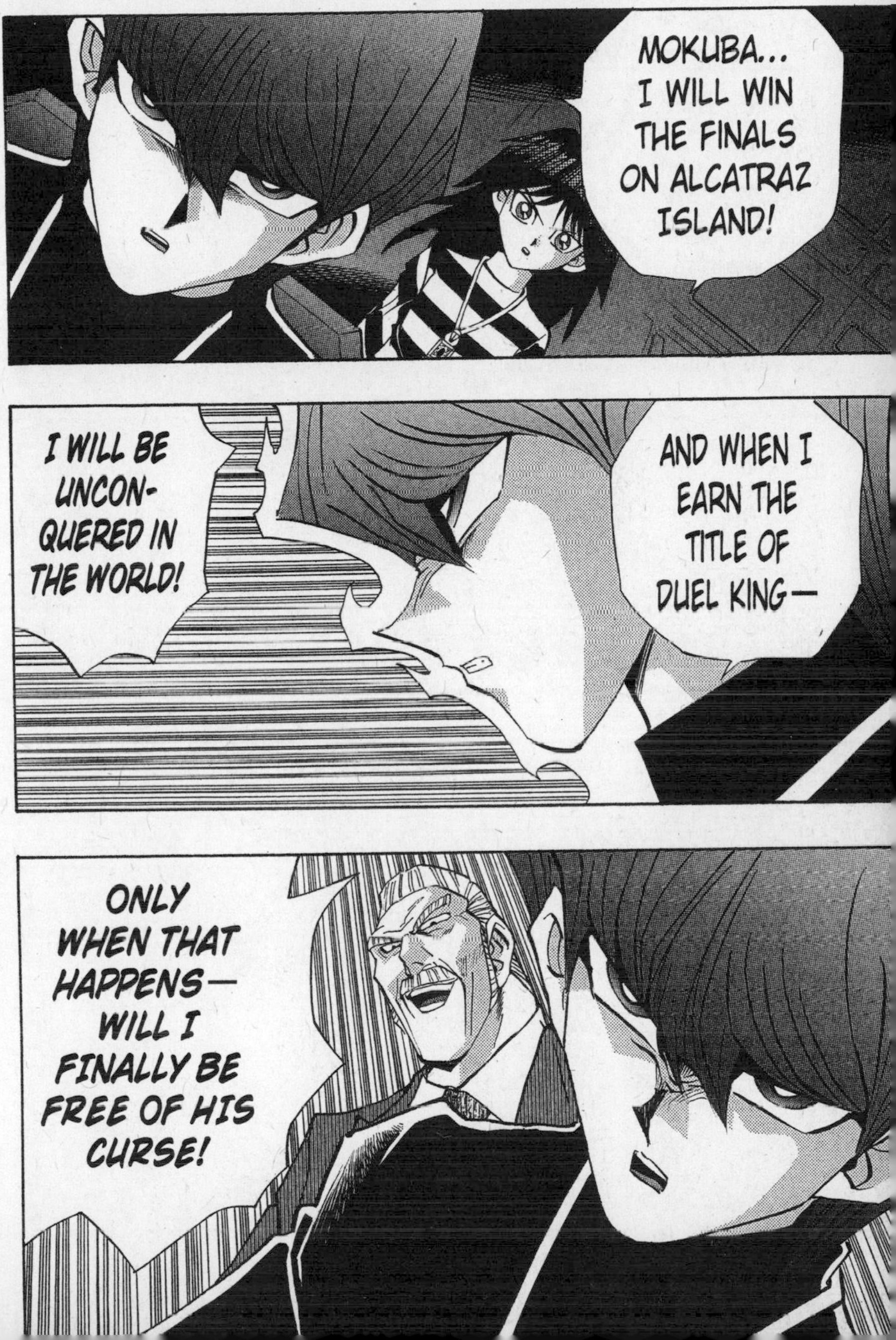
MOKUBA... I WILL WIN THE FINALS ON ALCATRAZ ISLAND!
AND WHEN I EARN THE TITLE OF DUEL KING—
I WILL BE UNCON-QUERED IN THE WORLD!
ONLY WHEN THAT HAPPENS—WILL I FINALLY BE FREE OF HIS CURSE!

READ THIS WAY

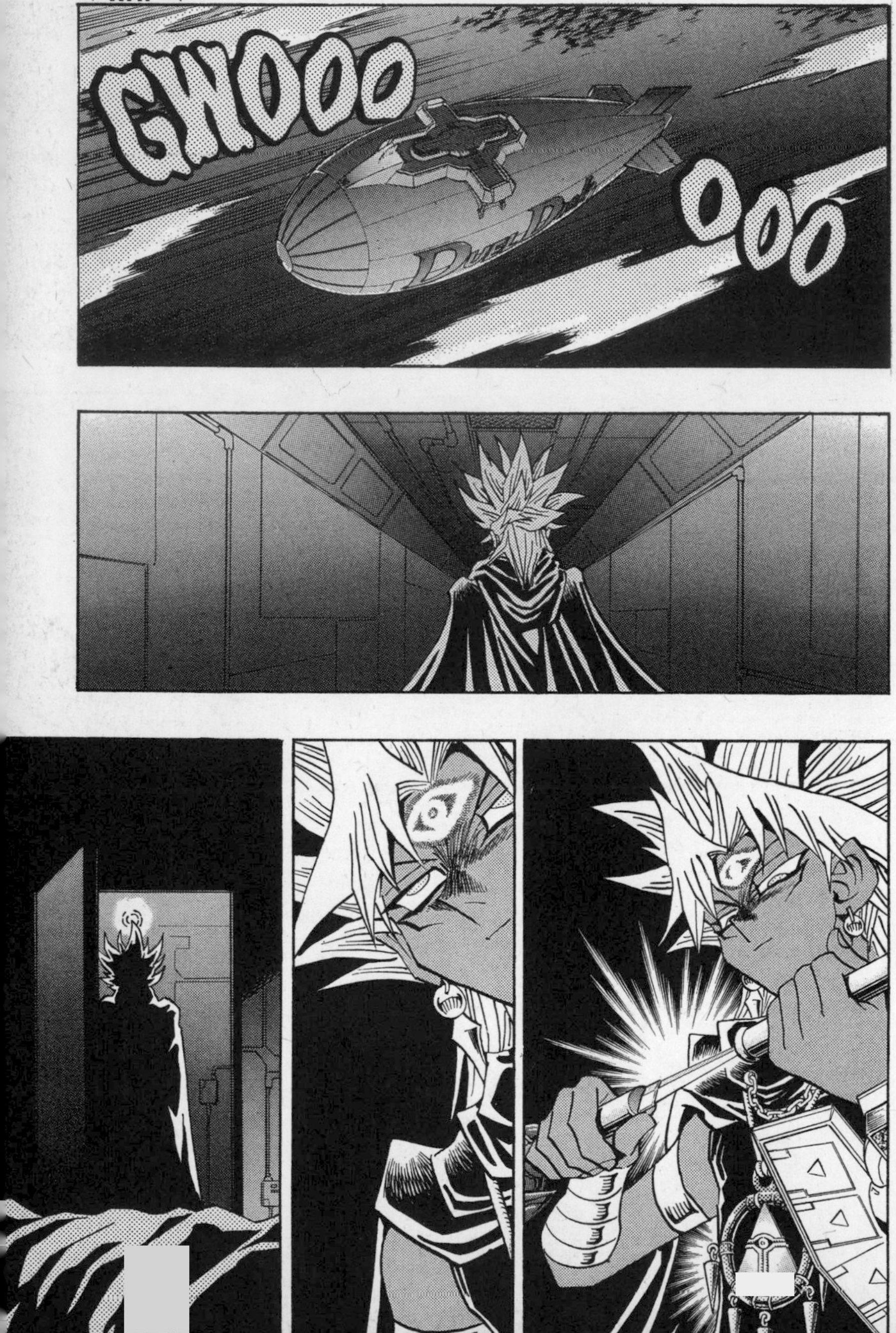
GWOOO
OOO

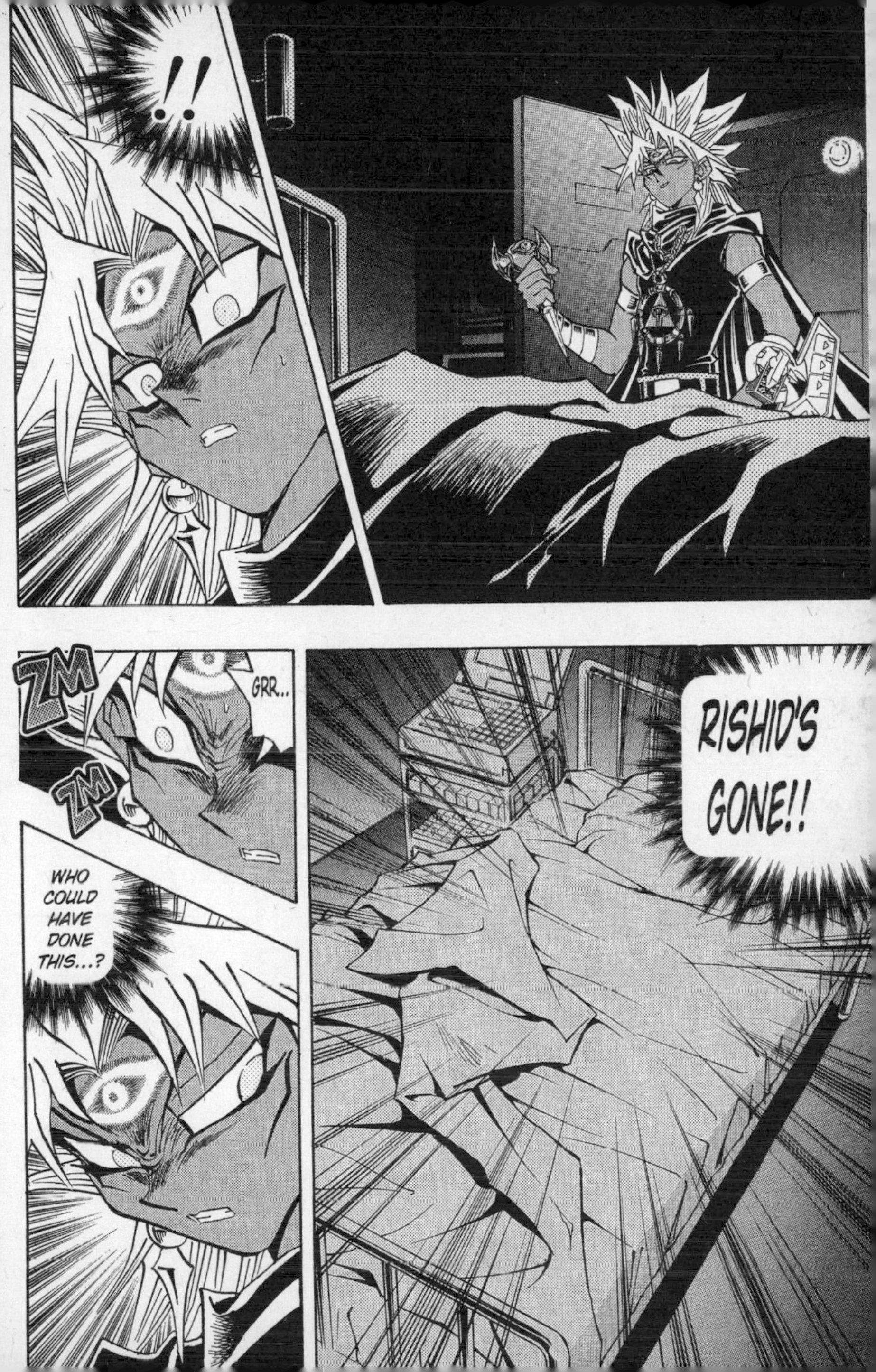
!!
RISHID'S GONE!!
ZM
ZM
GRR...
WHO COULD HAVE DONE THIS...?

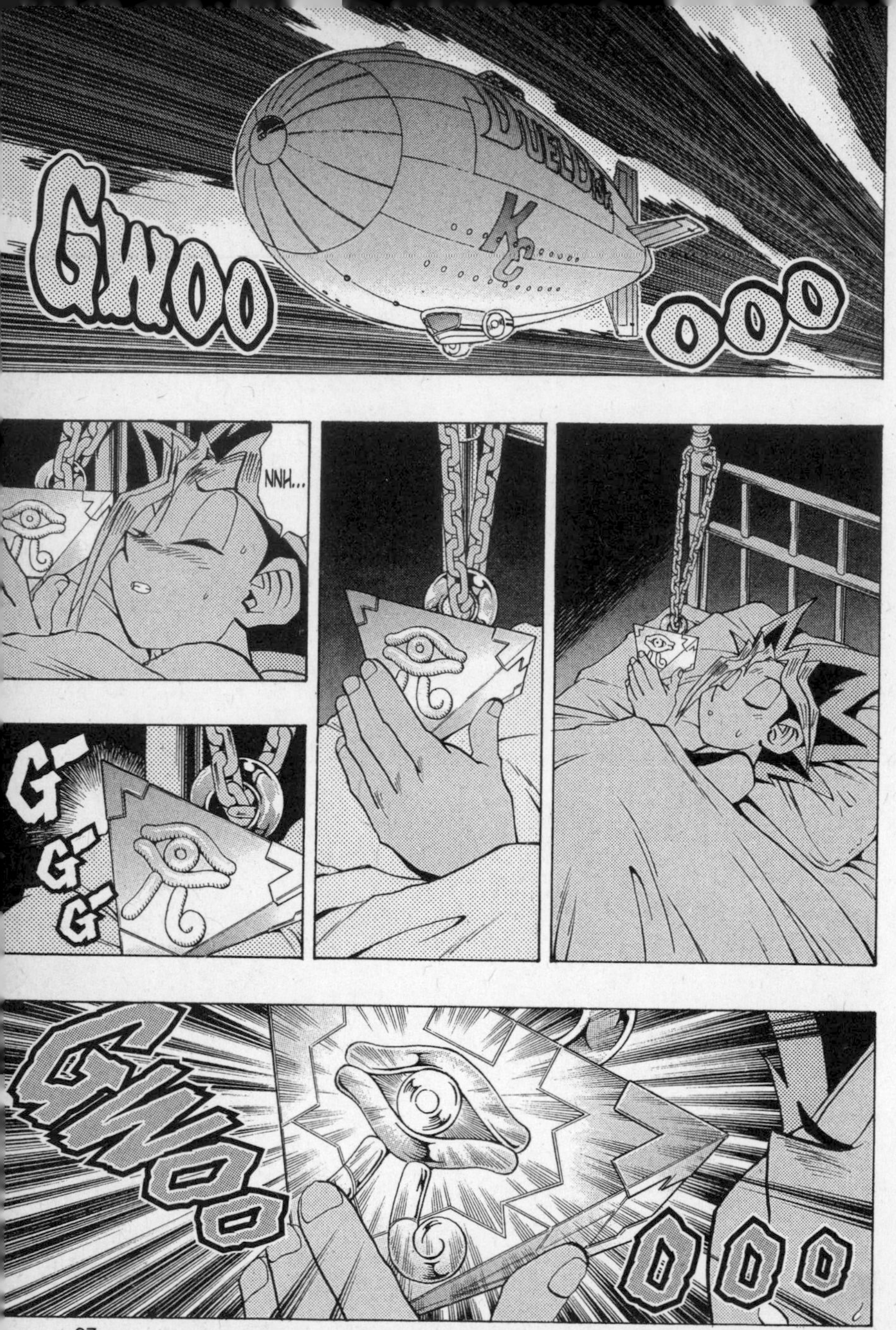
GWOOOOO
NNH...
G-G-G-
GWOOOOO

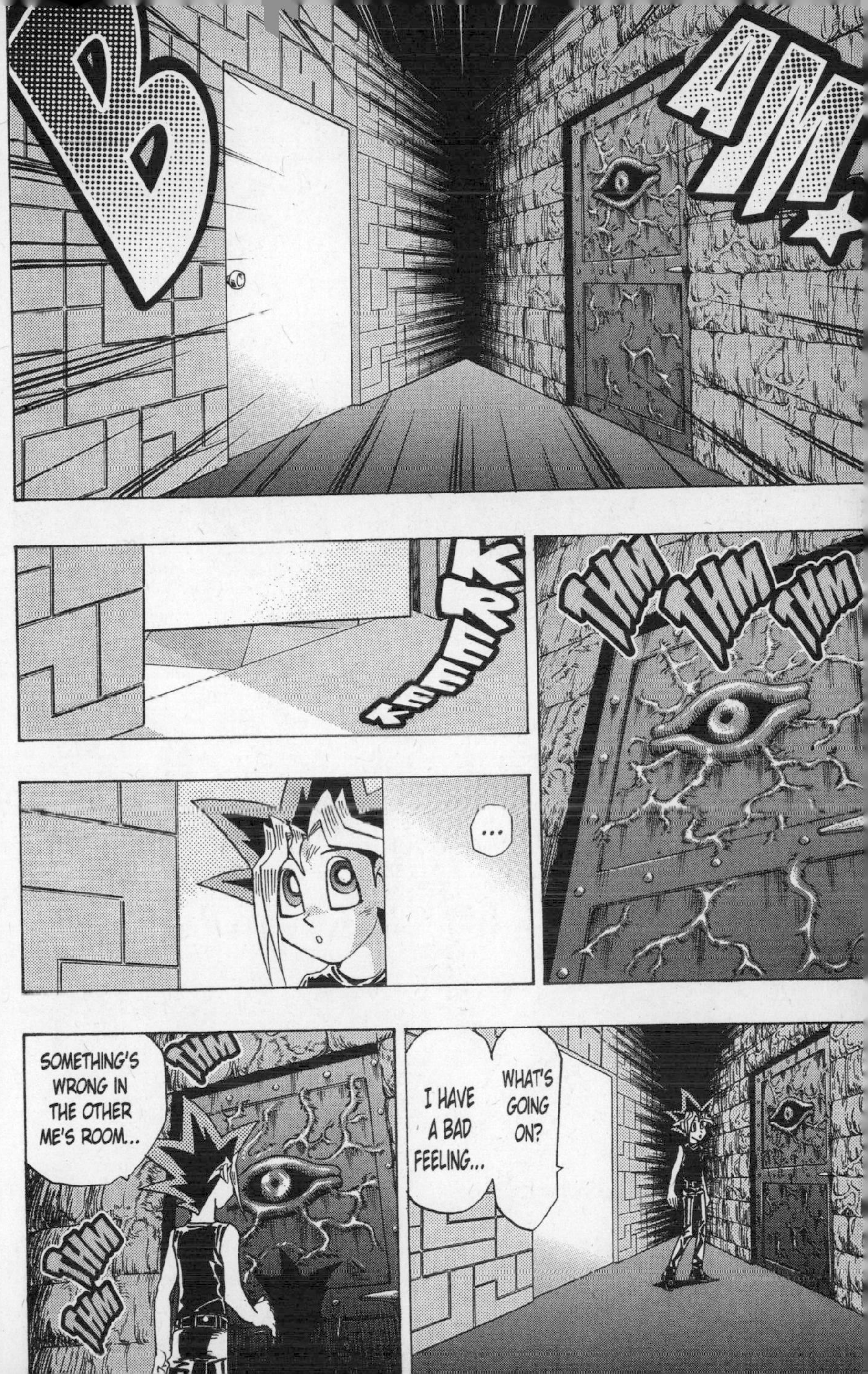
BAM!
THM THM THM
KREEEEK
...
WHAT'S GOING ON?
I HAVE A BAD FEELING...
THM
SOMETHING'S WRONG IN THE OTHER ME'S ROOM...
THM THM

READ THIS WAY

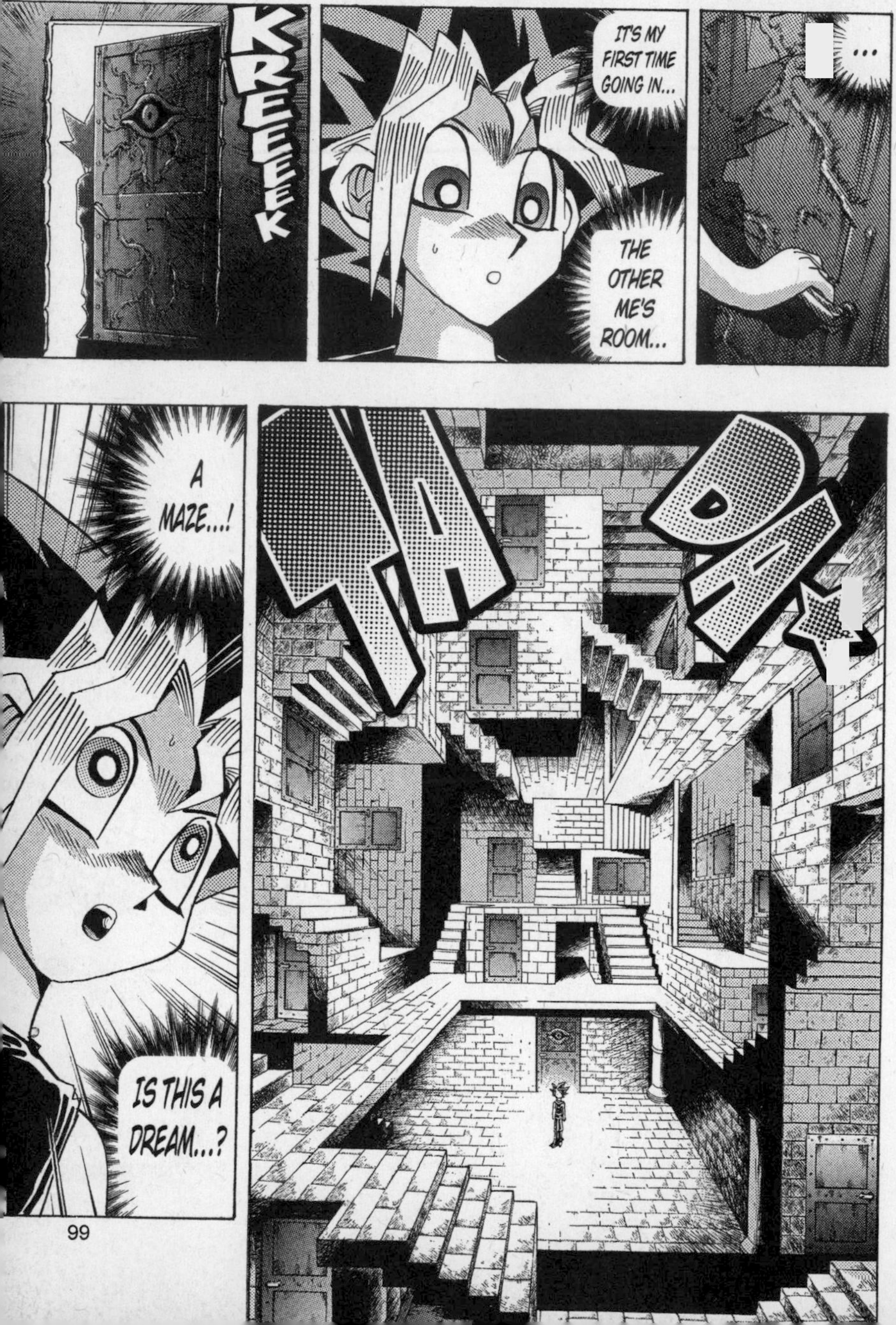
...
IT'S MY FIRST TIME GOING IN...
THE OTHER ME'S ROOM...
KREEEEK
TA DA
A MAZE...!
IS THIS A DREAM...?

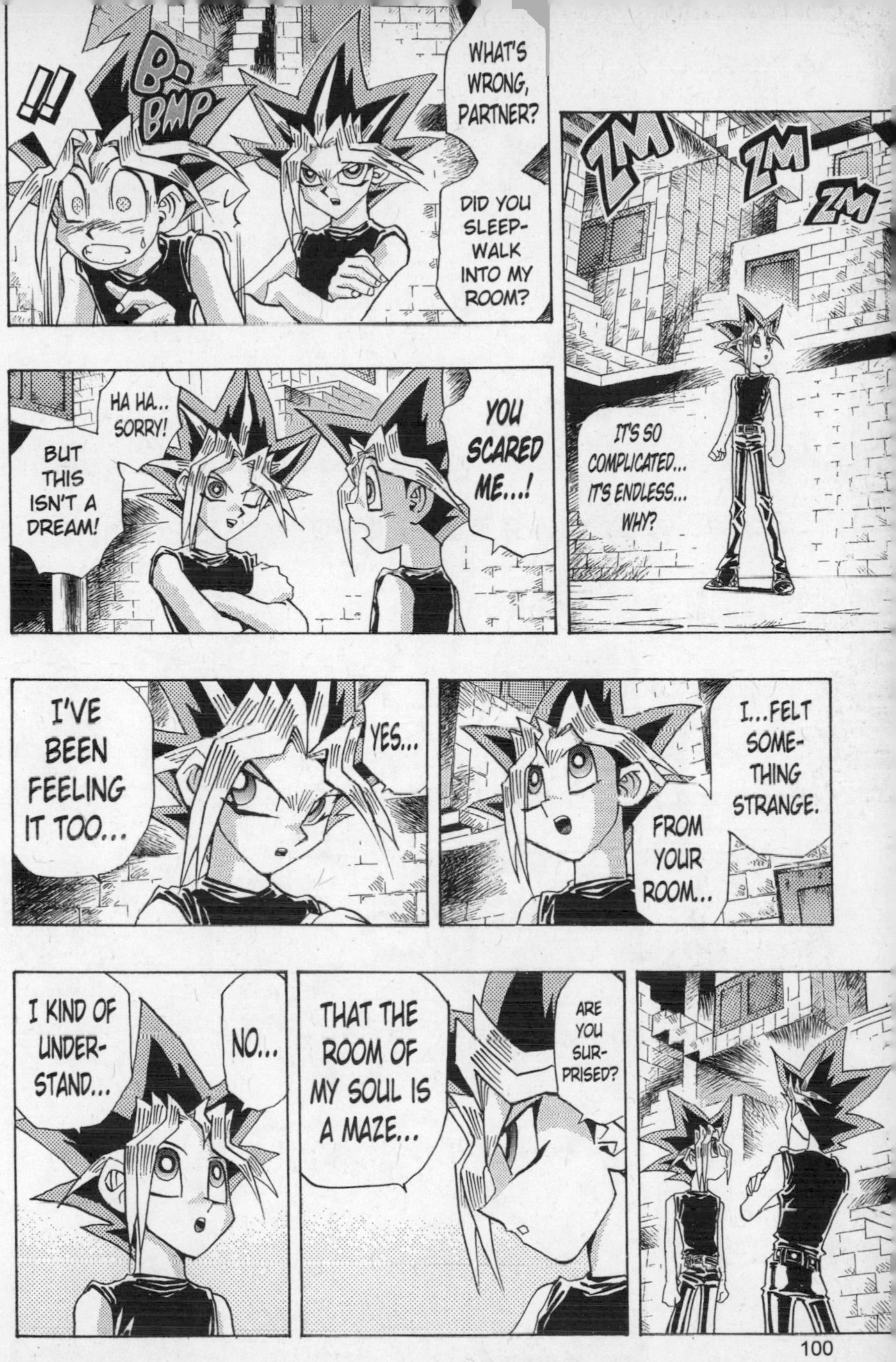
ZM ZM ZM
IT'S SO COMPLICATED... IT'S ENDLESS... WHY?
!!
B-BMP
WHAT'S WRONG, PARTNER?
DID YOU SLEEP-WALK INTO MY ROOM?
YOU SCARED ME...!
HA HA... SORRY!
BUT THIS ISN'T A DREAM!
I...FELT SOME-THING STRANGE.
FROM YOUR ROOM...
YES...
I'VE BEEN FEELING IT TOO...
ARE YOU SUR-PRISED?
THAT THE ROOM OF MY SOUL IS A MAZE...
NO...
I KIND OF UNDER-STAND...

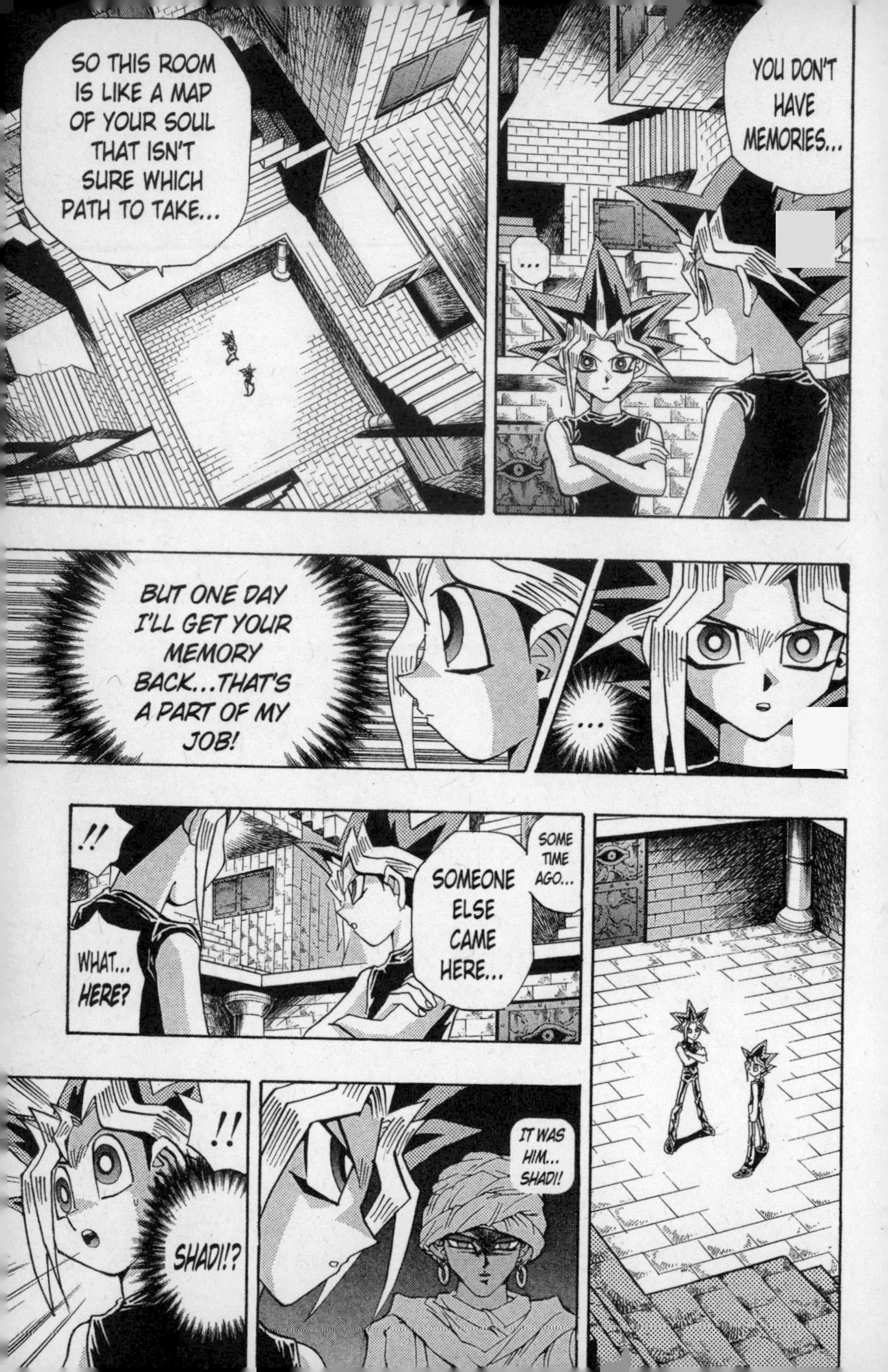
YOU DON'T HAVE MEMORIES...
...
SO THIS ROOM IS LIKE A MAP OF YOUR SOUL THAT ISN'T SURE WHICH PATH TO TAKE...
...
BUT ONE DAY I'LL GET YOUR MEMORY BACK...THAT'S A PART OF MY JOB!
SOME TIME AGO...
SOMEONE ELSE CAME HERE...
!!
WHAT... HERE?
IT WAS HIM... SHADI!
!!
SHADI!?

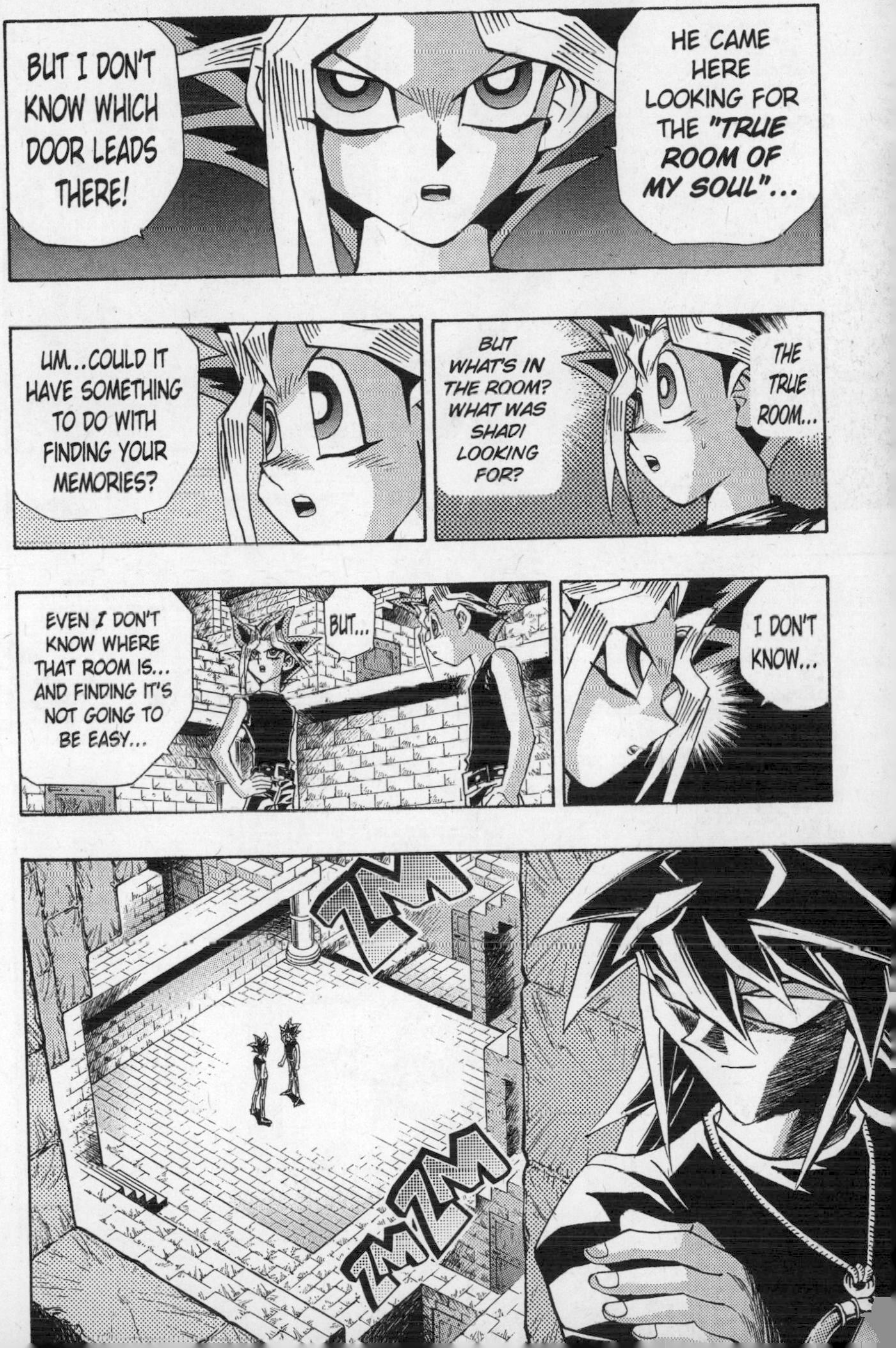
HE CAME HERE LOOKING FOR THE "TRUE ROOM OF MY SOUL"...
BUT I DON'T KNOW WHICH DOOR LEADS THERE!
THE TRUE ROOM...
BUT WHAT'S IN THE ROOM? WHAT WAS SHADI LOOKING FOR?
UM...COULD IT HAVE SOMETHING TO DO WITH FINDING YOUR MEMORIES?
I DON'T KNOW...
BUT...
EVEN I DON'T KNOW WHERE THAT ROOM IS... AND FINDING IT'S NOT GOING TO BE EASY...
ZM
ZMZM

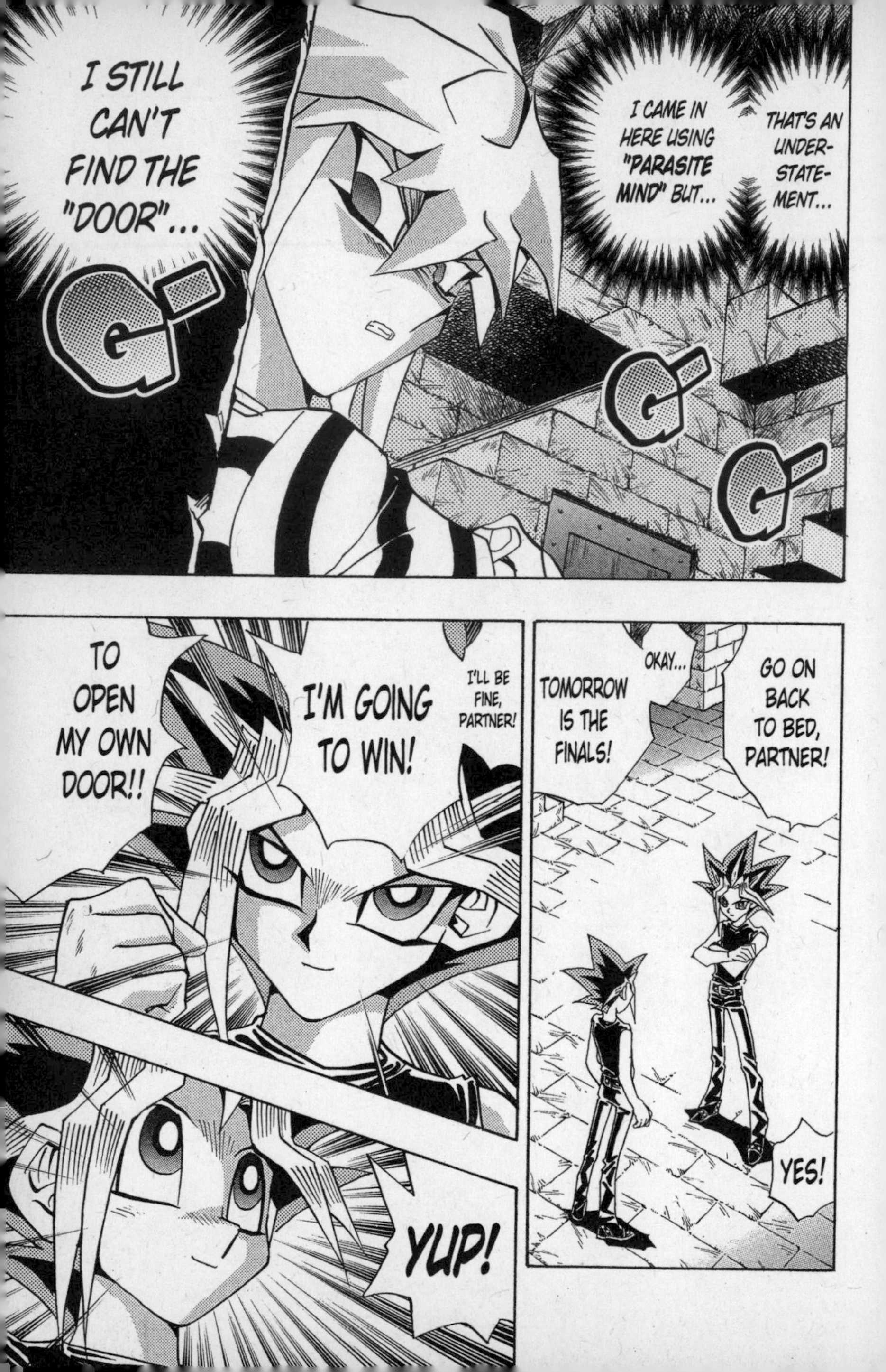
THAT'S AN UNDER-STATEMENT...
I CAME IN HERE USING "PARASITE MIND" BUT...
I STILL CAN'T FIND THE "DOOR"...
G
G
G
GO ON BACK TO BED, PARTNER!
OKAY...
TOMORROW IS THE FINALS!
YES!
I'LL BE FINE, PARTNER!
I'M GOING TO WIN!
TO OPEN MY OWN DOOR!!
YUP!

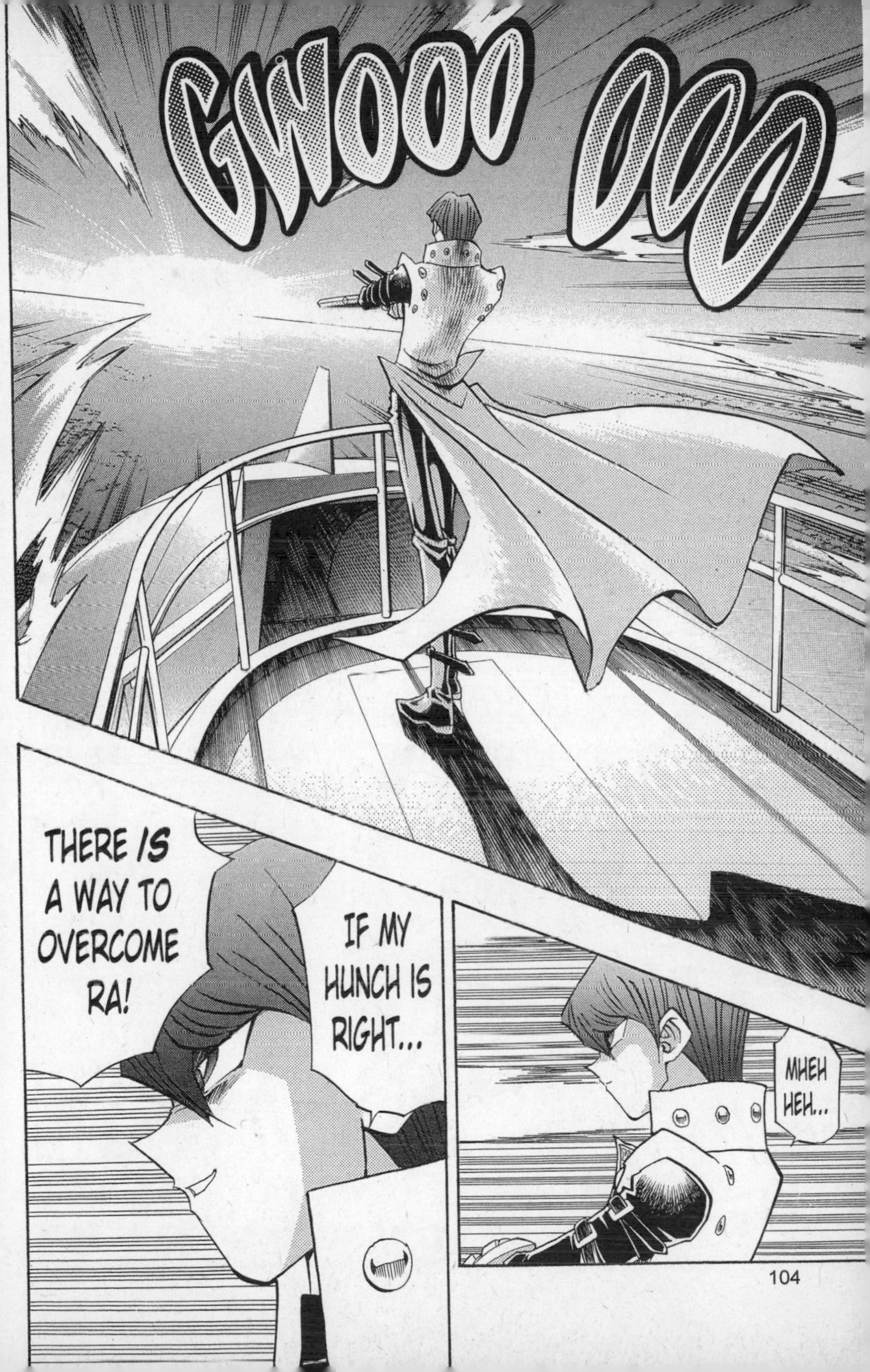
GWOOO OOO
MHEH HEH...
IF MY HUNCH IS RIGHT...
THERE *IS* A WAY TO OVERCOME RA!

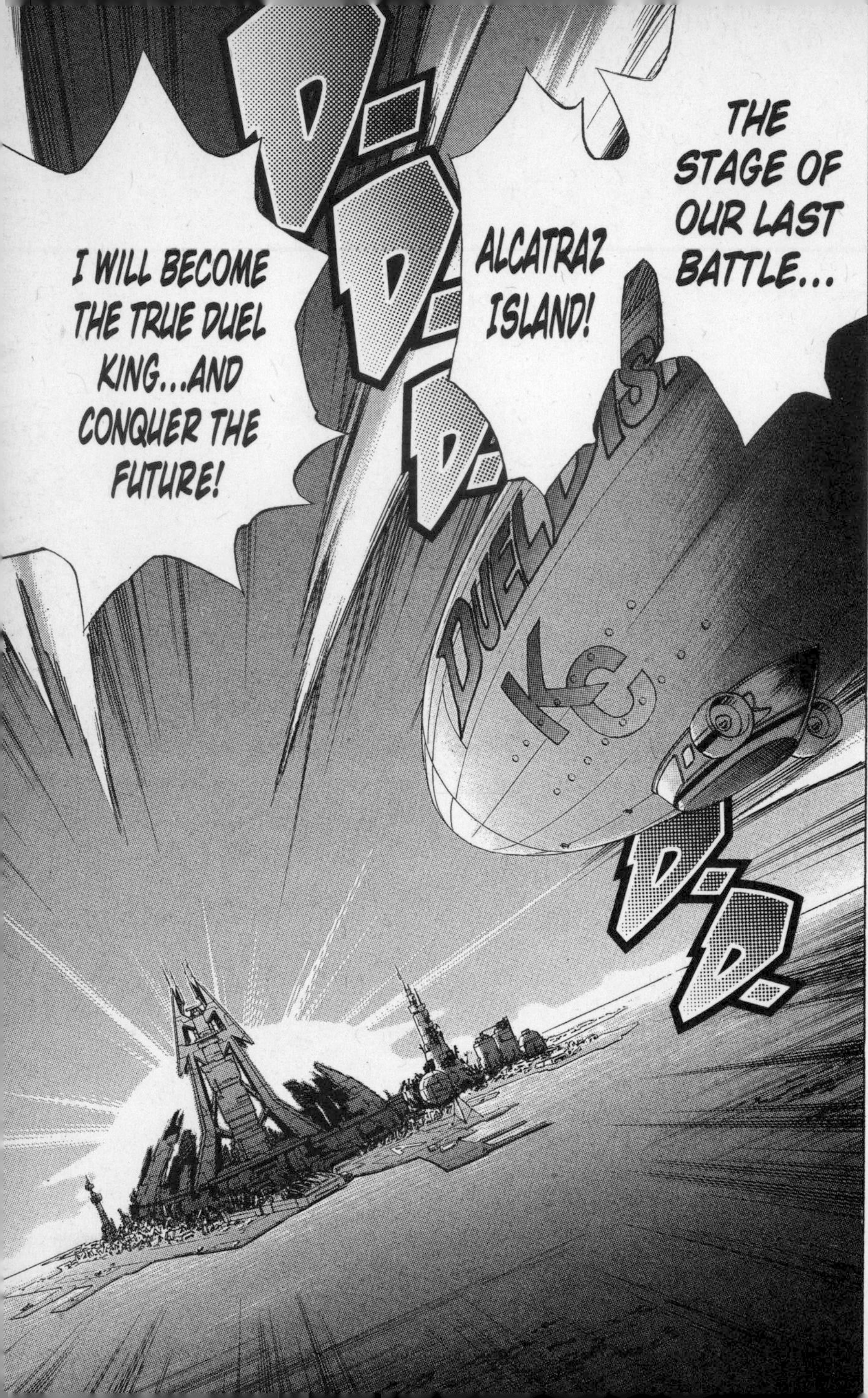
THE STAGE OF OUR LAST BATTLE...
ALCATRAZ ISLAND!
I WILL BECOME THE TRUE DUEL KING...AND CONQUER THE FUTURE!
KC

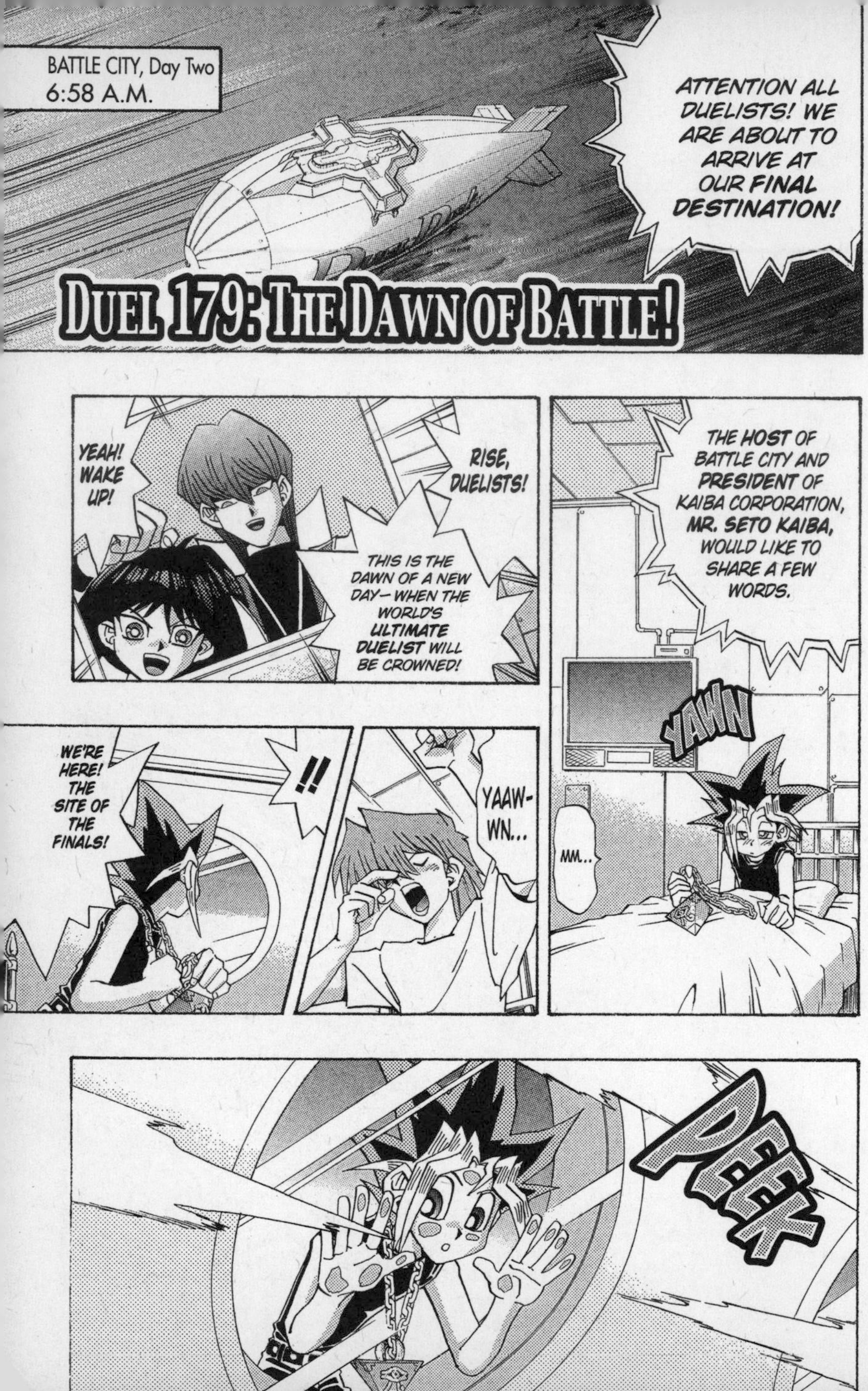
BATTLE CITY, Day Two
6:58 A.M.
ATTENTION ALL DUELISTS! WE ARE ABOUT TO ARRIVE AT OUR FINAL DESTINATION!
DUEL 179: THE DAWN OF BATTLE!
THE HOST OF BATTLE CITY AND PRESIDENT OF KAIBA CORPORATION, MR. SETO KAIBA, WOULD LIKE TO SHARE A FEW WORDS.
YAWN
MM...
RISE, DUELISTS!
YEAH! WAKE UP!
THIS IS THE DAWN OF A NEW DAY—WHEN THE WORLD'S ULTIMATE DUELIST WILL BE CROWNED!
YAAW-WN...
!!
WE'RE HERE! THE SITE OF THE FINALS!
PEEK

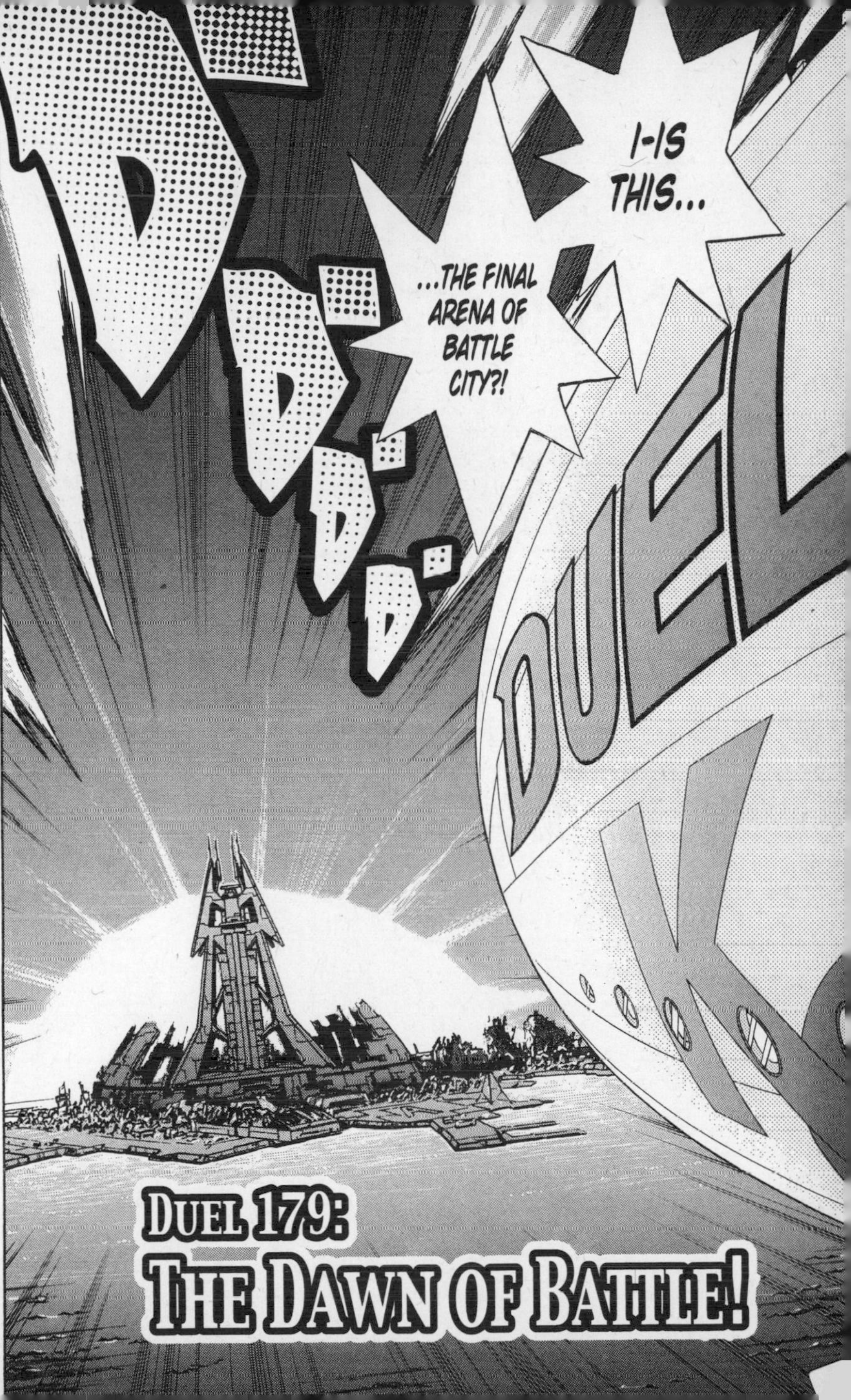
I-IS THIS...
...THE FINAL ARENA OF BATTLE CITY?!
DUEL
DUEL 179:
THE DAWN OF BATTLE!

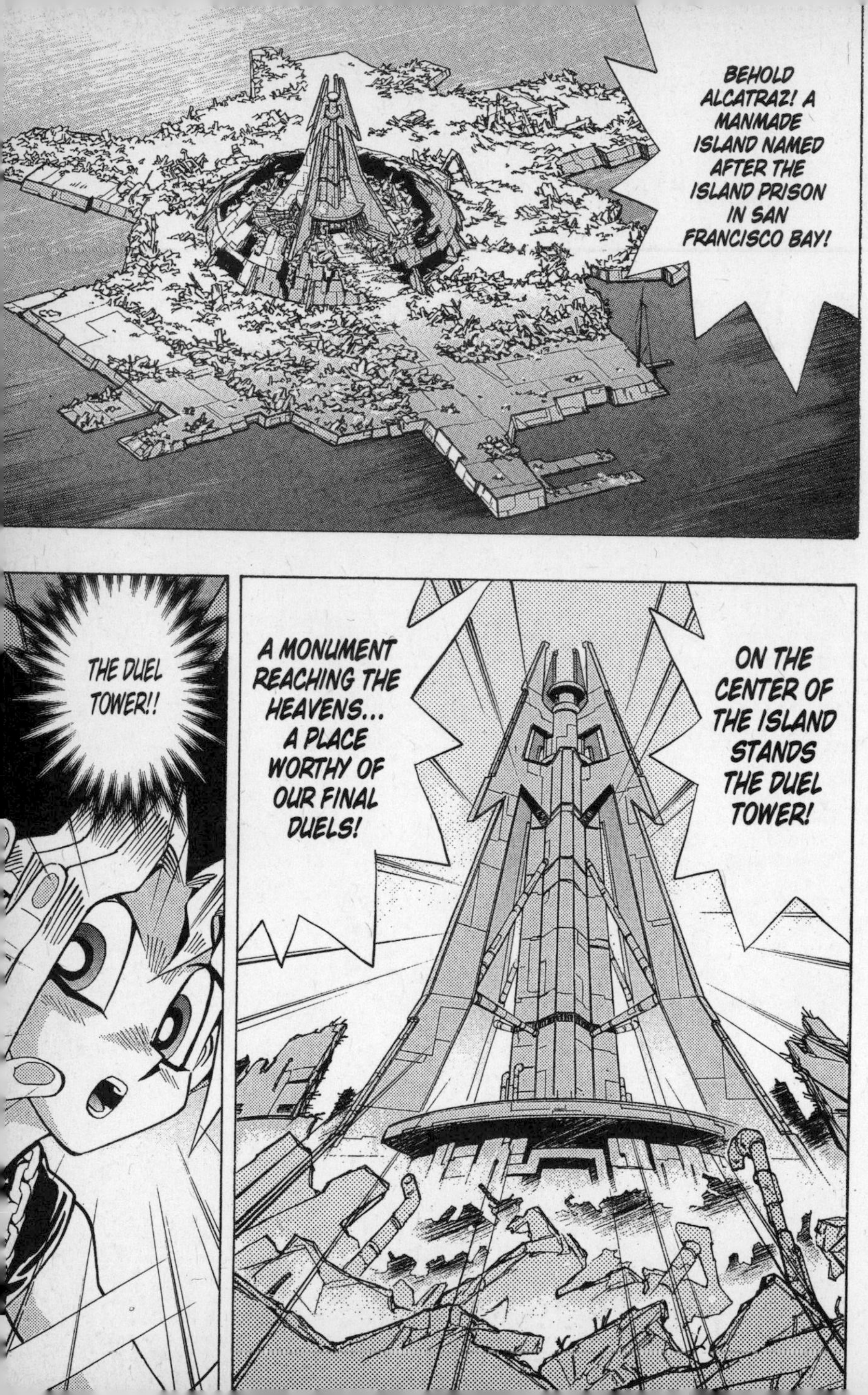
BEHOLD ALCATRAZ! A MANMADE ISLAND NAMED AFTER THE ISLAND PRISON IN SAN FRANCISCO BAY!
ON THE CENTER OF THE ISLAND STANDS THE DUEL TOWER!
A MONUMENT REACHING THE HEAVENS... A PLACE WORTHY OF OUR FINAL DUELS!
THE DUEL TOWER!!

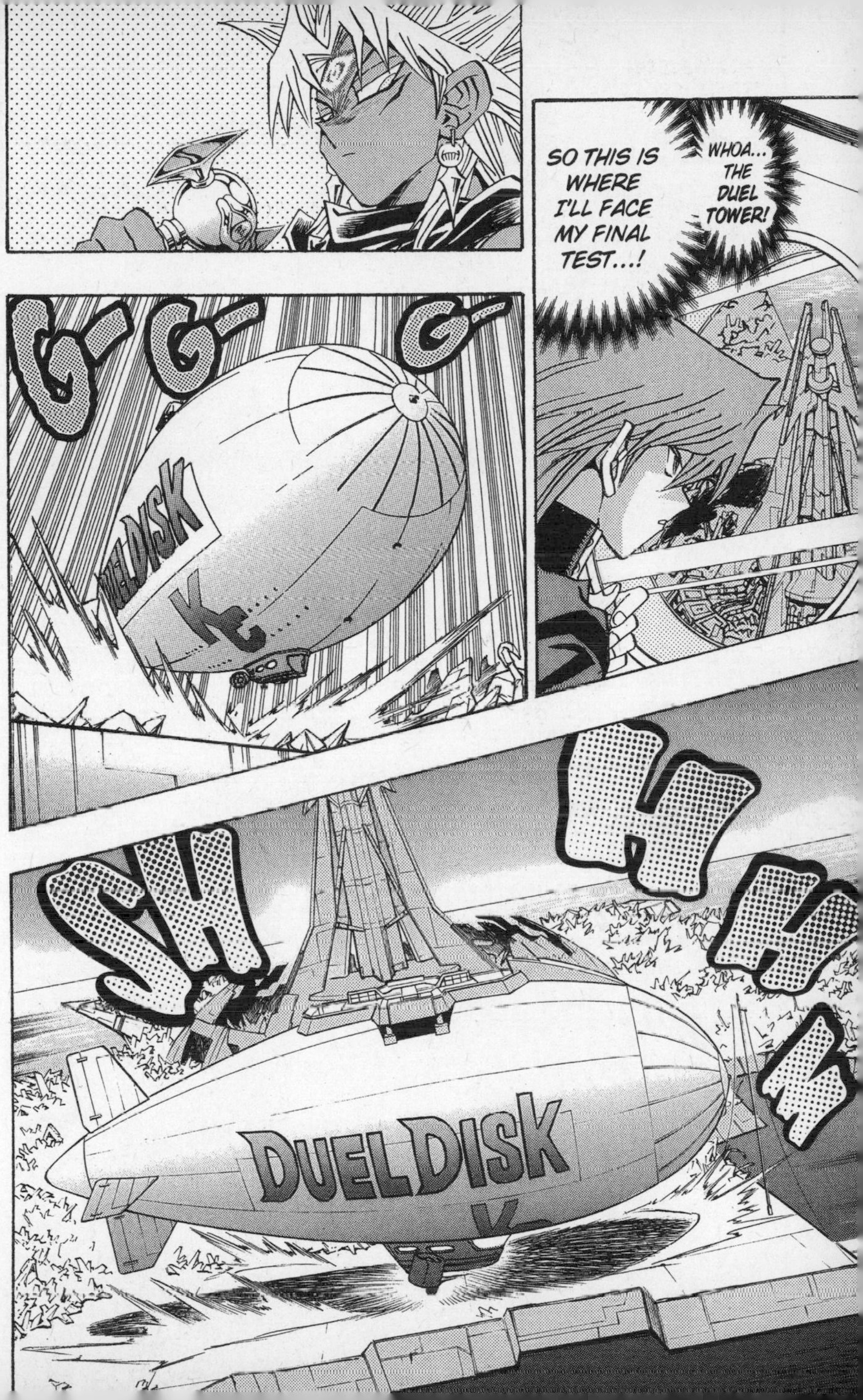
WHOA... THE DUEL TOWER!
SO THIS IS WHERE I'LL FACE MY FINAL TEST...!
G-G-G-
DUEL DISK
SH
DUELDISK

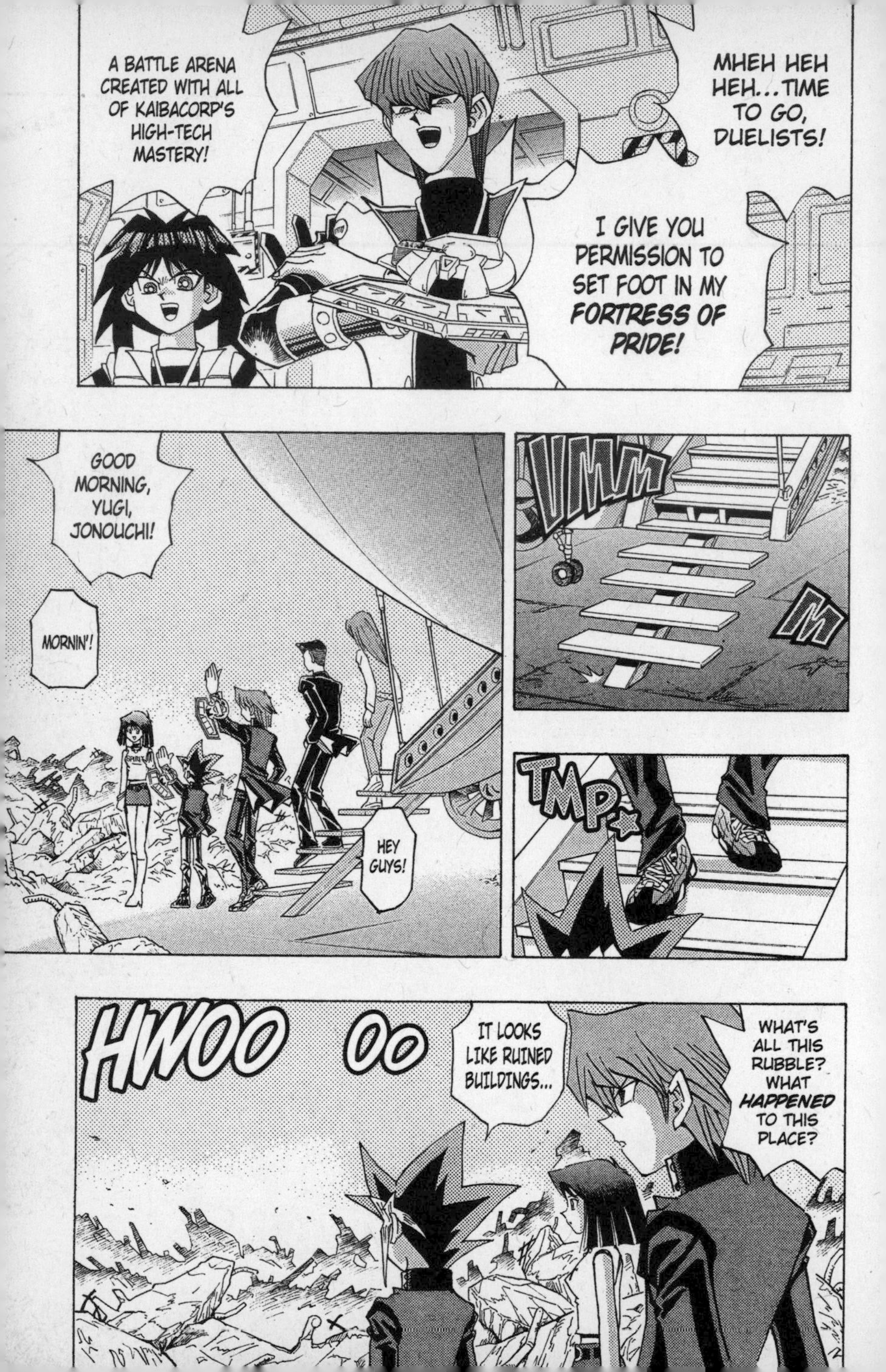
MHEH HEH HEH...TIME TO GO, DUELISTS!
I GIVE YOU PERMISSION TO SET FOOT IN MY ***FORTRESS OF PRIDE!***
A BATTLE ARENA CREATED WITH ALL OF KAIBACORP'S HIGH-TECH MASTERY!
VMMM
M
TMP
GOOD MORNING, YUGI, JONOUCHI!
HEY GUYS!
MORNIN'!
WHAT'S ALL THIS RUBBLE? WHAT ***HAPPENED*** TO THIS PLACE?
IT LOOKS LIKE RUINED BUILDINGS...
HWOO OO

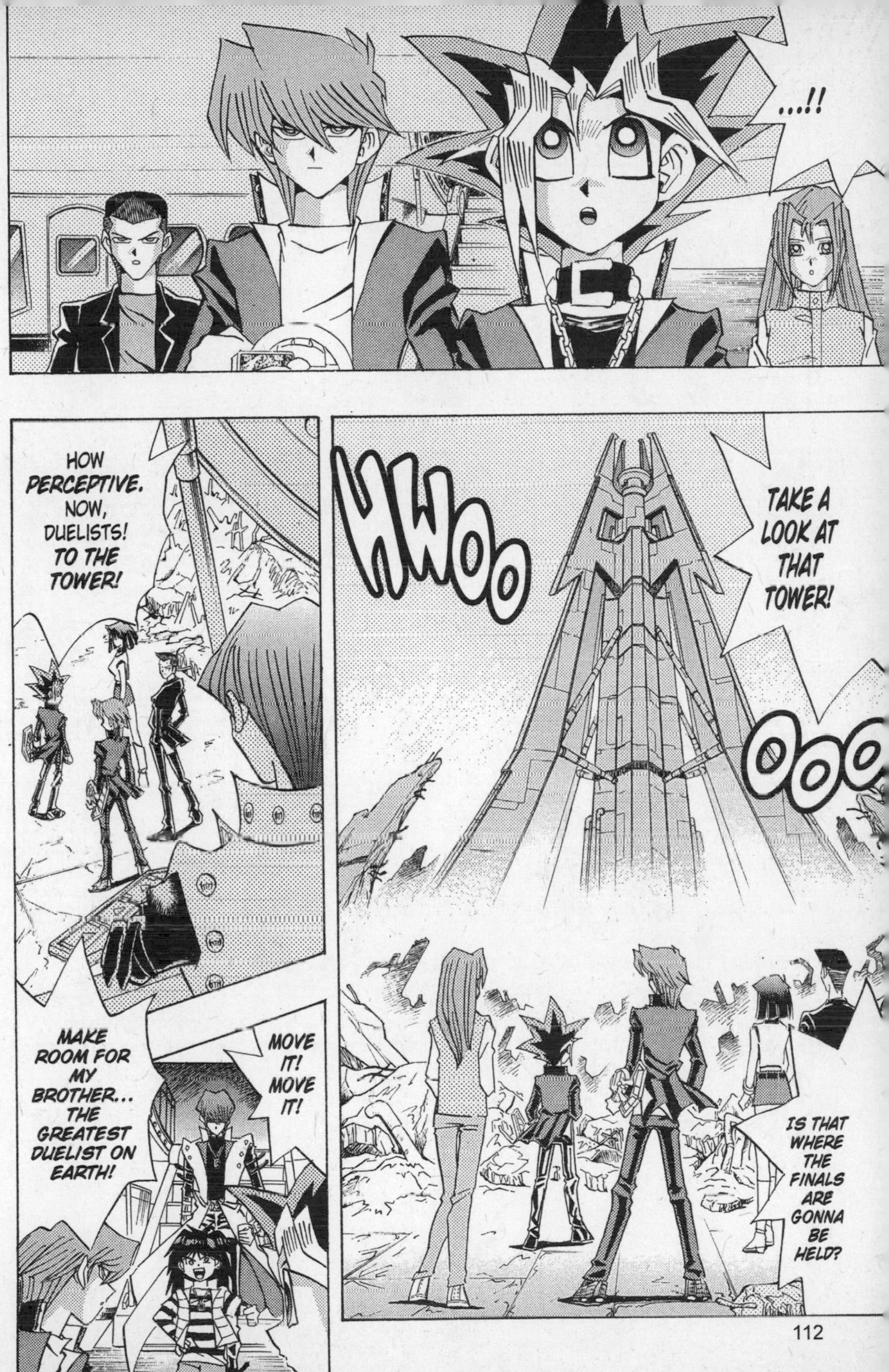
...!!
TAKE A LOOK AT THAT TOWER!
HWOOOOO
IS THAT WHERE THE FINALS ARE GONNA BE HELD?
HOW PERCEPTIVE. NOW, DUELISTS! TO THE TOWER!
MOVE IT! MOVE IT!
MAKE ROOM FOR MY BROTHER... THE GREATEST DUELIST ON EARTH!

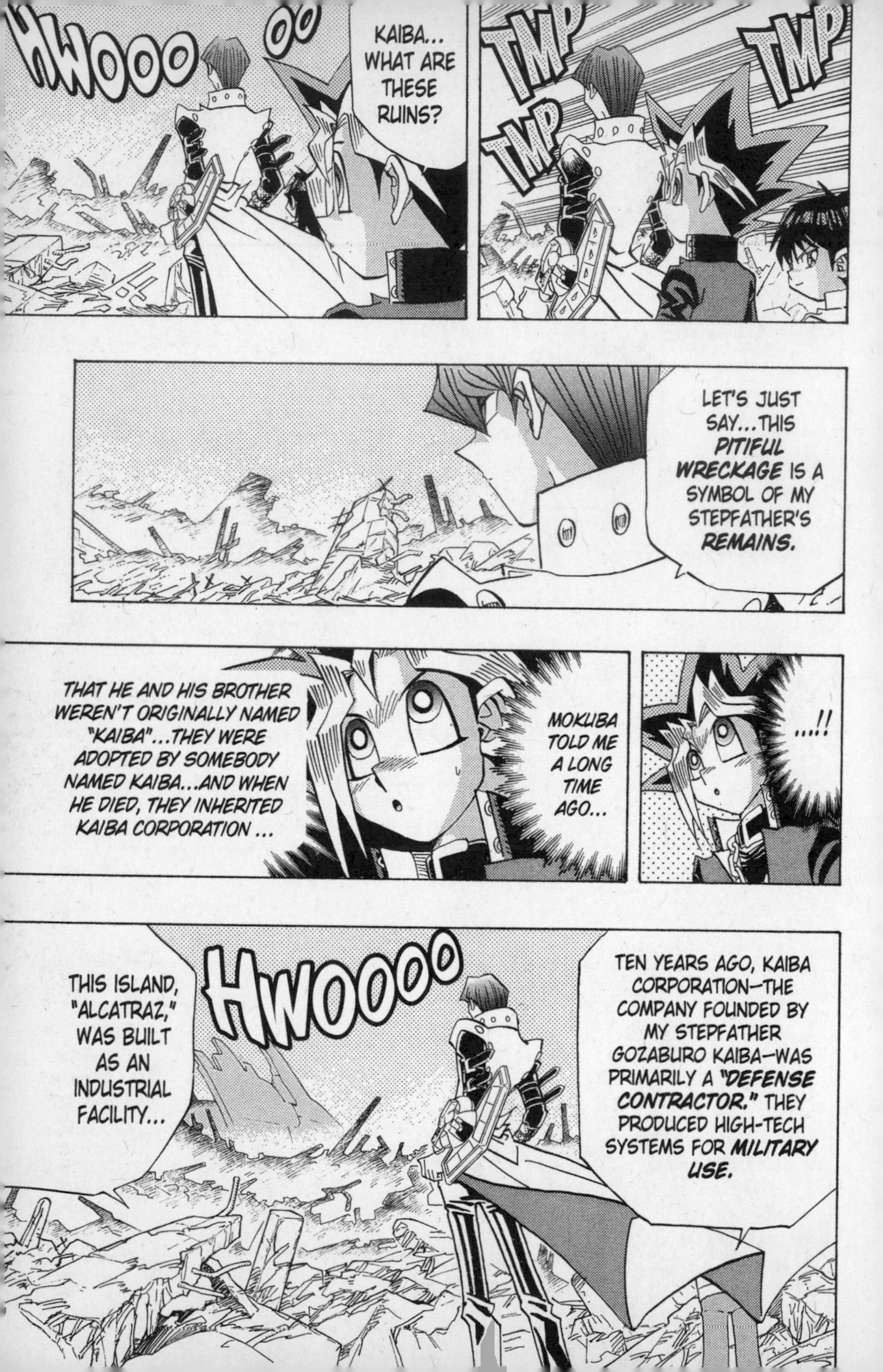
TMP
TMP
TMP
TMP
HWOOOO
KAIBA... WHAT ARE THESE RUINS?
LET'S JUST SAY...THIS **PITIFUL WRECKAGE** IS A SYMBOL OF MY STEPFATHER'S **REMAINS.**
...!!
MOKUBA TOLD ME A LONG TIME AGO...
THAT HE AND HIS BROTHER WEREN'T ORIGINALLY NAMED "KAIBA"...THEY WERE ADOPTED BY SOMEBODY NAMED KAIBA...AND WHEN HE DIED, THEY INHERITED KAIBA CORPORATION ...
TEN YEARS AGO, KAIBA CORPORATION—THE COMPANY FOUNDED BY MY STEPFATHER GOZABURO KAIBA—WAS PRIMARILY A **"DEFENSE CONTRACTOR."** THEY PRODUCED HIGH-TECH SYSTEMS FOR **MILITARY USE.**
HWOOOO
THIS ISLAND, "ALCATRAZ," WAS BUILT AS AN INDUSTRIAL FACILITY...

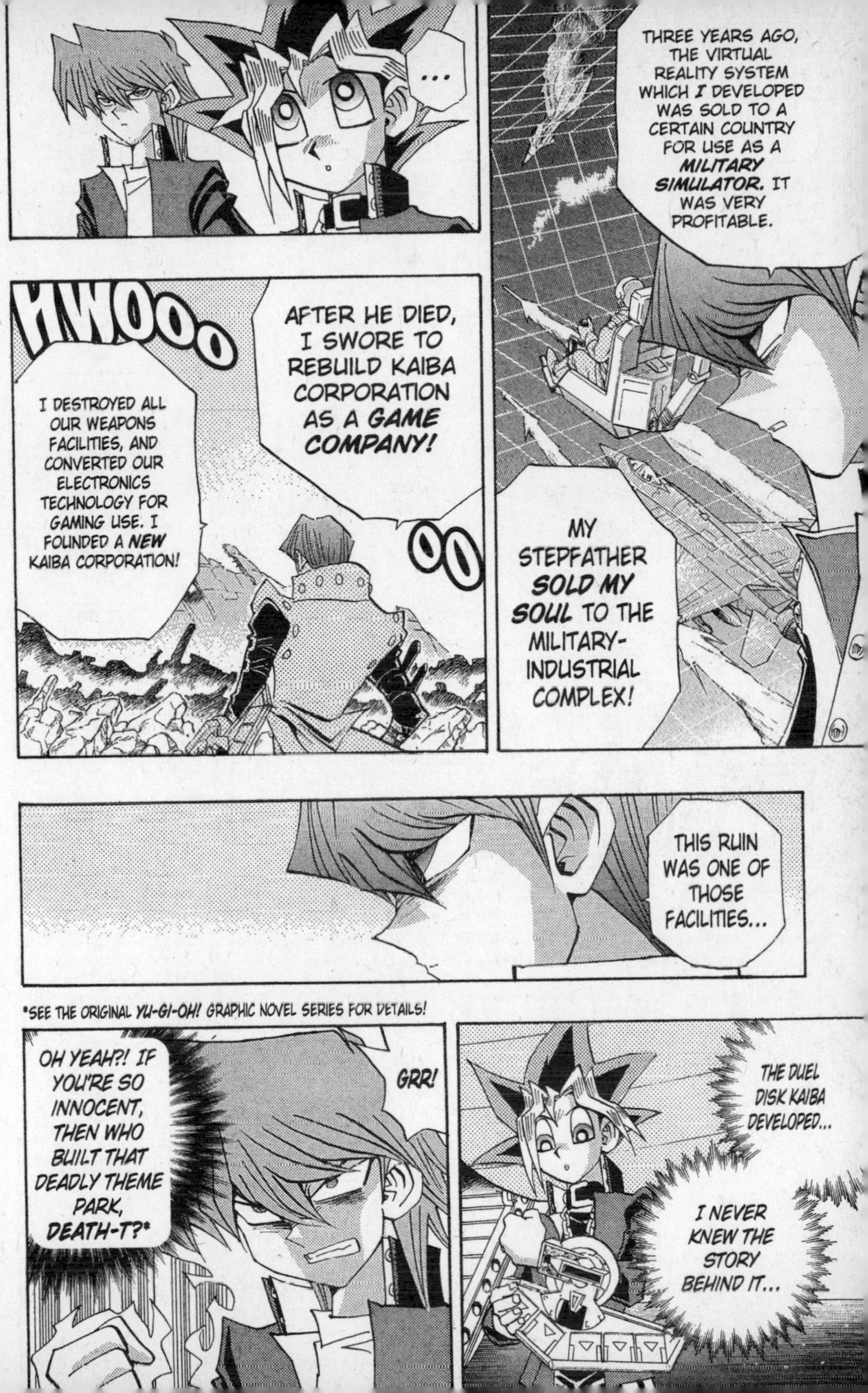
THREE YEARS AGO, THE VIRTUAL REALITY SYSTEM WHICH *I* DEVELOPED WAS SOLD TO A CERTAIN COUNTRY FOR USE AS A ***MILITARY SIMULATOR.*** IT WAS VERY PROFITABLE.
MY STEPFATHER ***SOLD MY SOUL*** TO THE MILITARY-INDUSTRIAL COMPLEX!
...
AFTER HE DIED, I SWORE TO REBUILD KAIBA CORPORATION AS A ***GAME COMPANY!***
I DESTROYED ALL OUR WEAPONS FACILITIES, AND CONVERTED OUR ELECTRONICS TECHNOLOGY FOR GAMING USE. I FOUNDED A ***NEW*** KAIBA CORPORATION!
HWOOOOO
THIS RUIN WAS ONE OF THOSE FACILITIES...
*SEE THE ORIGINAL *YU-GI-OH!* GRAPHIC NOVEL SERIES FOR DETAILS!
THE DUEL DISK KAIBA DEVELOPED...
I NEVER KNEW THE STORY BEHIND IT...
GRR!
OH YEAH?! IF YOU'RE SO INNOCENT, THEN WHO BUILT THAT DEADLY THEME PARK, **DEATH-T?***

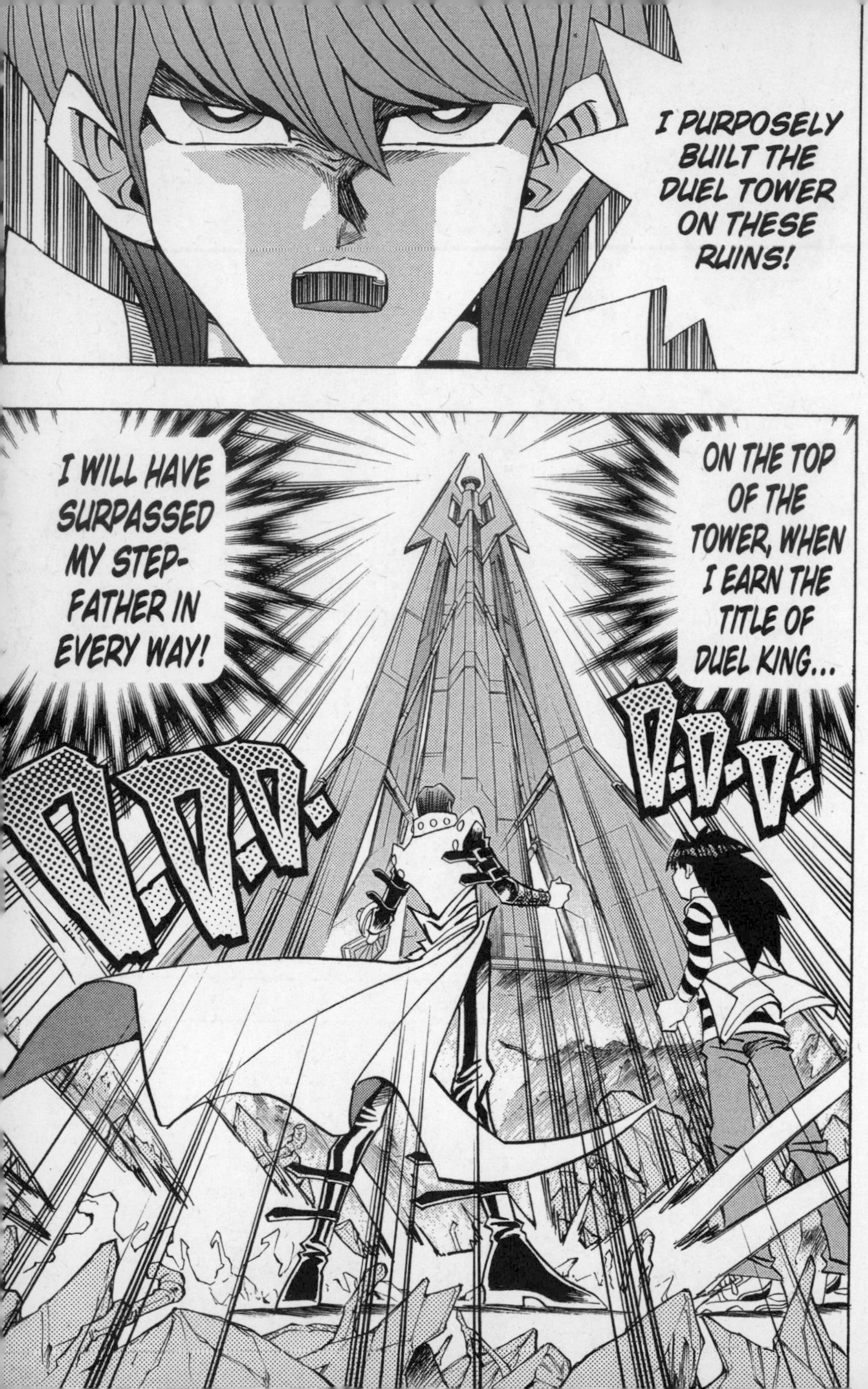
I PURPOSELY BUILT THE DUEL TOWER ON THESE RUINS!
ON THE TOP OF THE TOWER, WHEN I EARN THE TITLE OF DUEL KING...
I WILL HAVE SURPASSED MY STEP-FATHER IN EVERY WAY!
D.D.D.
D.D.D.

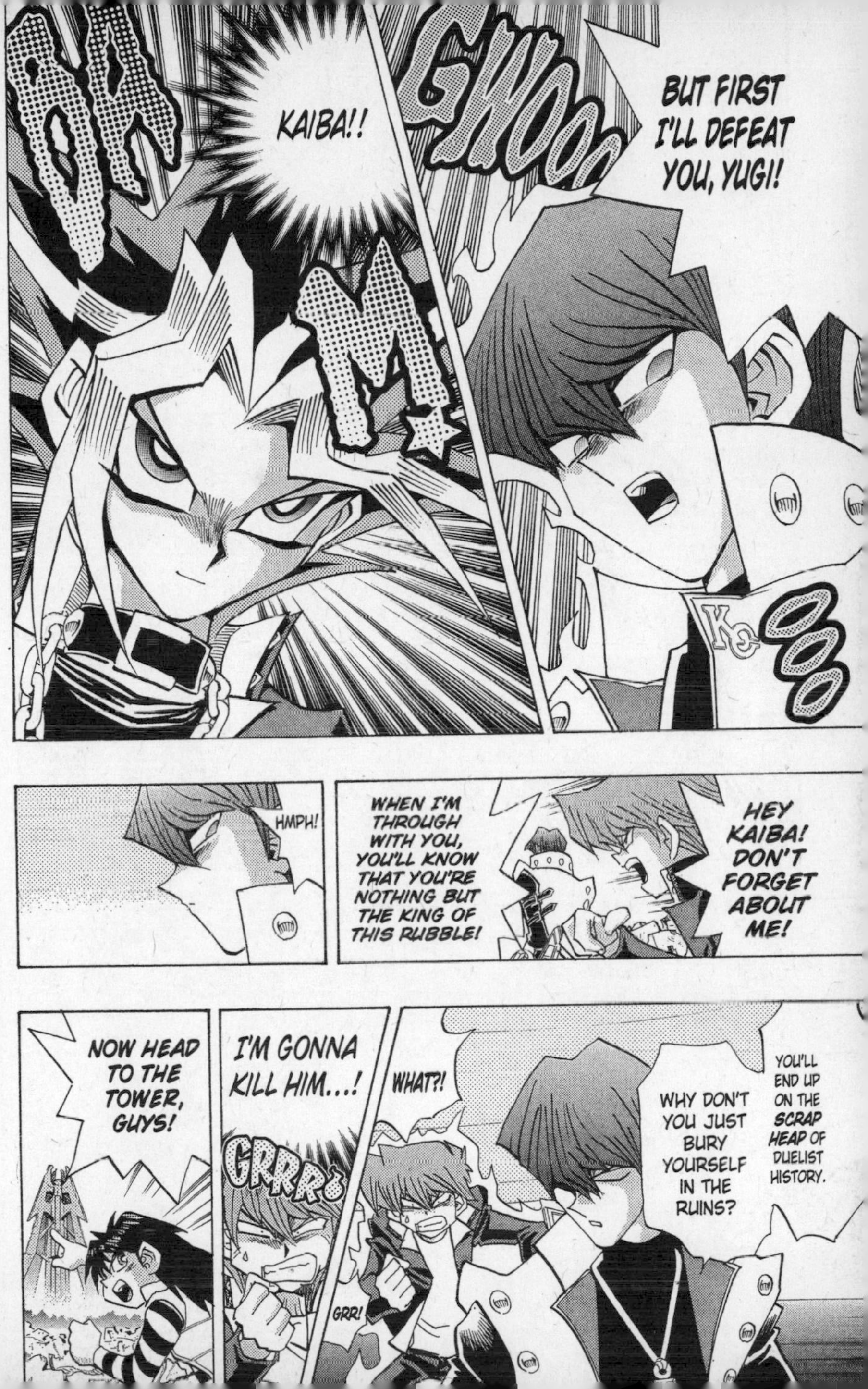
GWOOO
BUT FIRST I'LL DEFEAT YOU, YUGI!
KAIBA!!
HEY KAIBA! DON'T FORGET ABOUT ME!
WHEN I'M THROUGH WITH YOU, YOU'LL KNOW THAT YOU'RE NOTHING BUT THE KING OF THIS RUBBLE!
HMPH!
YOU'LL END UP ON THE SCRAP HEAP OF DUELIST HISTORY.
WHY DON'T YOU JUST BURY YOURSELF IN THE RUINS?
WHAT?!
GRR!
I'M GONNA KILL HIM...!
GRRRR
NOW HEAD TO THE TOWER, GUYS!

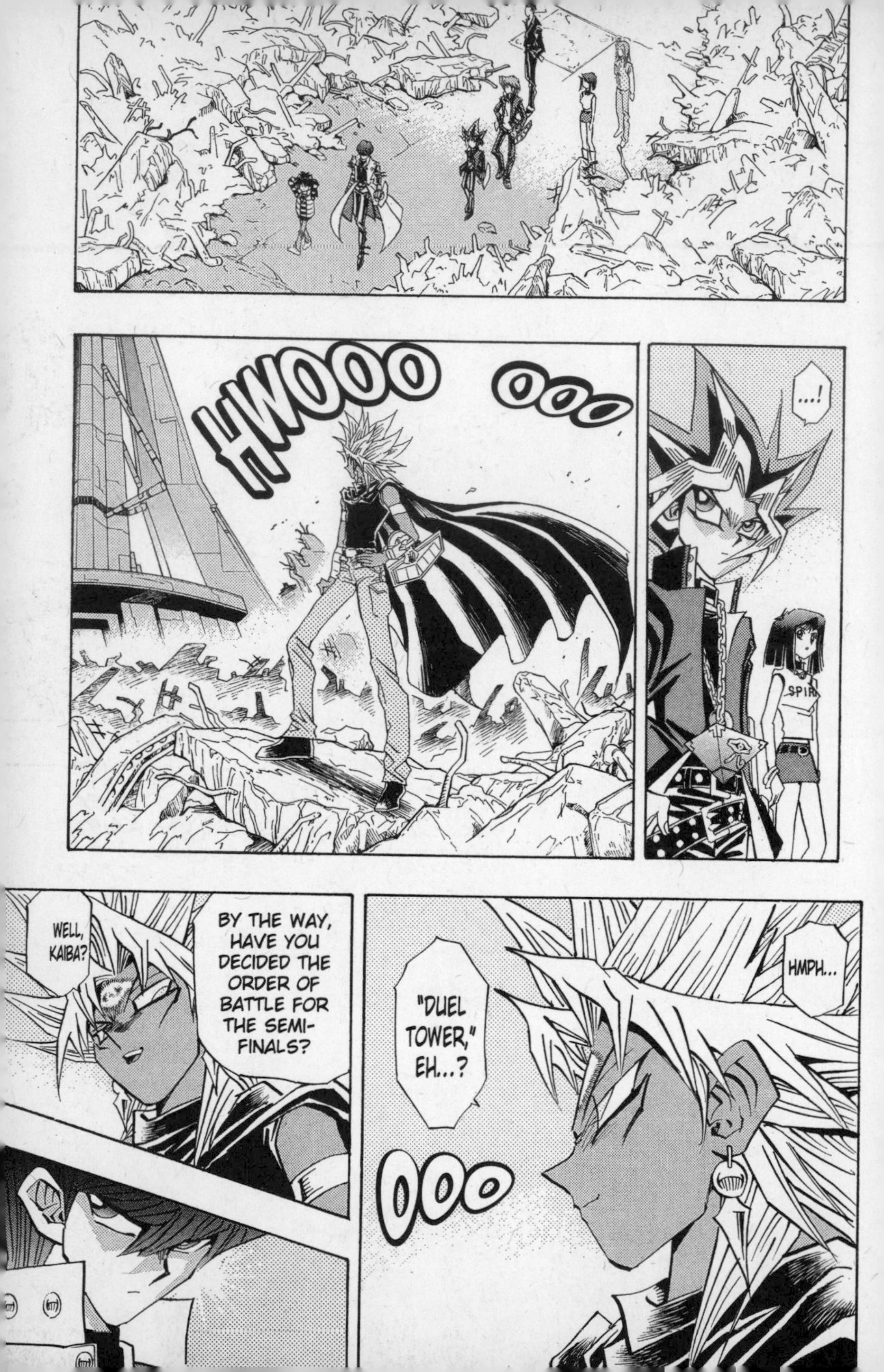

...!
HWOOOO OOO
HMPH...
"DUEL TOWER," EH...?
OOO
BY THE WAY, HAVE YOU DECIDED THE ORDER OF BATTLE FOR THE SEMI-FINALS?
WELL, KAIBA?
SPIRI

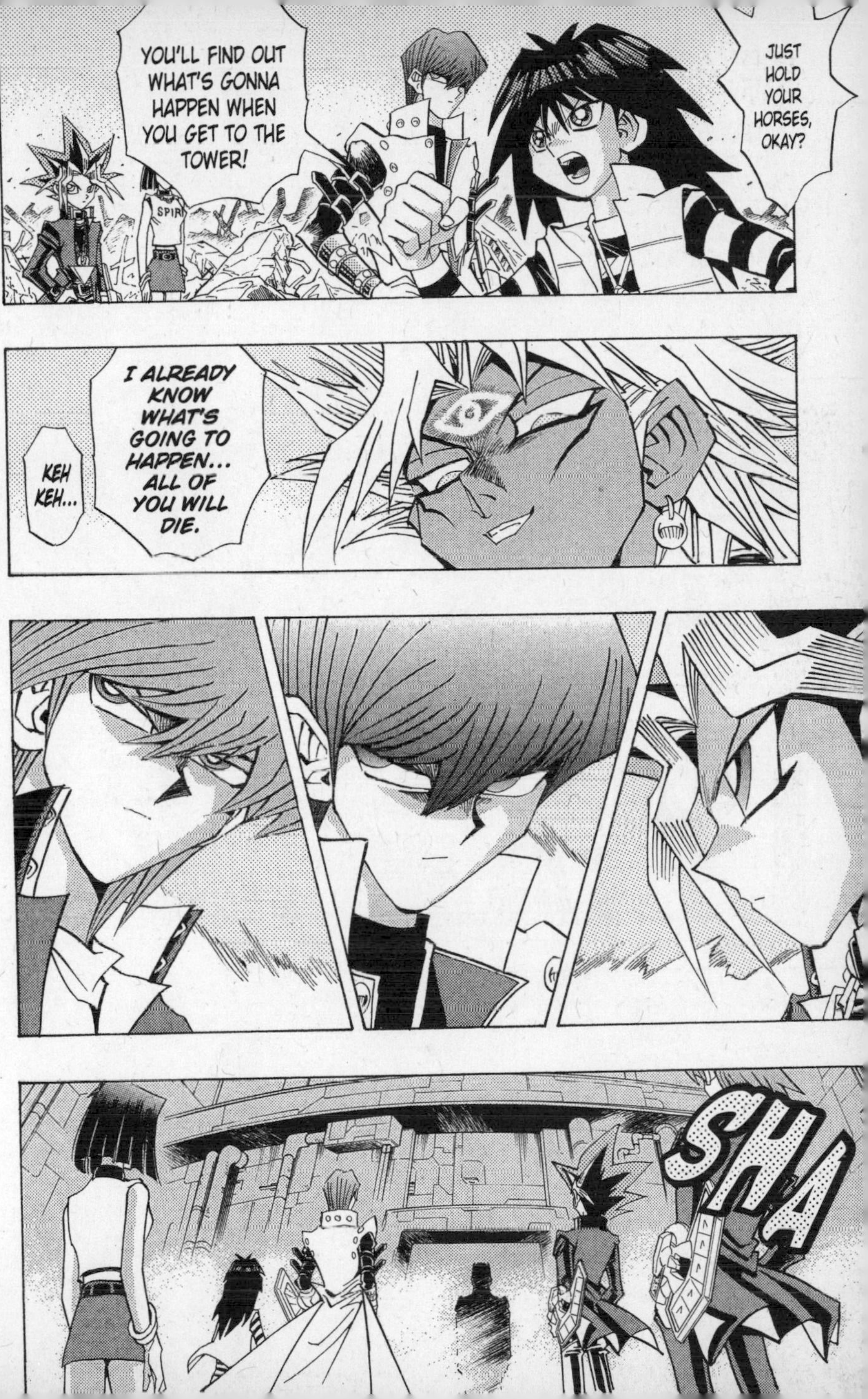
JUST HOLD YOUR HORSES, OKAY?
YOU'LL FIND OUT WHAT'S GONNA HAPPEN WHEN YOU GET TO THE TOWER!
I ALREADY KNOW WHAT'S GOING TO HAPPEN... ALL OF YOU WILL DIE.
KEH KEH...
SHA

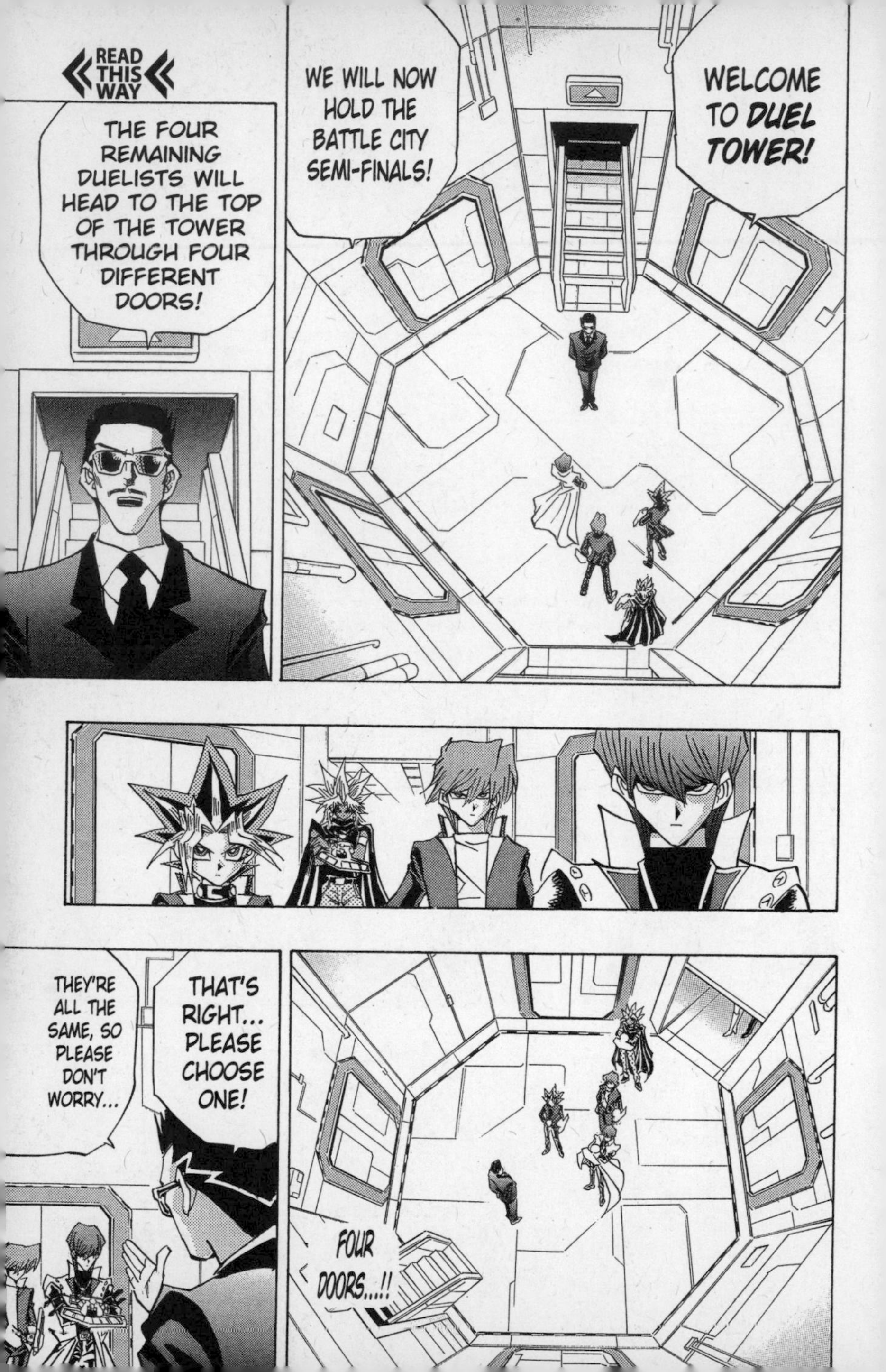
READ THIS WAY
WELCOME TO DUEL TOWER!
WE WILL NOW HOLD THE BATTLE CITY SEMI-FINALS!
THE FOUR REMAINING DUELISTS WILL HEAD TO THE TOP OF THE TOWER THROUGH FOUR DIFFERENT DOORS!
FOUR DOORS...!!
THAT'S RIGHT... PLEASE CHOOSE ONE!
THEY'RE ALL THE SAME, SO PLEASE DON'T WORRY...

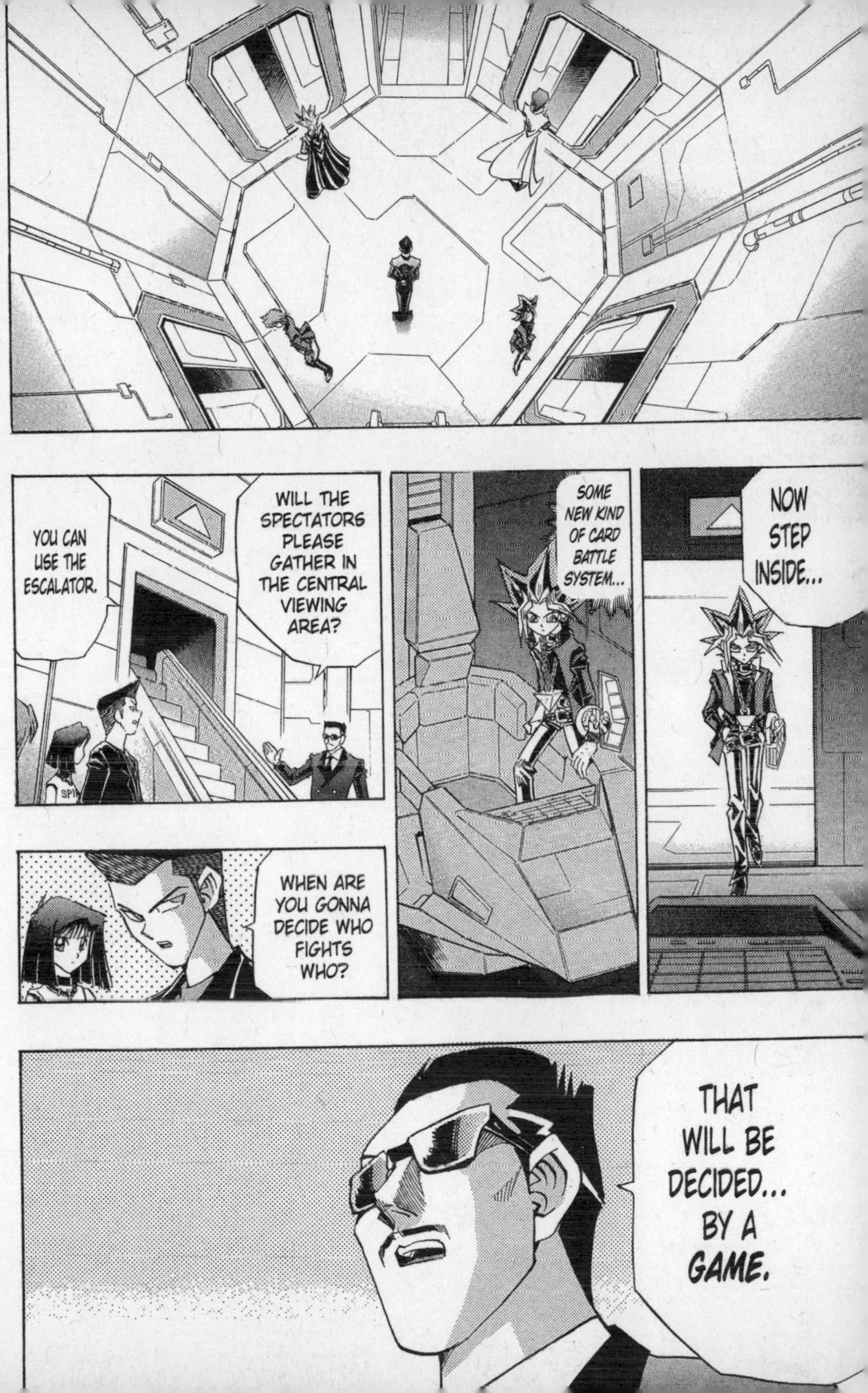
NOW STEP INSIDE...
SOME NEW KIND OF CARD BATTLE SYSTEM...
WILL THE SPECTATORS PLEASE GATHER IN THE CENTRAL VIEWING AREA?
YOU CAN USE THE ESCALATOR.
WHEN ARE YOU GONNA DECIDE WHO FIGHTS WHO?
THAT WILL BE DECIDED... BY A GAME.

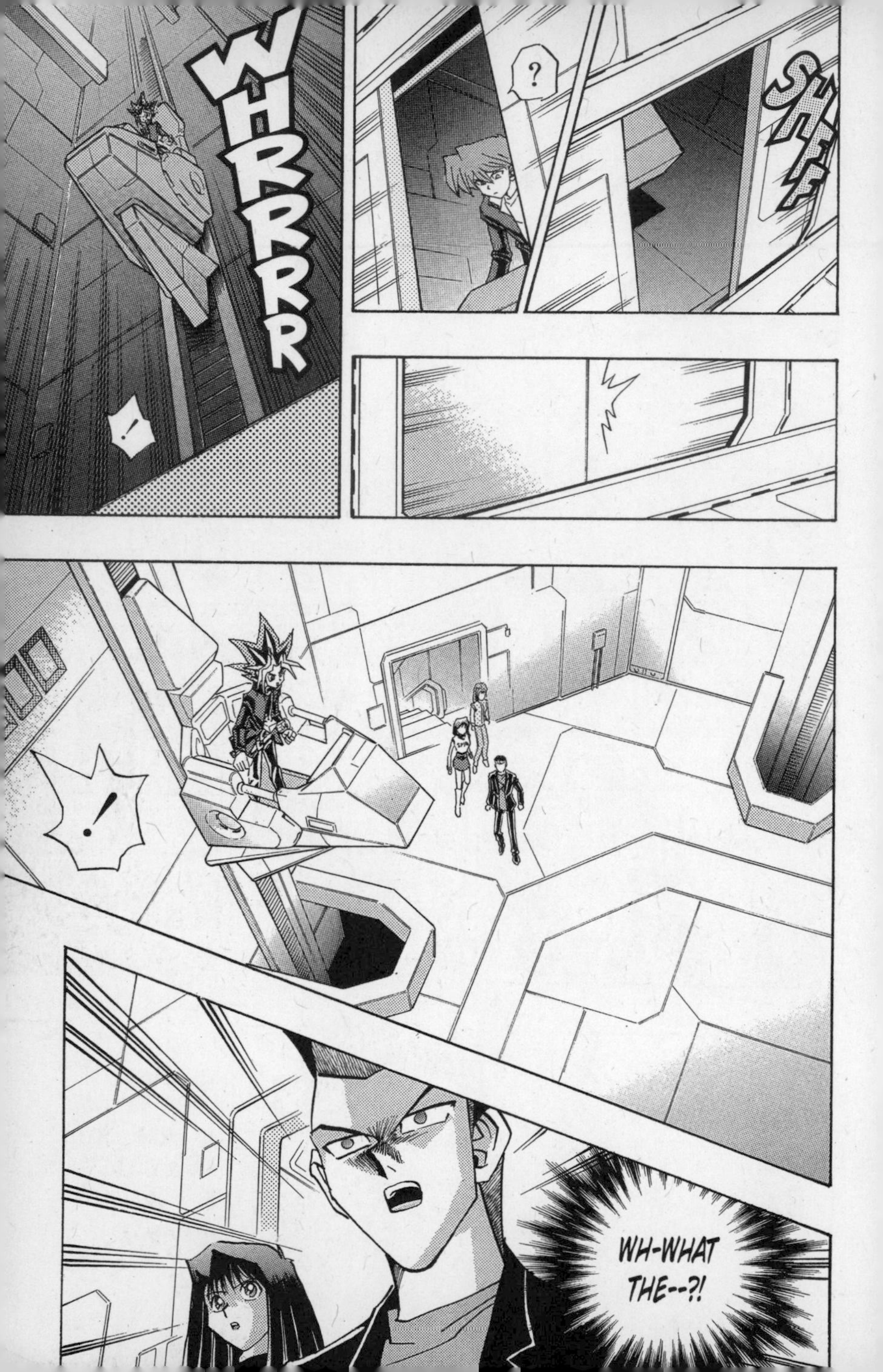
SHFF
?
WHRRRR
!
!
WH-WHAT THE--?!

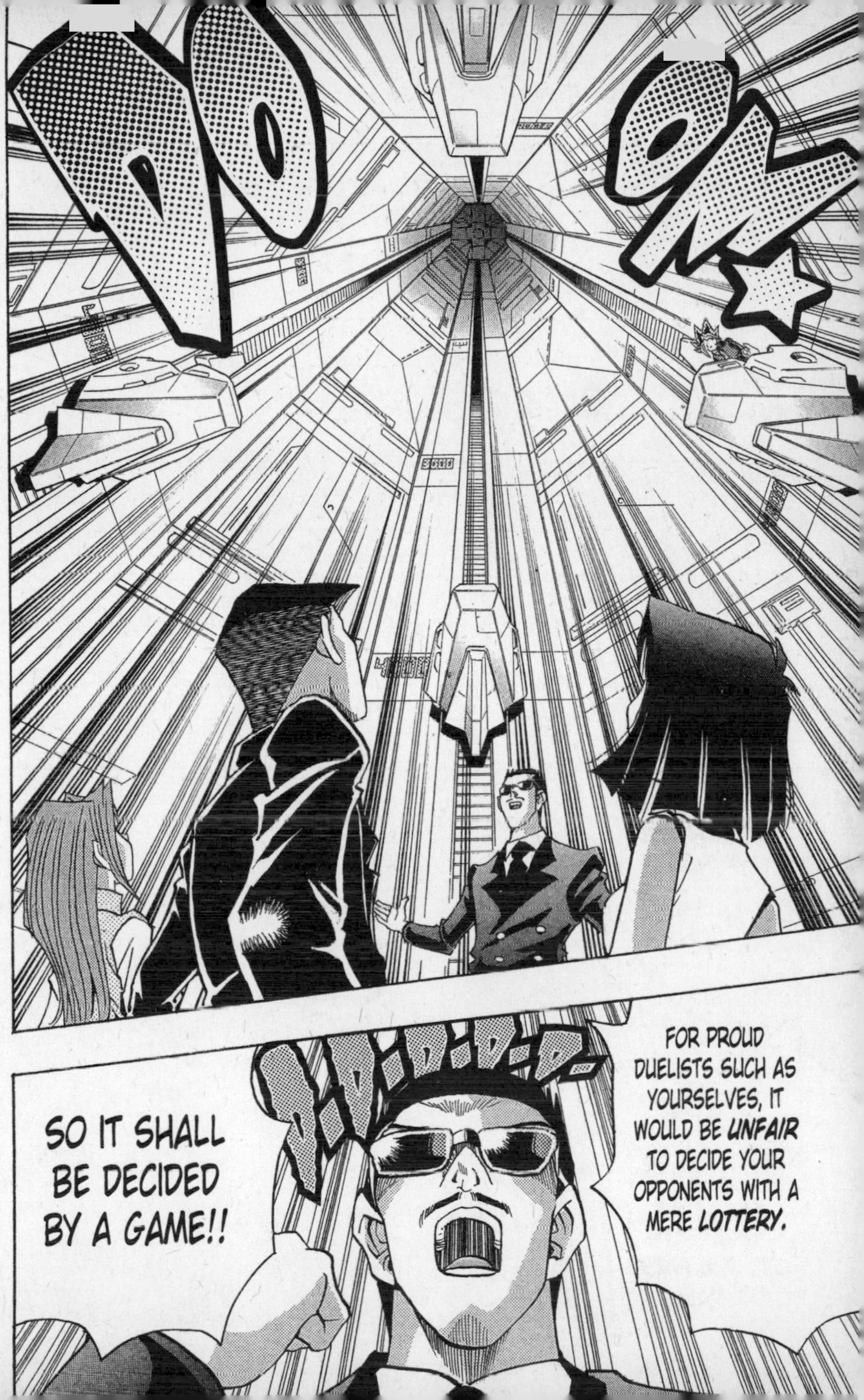
DOOM
FOR PROUD DUELISTS SUCH AS YOURSELVES, IT WOULD BE *UNFAIR* TO DECIDE YOUR OPPONENTS WITH A MERE *LOTTERY.*
SO IT SHALL BE DECIDED BY A GAME!!

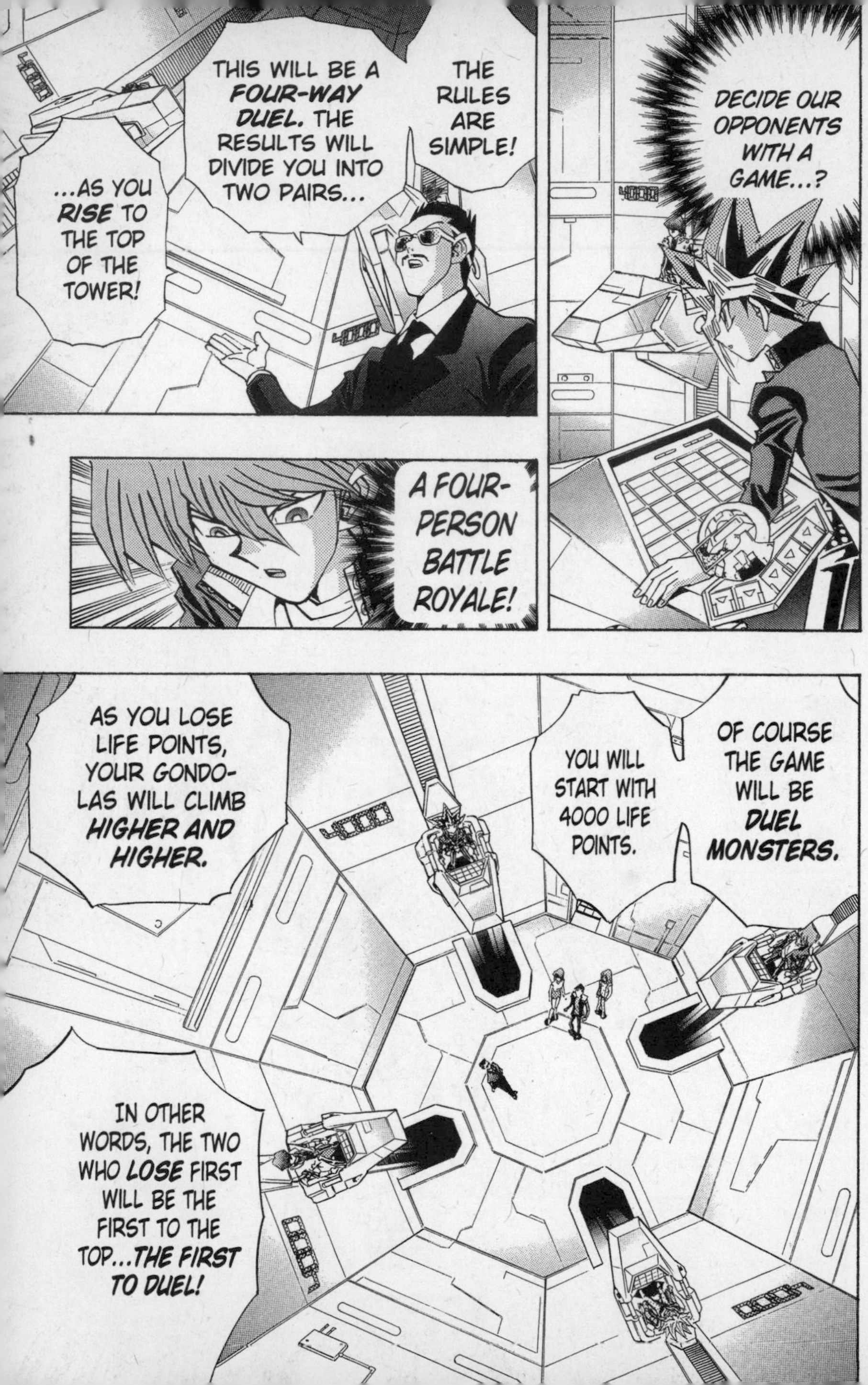
DECIDE OUR OPPONENTS WITH A GAME...?
THE RULES ARE SIMPLE!
THIS WILL BE A FOUR-WAY DUEL. THE RESULTS WILL DIVIDE YOU INTO TWO PAIRS...
...AS YOU RISE TO THE TOP OF THE TOWER!
A FOUR-PERSON BATTLE ROYALE!
OF COURSE THE GAME WILL BE DUEL MONSTERS.
YOU WILL START WITH 4000 LIFE POINTS.
AS YOU LOSE LIFE POINTS, YOUR GONDO-LAS WILL CLIMB HIGHER AND HIGHER.
IN OTHER WORDS, THE TWO WHO LOSE FIRST WILL BE THE FIRST TO THE TOP...THE FIRST TO DUEL!

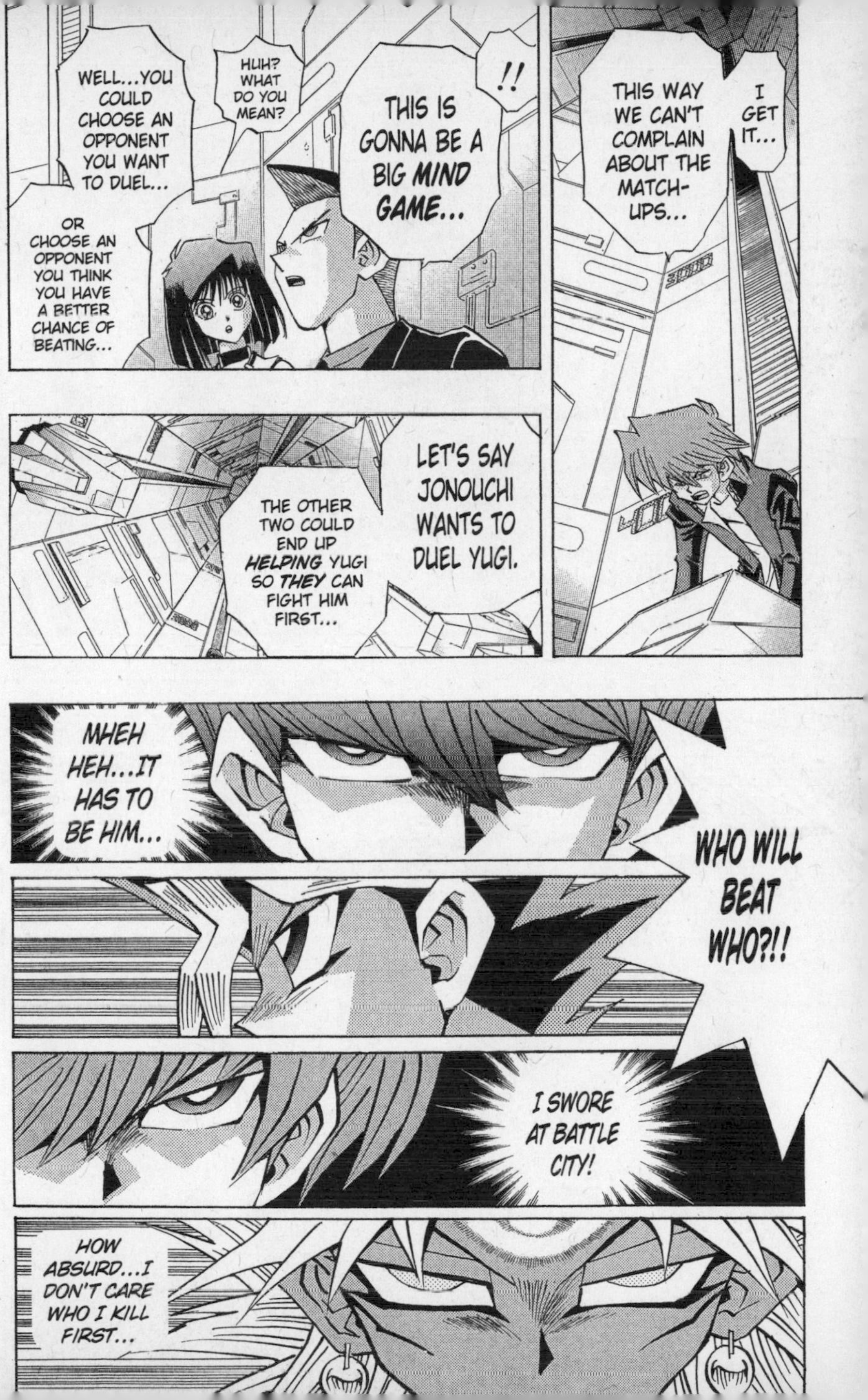
I GET IT...
THIS WAY WE CAN'T COMPLAIN ABOUT THE MATCH-UPS...
!!
THIS IS GONNA BE A BIG *MIND GAME*...
HUH? WHAT DO YOU MEAN?
WELL...YOU COULD CHOOSE AN OPPONENT YOU WANT TO DUEL...
OR CHOOSE AN OPPONENT YOU THINK YOU HAVE A BETTER CHANCE OF BEATING...
LET'S SAY JONOUCHI WANTS TO DUEL YUGI.
THE OTHER TWO COULD END UP *HELPING* YUGI SO *THEY* CAN FIGHT HIM FIRST...
MHEH HEH...IT HAS TO BE HIM...
WHO WILL BEAT WHO?!!
I SWORE AT BATTLE CITY!
HOW ABSURD...I DON'T CARE WHO I KILL FIRST...

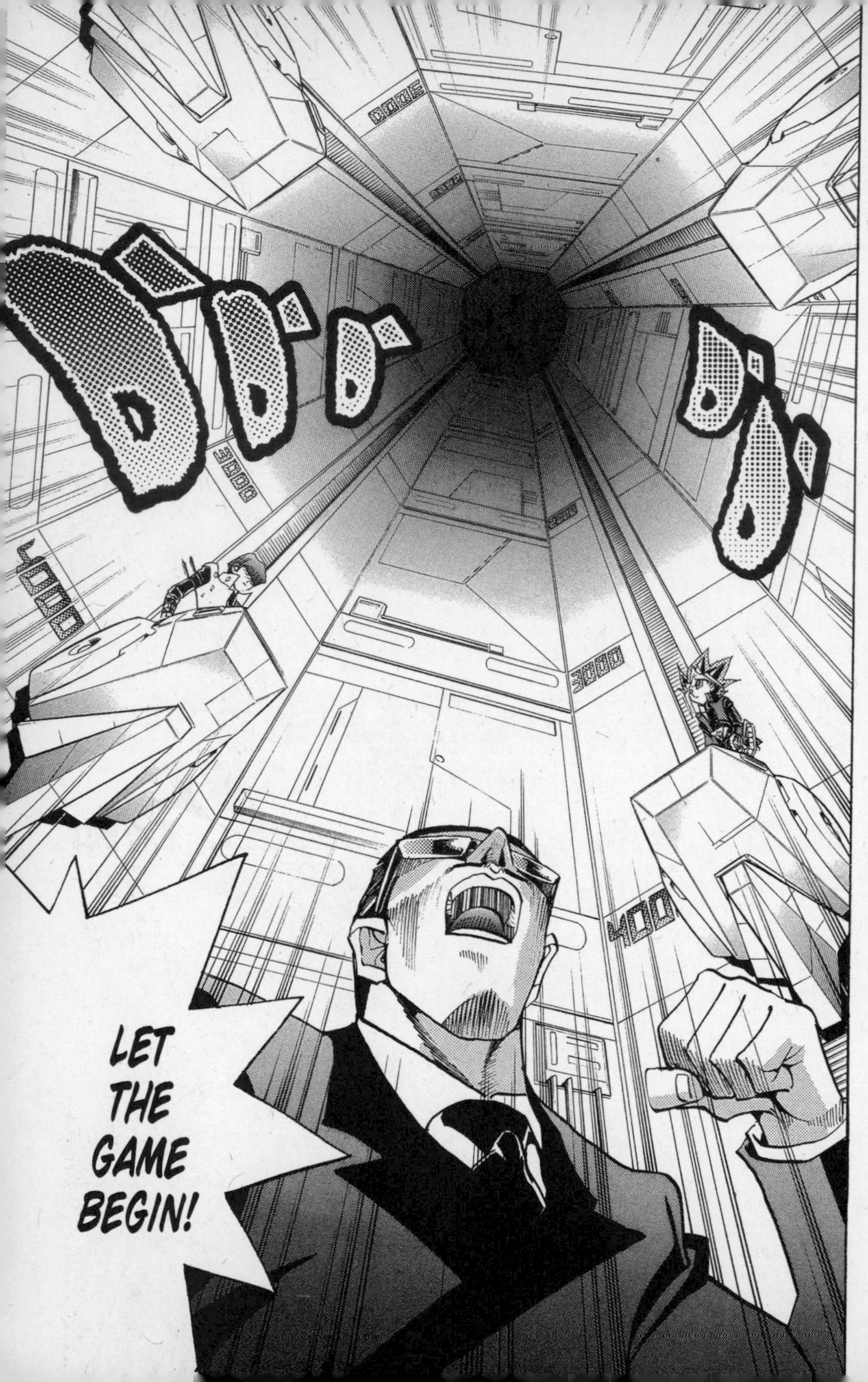
LET THE GAME BEGIN!

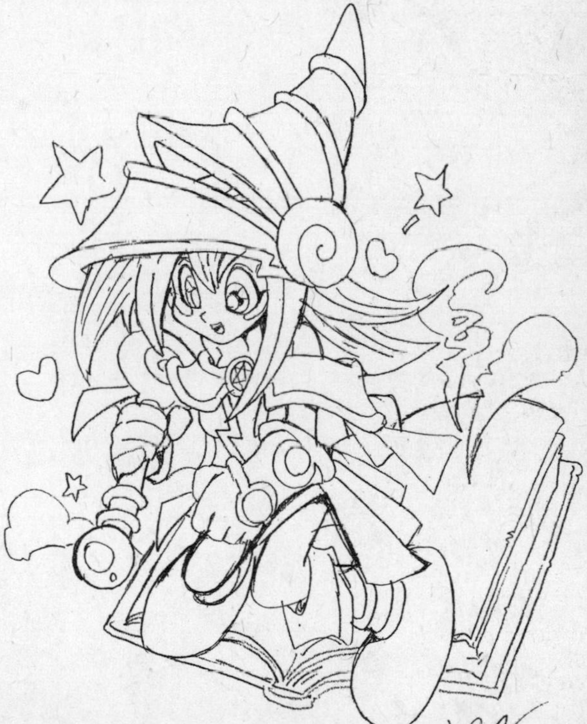
Kaz

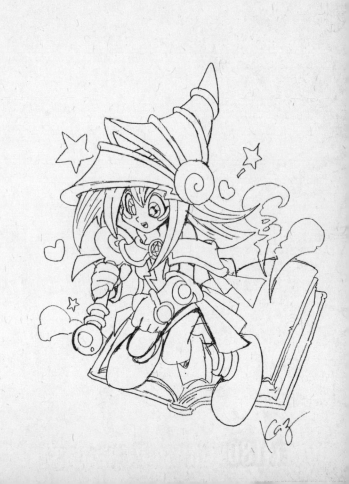

READ THIS WAY

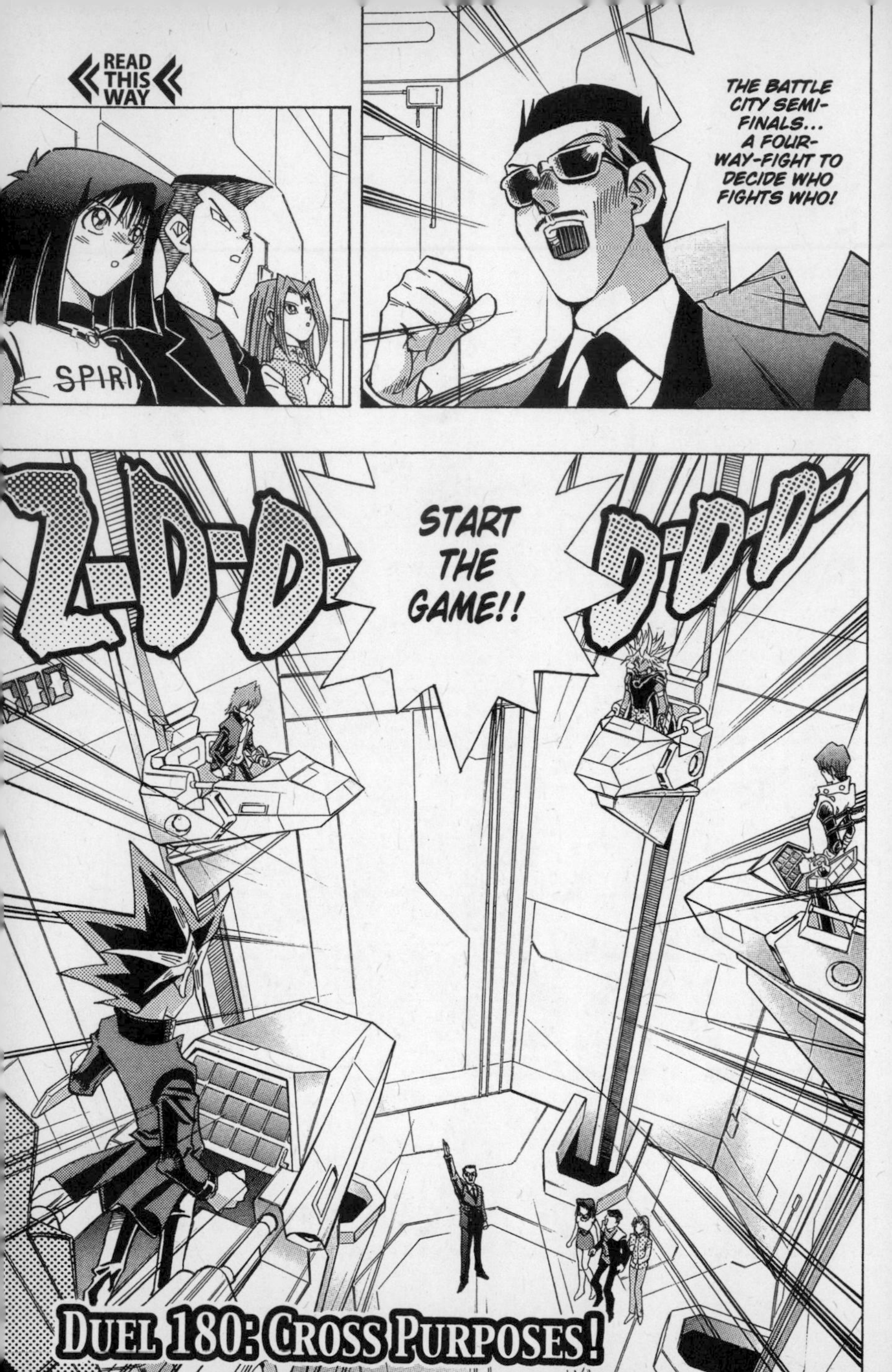
THE BATTLE CITY SEMI-FINALS... A FOUR-WAY-FIGHT TO DECIDE WHO FIGHTS WHO!
SPIRI
D-D-D
START THE GAME!!
Z-D-D

Duel 180: Cross Purposes!

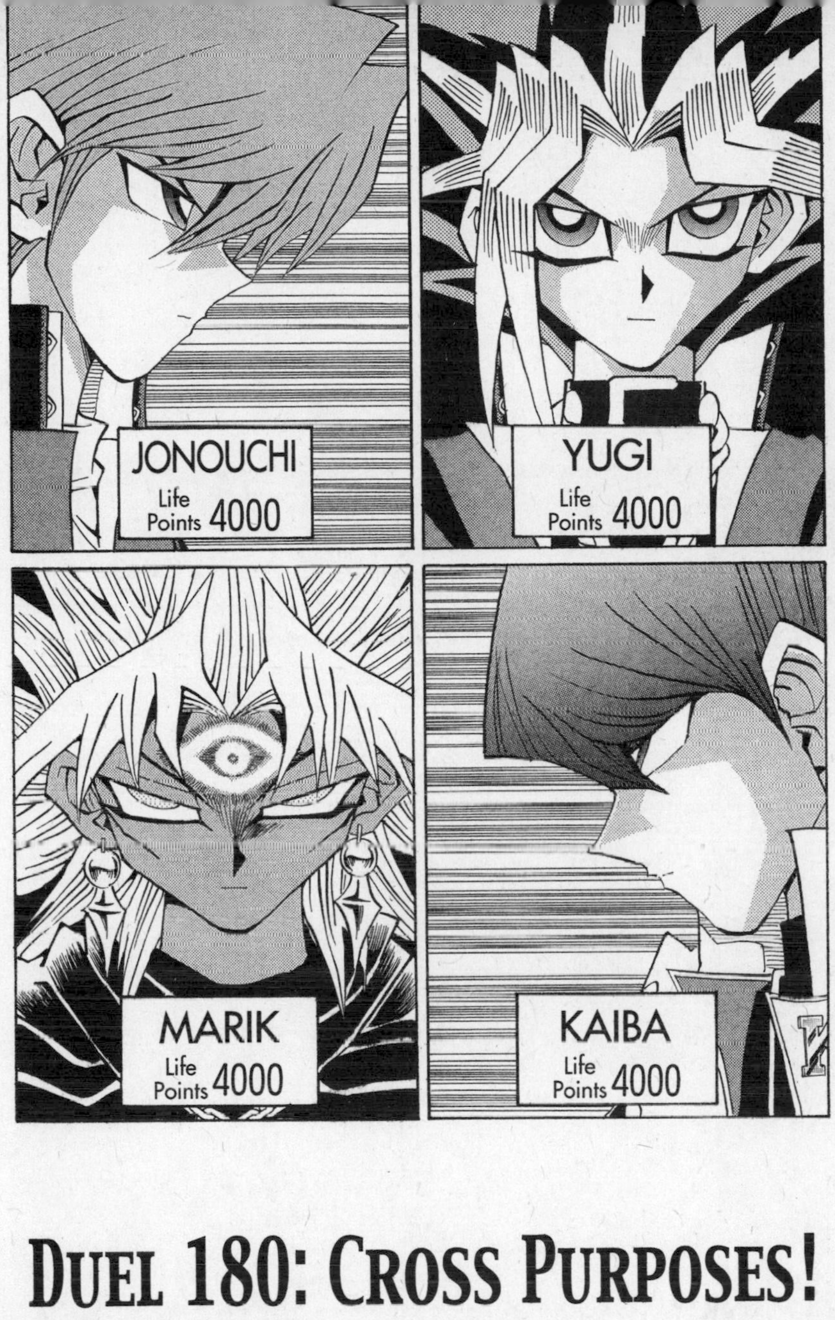
YUGI
Life Points 4000
JONOUCHI
Life Points 4000
KAIBA
Life Points 4000
MARIK
Life Points 4000

DUEL 180: CROSS PURPOSES!

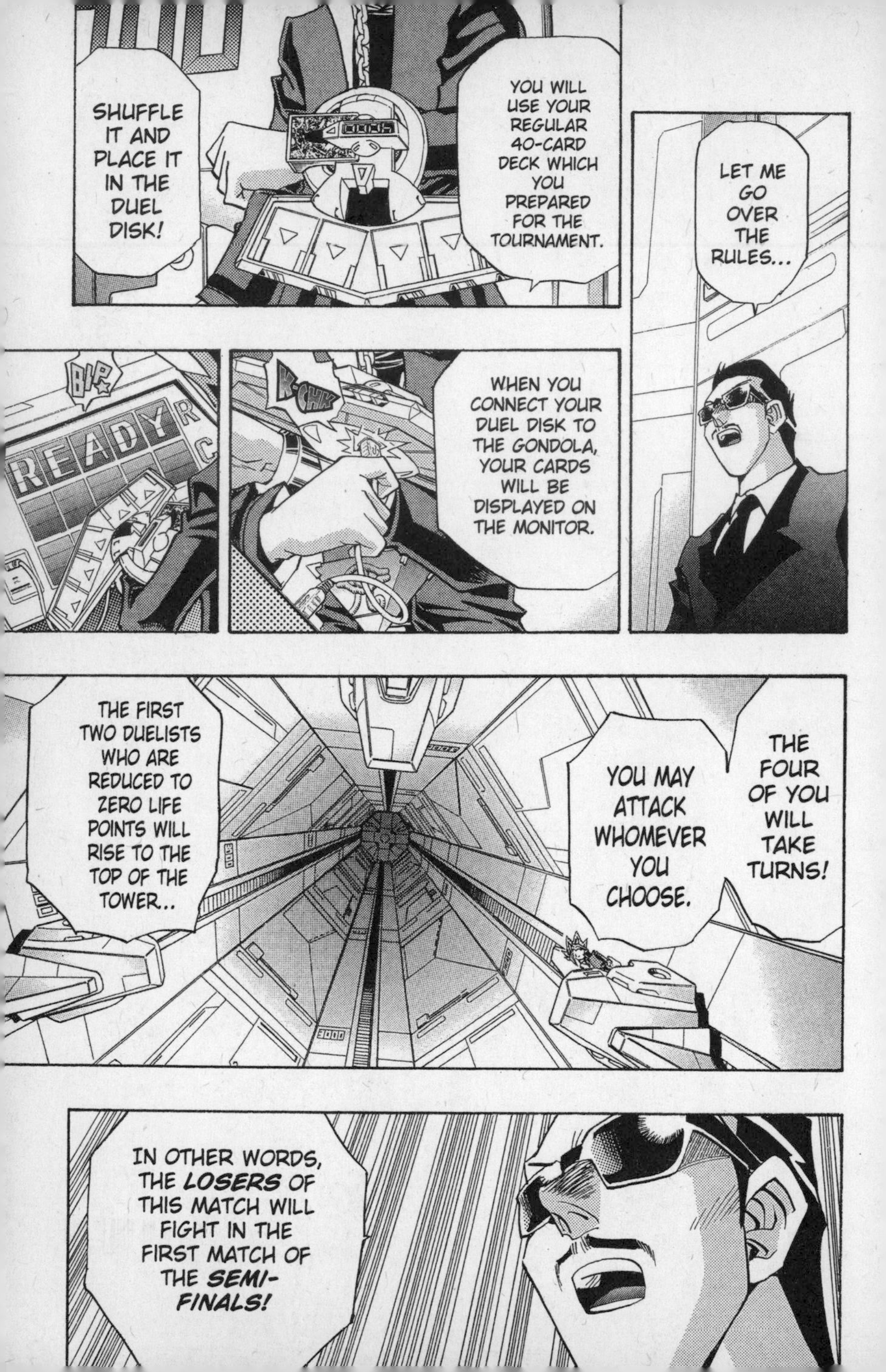
LET ME GO OVER THE RULES...
YOU WILL USE YOUR REGULAR 40-CARD DECK WHICH YOU PREPARED FOR THE TOURNAMENT.
SHUFFLE IT AND PLACE IT IN THE DUEL DISK!
K-CHK
WHEN YOU CONNECT YOUR DUEL DISK TO THE GONDOLA, YOUR CARDS WILL BE DISPLAYED ON THE MONITOR.
BIP
READY
THE FOUR OF YOU WILL TAKE TURNS!
YOU MAY ATTACK WHOMEVER YOU CHOOSE.
THE FIRST TWO DUELISTS WHO ARE REDUCED TO ZERO LIFE POINTS WILL RISE TO THE TOP OF THE TOWER...
IN OTHER WORDS, THE *LOSERS* OF THIS MATCH WILL FIGHT IN THE FIRST MATCH OF THE *SEMI-FINALS!*

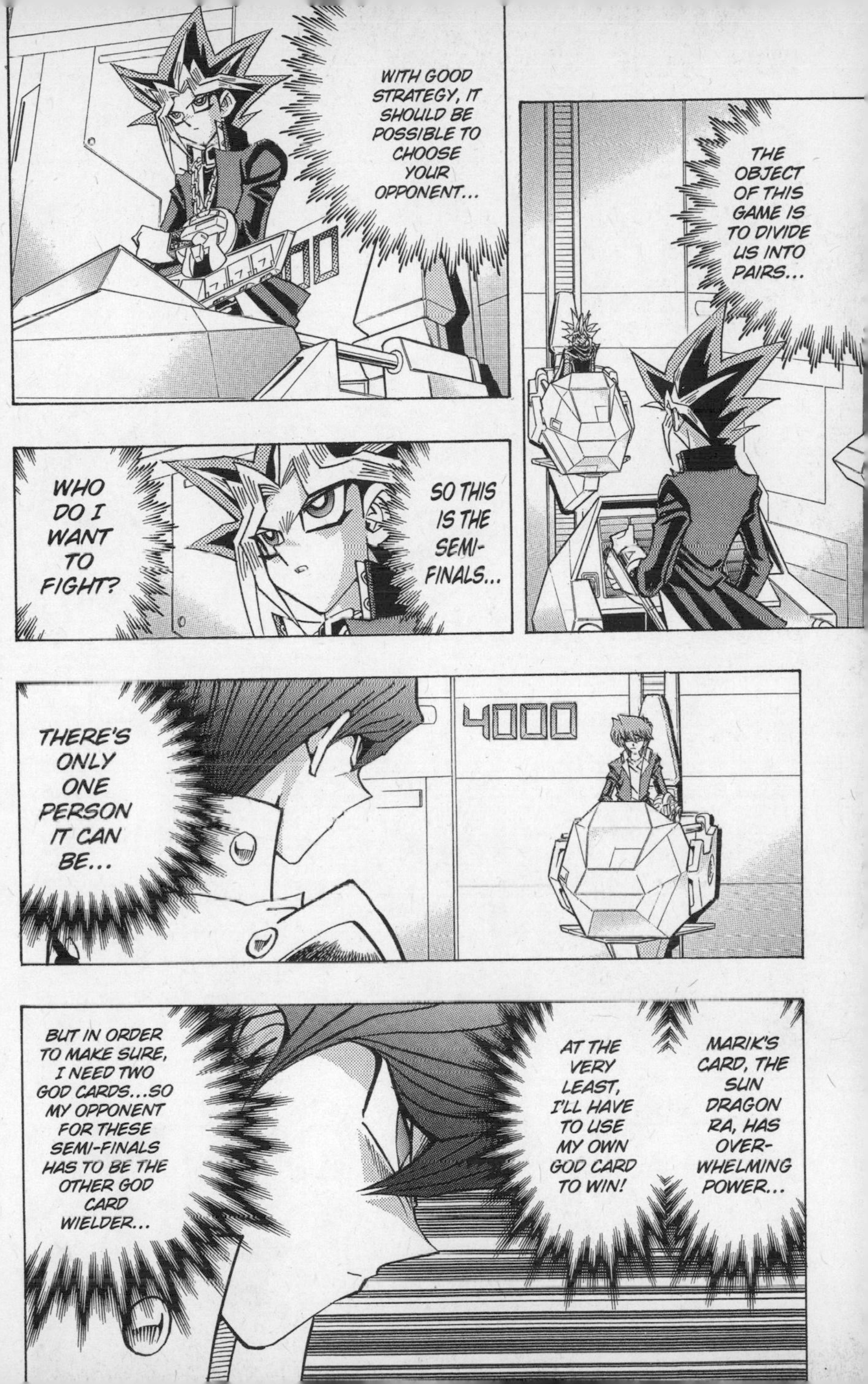
THE OBJECT OF THIS GAME IS TO DIVIDE US INTO PAIRS...
WITH GOOD STRATEGY, IT SHOULD BE POSSIBLE TO CHOOSE YOUR OPPONENT...
SO THIS IS THE SEMI-FINALS...
WHO DO I WANT TO FIGHT?
4000
THERE'S ONLY ONE PERSON IT CAN BE...
MARIK'S CARD, THE SUN DRAGON RA, HAS OVER-WHELMING POWER...
AT THE VERY LEAST, I'LL HAVE TO USE MY OWN GOD CARD TO WIN!
BUT IN ORDER TO MAKE SURE, I NEED TWO GOD CARDS...SO MY OPPONENT FOR THESE SEMI-FINALS HAS TO BE THE OTHER GOD CARD WIELDER...

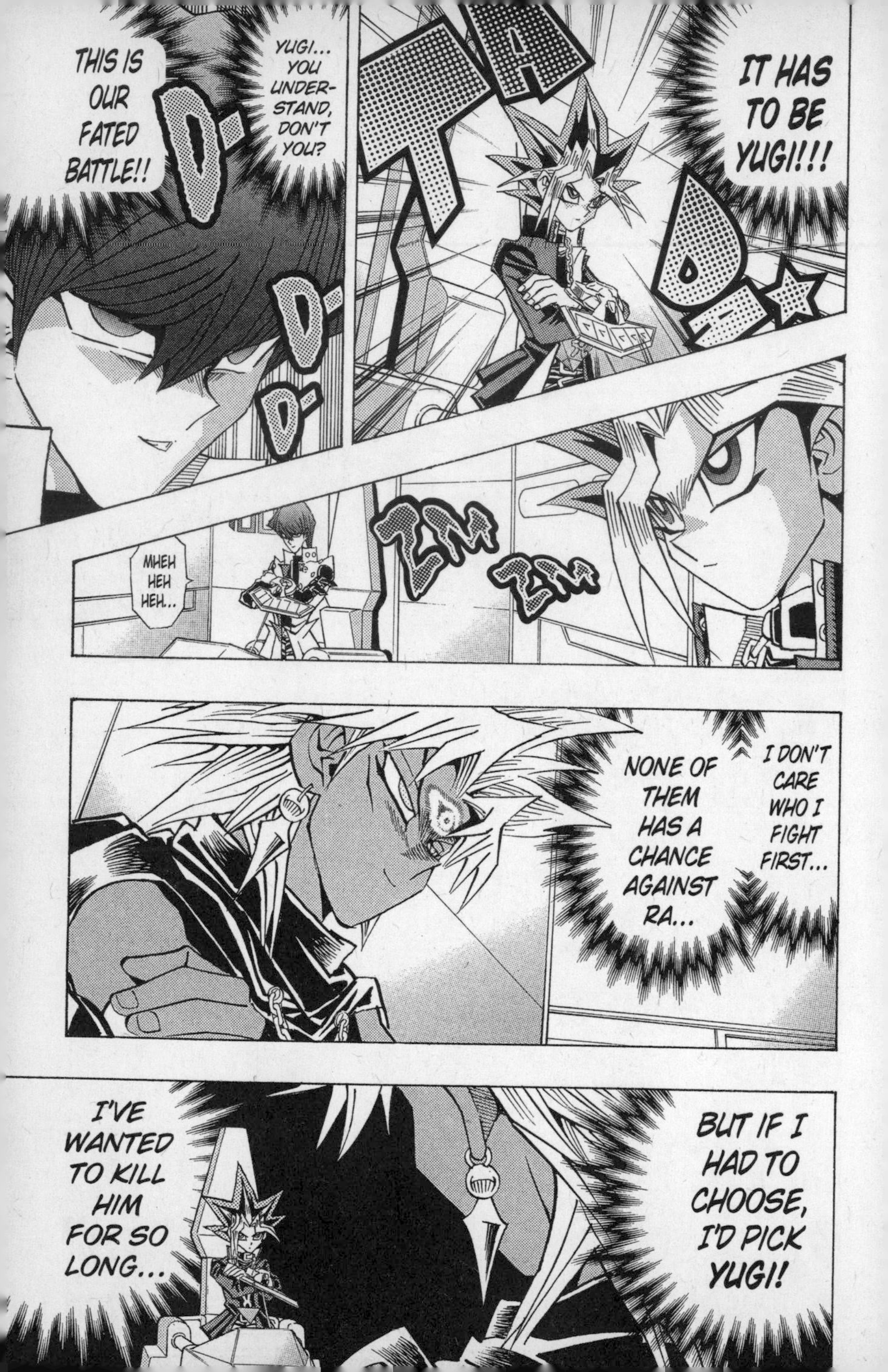
IT HAS TO BE YUGI!!!
YUGI... YOU UNDERSTAND, DON'T YOU?
THIS IS OUR FATED BATTLE!!
MHEH HEH HEH...
I DON'T CARE WHO I FIGHT FIRST...
NONE OF THEM HAS A CHANCE AGAINST RA...
BUT IF I HAD TO CHOOSE, I'D PICK YUGI!
I'VE WANTED TO KILL HIM FOR SO LONG...

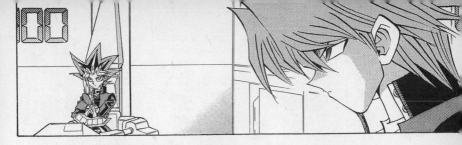

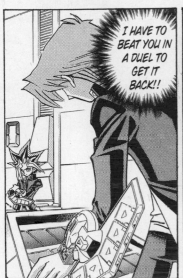

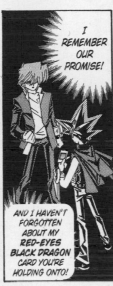

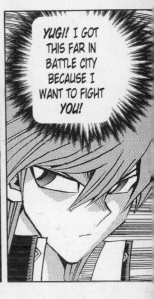

YUGI! I GOT THIS FAR IN BATTLE CITY BECAUSE I WANT TO FIGHT YOU!
I REMEMBER OUR PROMISE!
AND I HAVEN'T FORGOTTEN ABOUT MY RED-EYES BLACK DRAGON CARD YOU'RE HOLDING ONTO!
I HAVE TO BEAT YOU IN A DUEL TO GET IT BACK!!
BUT...
...
BEEP BEEP BEEP

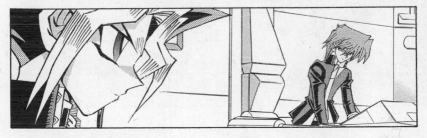

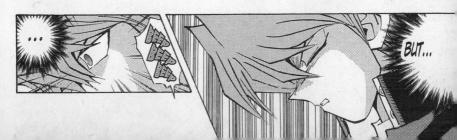

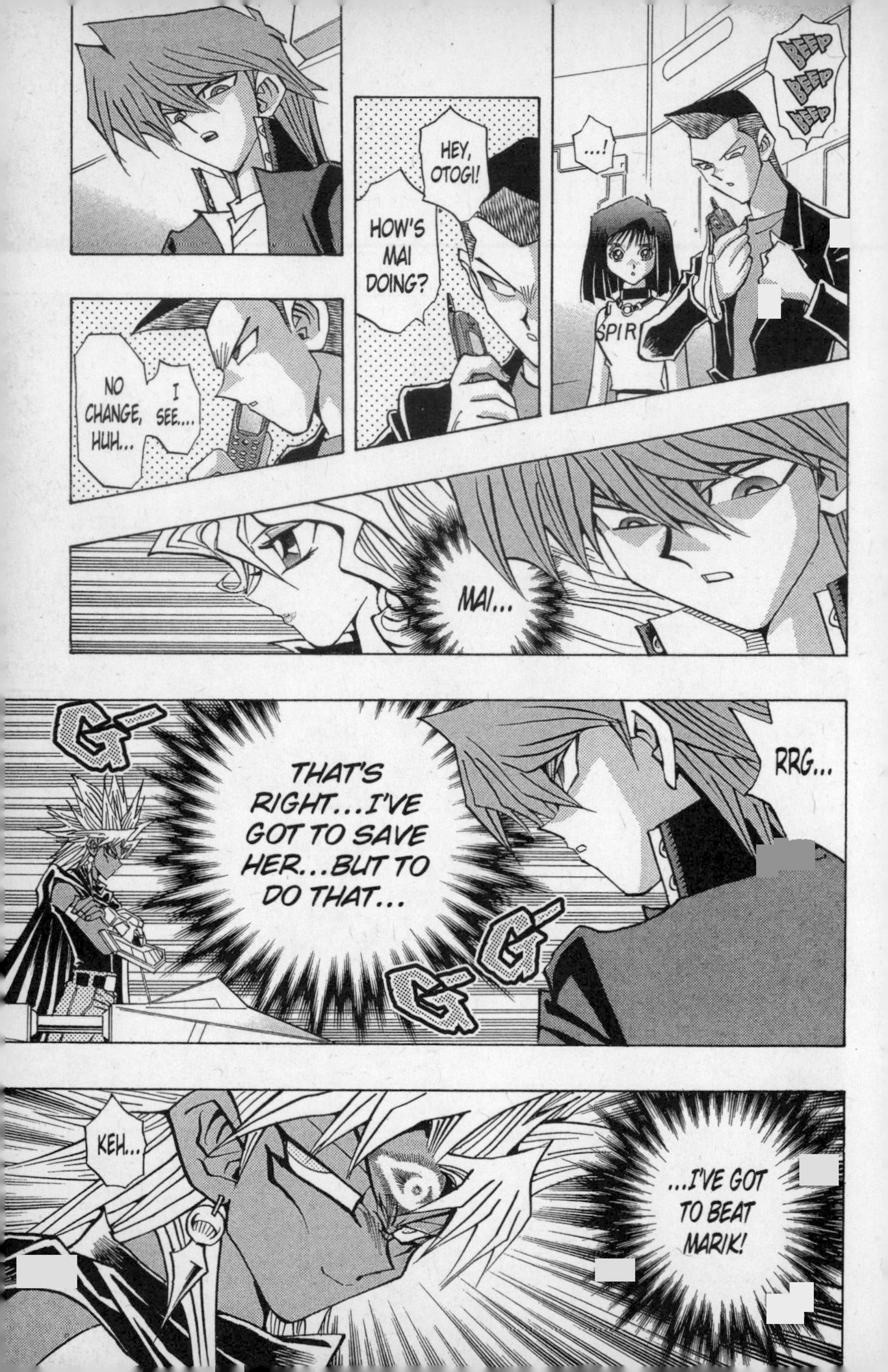
BEEP
BEEP
BEEP
...!
HEY, OTOGI!
HOW'S MAI DOING?
I SEE....
NO CHANGE, HUH...
MAI...
RRG...
THAT'S RIGHT...I'VE GOT TO SAVE HER...BUT TO DO THAT...
G
G
G
...I'VE GOT TO BEAT MARIK!
KEH...

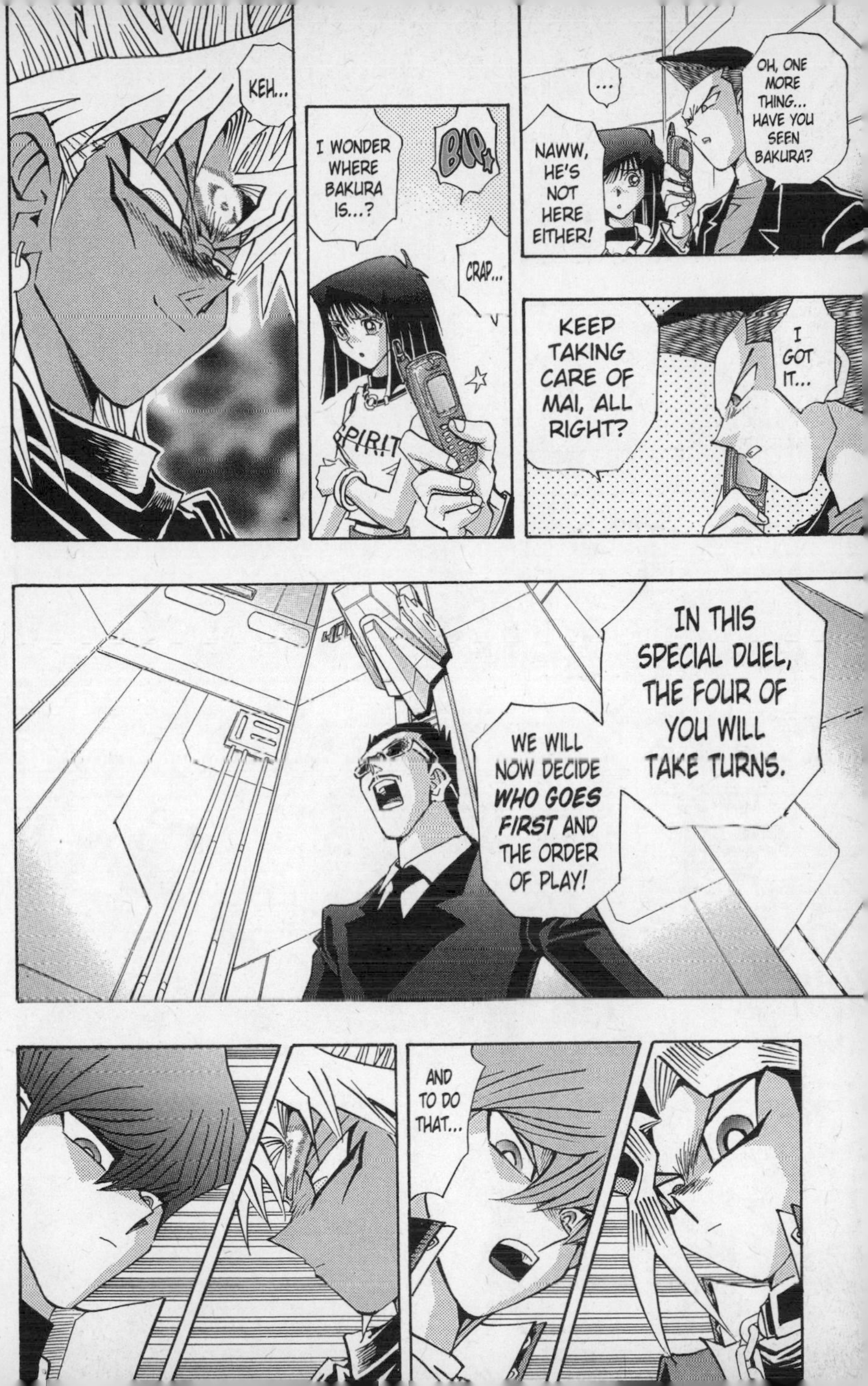
OH, ONE MORE THING... HAVE YOU SEEN BAKURA?
...
NAWW, HE'S NOT HERE EITHER!
I GOT IT...
KEEP TAKING CARE OF MAI, ALL RIGHT?
BLIP
CRAP...
I WONDER WHERE BAKURA IS...?
KEH...
IN THIS SPECIAL DUEL, THE FOUR OF YOU WILL TAKE TURNS.
WE WILL NOW DECIDE *WHO GOES FIRST* AND THE ORDER OF PLAY!
AND TO DO THAT...

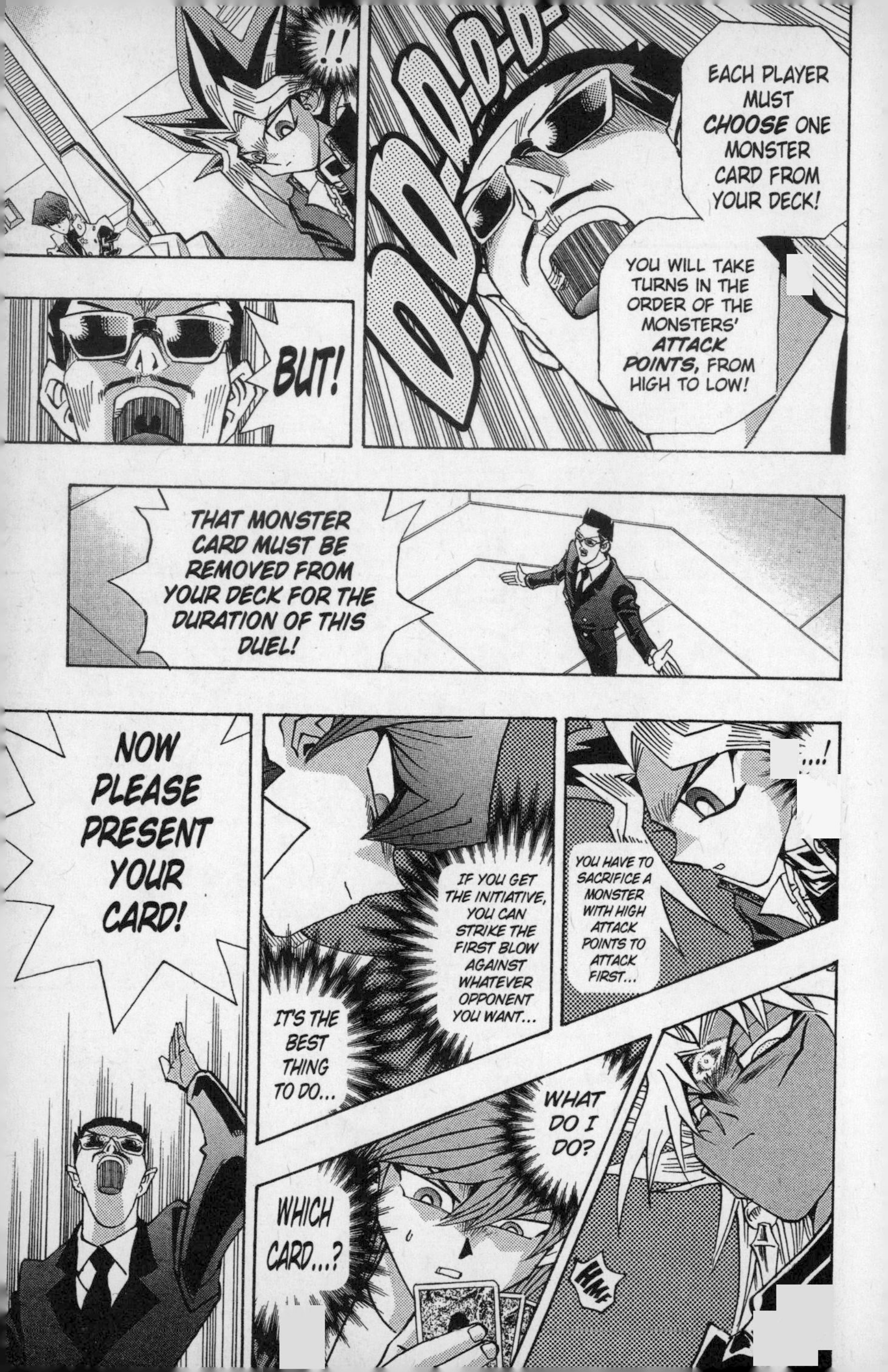
EACH PLAYER MUST CHOOSE ONE MONSTER CARD FROM YOUR DECK!
YOU WILL TAKE TURNS IN THE ORDER OF THE MONSTERS' ATTACK POINTS, FROM HIGH TO LOW!
D-D-D-D-D-D-
!!
BUT!
THAT MONSTER CARD MUST BE REMOVED FROM YOUR DECK FOR THE DURATION OF THIS DUEL!
...!
YOU HAVE TO SACRIFICE A MONSTER WITH HIGH ATTACK POINTS TO ATTACK FIRST...
IF YOU GET THE INITIATIVE, YOU CAN STRIKE THE FIRST BLOW AGAINST WHATEVER OPPONENT YOU WANT...
IT'S THE BEST THING TO DO...
WHAT DO I DO?
HMF
WHICH CARD...?
NOW PLEASE PRESENT YOUR CARD!

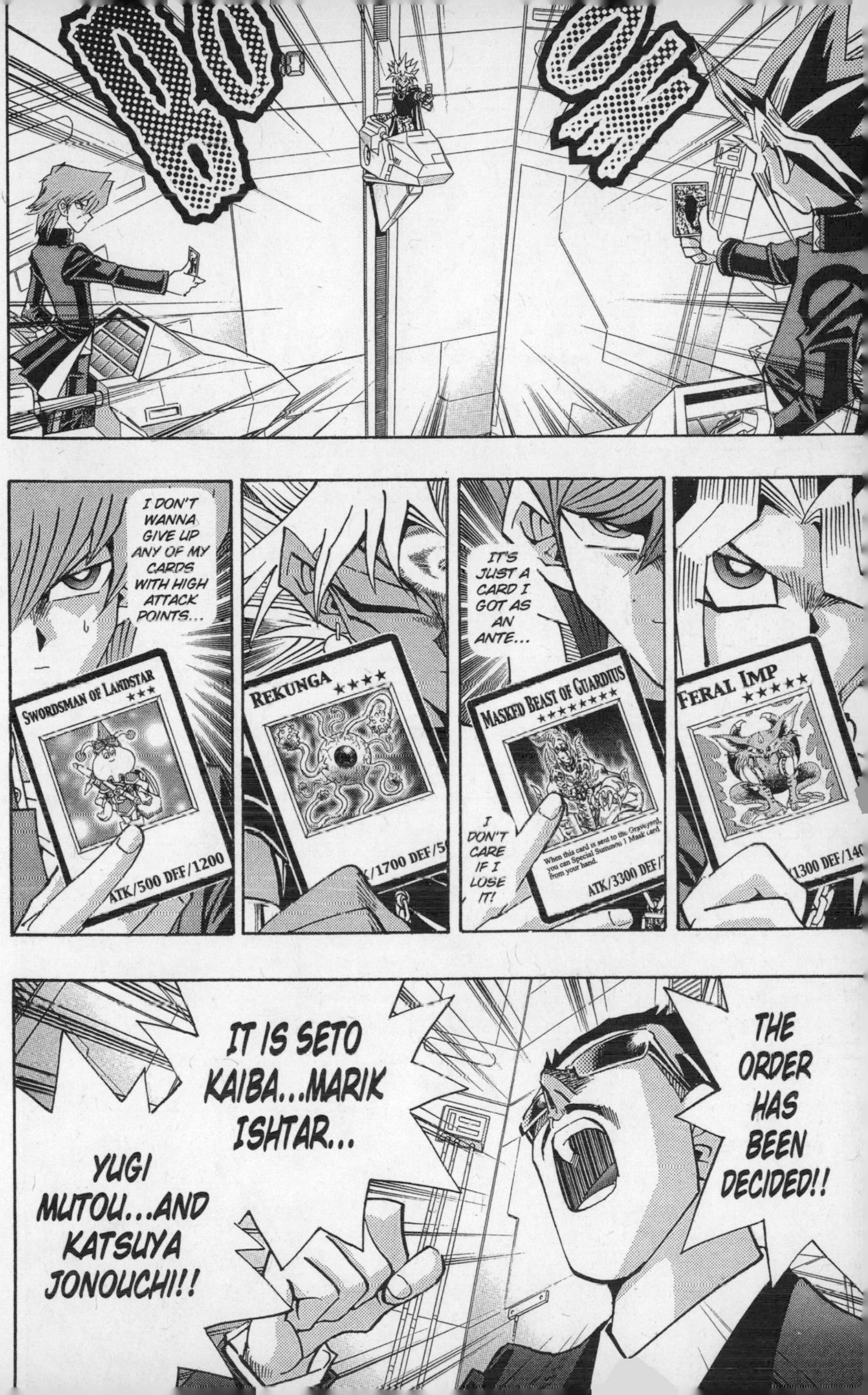
FERAL IMP
/1300 DEF/140
IT'S JUST A CARD I GOT AS AN ANTE...
MASKED BEAST OF GUARDIUS
When this card is sent to the Graveyard, you can Special Summon 1 Mask card from your hand.
ATK/3300 DEF/
I DON'T CARE IF I LOSE IT!
REKUNGA
/1700 DEF/5
I DON'T WANNA GIVE UP ANY OF MY CARDS WITH HIGH ATTACK POINTS...
SWORDSMAN OF LANDSTAR
ATK/500 DEF/1200
THE ORDER HAS BEEN DECIDED!!
IT IS SETO KAIBA...MARIK ISHTAR...
YUGI MUTOU...AND KATSUYA JONOUCHI!!

READ THIS WAY

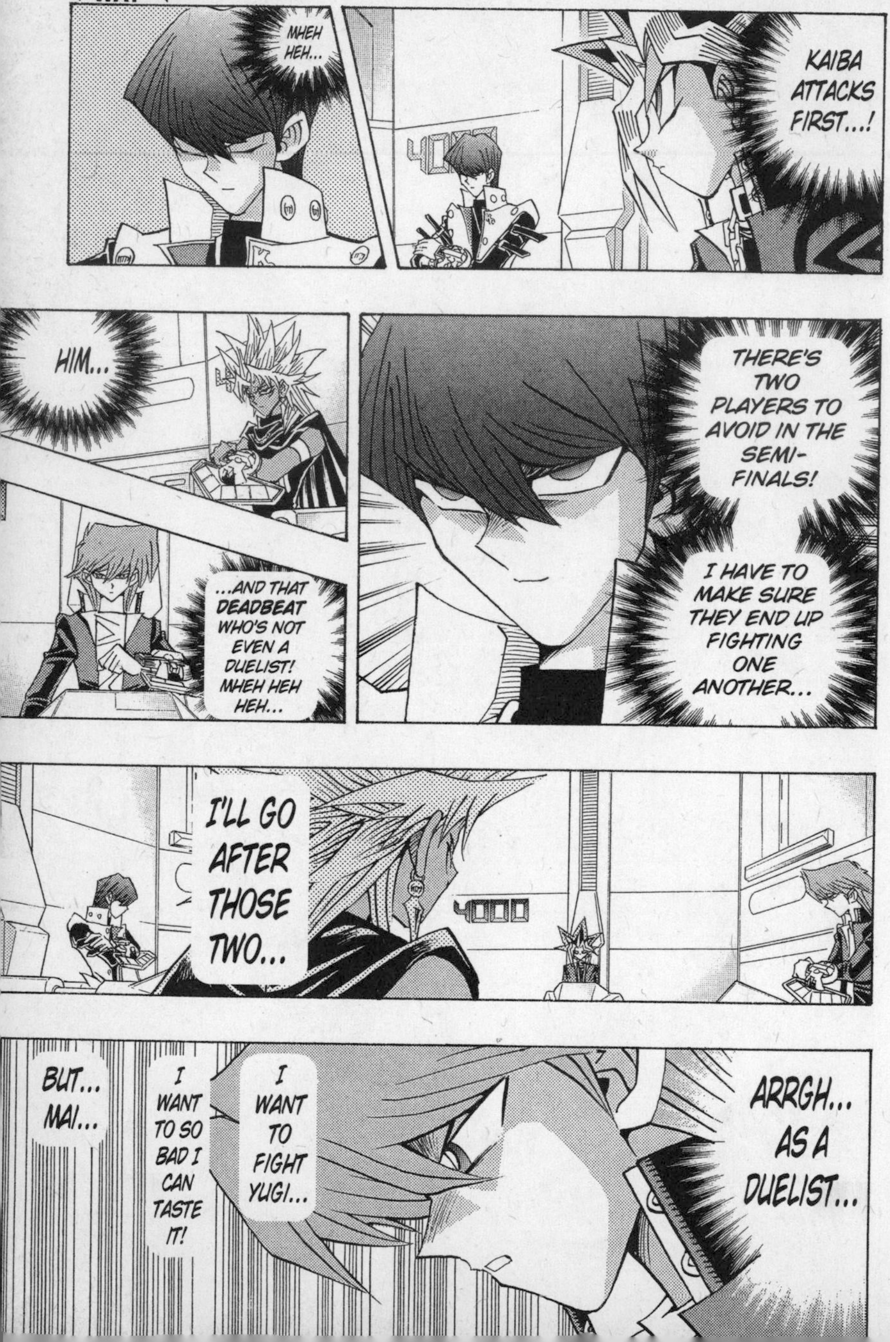
KAIBA ATTACKS FIRST...!
MHEH HEH...
THERE'S TWO PLAYERS TO AVOID IN THE SEMI-FINALS!
I HAVE TO MAKE SURE THEY END UP FIGHTING ONE ANOTHER...
HIM...
...AND THAT DEADBEAT WHO'S NOT EVEN A DUELIST! MHEH HEH HEH...
I'LL GO AFTER THOSE TWO...
ARRGH... AS A DUELIST...
I WANT TO FIGHT YUGI...
I WANT TO SO BAD I CAN TASTE IT!
BUT... MAI...

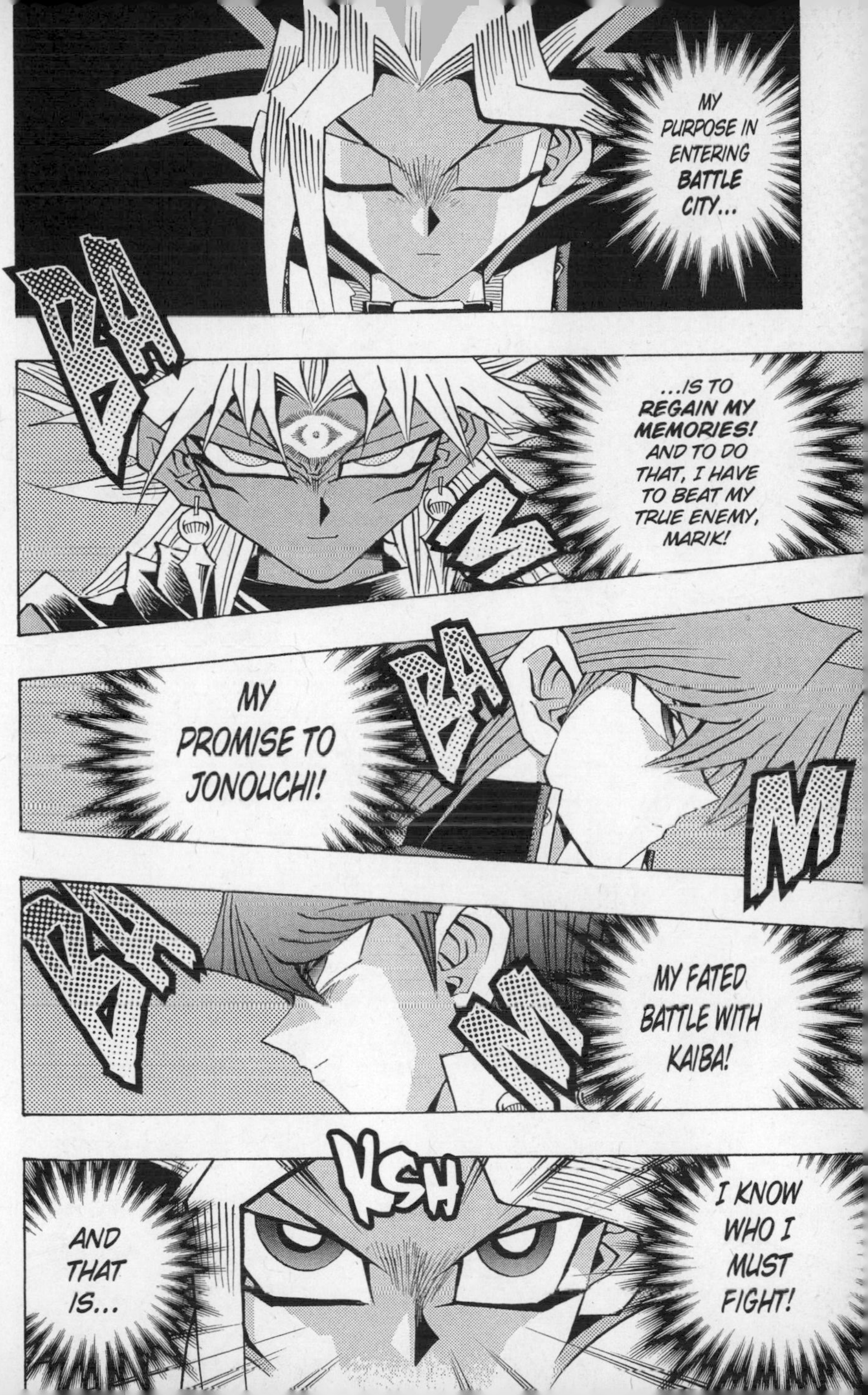
MY PURPOSE IN ENTERING BATTLE CITY...
BA
BAM
...IS TO REGAIN MY MEMORIES! AND TO DO THAT, I HAVE TO BEAT MY TRUE ENEMY, MARIK!
MY PROMISE TO JONOUCHI!
BA
M
BA
BAM
MY FATED BATTLE WITH KAIBA!
AND THAT IS...
KSH
I KNOW WHO I MUST FIGHT!

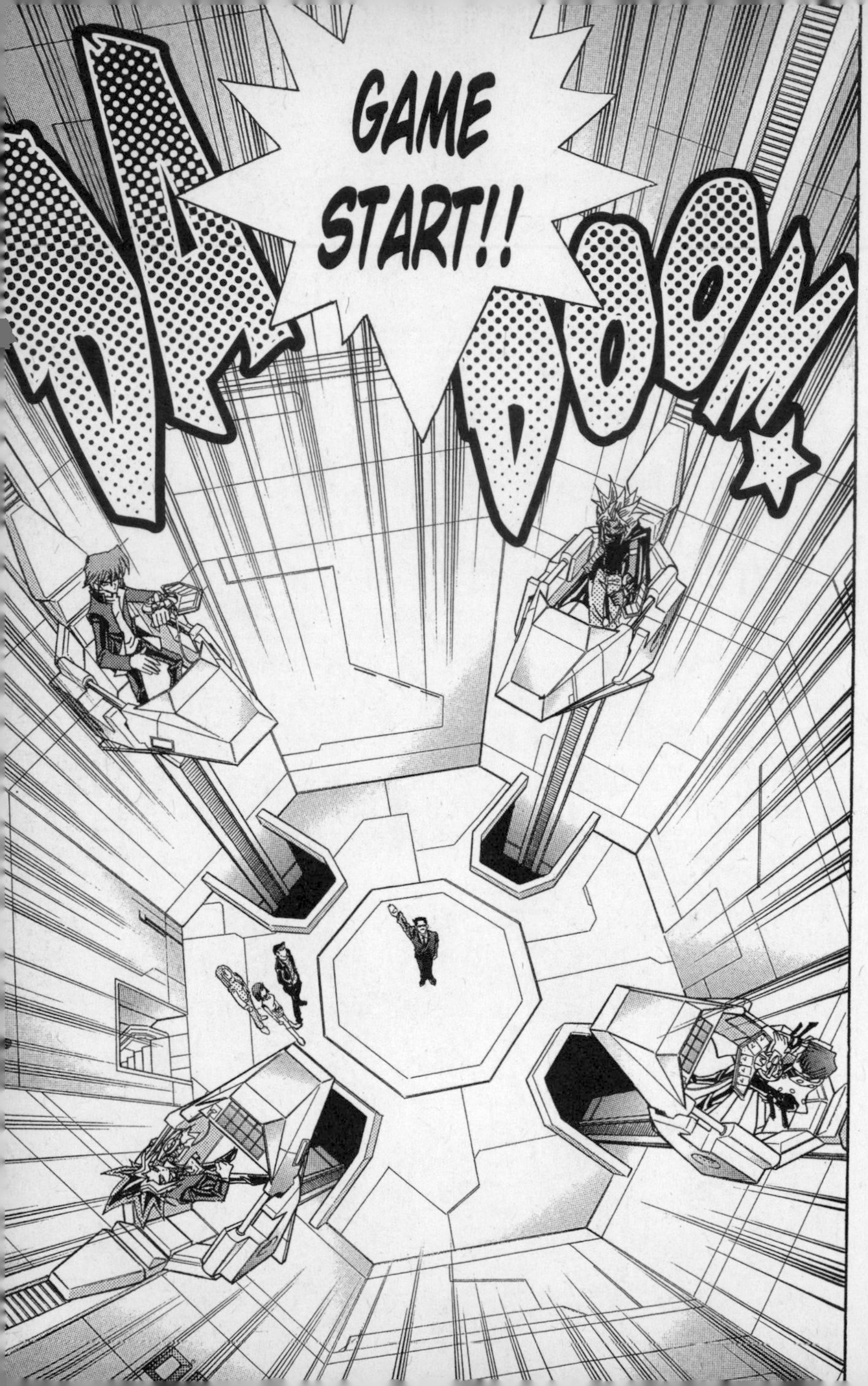
GAME START!!

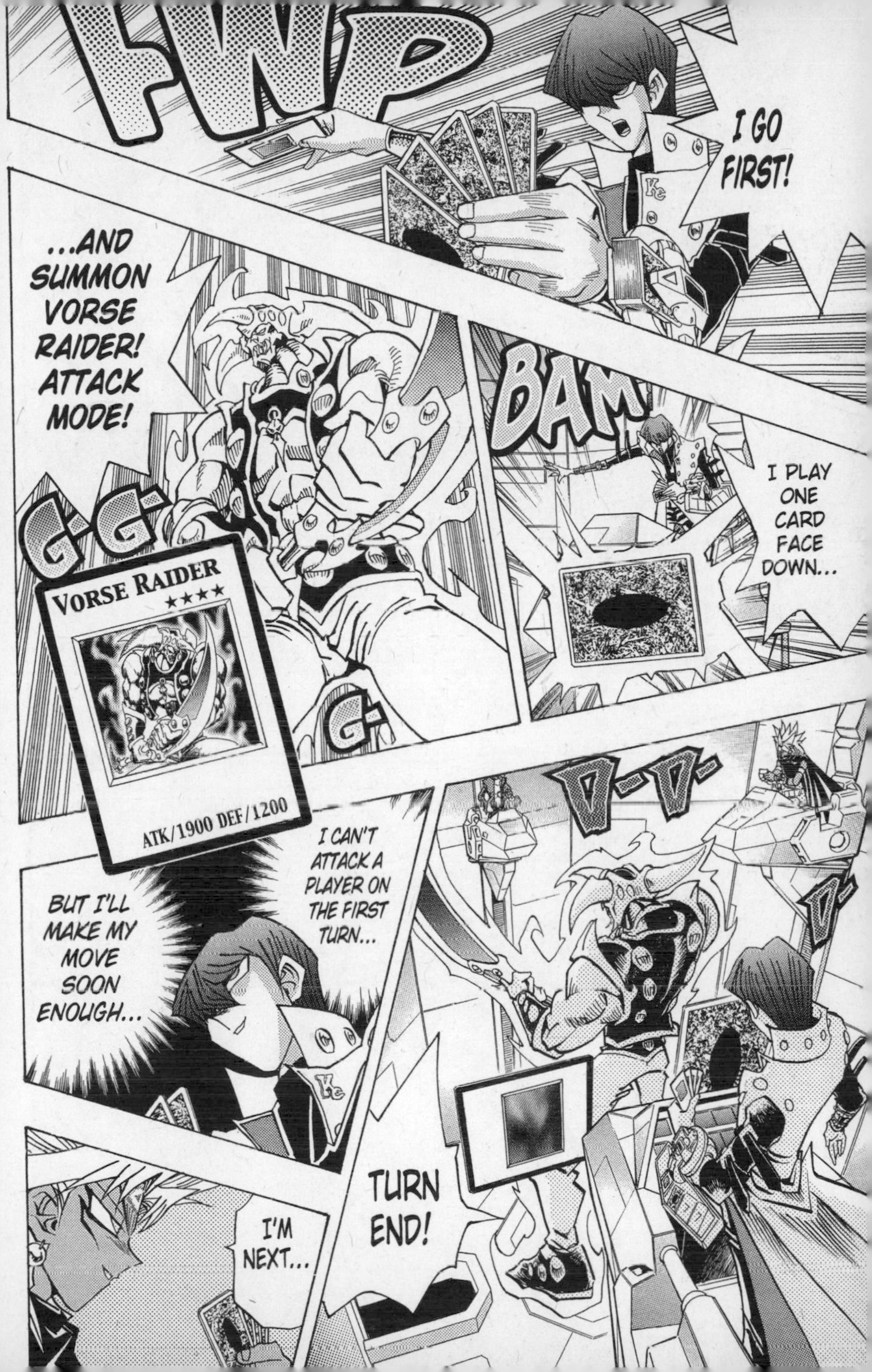
FWP
I GO FIRST!
BAM
I PLAY ONE CARD FACE DOWN...
...AND SUMMON VORSE RAIDER! ATTACK MODE!
G-G-
VORSE RAIDER ★★★★
ATK/1900 DEF/1200
G-
D-D-
D-
TURN END!
I CAN'T ATTACK A PLAYER ON THE FIRST TURN...
BUT I'LL MAKE MY MOVE SOON ENOUGH...
I'M NEXT...

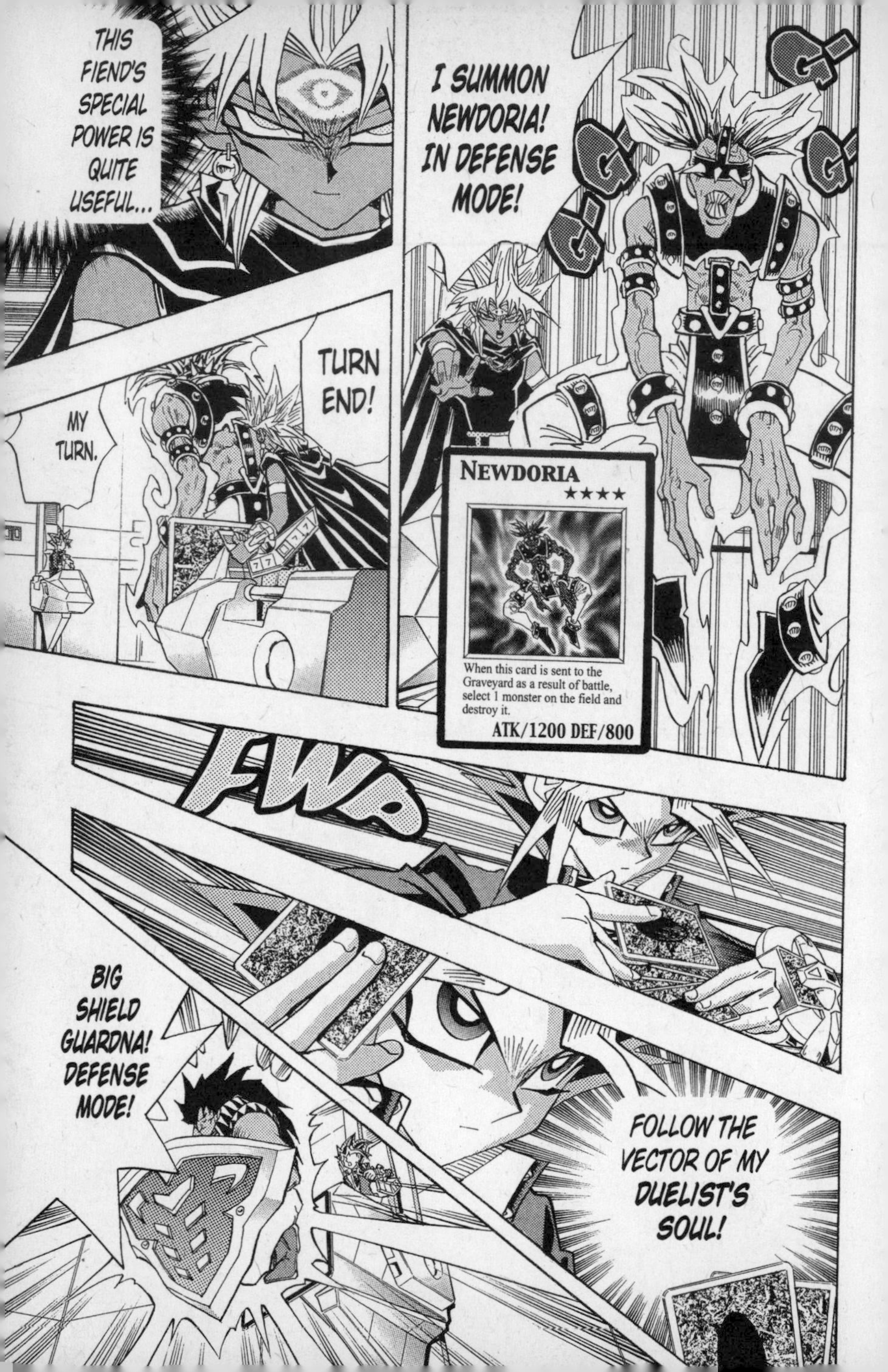
I SUMMON NEWDORIA! IN DEFENSE MODE!
G- G- G- G-
NEWDORIA
★★★★
When this card is sent to the Graveyard as a result of battle, select 1 monster on the field and destroy it.
ATK/1200 DEF/800
THIS FIEND'S SPECIAL POWER IS QUITE USEFUL...
TURN END!
MY TURN.
FWP
FOLLOW THE VECTOR OF MY DUELIST'S SOUL!
BIG SHIELD GUARDNA! DEFENSE MODE!

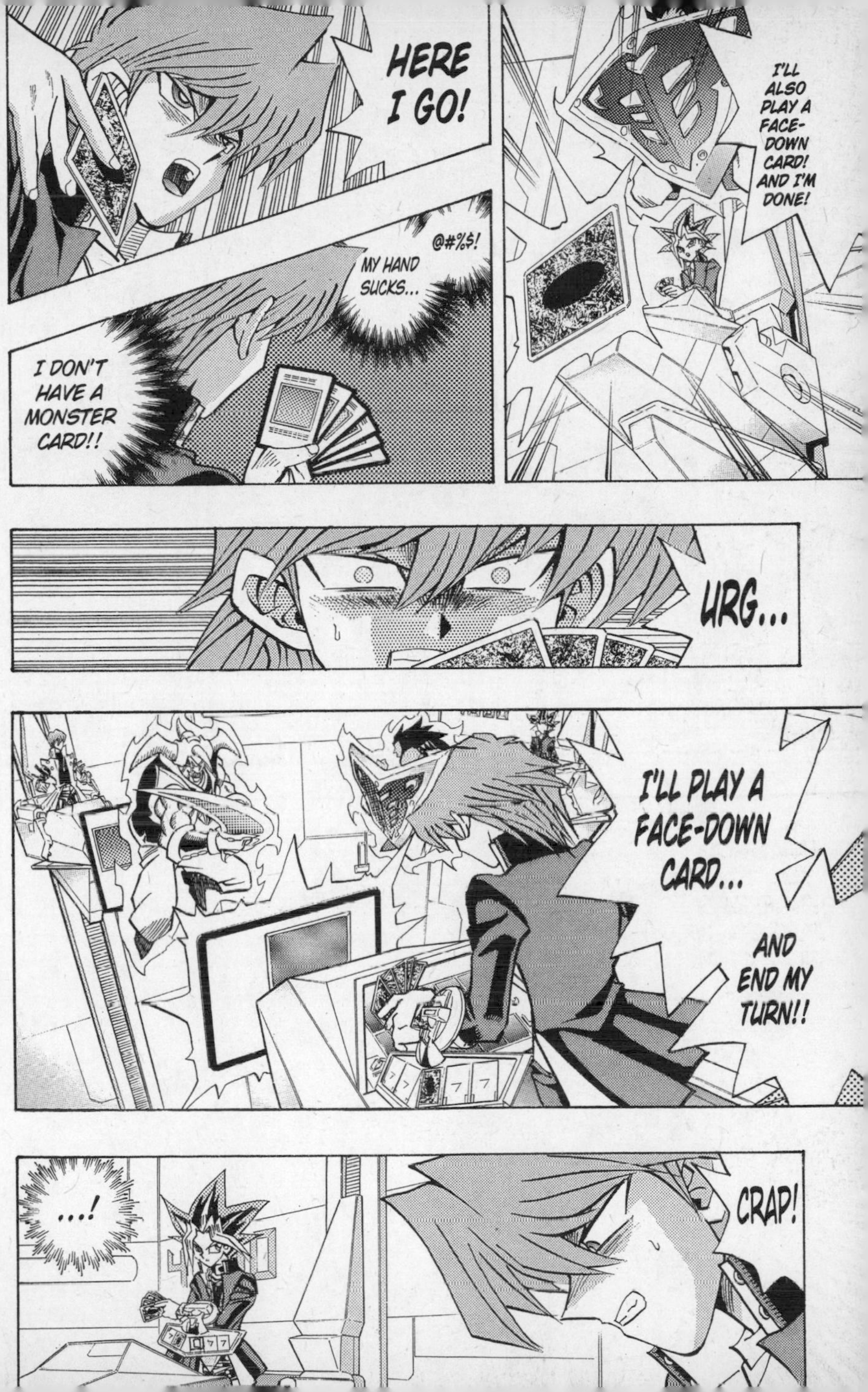
I'LL ALSO PLAY A FACE-DOWN CARD! AND I'M DONE!
HERE I GO!
@#%$!
MY HAND SUCKS...
I DON'T HAVE A MONSTER CARD!!
URG...
I'LL PLAY A FACE-DOWN CARD...
AND END MY TURN!!
CRAP!
...!

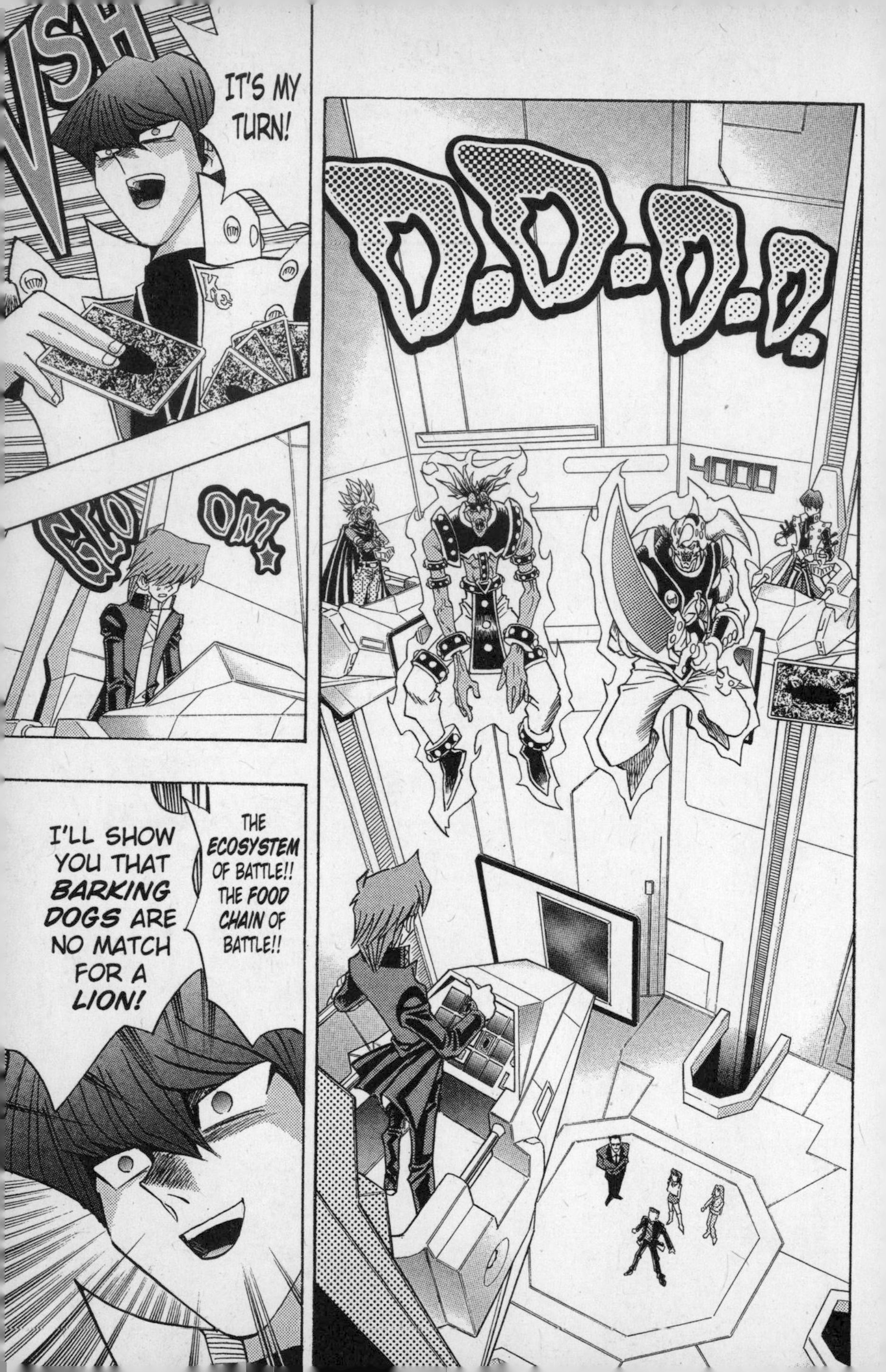
D.D.D.D.
4000
IT'S MY TURN!
THE ECOSYSTEM OF BATTLE!! THE FOOD CHAIN OF BATTLE!!
I'LL SHOW YOU THAT BARKING DOGS ARE NO MATCH FOR A LION!

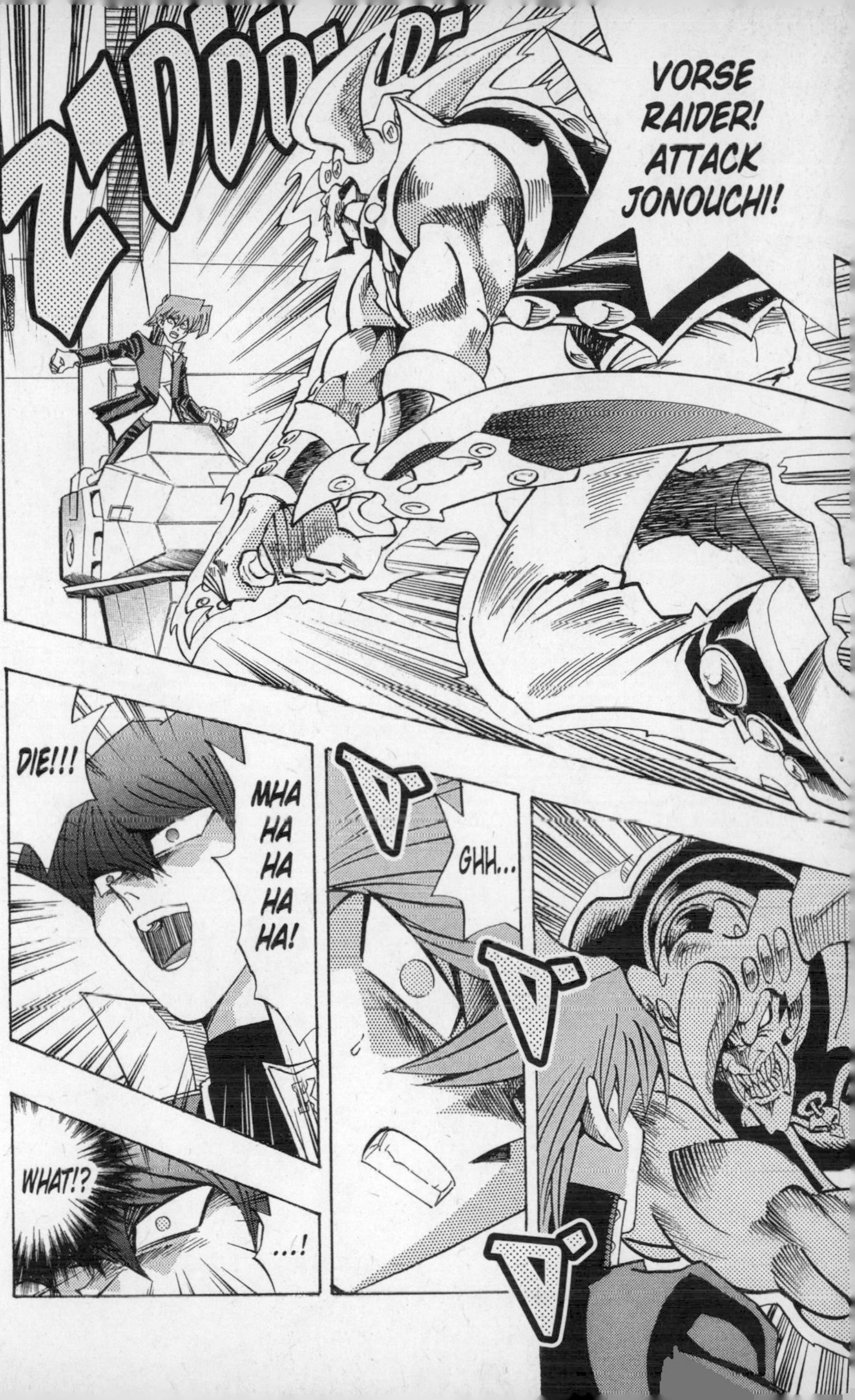
VORSE RAIDER! ATTACK JONOUCHI!
Z-DDD-D-
D
D
GHH...
D
DIE!!!
MHA HA HA HA HA!
WHAT!?
...!

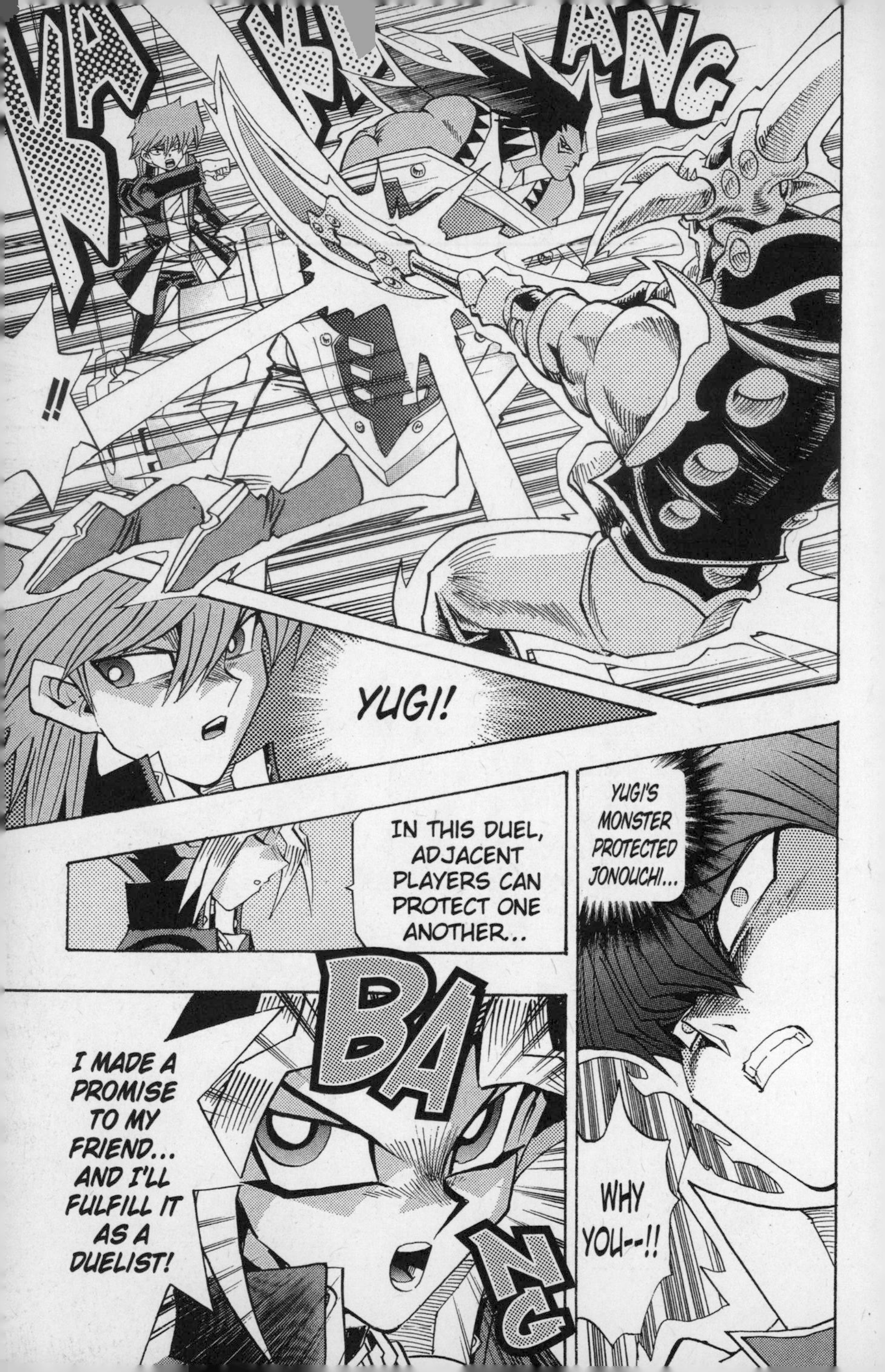
!!
YUGI!
YUGI'S MONSTER PROTECTED JONOUCHI...
IN THIS DUEL, ADJACENT PLAYERS CAN PROTECT ONE ANOTHER..
WHY YOU--!!
BANG
I MADE A PROMISE TO MY FRIEND... AND I'LL FULFILL IT AS A DUELIST!

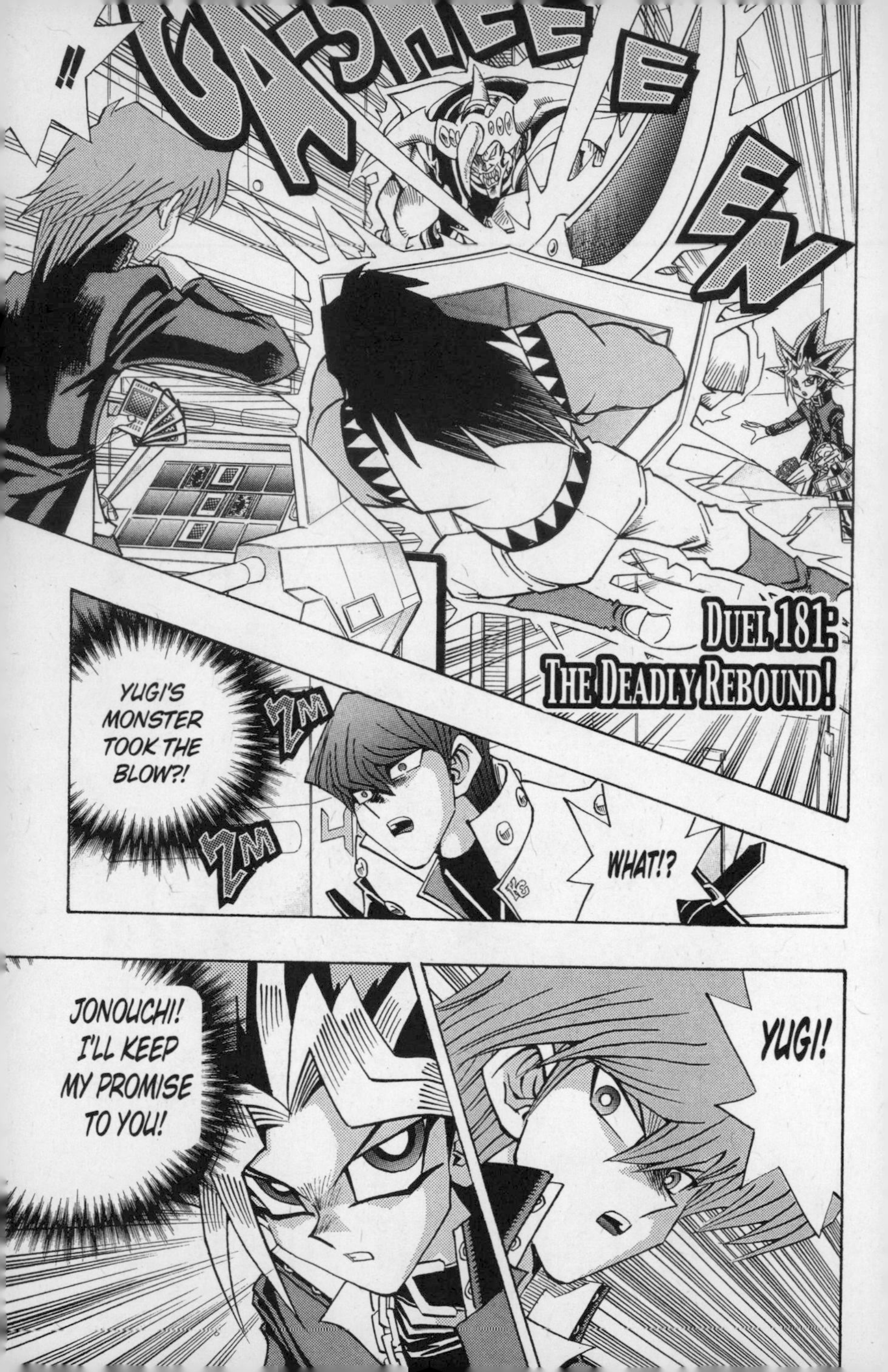
GASHEEEEN
!!
DUEL 181:
THE DEADLY REBOUND!
WHAT!?
ZM
ZM
YUGI'S MONSTER TOOK THE BLOW?!
YUGI!
JONOUCHI! I'LL KEEP MY PROMISE TO YOU!

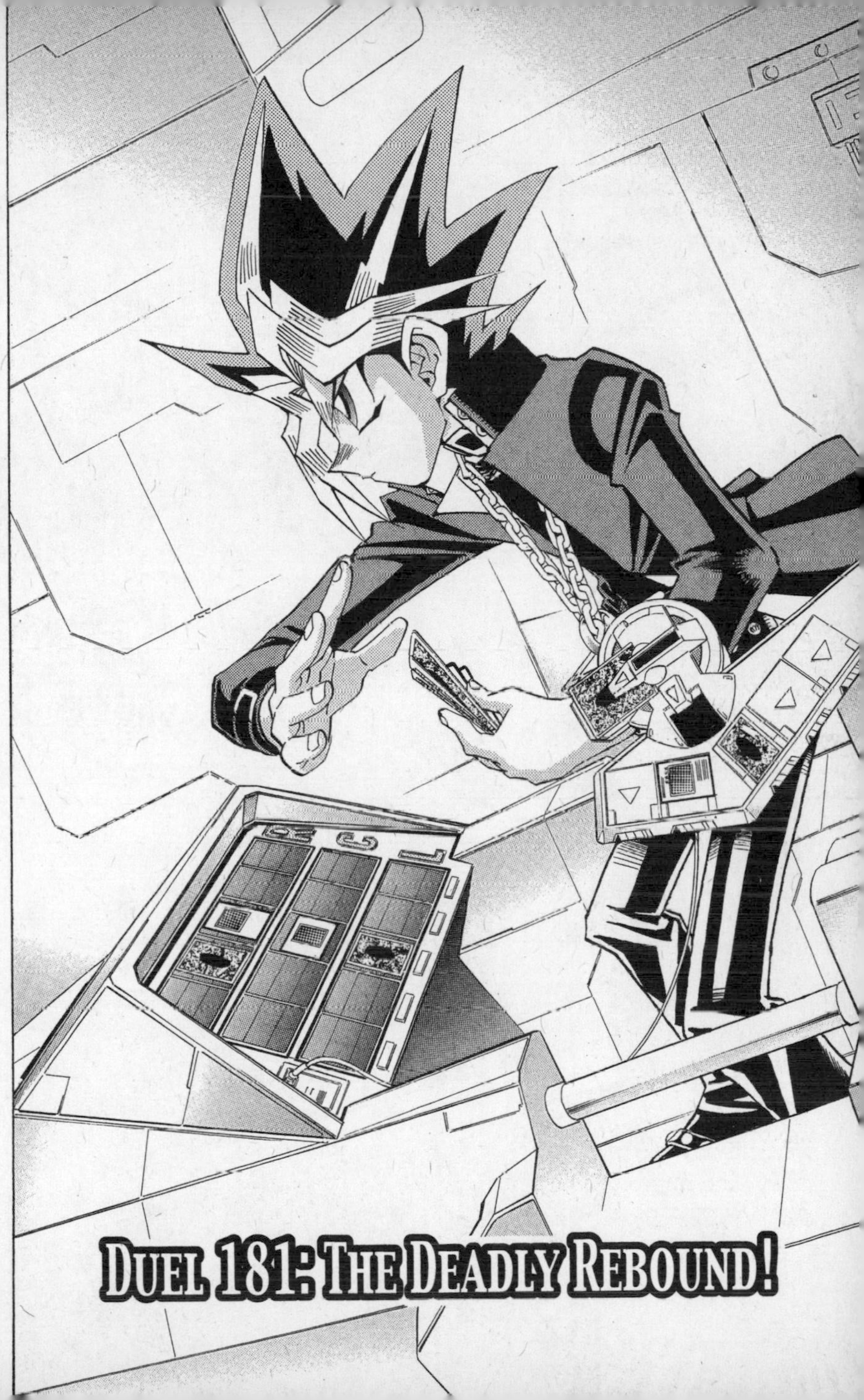

Duel 181: The Deadly Rebound!

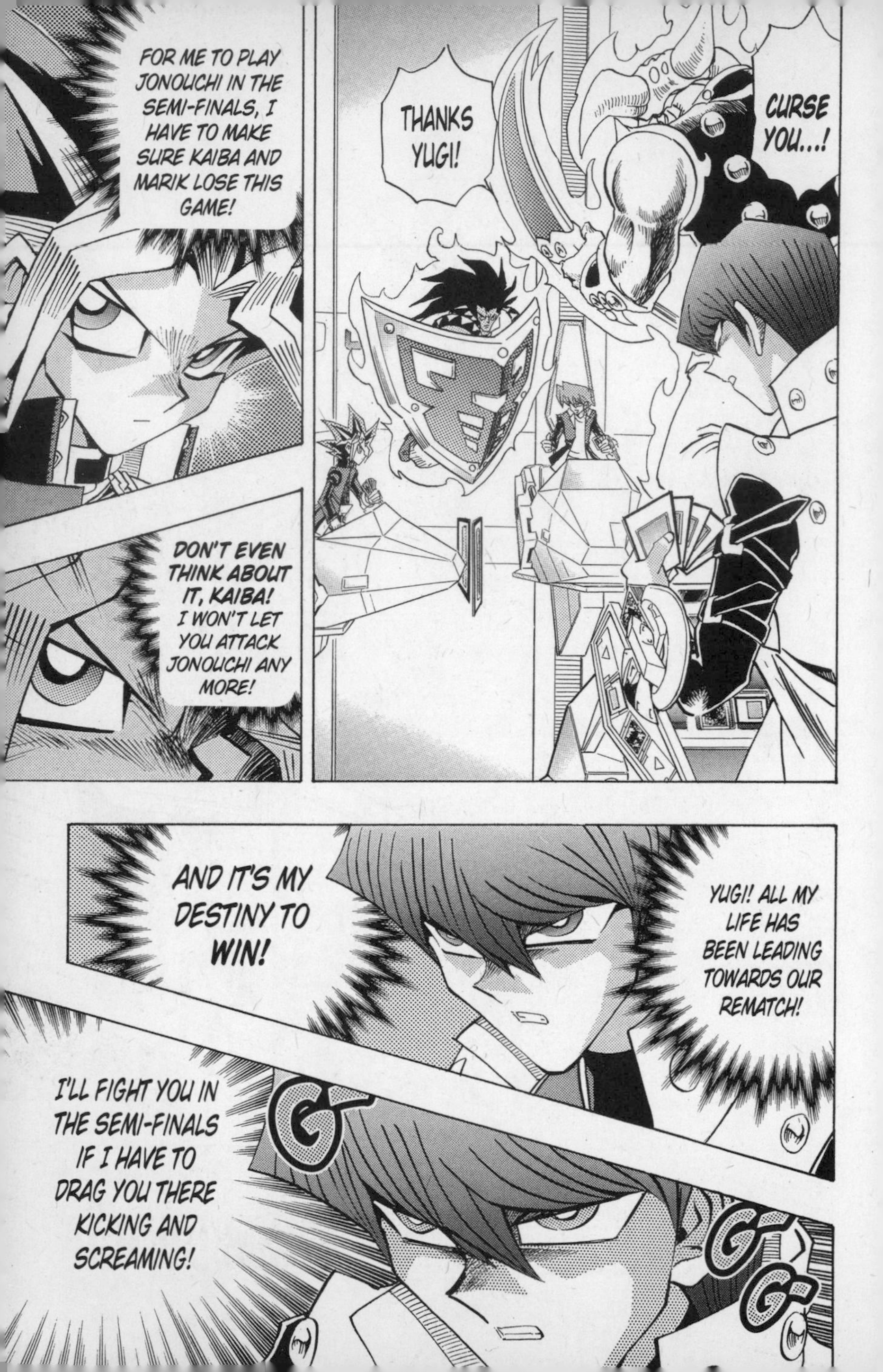
CURSE YOU...!
THANKS YUGI!
FOR ME TO PLAY JONOUCHI IN THE SEMI-FINALS, I HAVE TO MAKE SURE KAIBA AND MARIK LOSE THIS GAME!
DON'T EVEN THINK ABOUT IT, KAIBA! I WON'T LET YOU ATTACK JONOUCHI ANY MORE!
YUGI! ALL MY LIFE HAS BEEN LEADING TOWARDS OUR REMATCH!
AND IT'S MY DESTINY TO WIN!
I'LL FIGHT YOU IN THE SEMI-FINALS IF I HAVE TO DRAG YOU THERE KICKING AND SCREAMING!

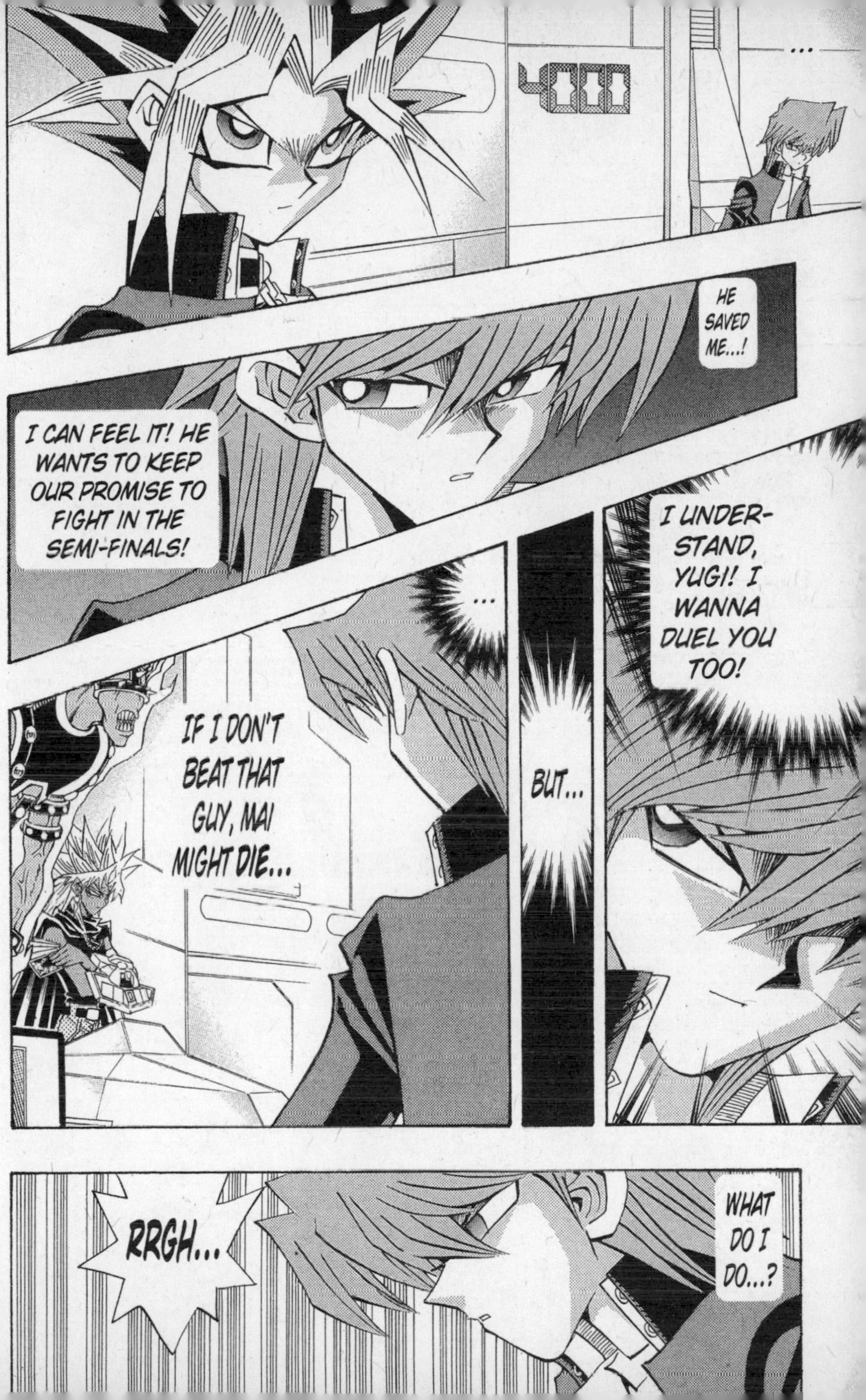
...
HE SAVED ME...!
I CAN FEEL IT! HE WANTS TO KEEP OUR PROMISE TO FIGHT IN THE SEMI-FINALS!
I UNDER-STAND, YUGI! I WANNA DUEL YOU TOO!
BUT...
...
IF I DON'T BEAT THAT GUY, MAI MIGHT DIE...
WHAT DO I DO...?
RRGH...

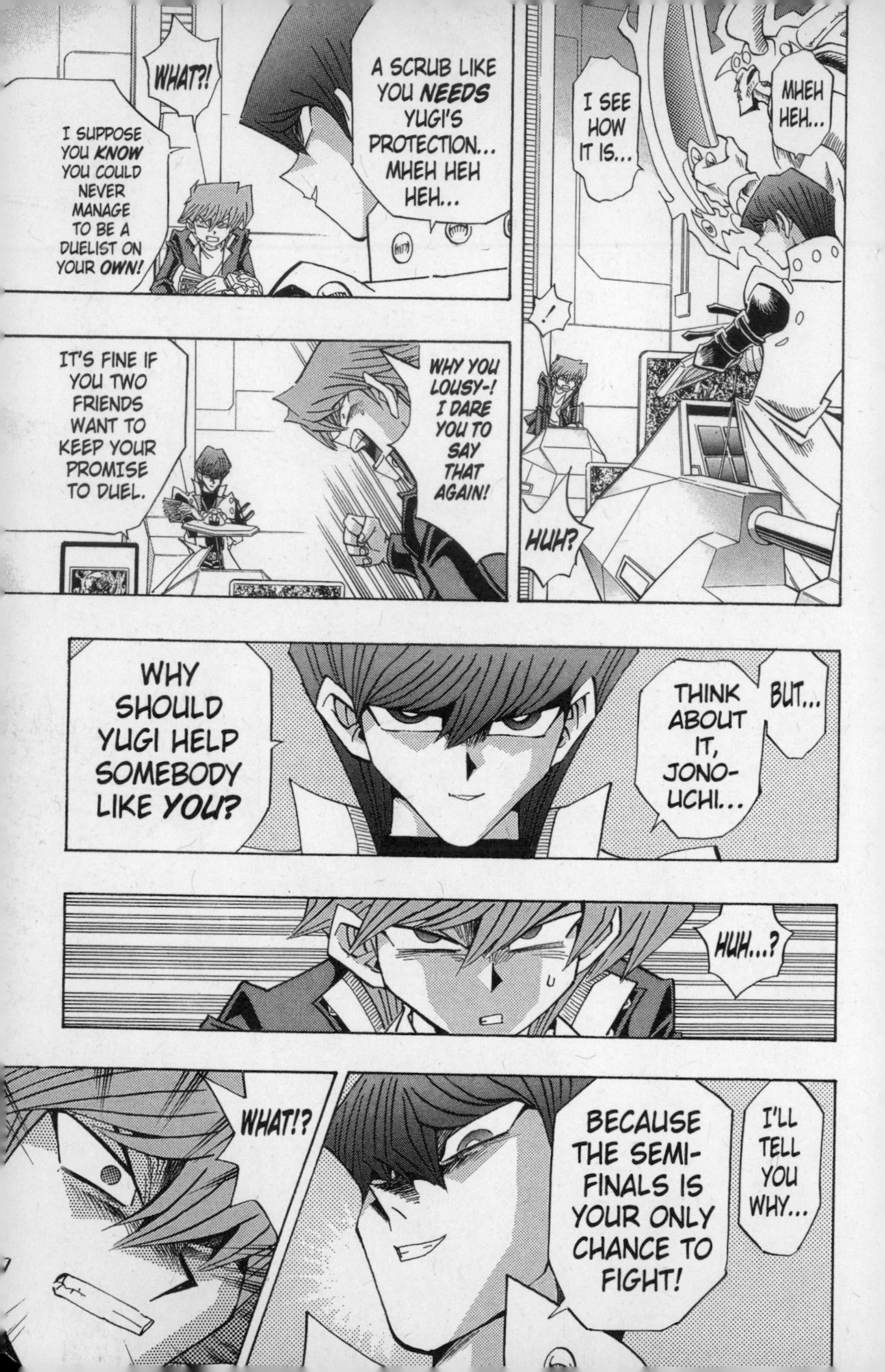
MHEH HEH...
I SEE HOW IT IS...
!
HUH?
A SCRUB LIKE YOU NEEDS YUGI'S PROTECTION... MHEH HEH HEH...
WHAT?!
I SUPPOSE YOU KNOW YOU COULD NEVER MANAGE TO BE A DUELIST ON YOUR OWN!
WHY YOU LOUSY-! I DARE YOU TO SAY THAT AGAIN!
IT'S FINE IF YOU TWO FRIENDS WANT TO KEEP YOUR PROMISE TO DUEL.
BUT...
THINK ABOUT IT, JONO-UCHI...
WHY SHOULD YUGI HELP SOMEBODY LIKE YOU?
HUH...?
I'LL TELL YOU WHY...
BECAUSE THE SEMI-FINALS IS YOUR ONLY CHANCE TO FIGHT!
WHAT!?

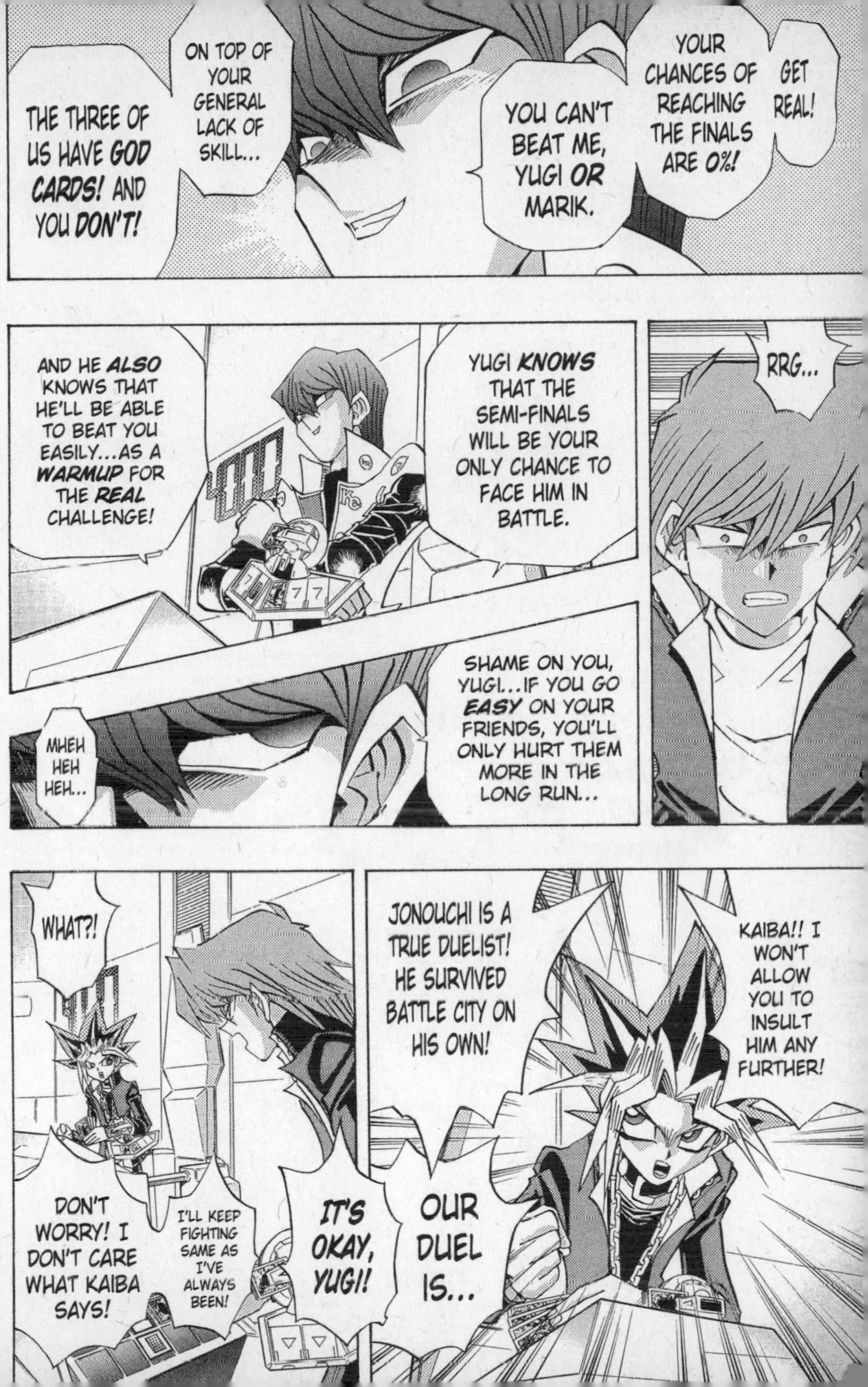
GET REAL!
YOUR CHANCES OF REACHING THE FINALS ARE 0%!
YOU CAN'T BEAT ME, YUGI OR MARIK.
ON TOP OF YOUR GENERAL LACK OF SKILL...
THE THREE OF US HAVE GOD CARDS! AND YOU DON'T!
RRG...
YUGI KNOWS THAT THE SEMI-FINALS WILL BE YOUR ONLY CHANCE TO FACE HIM IN BATTLE.
AND HE ALSO KNOWS THAT HE'LL BE ABLE TO BEAT YOU EASILY...AS A WARMUP FOR THE REAL CHALLENGE!
SHAME ON YOU, YUGI...IF YOU GO EASY ON YOUR FRIENDS, YOU'LL ONLY HURT THEM MORE IN THE LONG RUN...
MHEH HEH HEH...
KAIBA!! I WON'T ALLOW YOU TO INSULT HIM ANY FURTHER!
JONOUCHI IS A TRUE DUELIST! HE SURVIVED BATTLE CITY ON HIS OWN!
OUR DUEL IS...
WHAT?!
IT'S OKAY, YUGI!
I'LL KEEP FIGHTING SAME AS I'VE ALWAYS BEEN!
DON'T WORRY! I DON'T CARE WHAT KAIBA SAYS!

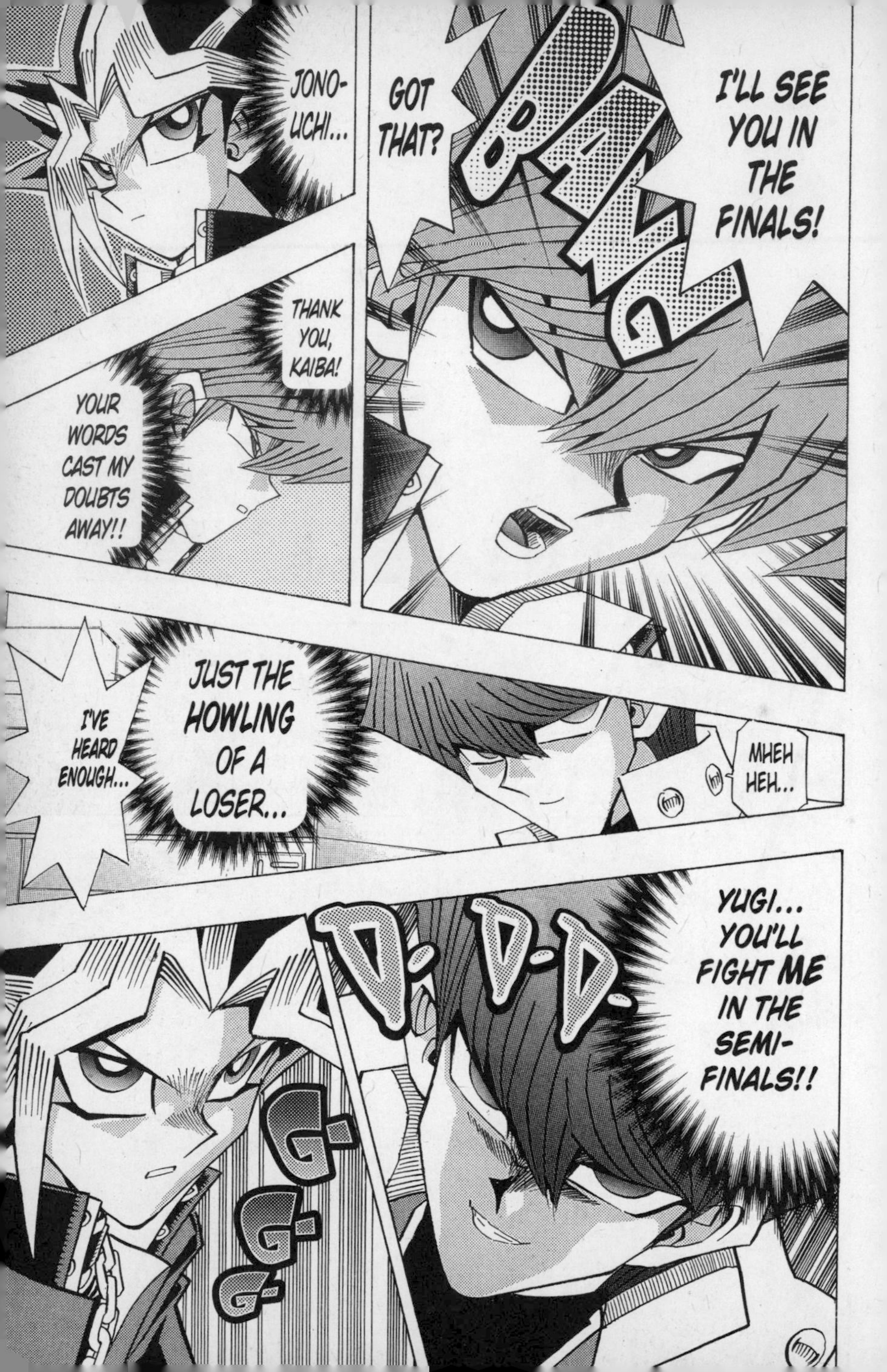
I'LL SEE YOU IN THE FINALS!
GOT THAT?
JONO-UCHI...
THANK YOU, KAIBA!
YOUR WORDS CAST MY DOUBTS AWAY!!
MHEH HEH...
JUST THE HOWLING OF A LOSER...
I'VE HEARD ENOUGH...
YUGI... YOU'LL FIGHT ME IN THE SEMI-FINALS!!
D-D-D
G-G-G

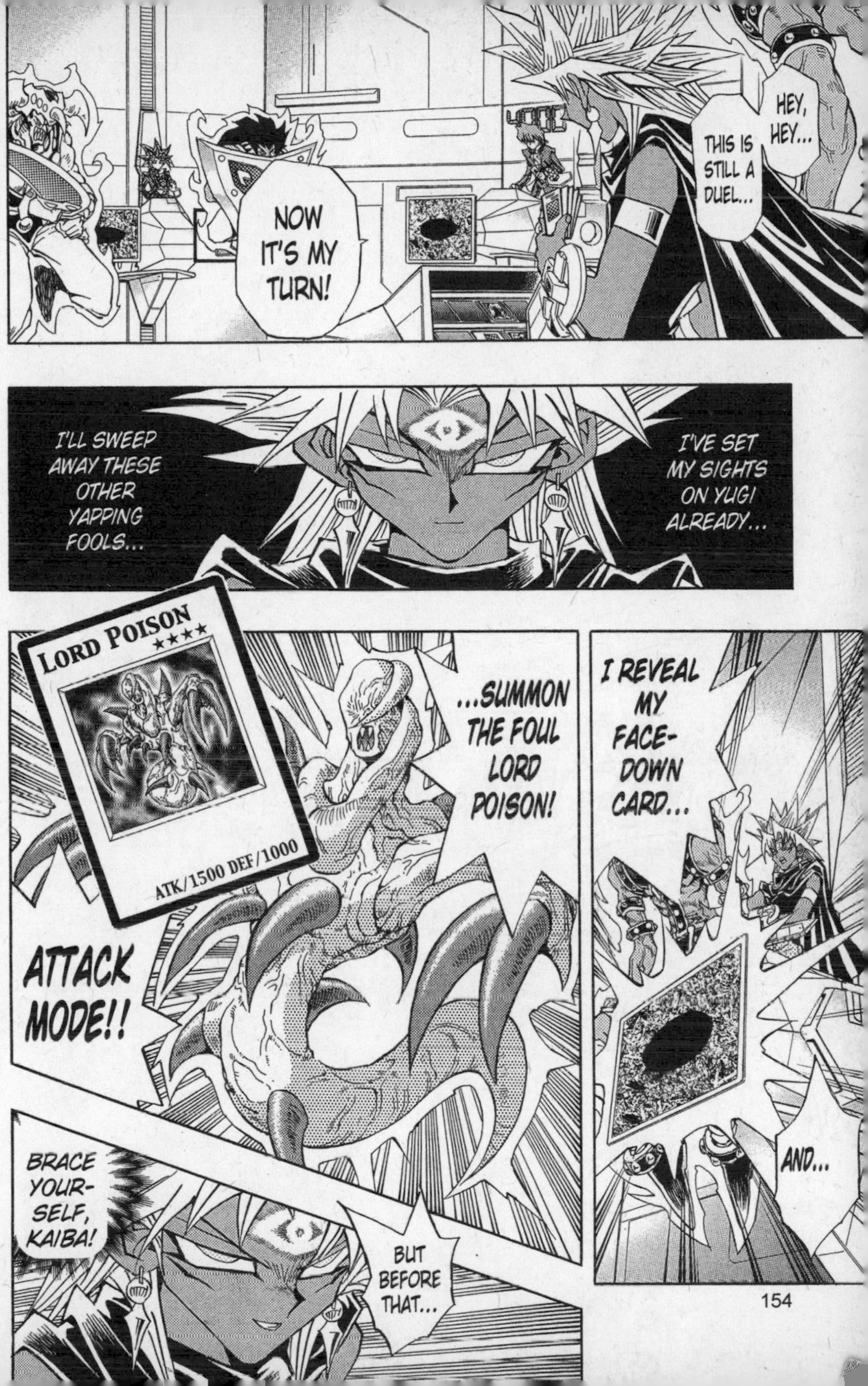
HEY, HEY...
THIS IS STILL A DUEL...
NOW IT'S MY TURN!
I'VE SET MY SIGHTS ON YUGI ALREADY...
I'LL SWEEP AWAY THESE OTHER YAPPING FOOLS...
I REVEAL MY FACE-DOWN CARD...
AND...
...SUMMON THE FOUL LORD POISON!
LORD POISON
ATK/1500 DEF/1000
ATTACK MODE!!
BUT BEFORE THAT...
BRACE YOURSELF, KAIBA!

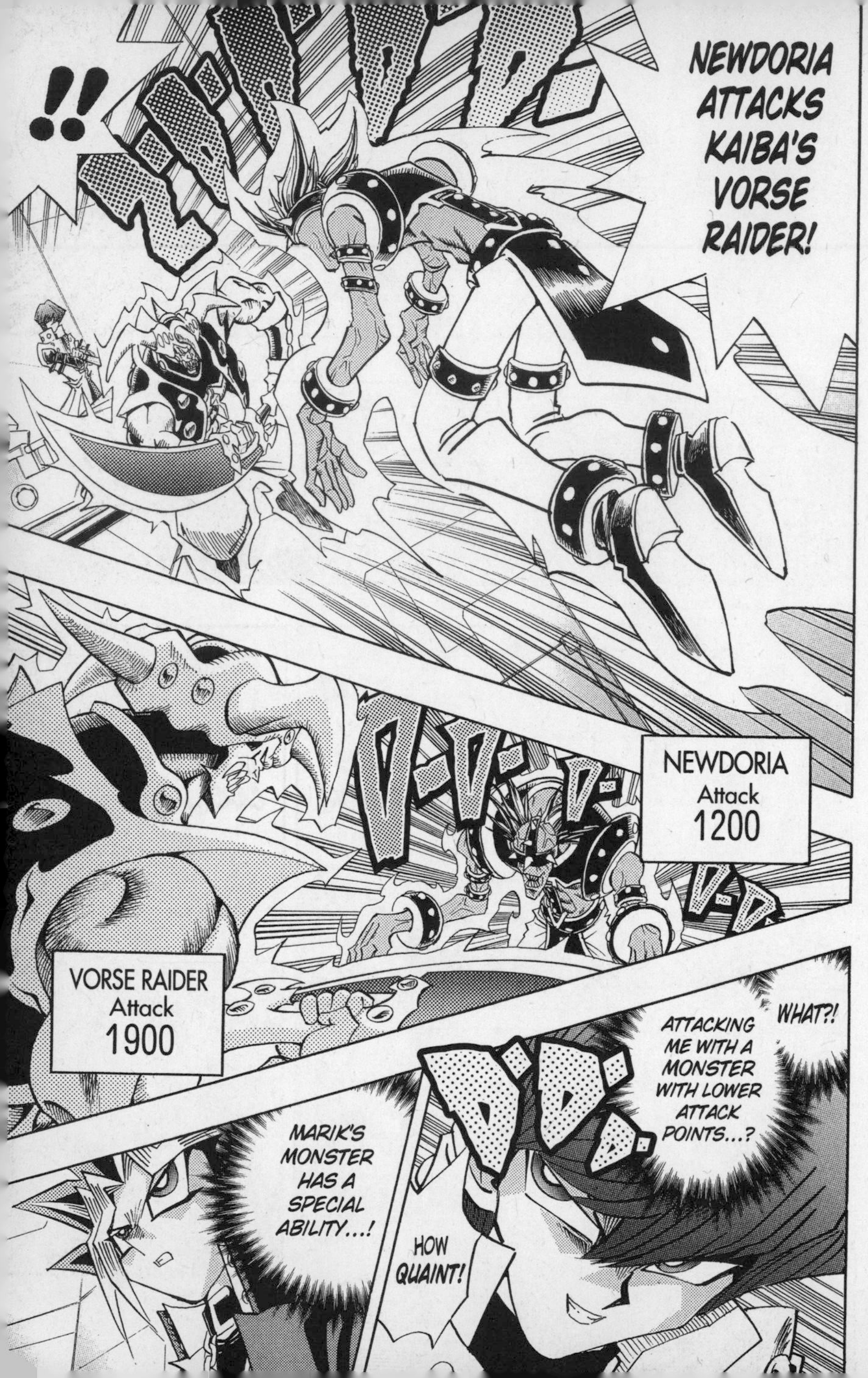
NEWDORIA ATTACKS KAIBA'S VORSE RAIDER!
!!
NEWDORIA Attack 1200
VORSE RAIDER Attack 1900
WHAT?!
ATTACKING ME WITH A MONSTER WITH LOWER ATTACK POINTS...?
HOW QUAINT!
MARIK'S MONSTER HAS A SPECIAL ABILITY...!

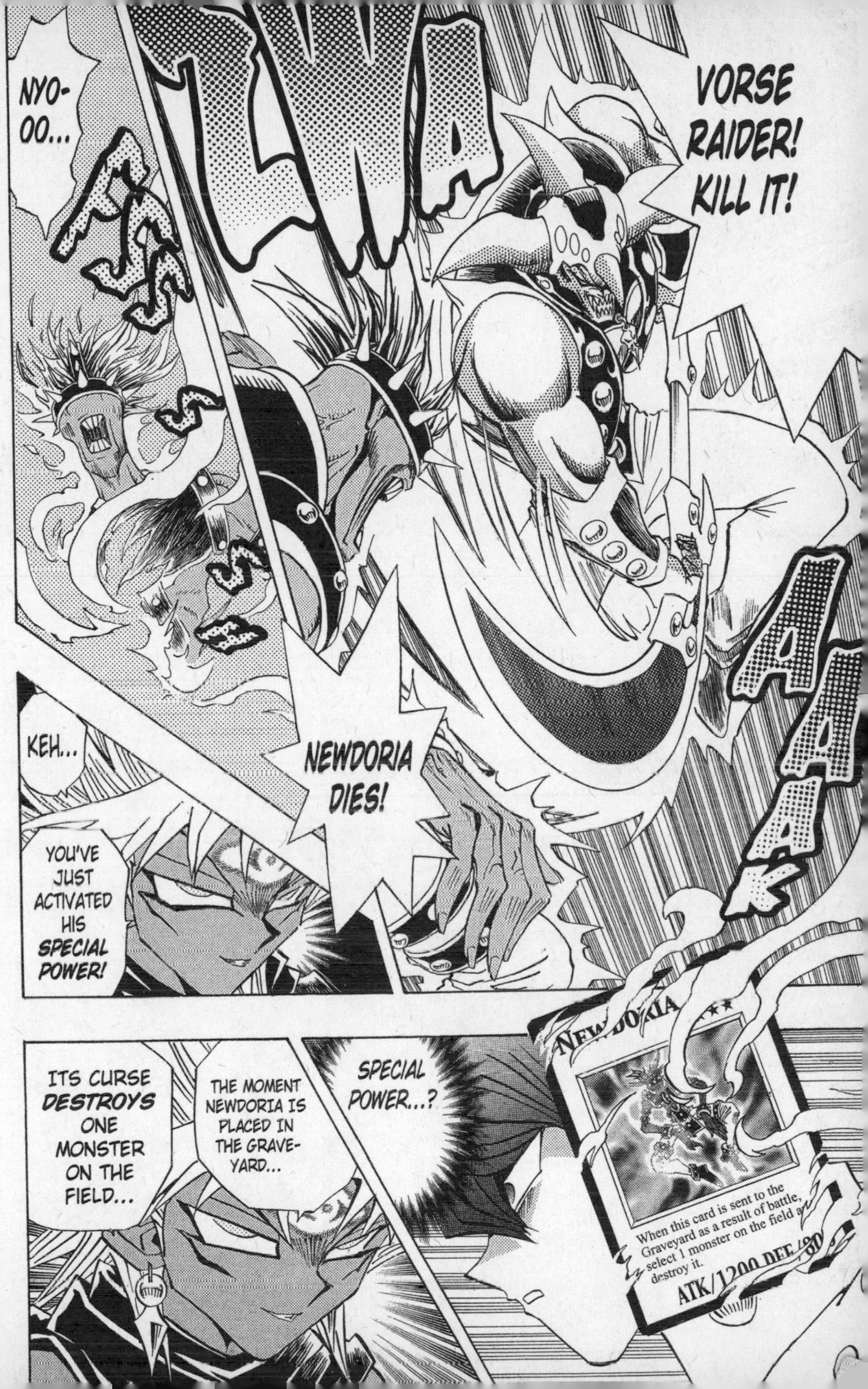
VORSE RAIDER! KILL IT!
AAAAK
NYO-OO...
NEWDORIA DIES!
KEH...
YOU'VE JUST ACTIVATED HIS SPECIAL POWER!
NEWDORIA
When this card is sent to the Graveyard as a result of battle, select 1 monster on the field
destroy it.
ATK/1200
SPECIAL POWER...?
THE MOMENT NEWDORIA IS PLACED IN THE GRAVEYARD...
ITS CURSE DESTROYS ONE MONSTER ON THE FIELD...

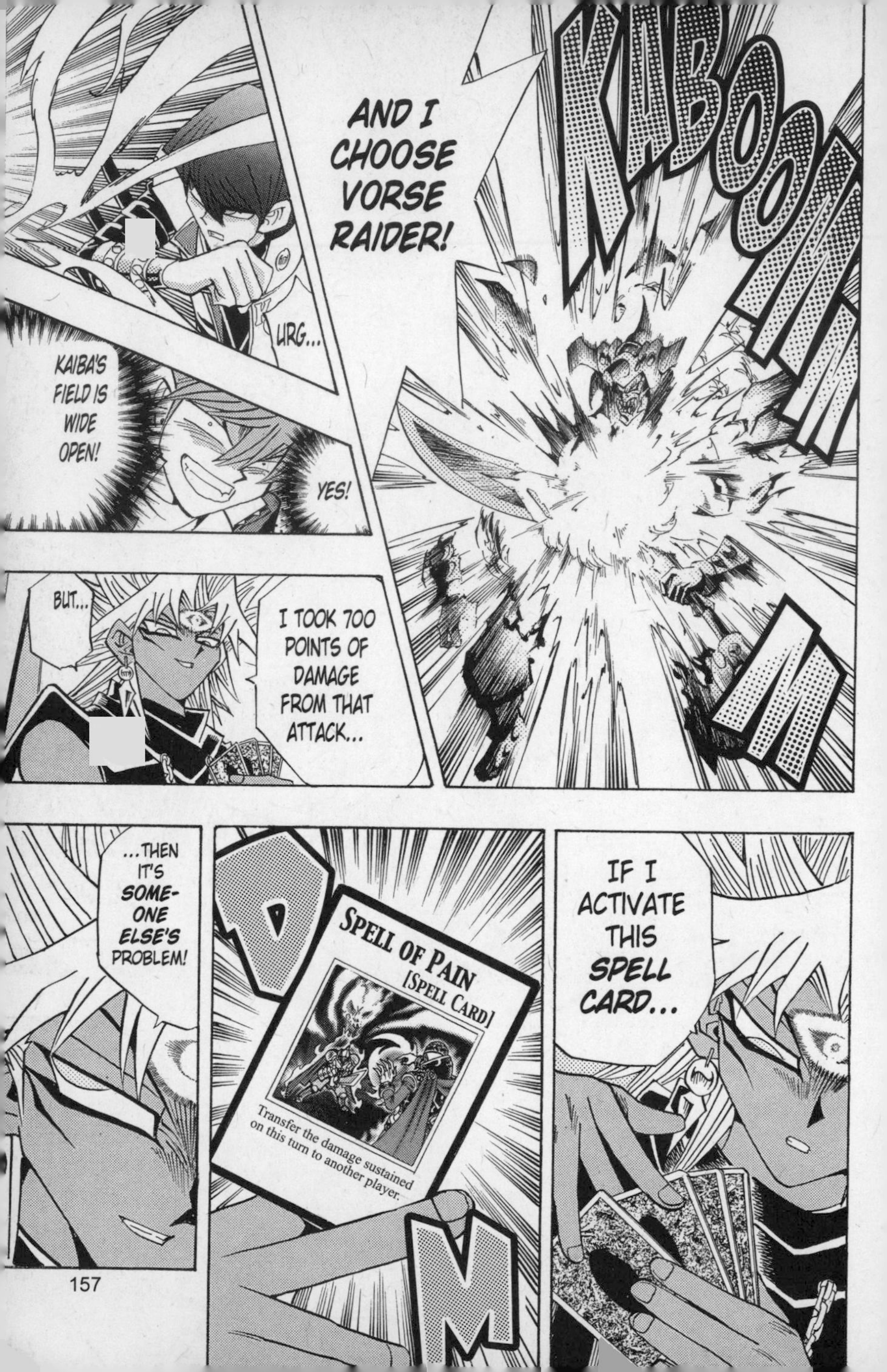
KABOOM
AND I CHOOSE VORSE RAIDER!
URG...
KAIBA'S FIELD IS WIDE OPEN!
YES!
BUT...
I TOOK 700 POINTS OF DAMAGE FROM THAT ATTACK...
IF I ACTIVATE THIS SPELL CARD...
SPELL OF PAIN
[SPELL CARD]
Transfer the damage sustained on this turn to another player.
...THEN IT'S SOMEONE-ONE ELSE'S PROBLEM!

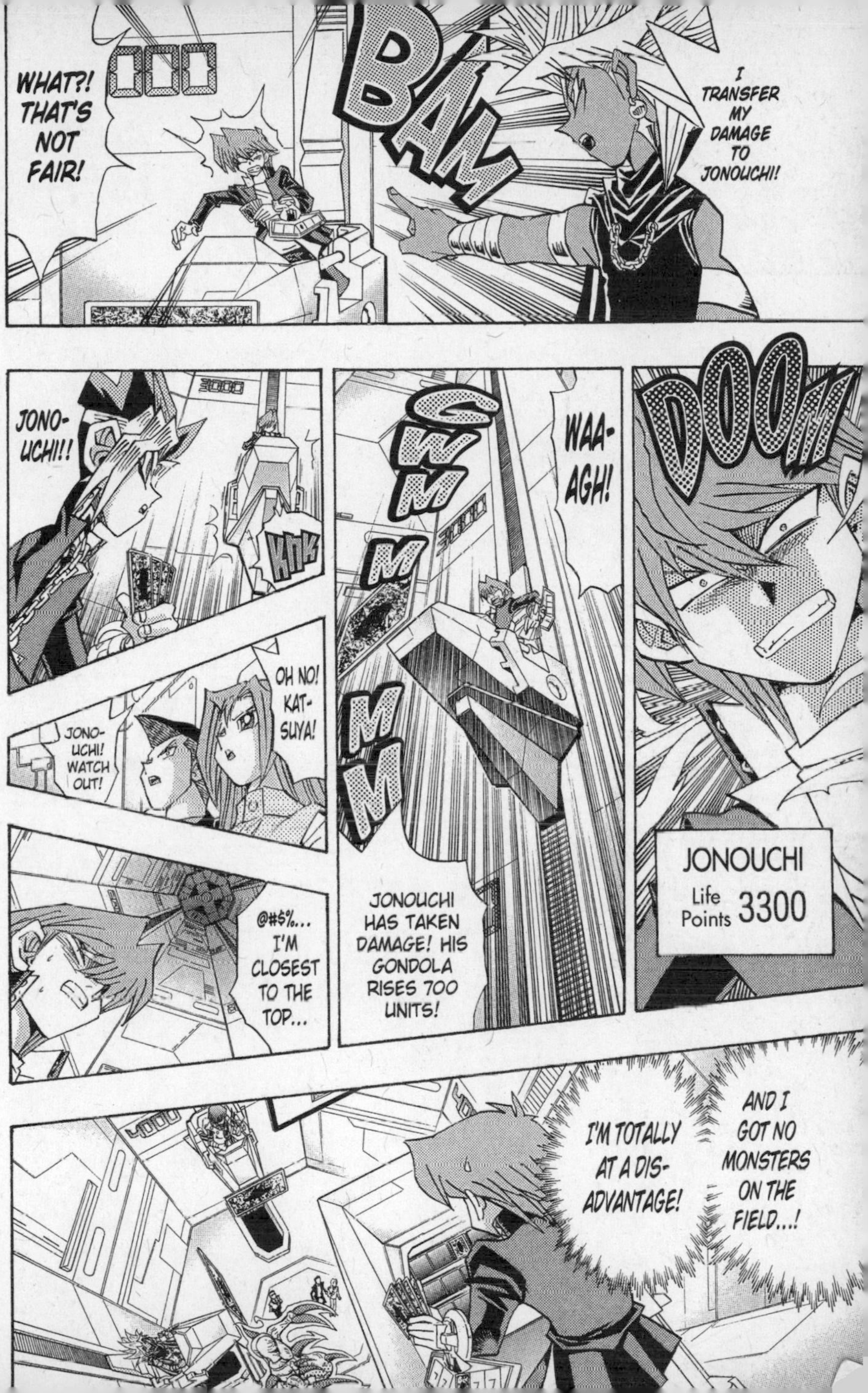
I TRANSFER MY DAMAGE TO JONOUCHI!
BAM
WHAT?! THAT'S NOT FAIR!
DOOM
JONOUCHI
Life Points 3300
WAA-AGH!
GWMMMMM
JONOUCHI HAS TAKEN DAMAGE! HIS GONDOLA RISES 700 UNITS!
JONO-UCHI!!
KNK
OH NO! KAT-SUYA!
JONO-UCHI! WATCH OUT!
@#$%... I'M CLOSEST TO THE TOP...
I'M TOTALLY AT A DIS-ADVANTAGE!
AND I GOT NO MONSTERS ON THE FIELD...!

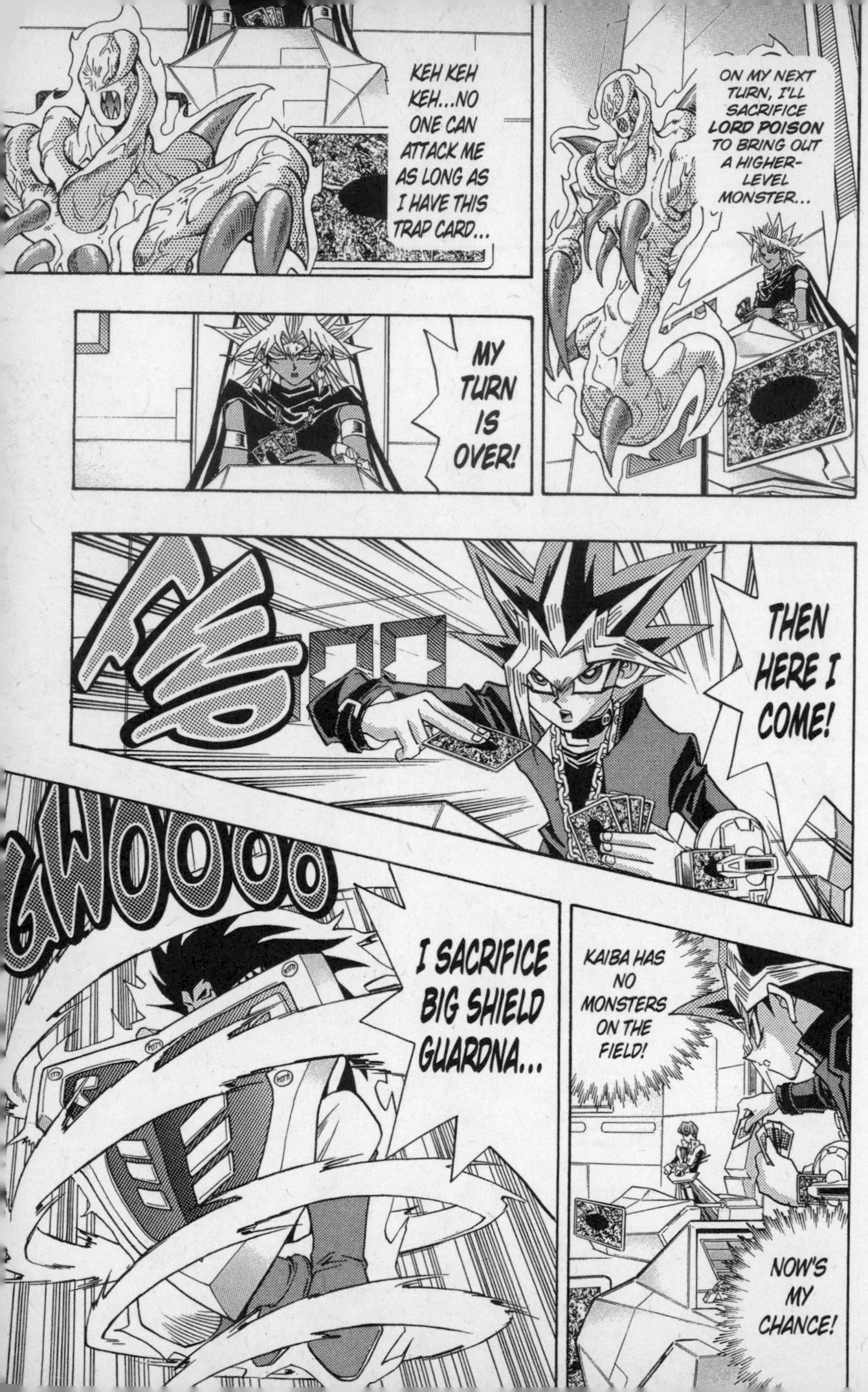
ON MY NEXT TURN, I'LL SACRIFICE **LORD POISON** TO BRING OUT A HIGHER-LEVEL MONSTER...
KEH KEH KEH...NO ONE CAN ATTACK ME AS LONG AS I HAVE THIS TRAP CARD...
MY TURN IS OVER!
THEN HERE I COME!
KAIBA HAS NO MONSTERS ON THE FIELD!
NOW'S MY CHANCE!
I SACRIFICE BIG SHIELD GUARDNA...

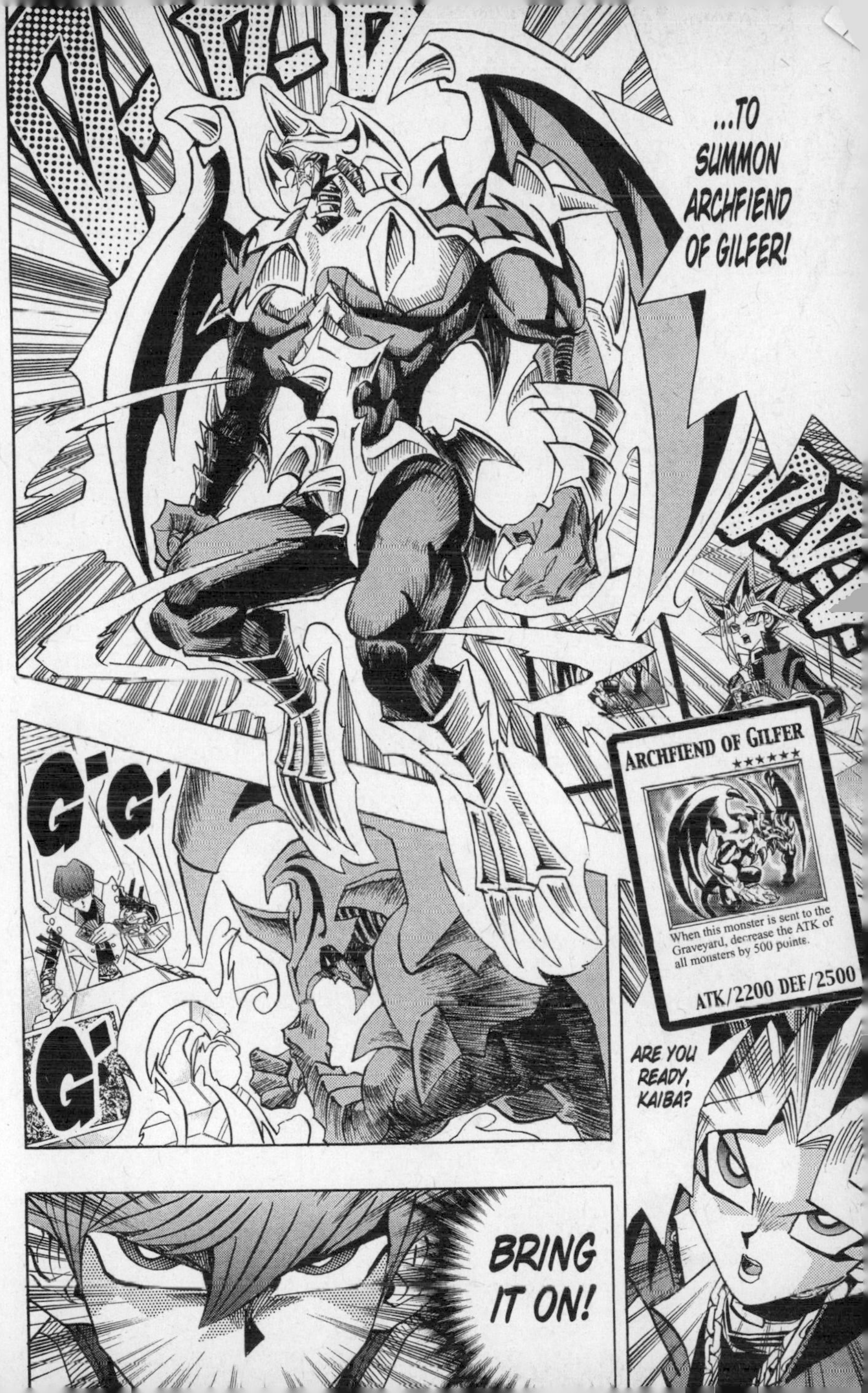
...TO SUMMON ARCHFIEND OF GILFER!
ARCHFIEND OF GILFER
When this monster is sent to the Graveyard, decrease the ATK of all monsters by 500 points.
ATK/2200 DEF/2500
ARE YOU READY, KAIBA?
BRING IT ON!

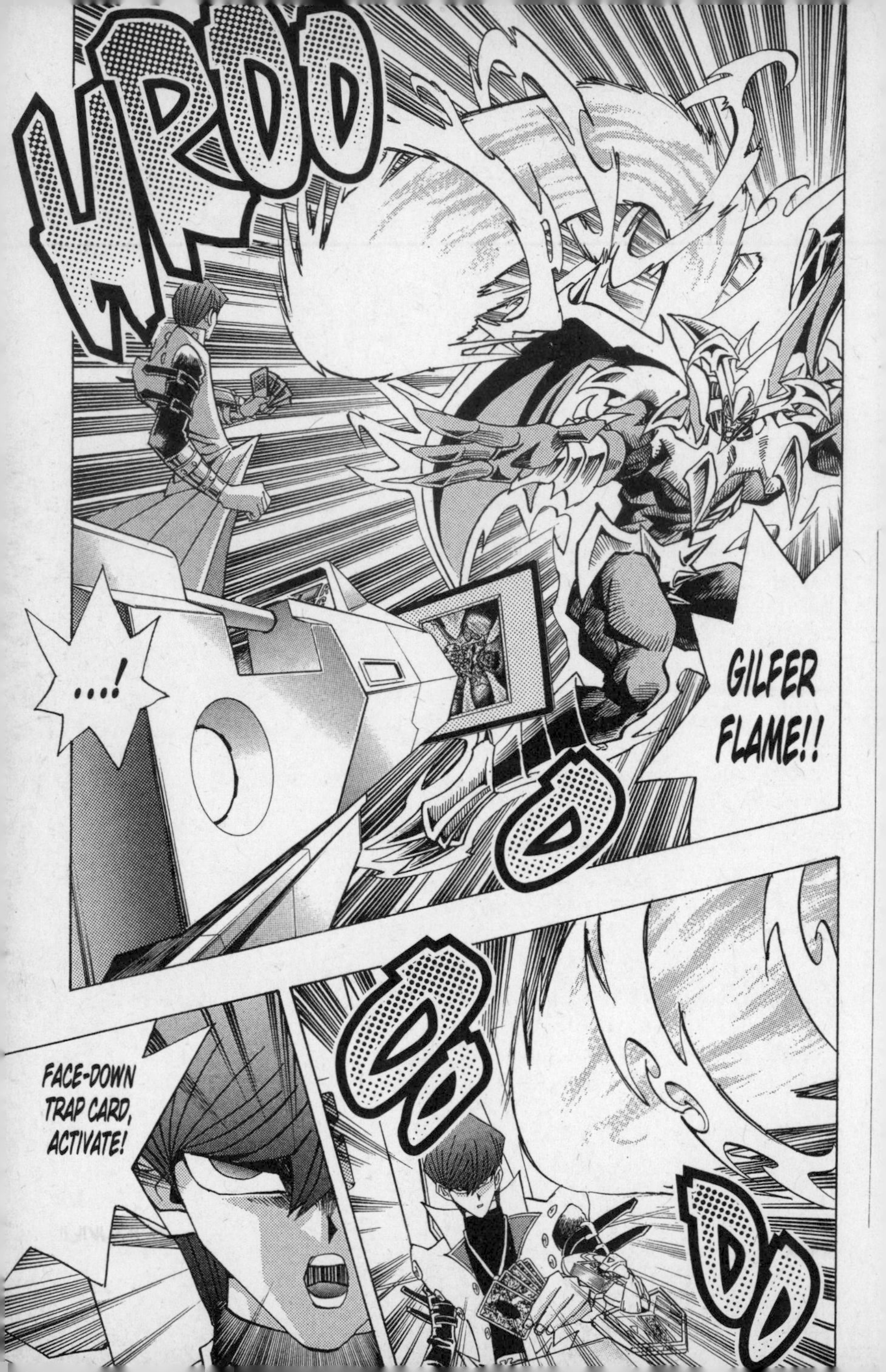
GILFER FLAME!!
...!
FACE-DOWN TRAP CARD, ACTIVATE!

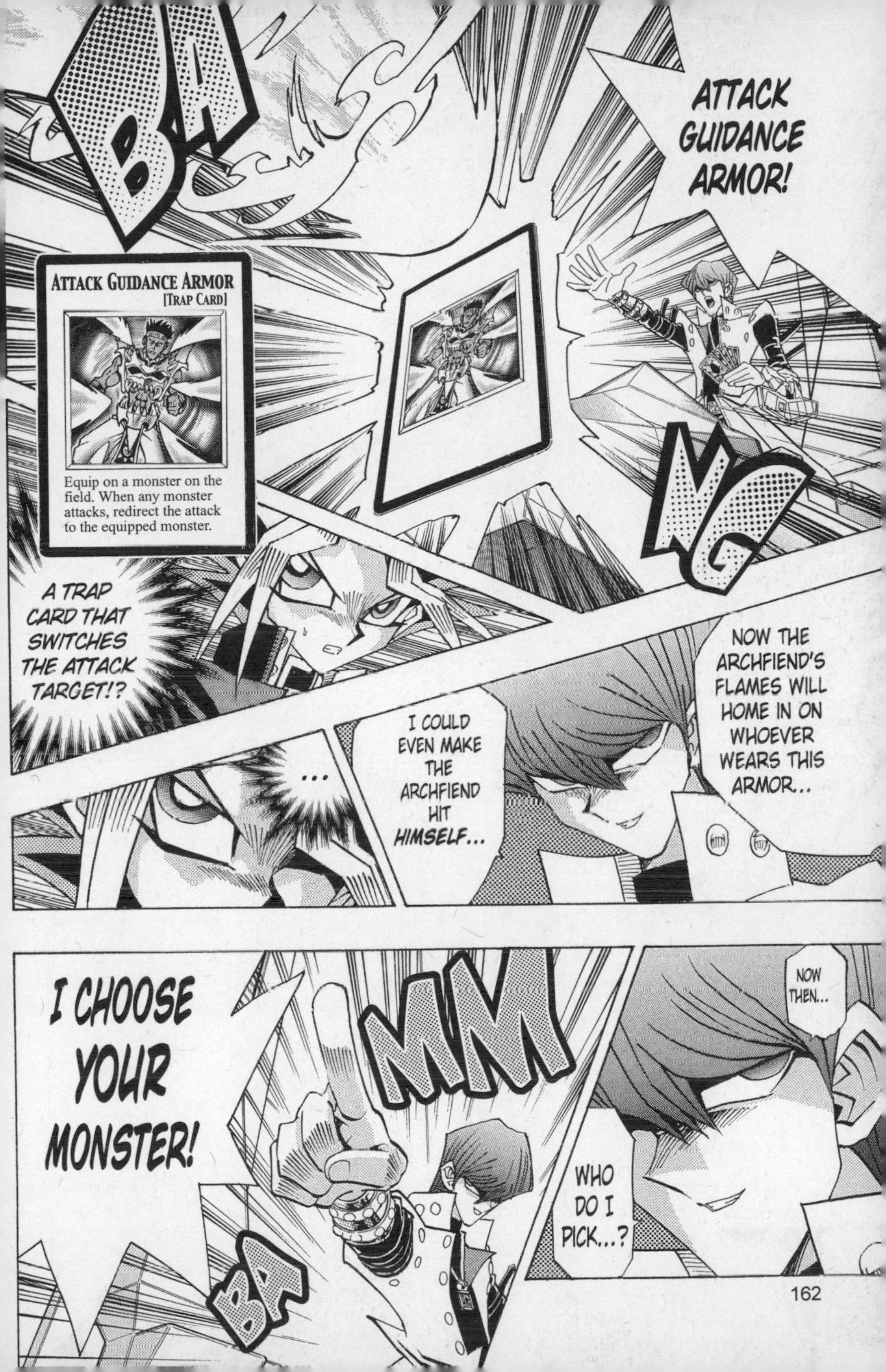
ATTACK GUIDANCE ARMOR!
BA
MG
ATTACK GUIDANCE ARMOR
[TRAP CARD]
Equip on a monster on the field. When any monster attacks, redirect the attack to the equipped monster.
A TRAP CARD THAT SWITCHES THE ATTACK TARGET!?
NOW THE ARCHFIEND'S FLAMES WILL HOME IN ON WHOEVER WEARS THIS ARMOR...
I COULD EVEN MAKE THE ARCHFIEND HIT *HIMSELF*...
...
NOW THEN...
WHO DO I PICK...?
I CHOOSE YOUR MONSTER!
MM
BA

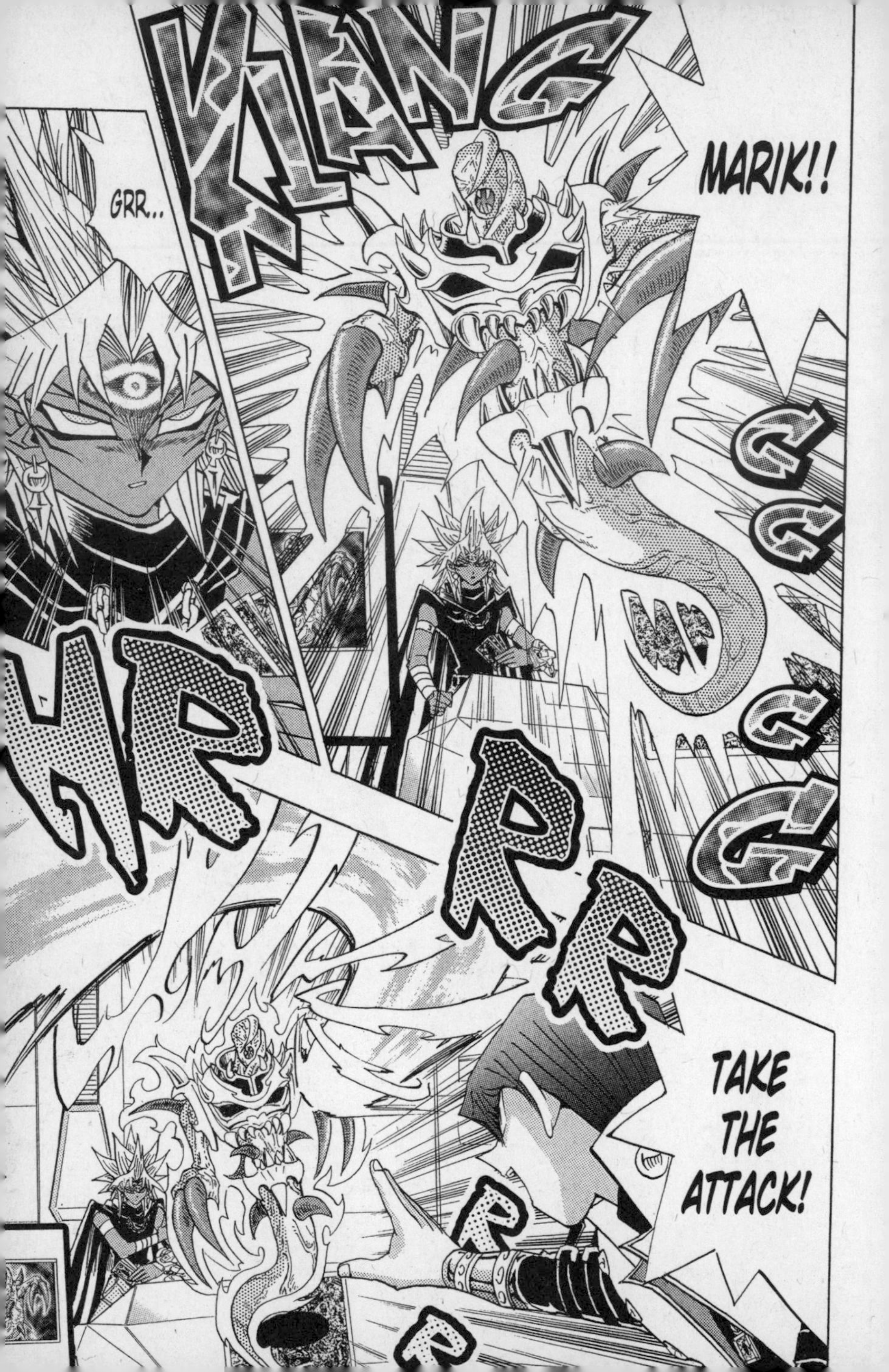
KLANG
MARIK!!
GRR...
GGGG
TAKE THE ATTACK!

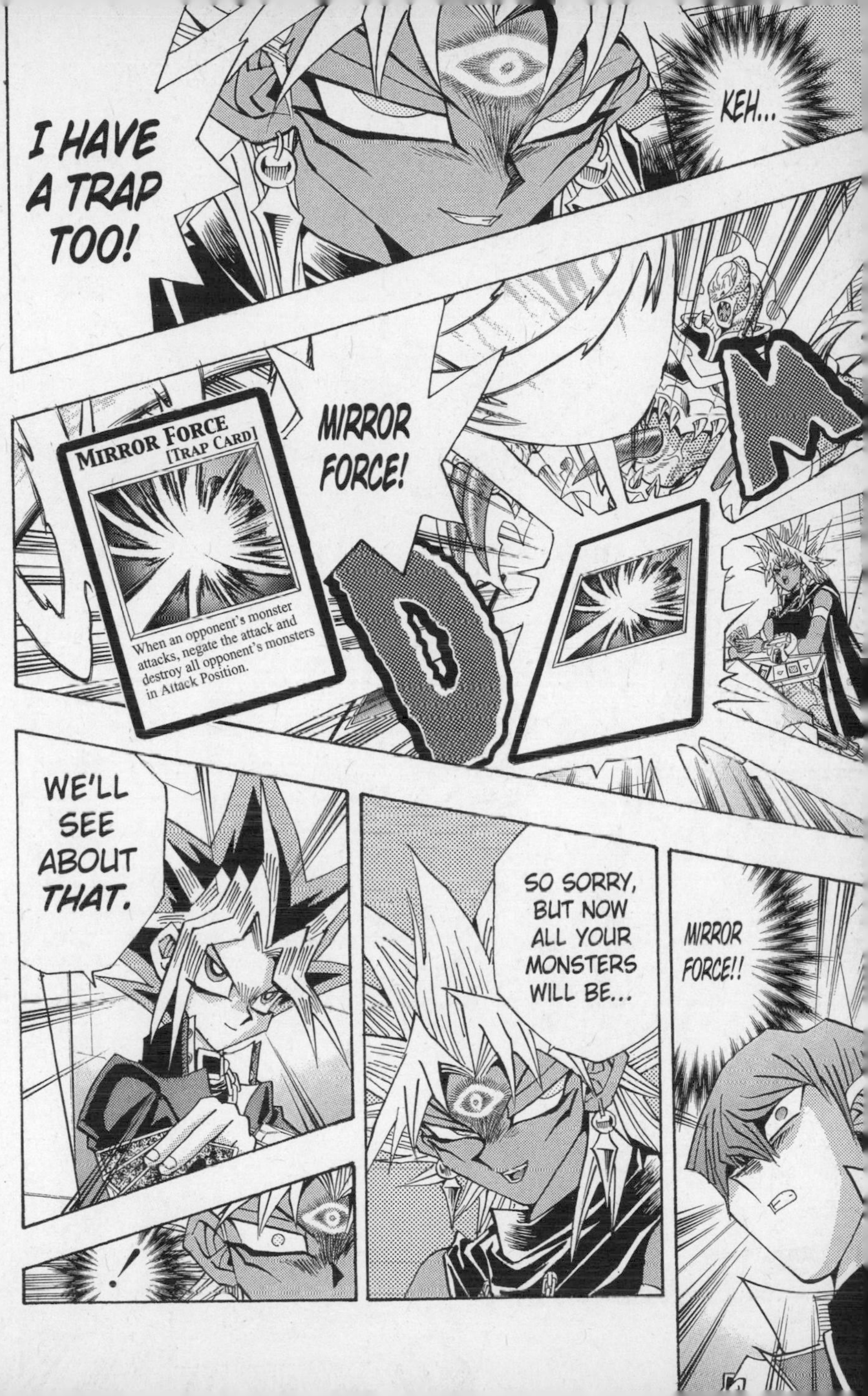
KEH...
I HAVE A TRAP TOO!
MIRROR FORCE!
MIRROR FORCE [TRAP CARD]
When an opponent's monster attacks, negate the attack and destroy all opponent's monsters in Attack Position.
MIRROR FORCE!!
SO SORRY, BUT NOW ALL YOUR MONSTERS WILL BE...
WE'LL SEE ABOUT THAT.
!

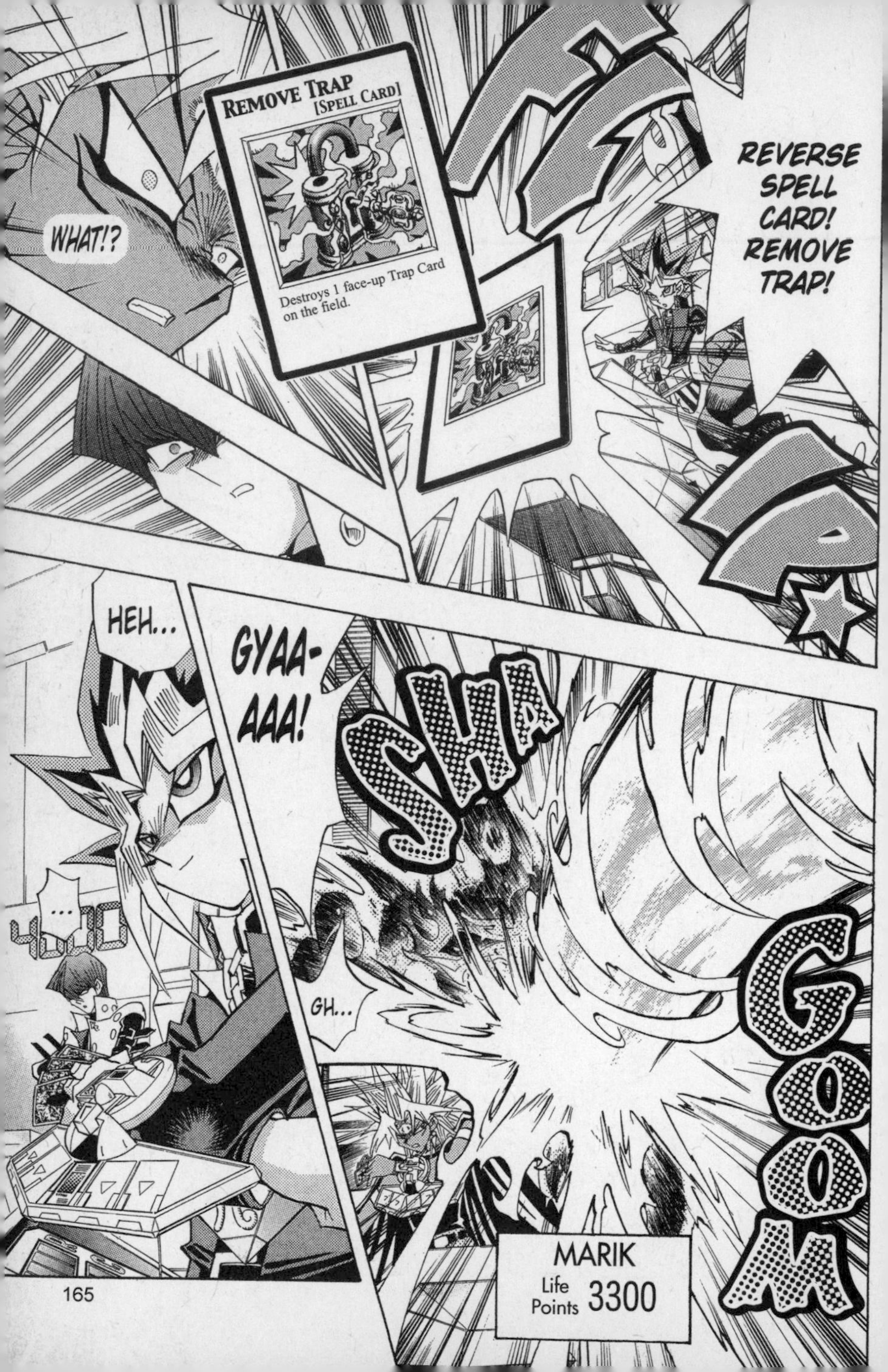
REVERSE SPELL CARD! REMOVE TRAP!
REMOVE TRAP
[SPELL CARD]
Destroys 1 face-up Trap Card on the field.
WHAT!?
GYAAA-AAA!
SHA
GOOOM
GH...
MARIK
Life Points 3300
HEH...
...
4000

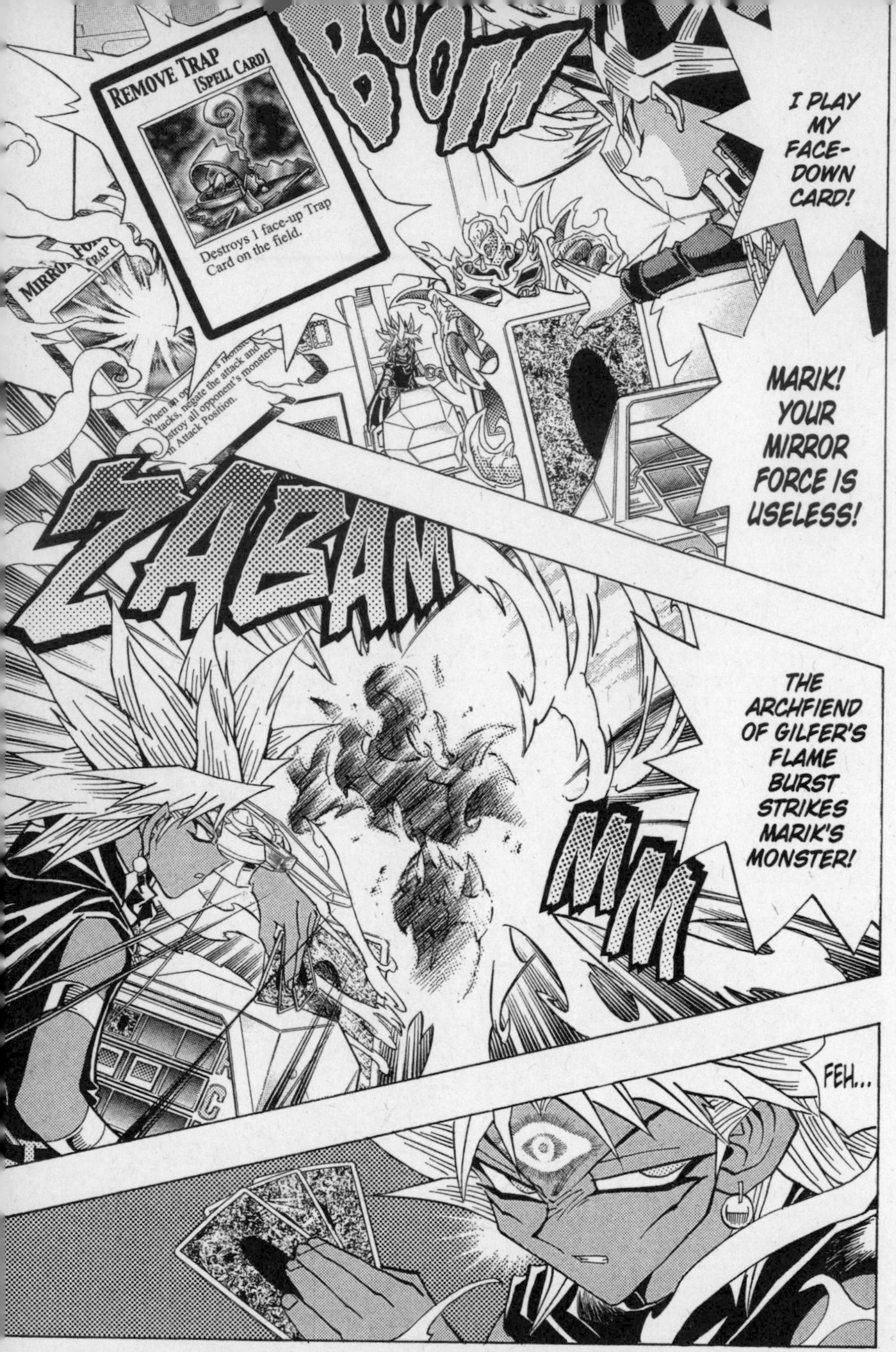
I PLAY MY FACE-DOWN CARD!
BOOM
REMOVE TRAP
[SPELL CARD]
Destroys 1 face-up Trap Card on the field.
MARIK! YOUR MIRROR FORCE IS USELESS!
ZABAM
THE ARCHFIEND OF GILFER'S FLAME BURST STRIKES MARIK'S MONSTER!
MMM
FEH...

Duel 182: Eyes on the Target!

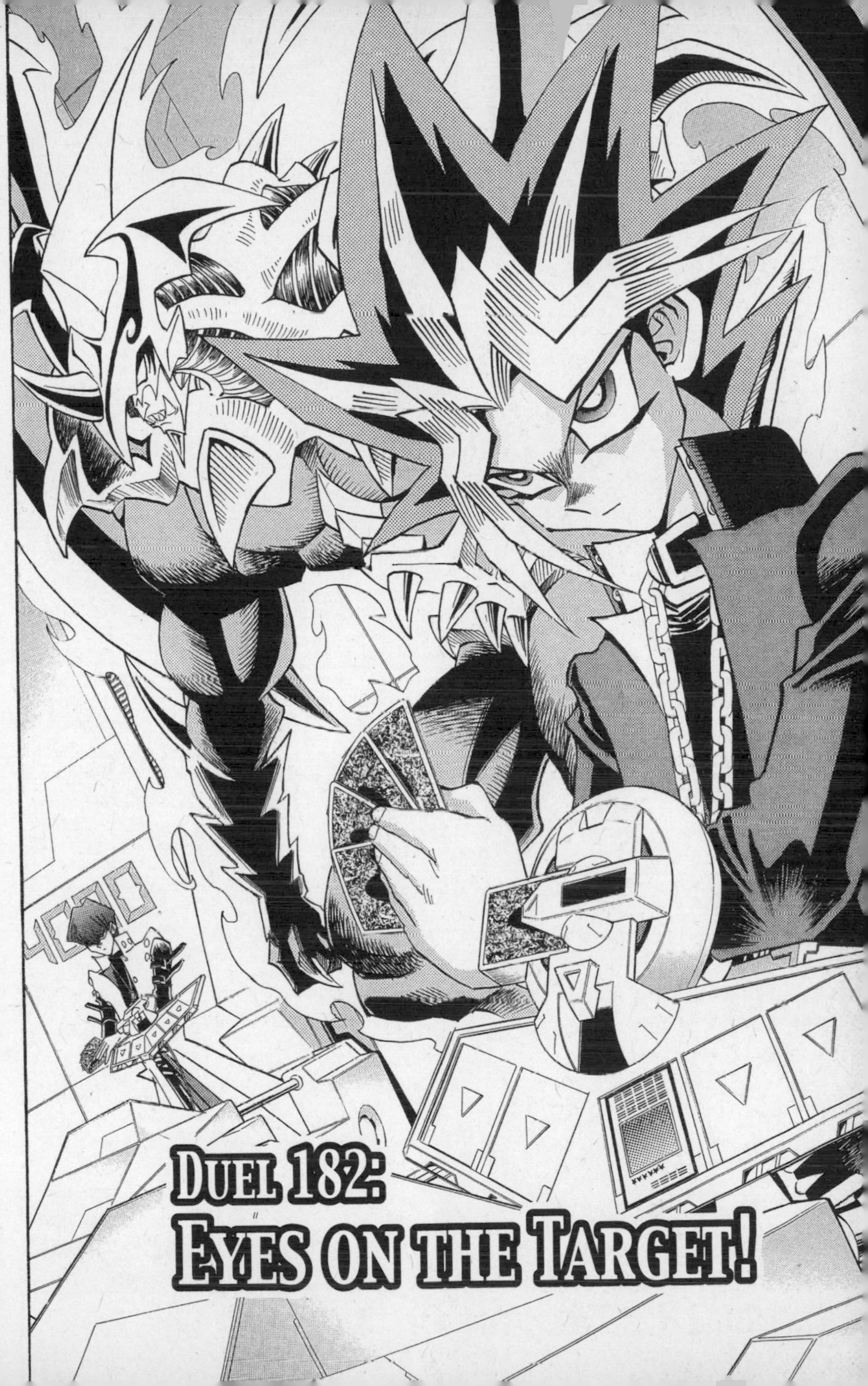
DUEL 182:
EYES ON THE TARGET!

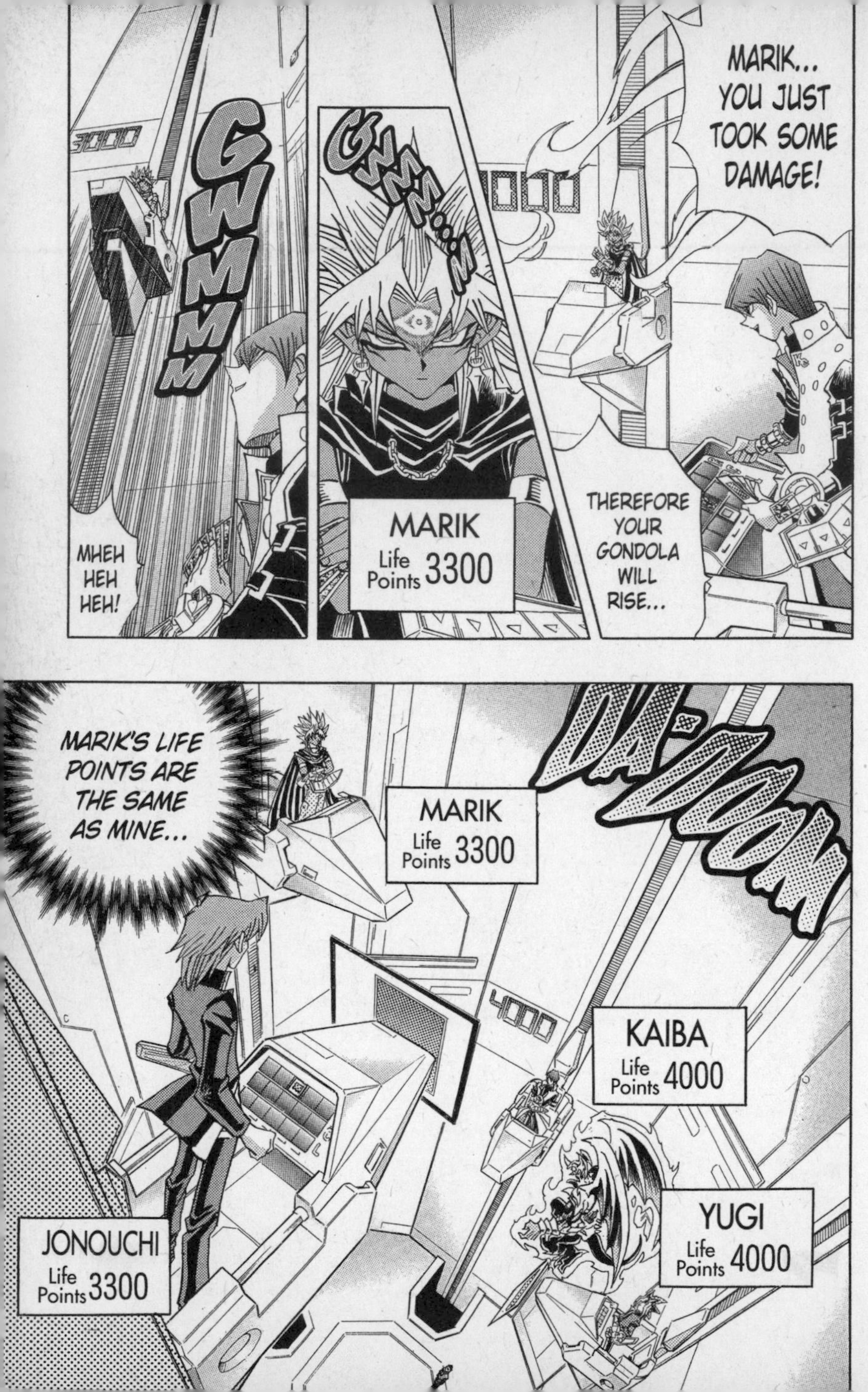
MARIK... YOU JUST TOOK SOME DAMAGE!
THEREFORE YOUR GONDOLA WILL RISE...
MARIK
Life Points 3300
GWMMM
MHEH HEH HEH!
DA-DOOM
MARIK'S LIFE POINTS ARE THE SAME AS MINE...
MARIK
Life Points 3300
KAIBA
Life Points 4000
YUGI
Life Points 4000
JONOUCHI
Life Points 3300

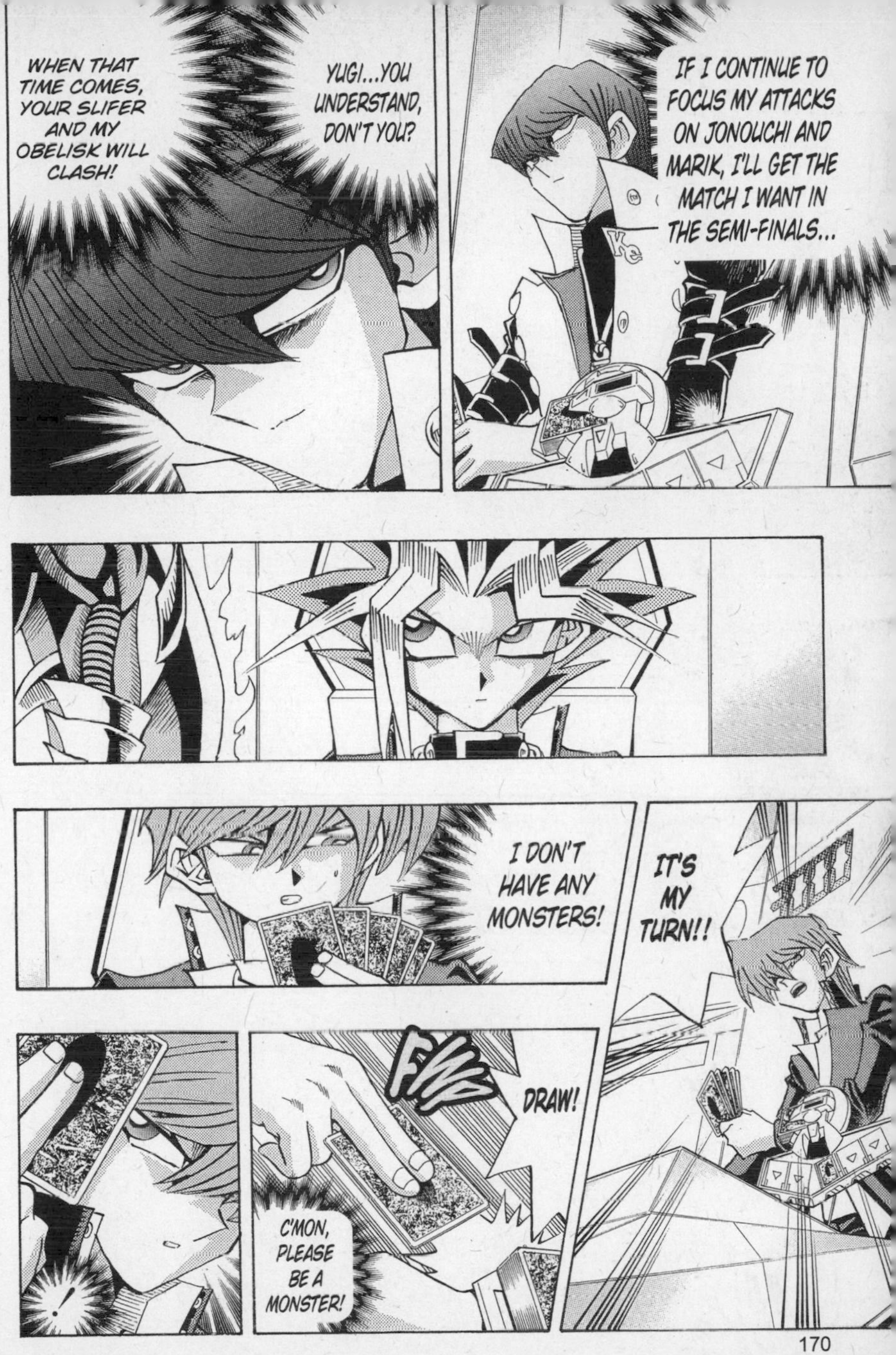
IF I CONTINUE TO FOCUS MY ATTACKS ON JONOUCHI AND MARIK, I'LL GET THE MATCH I WANT IN THE SEMI-FINALS...
YUGI...YOU UNDERSTAND, DON'T YOU?
WHEN THAT TIME COMES, YOUR SLIFER AND MY OBELISK WILL CLASH!
IT'S MY TURN!!
I DON'T HAVE ANY MONSTERS!
FWP
DRAW!
C'MON, PLEASE BE A MONSTER!
!

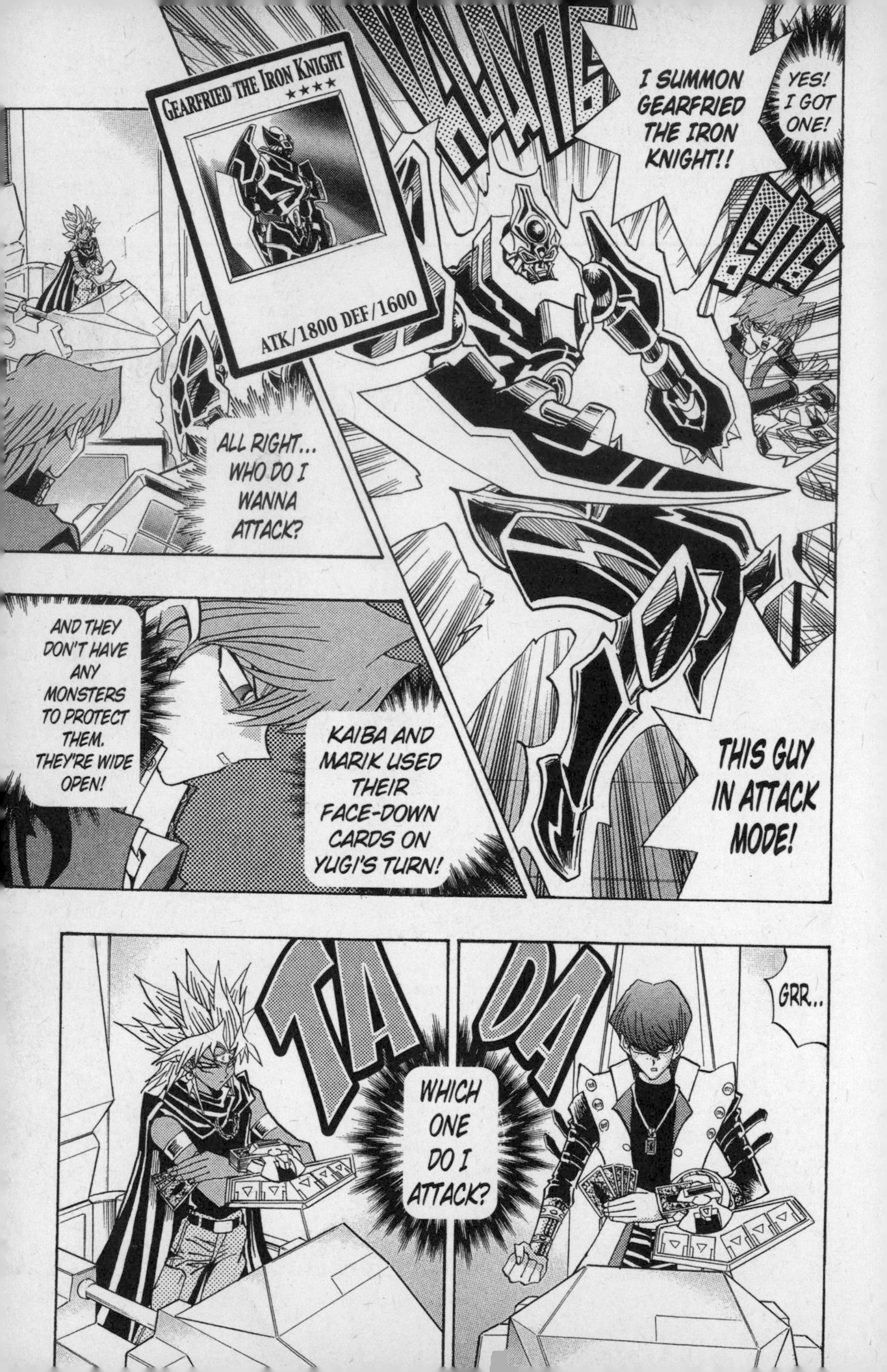
I SUMMON GEARFRIED THE IRON KNIGHT!!
YES! I GOT ONE!
GEARFRIED THE IRON KNIGHT
ATK/1800 DEF/1600
THIS GUY IN ATTACK MODE!
ALL RIGHT... WHO DO I WANNA ATTACK?
KAIBA AND MARIK USED THEIR FACE-DOWN CARDS ON YUGI'S TURN!
AND THEY DON'T HAVE ANY MONSTERS TO PROTECT THEM. THEY'RE WIDE OPEN!
GRR...
TA DA
WHICH ONE DO I ATTACK?

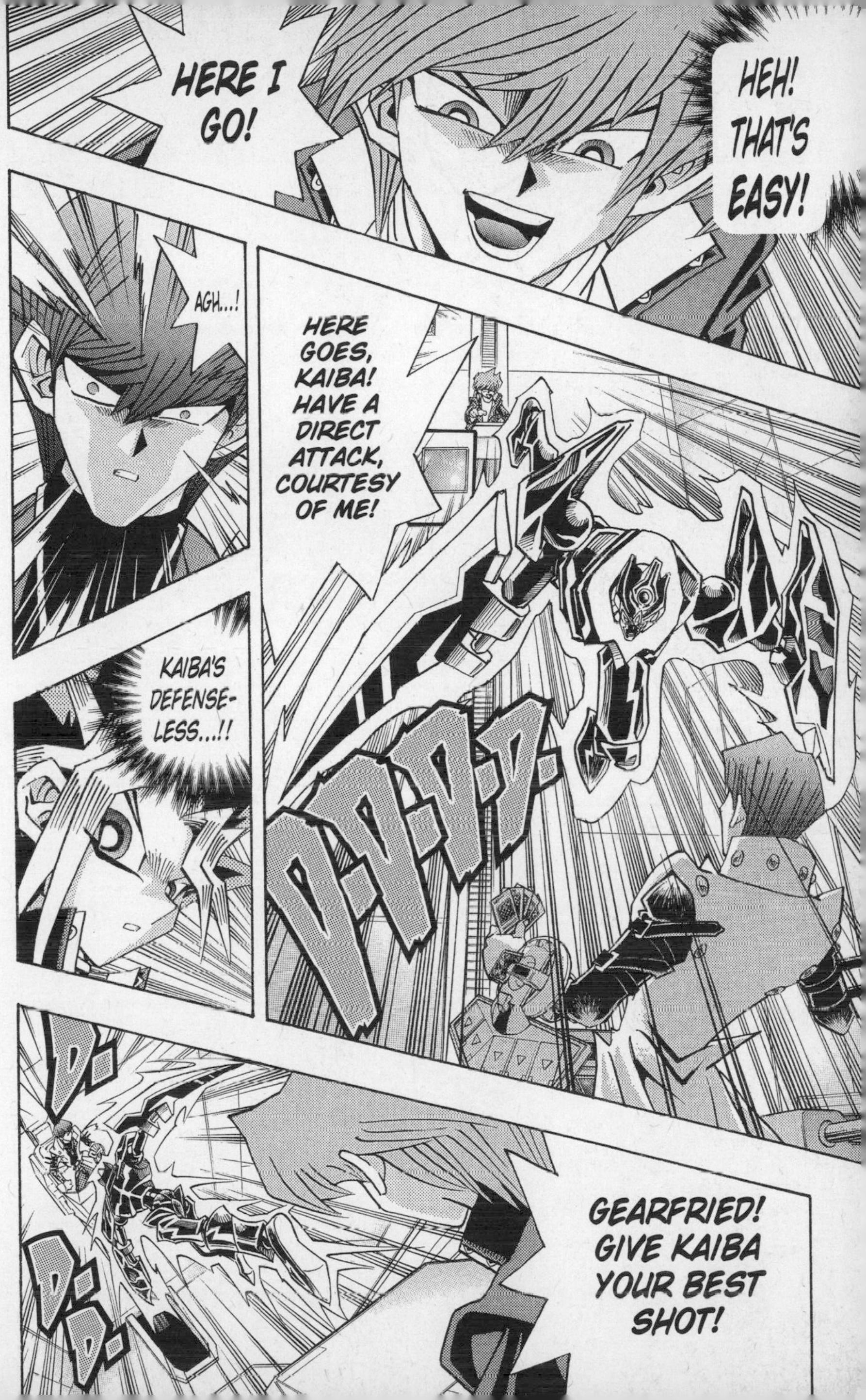
HEH! THAT'S EASY!
HERE I GO!
HERE GOES, KAIBA! HAVE A DIRECT ATTACK, COURTESY OF ME!
D-D-D-D.
AGH...!
KAIBA'S DEFENSE-LESS...!!
GEARFRIED! GIVE KAIBA YOUR BEST SHOT!
D.
D.
D.

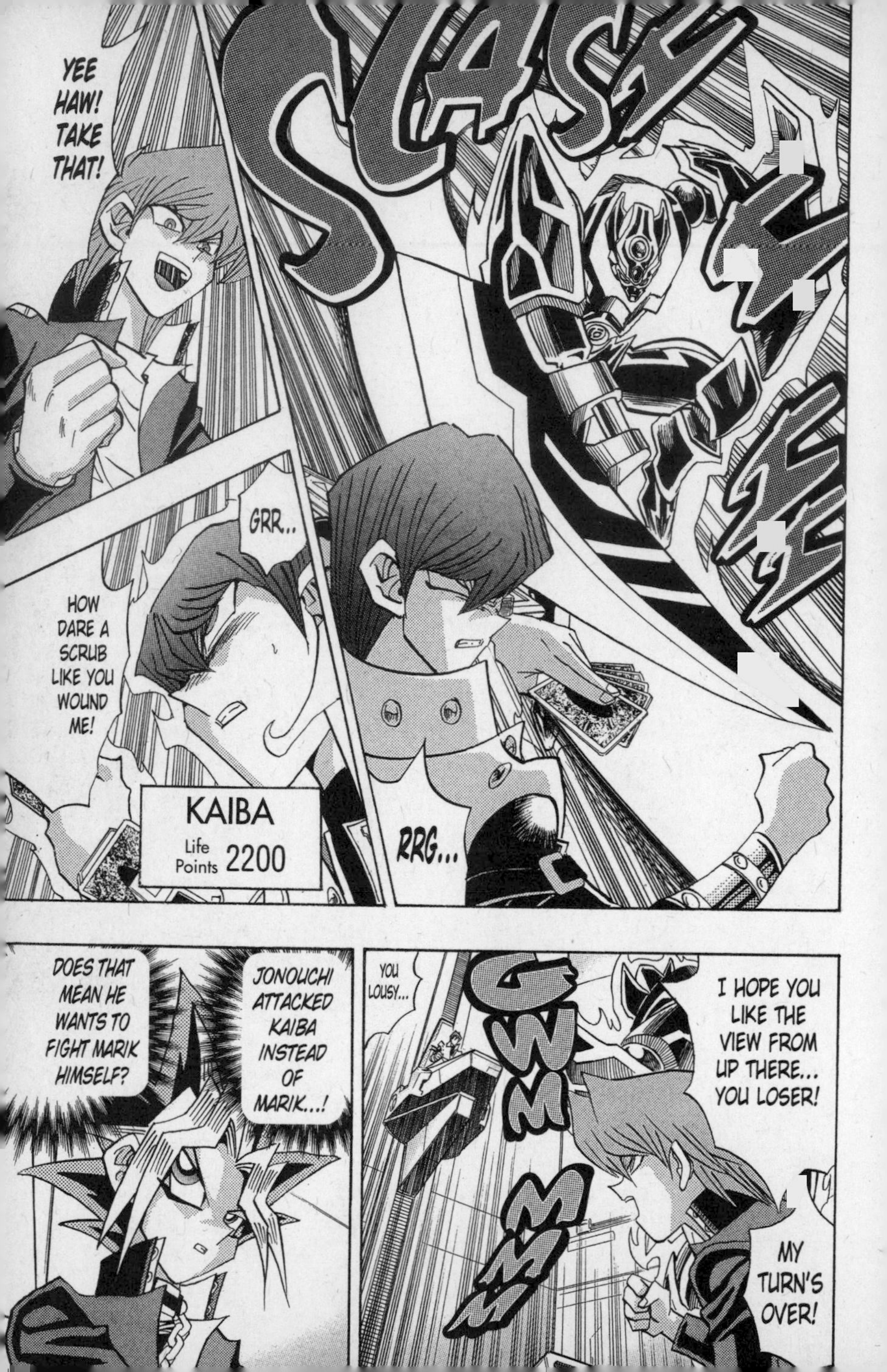
YEE HAW! TAKE THAT!
GRR...
HOW DARE A SCRUB LIKE YOU WOUND ME!
KAIBA
Life Points 2200
RRG...
I HOPE YOU LIKE THE VIEW FROM UP THERE... YOU LOSER!
YOU LOUSY...
MY TURN'S OVER!
JONOUCHI ATTACKED KAIBA INSTEAD OF MARIK...!
DOES THAT MEAN HE WANTS TO FIGHT MARIK HIMSELF?

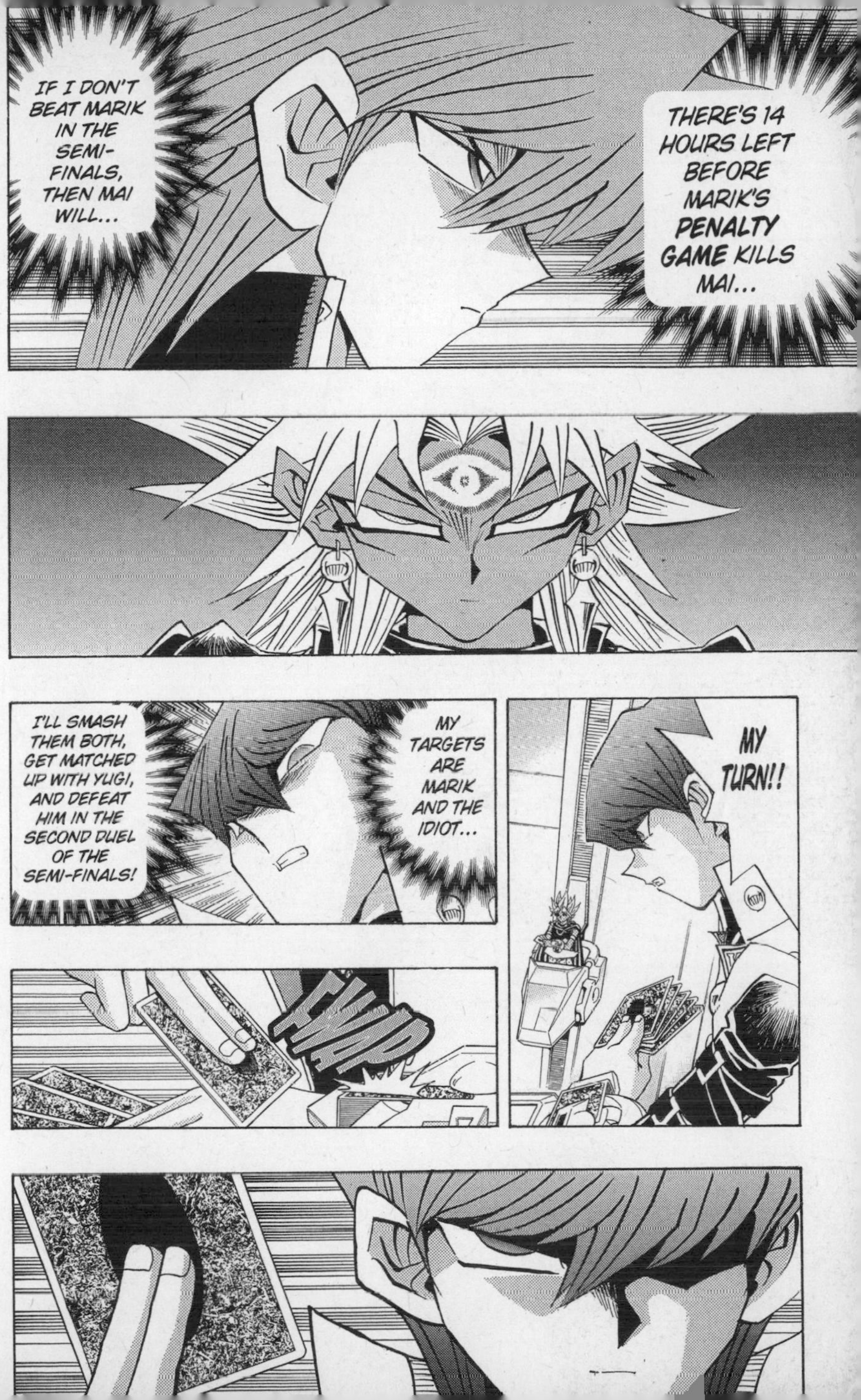
THERE'S 14 HOURS LEFT BEFORE MARIK'S PENALTY GAME KILLS MAI...
IF I DON'T BEAT MARIK IN THE SEMI-FINALS, THEN MAI WILL...
MY TURN!!
MY TARGETS ARE MARIK AND THE IDIOT...
I'LL SMASH THEM BOTH, GET MATCHED UP WITH YUGI, AND DEFEAT HIM IN THE SECOND DUEL OF THE SEMI-FINALS!

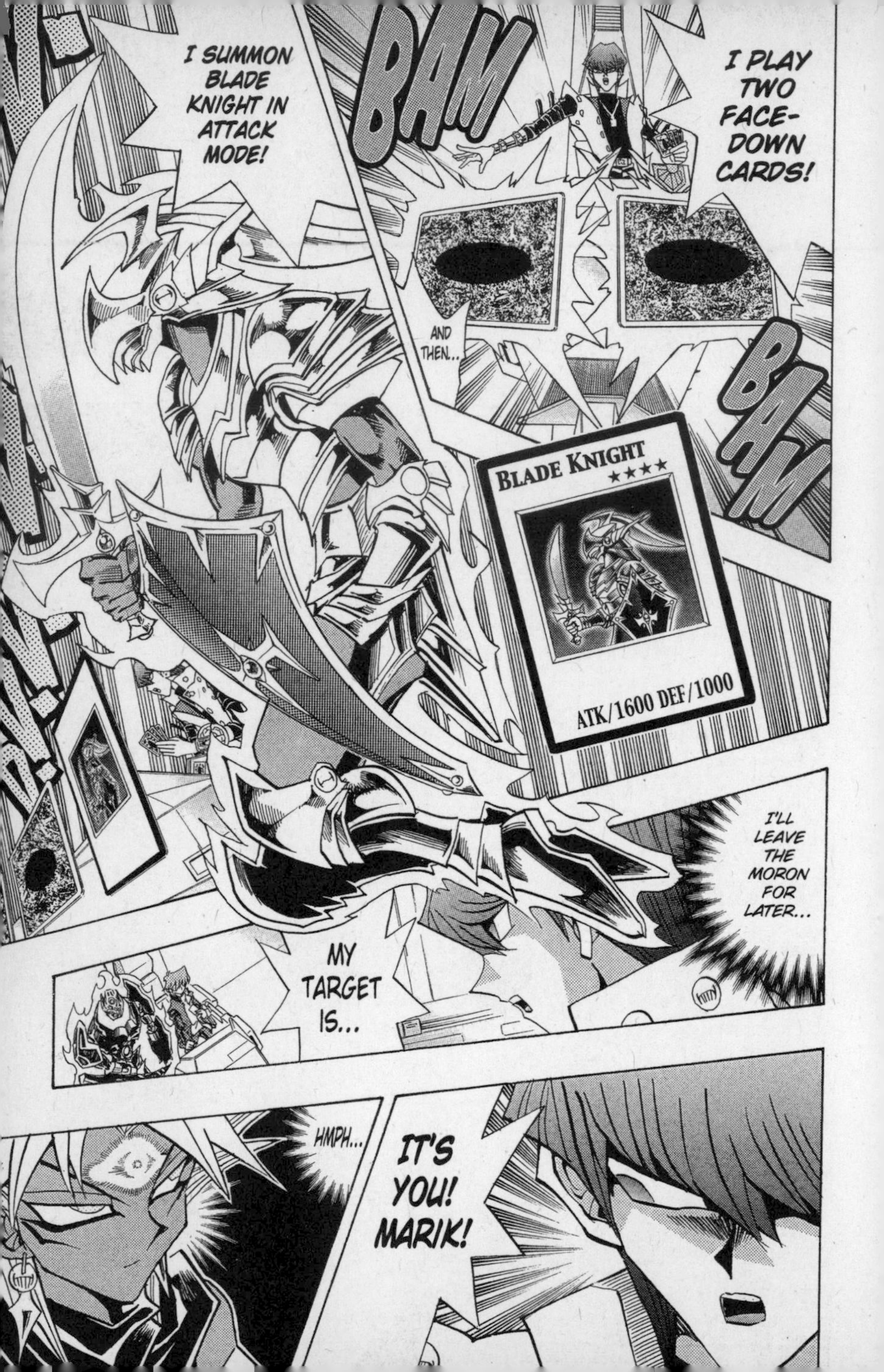
BAM
I PLAY TWO FACE-DOWN CARDS!
AND THEN...
BAM
BLADE KNIGHT ★★★★
ATK/1600 DEF/1000
I SUMMON BLADE KNIGHT IN ATTACK MODE!
I'LL LEAVE THE MORON FOR LATER...
MY TARGET IS...
IT'S YOU! MARIK!
HMPH...

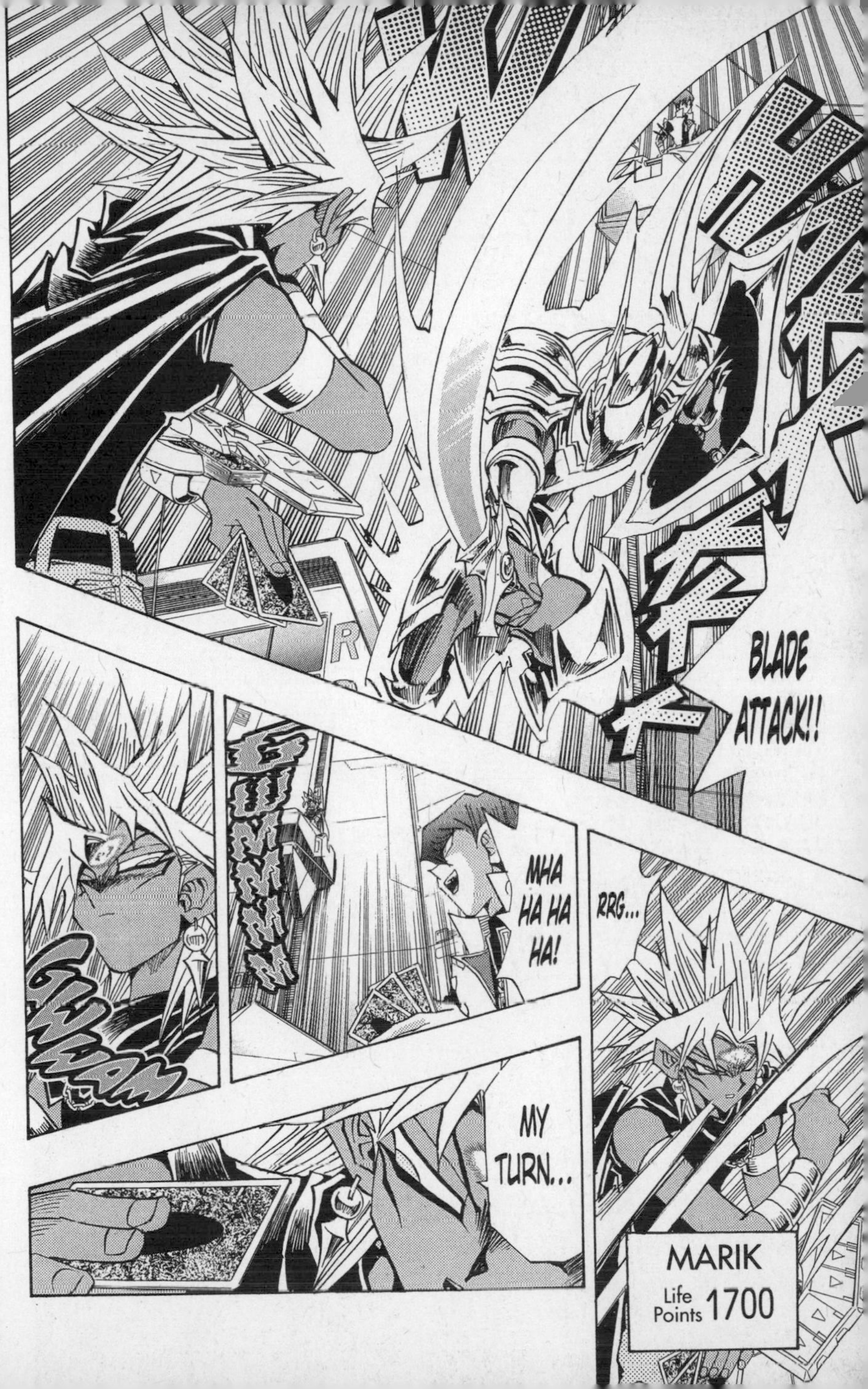
BLADE ATTACK!!
RRG...
MARIK
Life Points 1700
MHA HA HA HA!
MY TURN...

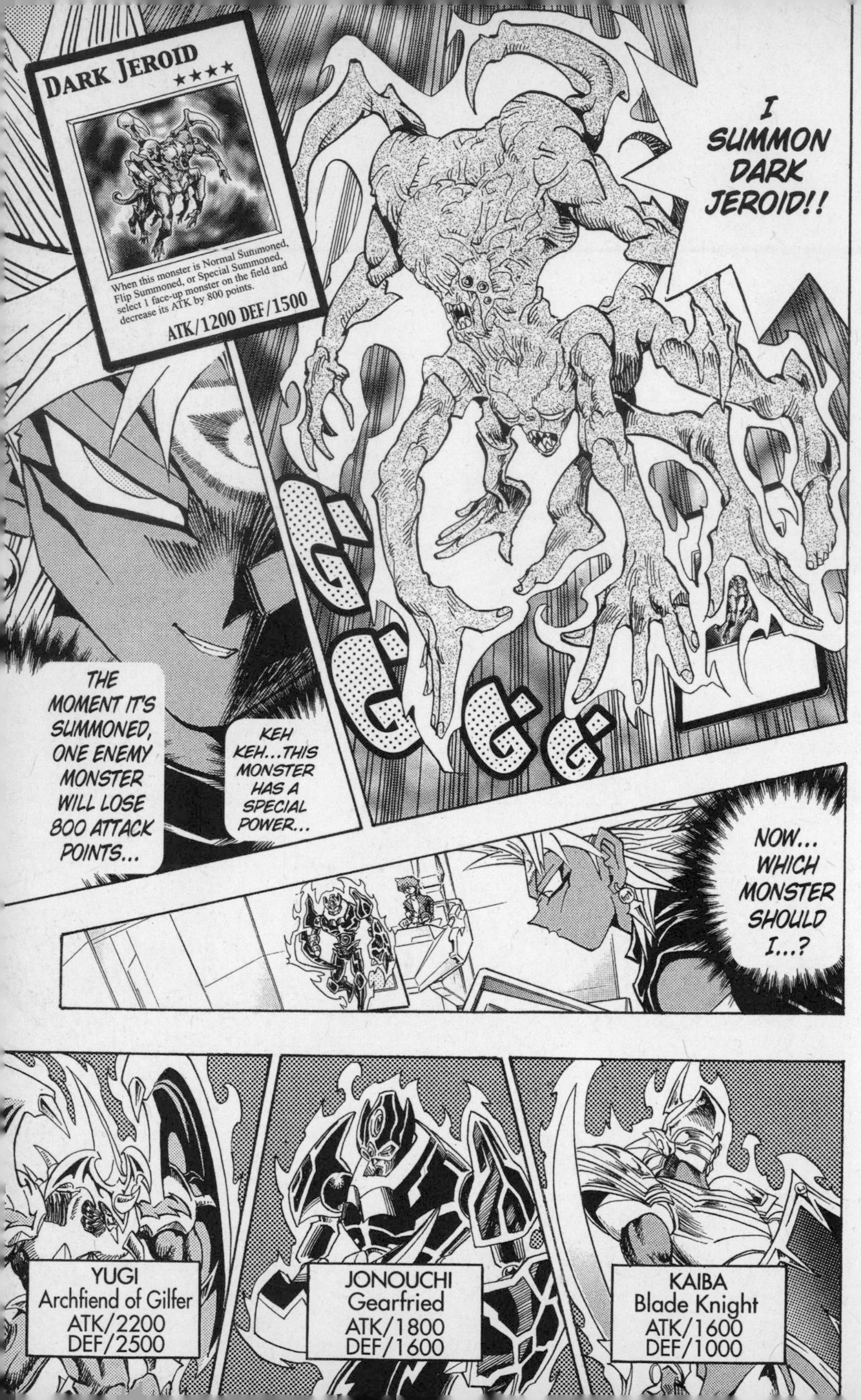
I SUMMON DARK JEROID!!
DARK JEROID ★★★★
When this monster is Normal Summoned, Flip Summoned, or Special Summoned, select 1 face-up monster on the field and decrease its ATK by 800 points.
ATK/1200 DEF/1500
KEH KEH...THIS MONSTER HAS A SPECIAL POWER...
THE MOMENT IT'S SUMMONED, ONE ENEMY MONSTER WILL LOSE 800 ATTACK POINTS...
NOW... WHICH MONSTER SHOULD I...?
KAIBA
Blade Knight
ATK/1600
DEF/1000
JONOUCHI
Gearfried
ATK/1800
DEF/1600
YUGI
Archfiend of Gilfer
ATK/2200
DEF/2500

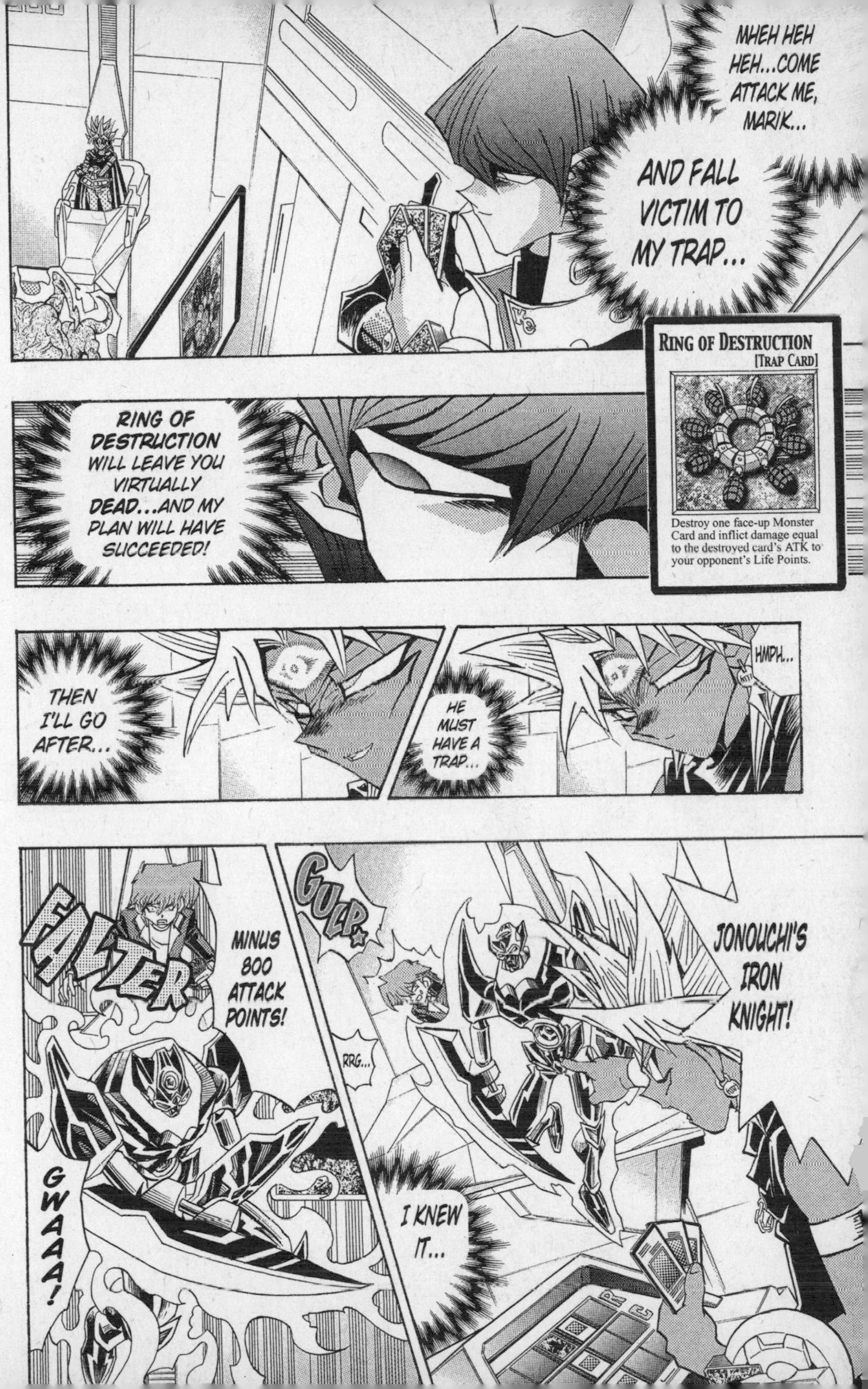
MHEH HEH HEH...COME ATTACK ME, MARIK...
AND FALL VICTIM TO MY TRAP...
RING OF DESTRUCTION
[TRAP CARD]
Destroy one face-up Monster Card and inflict damage equal to the destroyed card's ATK to your opponent's Life Points.
RING OF DESTRUCTION WILL LEAVE YOU VIRTUALLY DEAD...AND MY PLAN WILL HAVE SUCCEEDED!
HMPH...
HE MUST HAVE A TRAP...
THEN I'LL GO AFTER...
JONOUCHI'S IRON KNIGHT!
GULP
RRG...
I KNEW IT...
FALTER
MINUS 800 ATTACK POINTS!
GWAAAA!

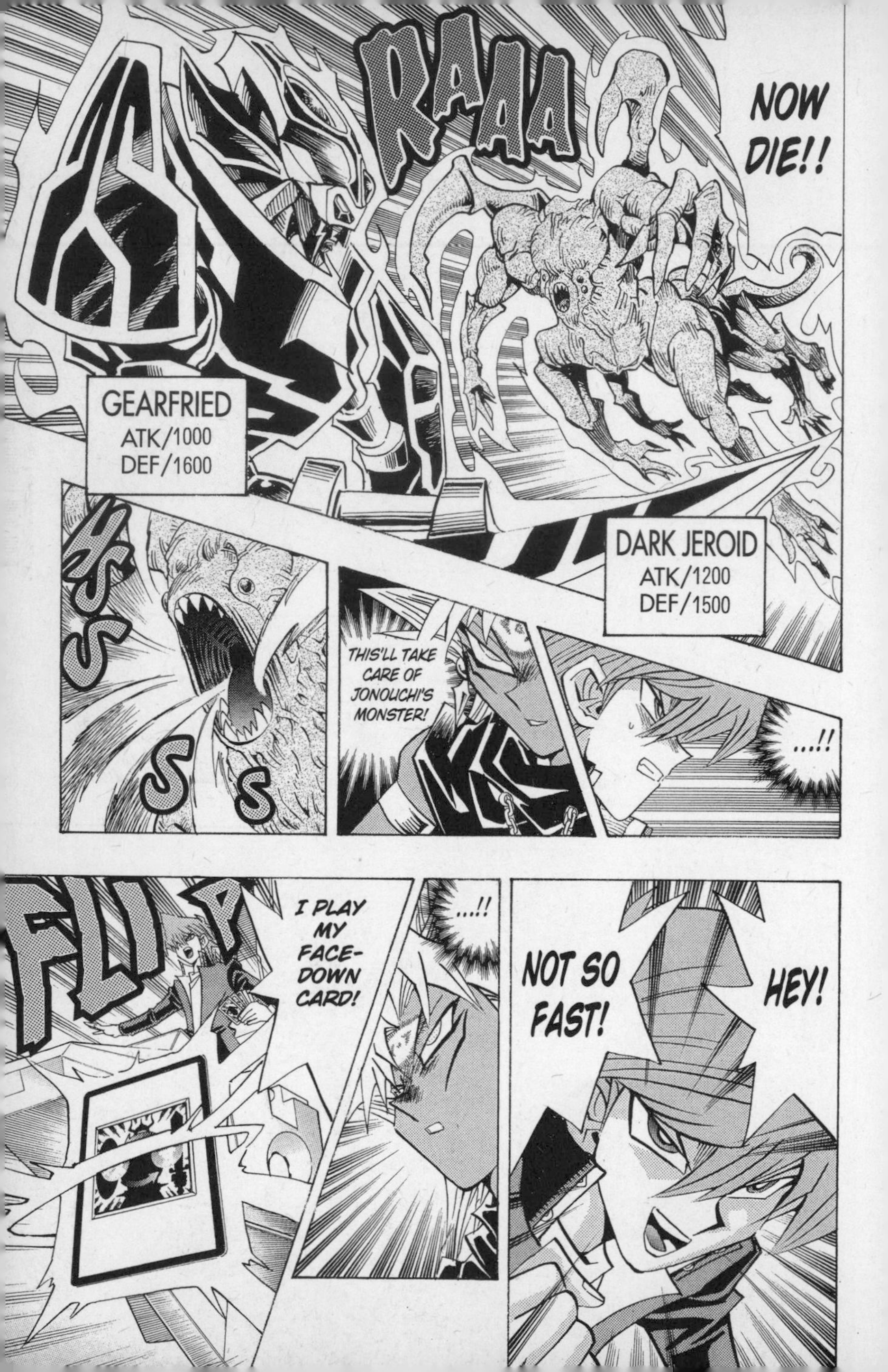
NOW DIE!!
RAAA
GEARFRIED ATK/1000 DEF/1600
DARK JEROID ATK/1200 DEF/1500
...!!
THIS'LL TAKE CARE OF JONOUCHI'S MONSTER!
HSSSS
HEY!
NOT SO FAST!
...!!
I PLAY MY FACE-DOWN CARD!
FLIP

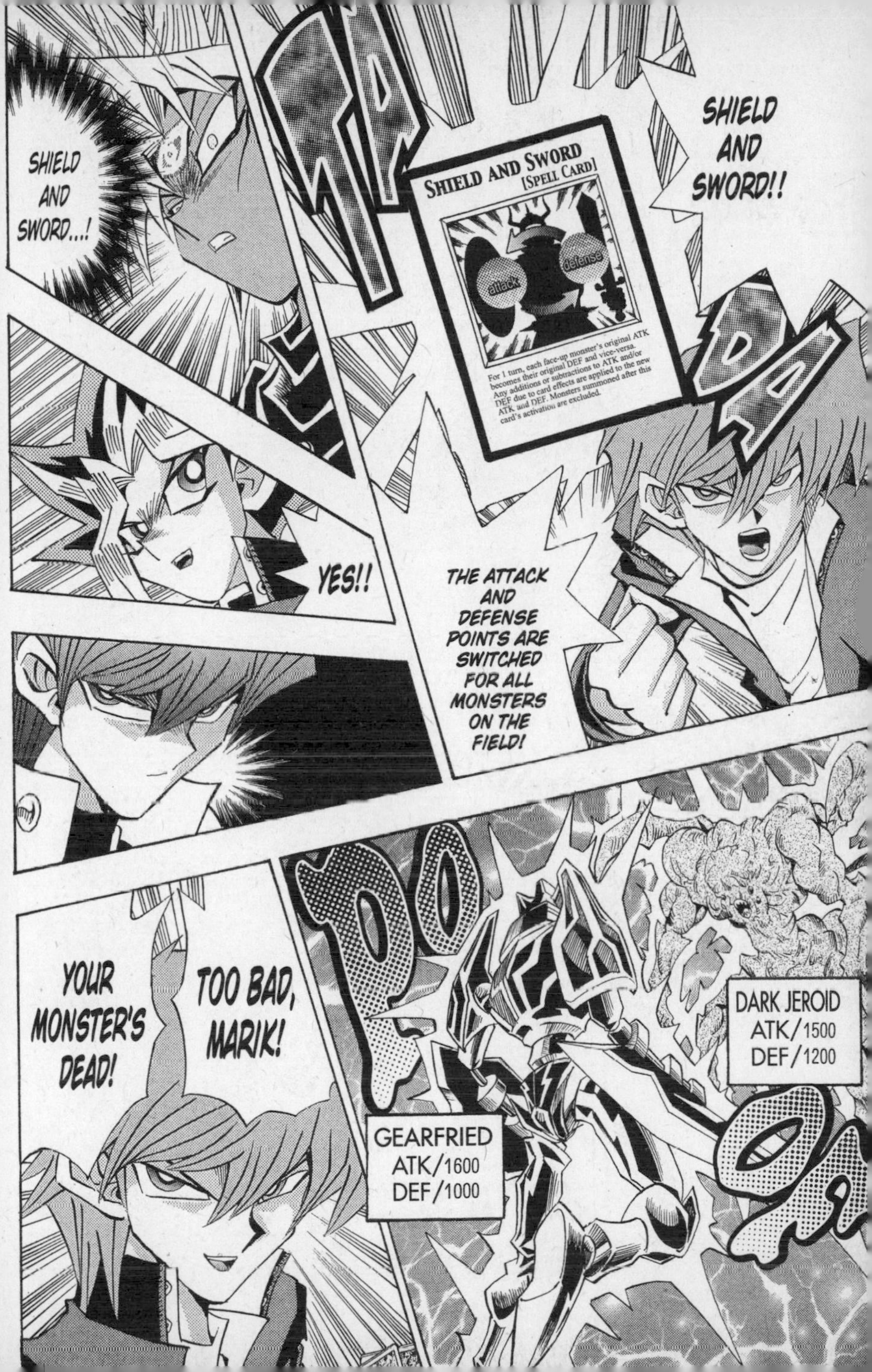
SHIELD AND SWORD!!
SHIELD AND SWORD
[SPELL CARD]
attack
defense
For 1 turn, each face-up monster's original ATK becomes their original DEF and vice-versa. Any additions or subtractions to ATK and/or DEF due to card effects are applied to the new ATK and DEF. Monsters summoned after this card's activation are excluded.
THE ATTACK AND DEFENSE POINTS ARE SWITCHED FOR ALL MONSTERS ON THE FIELD!
SHIELD AND SWORD...!
YES!!
DARK JEROID
ATK/1500
DEF/1200
GEARFRIED
ATK/1600
DEF/1000
TOO BAD, MARIK!
YOUR MONSTER'S DEAD!

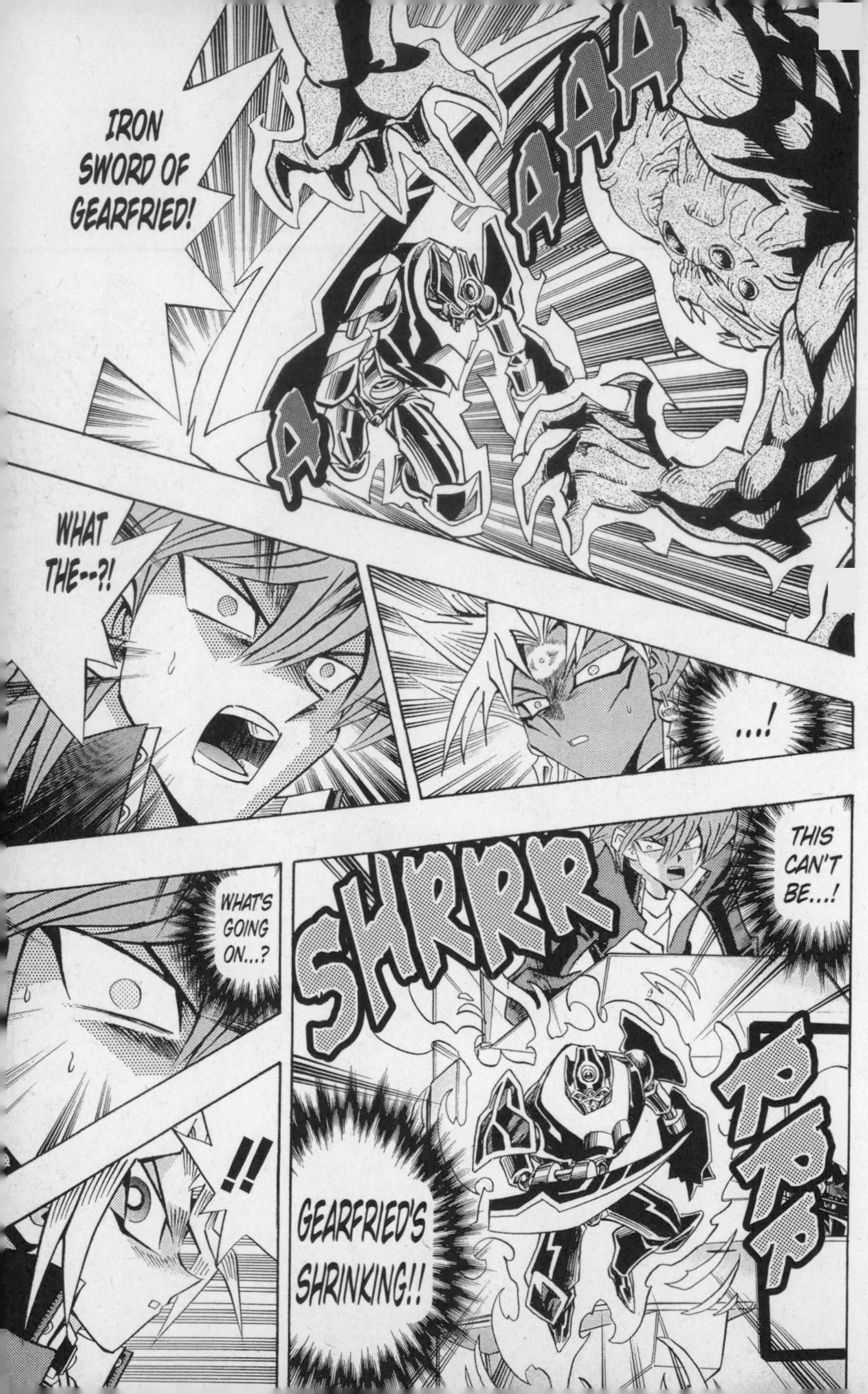
IRON SWORD OF GEARFRIED!
...!
WHAT THE--?!
THIS CAN'T BE...!
SHRRR
GEARFRIED'S SHRINKING!!
WHAT'S GOING ON...?
!!

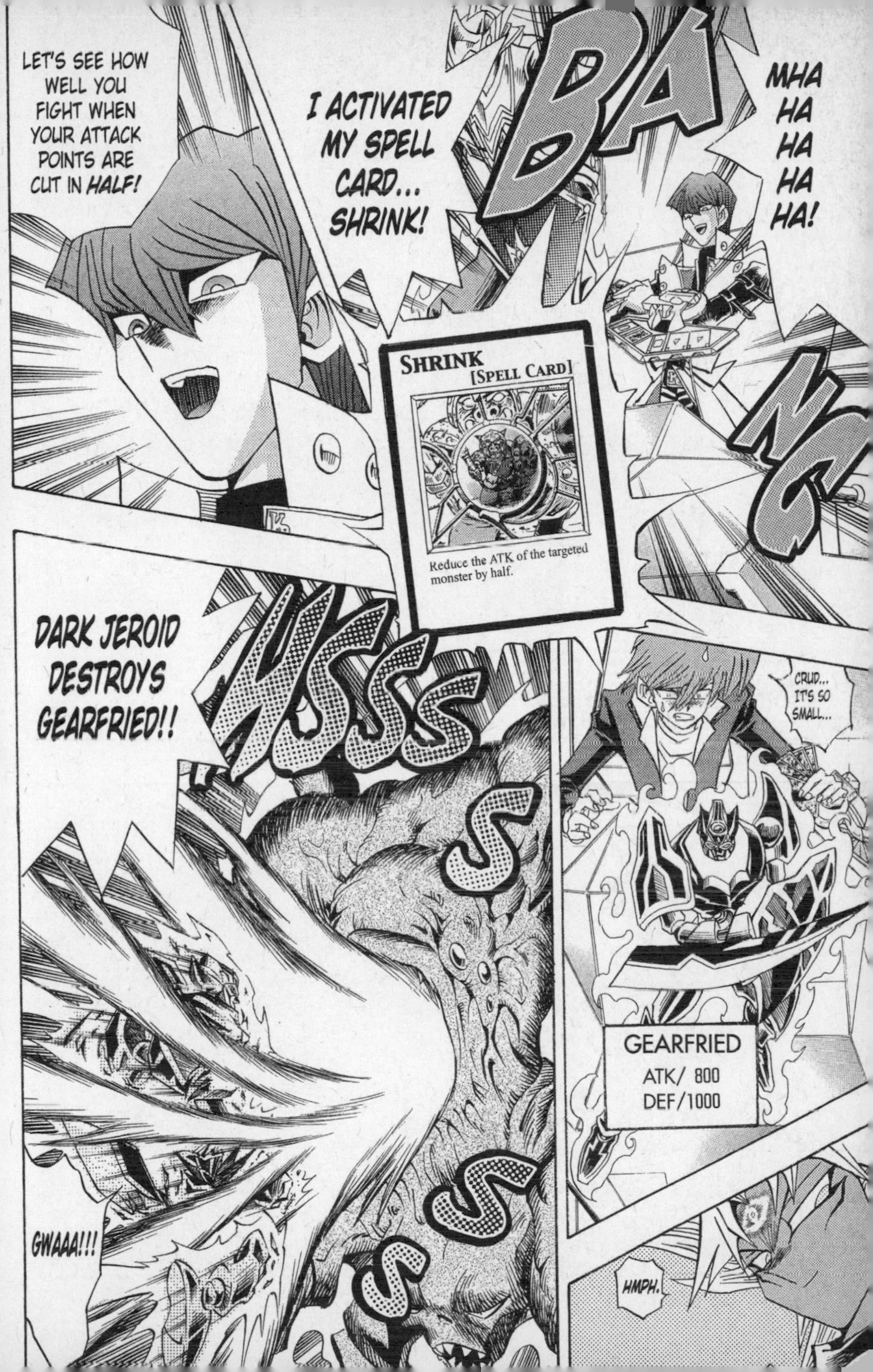
MHA HA HA HA HA!
BANG
I ACTIVATED MY SPELL CARD... SHRINK!
LET'S SEE HOW WELL YOU FIGHT WHEN YOUR ATTACK POINTS ARE CUT IN *HALF!*
SHRINK
[SPELL CARD]
Reduce the ATK of the targeted monster by half.
CRUD... IT'S SO SMALL...
GEARFRIED
ATK/ 800
DEF/1000
HMPH.
DARK JEROID DESTROYS GEARFRIED!!
WHSSS
GWAAA!!!

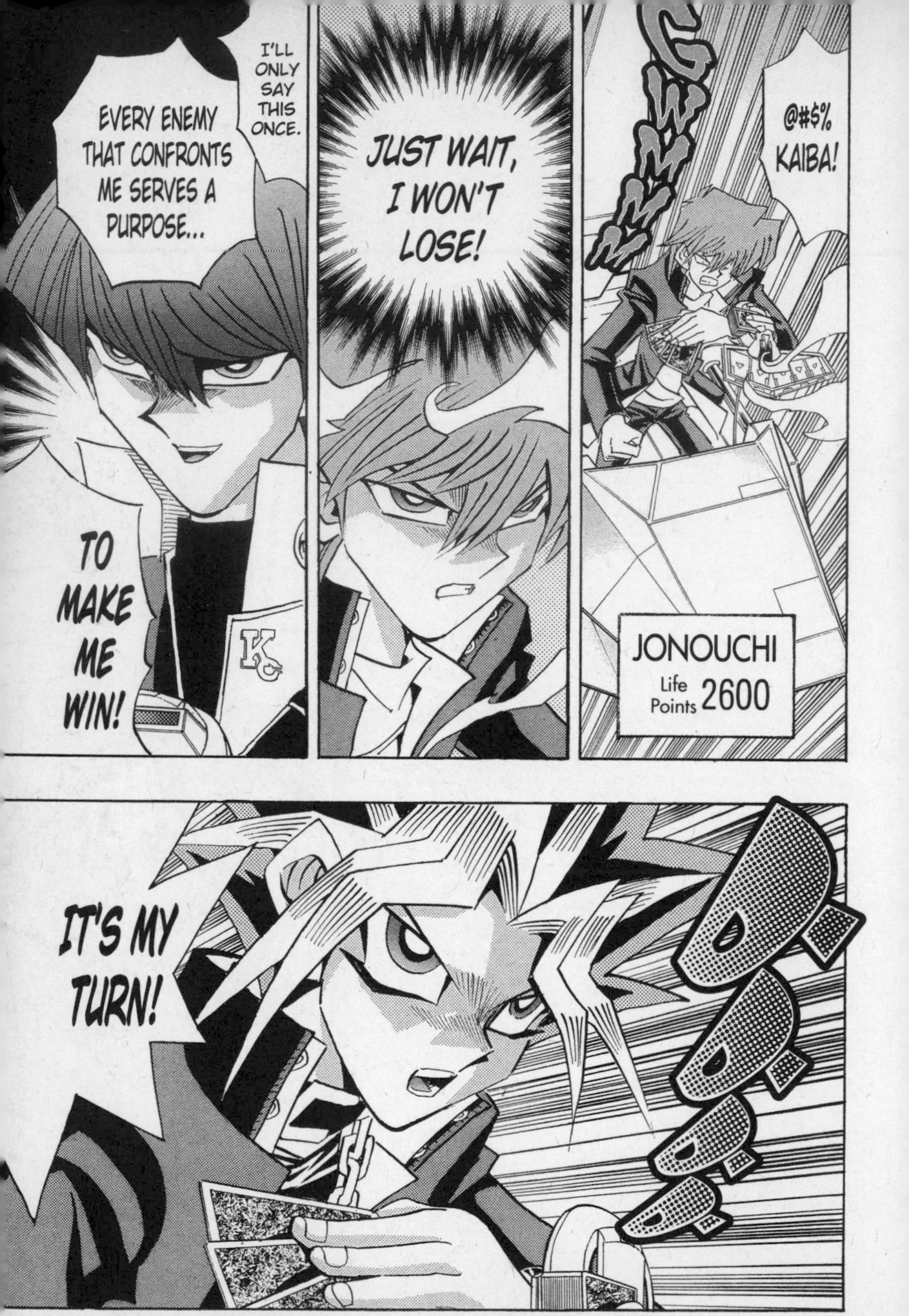
@#$% KAIBA!
JONOUCHI Life Points 2600
JUST WAIT, I WON'T LOSE!
I'LL ONLY SAY THIS ONCE.
EVERY ENEMY THAT CONFRONTS ME SERVES A PURPOSE...
TO MAKE ME WIN!
IT'S MY TURN!

TO BE CONTINUED IN *YU-GI-OH!: DUELIST* VOL. 21!

MASTER OF THE CARDS

The "Duel Monsters" card game first appeared in volume two of the original **Yu-Gi-Oh!** graphic novel series, but it's in **Yu-Gi-Oh!: Duelist** (originally printed in Japan as volumes 8-31 of **Yu-Gi-Oh!**) that it gets really important. As many fans know, some of the card names are different between the English and Japanese versions. In case you play the game, or you're interested in playing, here's a rundown of some of the cards in this graphic novel. Some cards only appear in the **Yu-Gi-Oh!** video games, not in the actual trading card game.

FIRST APPEARANCE IN THIS VOLUME	JAPANESE CARD NAME	ENGLISH CARD NAME
p.38	*Senritsu no Earthbound*	Fearful Earthbound (NOTE: Not a real game card)
p.38	*Goblin Zombie*	Goblin Zombie (NOTE: Not a real game card)
p.39	*Drillago*	Drillago
p.39	*Wana Hazushi* (Trap Jammer)	Trap Jammer
p.50	*Ouija Ban* (Ouija Board)	Destiny Board
p.50	*Dark Necrofear*	Dark Necrofear
p.53	*Gernia*	Gelnia (NOTE: Not a real game card)
p.54	*Ten yori no Hôsatsu* (Treasure from Heaven)	Card of Sanctity

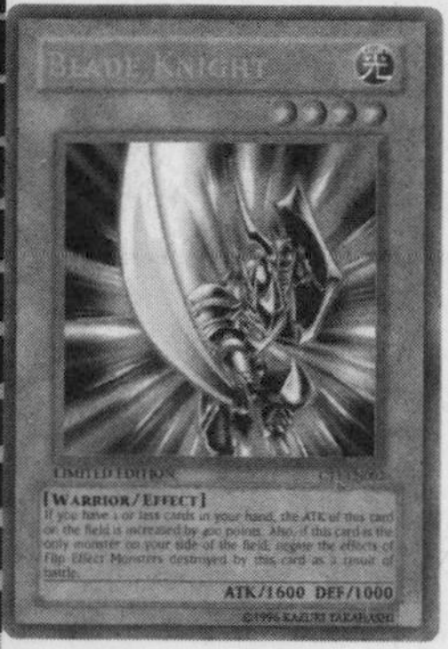
BLADE KNIGHT
LIMITED EDITION
[WARRIOR/EFFECT]
ATK/1600 DEF/1000
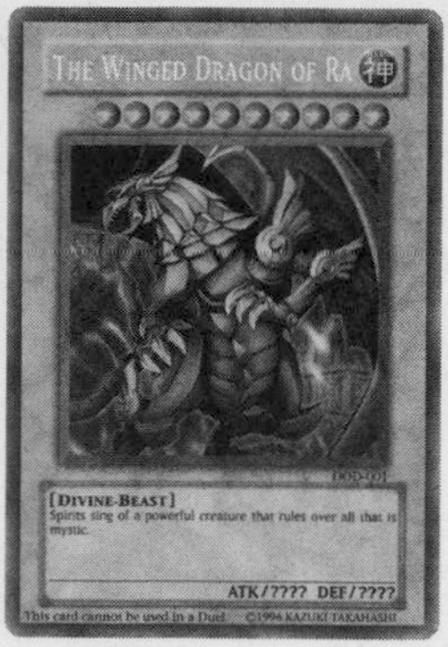
THE WINGED DRAGON OF RA
神
[DIVINE-BEAST]
Spirits sing of a powerful creature that rules over all that is mystic.
ATK/???? DEF/????
This card cannot be used in a Duel.
©1996 KAZUKI TAKAHASHI
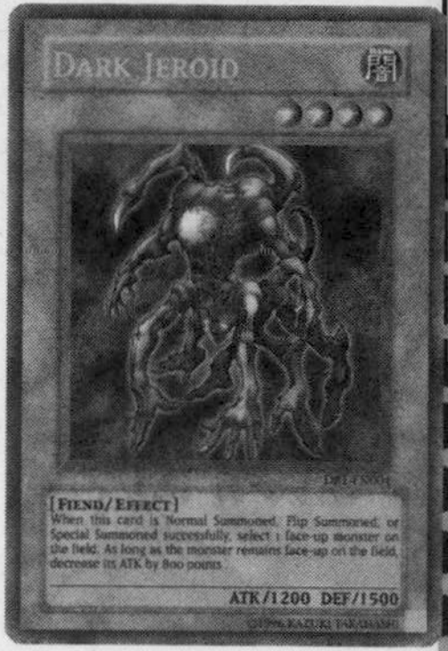
DARK JEROID
闇
[FIEND/EFFECT]
ATK/1200 DEF/1500

FIRST APPEARANCE IN THIS VOLUME	JAPANESE CARD NAME	ENGLISH CARD NAME
p.55	*Yami no Shimeisha* (Dark Designator)	Dark Designator
p.56	*Ra no Yokushinryû* (Ra the Winged God Dragon) (NOTE: The kanji for "sun god" is written beside the kanji for "Ra.")	The Sun Dragon Ra (NOTE: Called "The Winged Dragon of Ra" in the English anime and card game.)
p.56	*Shinaba Morotomo* (If We Die, We Die Together)	Multiple Destruction
p.60	*Shiryô Ayatsurishi—Puppet Master* (Puppeteer of Dead Spirits)	Puppet Master, Controller of the Dead (NOTE: Not a real game card)
p.61	*Kubi nashi Kishi* (Headless Knight)	Headless Knight
p.71	*Obelisk no Kyoshinhei* (Obelisk the Giant God Soldier)	The God of the Obelisk (NOTE: Called "Obelisk the Tormentor" in the English anime and card game.)
p.71	*Osiris no Tenkûryû* (Osiris the Heaven Dragon)	Slifer the Sky Dragon

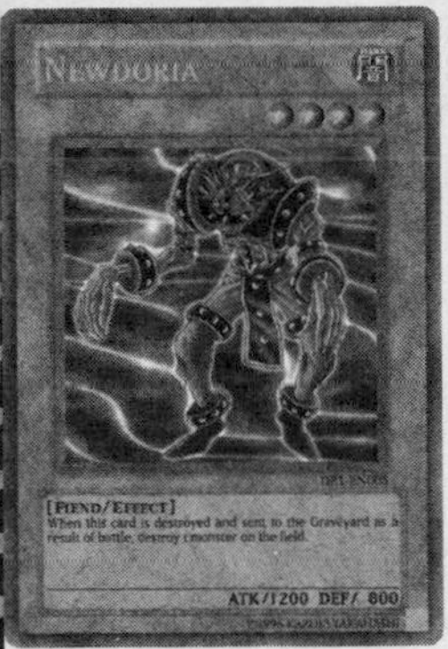
NEWDORIA
[FIEND/EFFECT]
ATK/1200 DEF/ 800

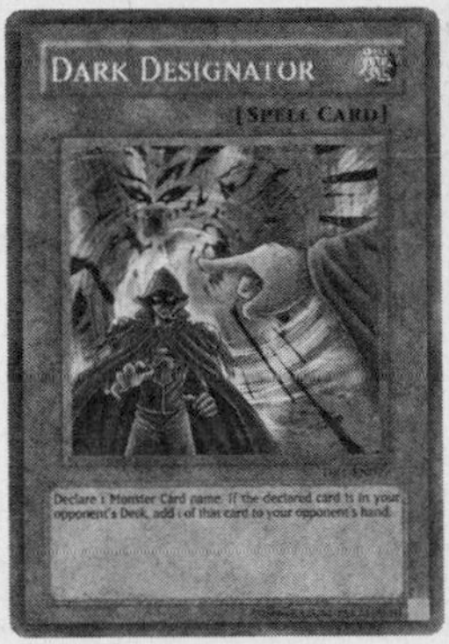
DARK DESIGNATOR
[SPELL CARD]

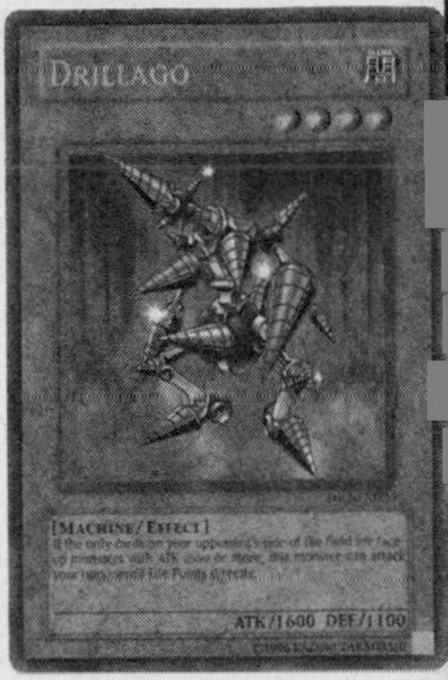
DRILLAGO
[MACHINE/EFFECT]
ATK/1600 DEF/1100

FIRST APPEARANCE IN THIS VOLUME	JAPANESE CARD NAME	ENGLISH CARD NAME
p.71	*Sei naru Barrier Mirror Force* (Holy Barrier Mirror Force)	Mirror Force
p.74	*Shisha Sosei* (Resurrection of the Dead)	Monster Reborn
p.91	*Blue-Eyes White Dragon*	Blue-Eyes White Dragon
p.136	*Kelbek*	Kelbek
p.136	*Gremlin*	Feral Imp
p.136	*Kamen Majû Des Guardius* (Masked Magical/Demon Beast Des Guardius)	Masked Beast of Guardius (NOTE: Not a real game card)
p.136	*Landstar no Kenshi* (Landstar Swordsman)	Swordsman of Landstar
p.140	*Blood Vorse*	Vorse Raider
p.141	*Newdoria*	Newdoria
p.141	*Big Shield Guardna*	Big Shield Guardna
p.154	*Lord Poison*	Lord Poison

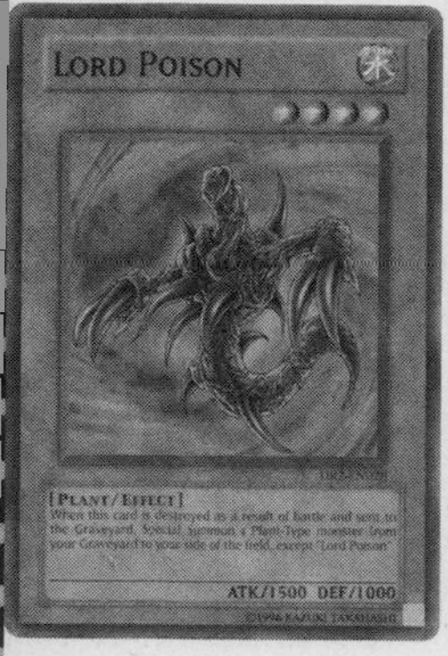
LORD POISON
[PLANT/EFFECT]
ATK/1500 DEF/1000
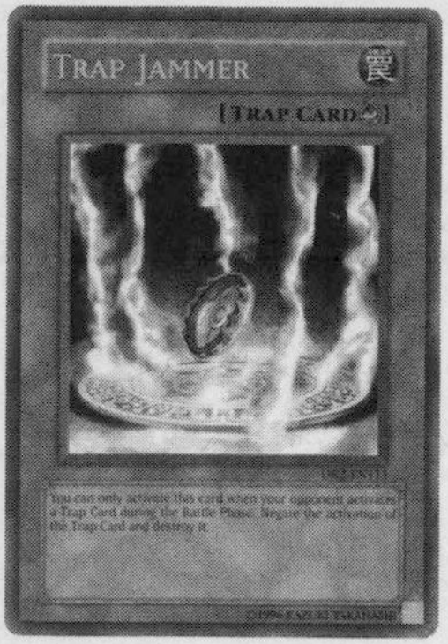
TRAP JAMMER
[TRAP CARD]
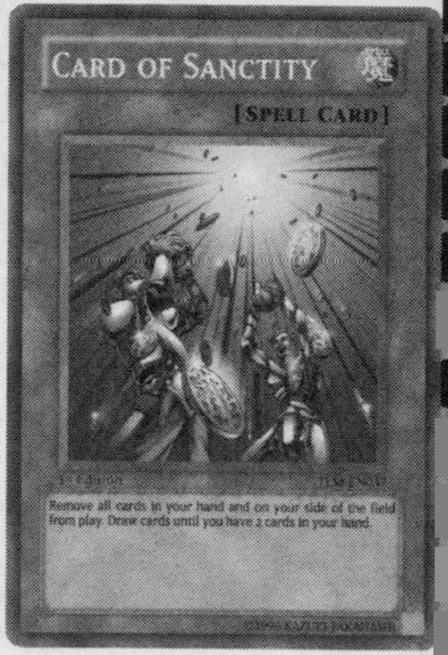
CARD OF SANCTITY
[SPELL CARD]

FIRST APPEARANCE IN THIS VOLUME	JAPANESE CARD NAME	ENGLISH CARD NAME
p.157	*Tsûkon no Jujutsu* (Spell/Technique of Pain)	Spell of Pain (NOTE: Not a real game card)
p.160	*Ankokumazoku Gilfer Demon* (Darkness/Black Magic/Demon Clan Gilfer Demon)	Archfiend of Gilfer
p.162	*Kôgeki Yûdô Armor* (Attack Guidance Armor)	Attack Guidance Armor (NOTE: Not a real game card)
p.171	*Tetsu no Kishi Gear Fried* (Iron Knight Gear Fried)	Gearfried the Iron Knight
p.175	*Blade Knight*	Blade Knight
p.177	*Dark Jeroid*	Dark Jeroid
p.178	*Hakairin* (Destruction Ring/Circle)	Ring of Destruction
p.179	*Migite ni Tate wo Hidarite ni Ken* (Shield in the Left Hand, Sword in the Right Hand)	Shield and Sword
p. 182	*Shûshuku* (Shrinking)	Shrink

IN THE NEXT VOLUME...

The order of the finals is determined, and Jonouchi's opponent is Marik! On the tower of Alcatraz, Jonouchi fights the evil Egyptian duelist whose grudge has smoldered for three thousand years. If he wins, he'll get his dream of facing Yugi in the finals. But if he loses, he'll get a one-way ticket to the grave!

COMING JUNE 2007!

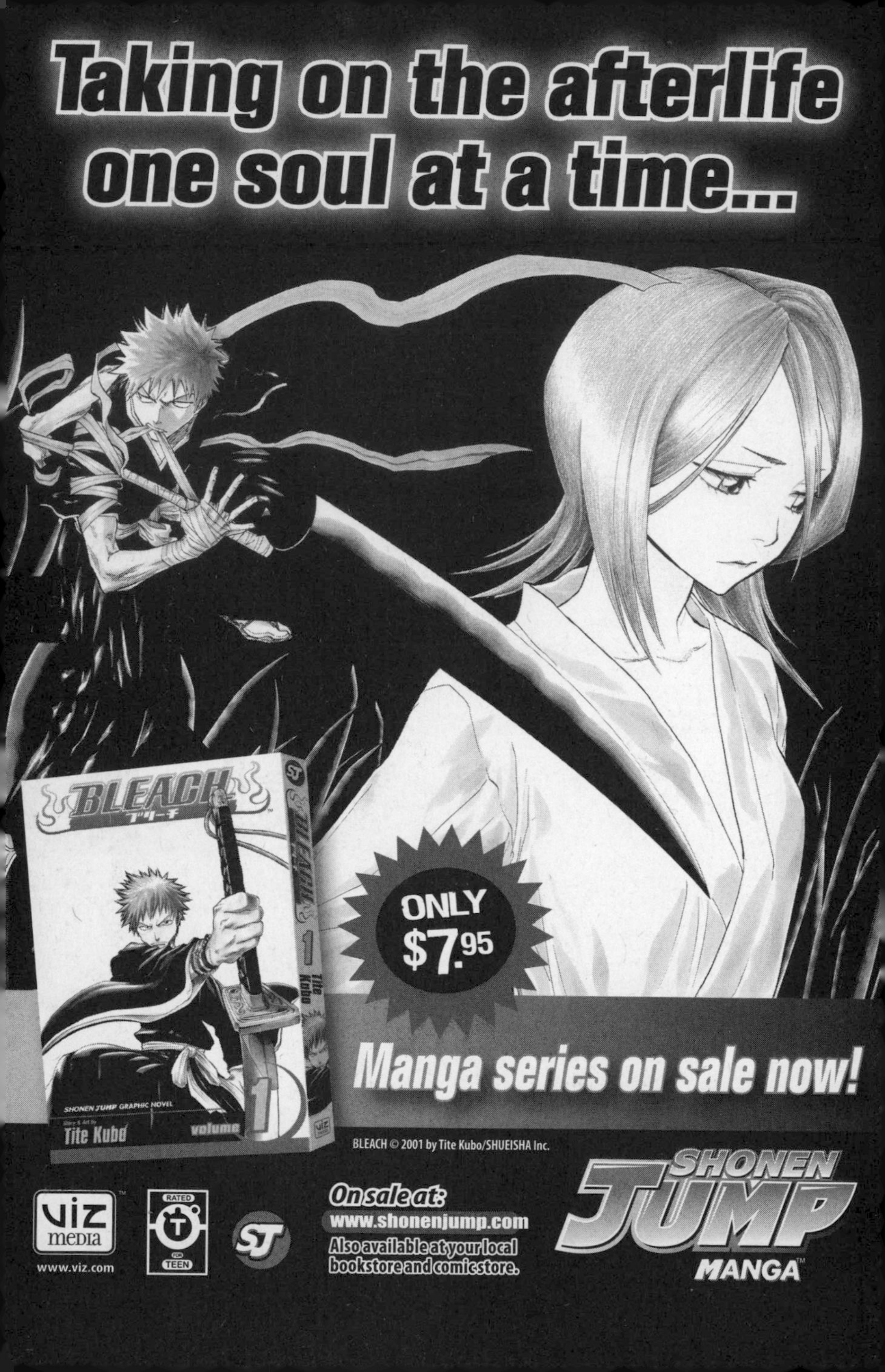

Taking on the afterlife one soul at a time...
BLEACH
ブリーチ
SHONEN JUMP GRAPHIC NOVEL
Tite Kubo
volume 1
ONLY $7.95
Manga series on sale now!
BLEACH © 2001 by Tite Kubo/SHUEISHA Inc.
viz media
www.viz.com
RATED T FOR TEEN
SJ
On sale at:
www.shonenjump.com
Also available at your local bookstore and comic store.
SHONEN JUMP MANGA

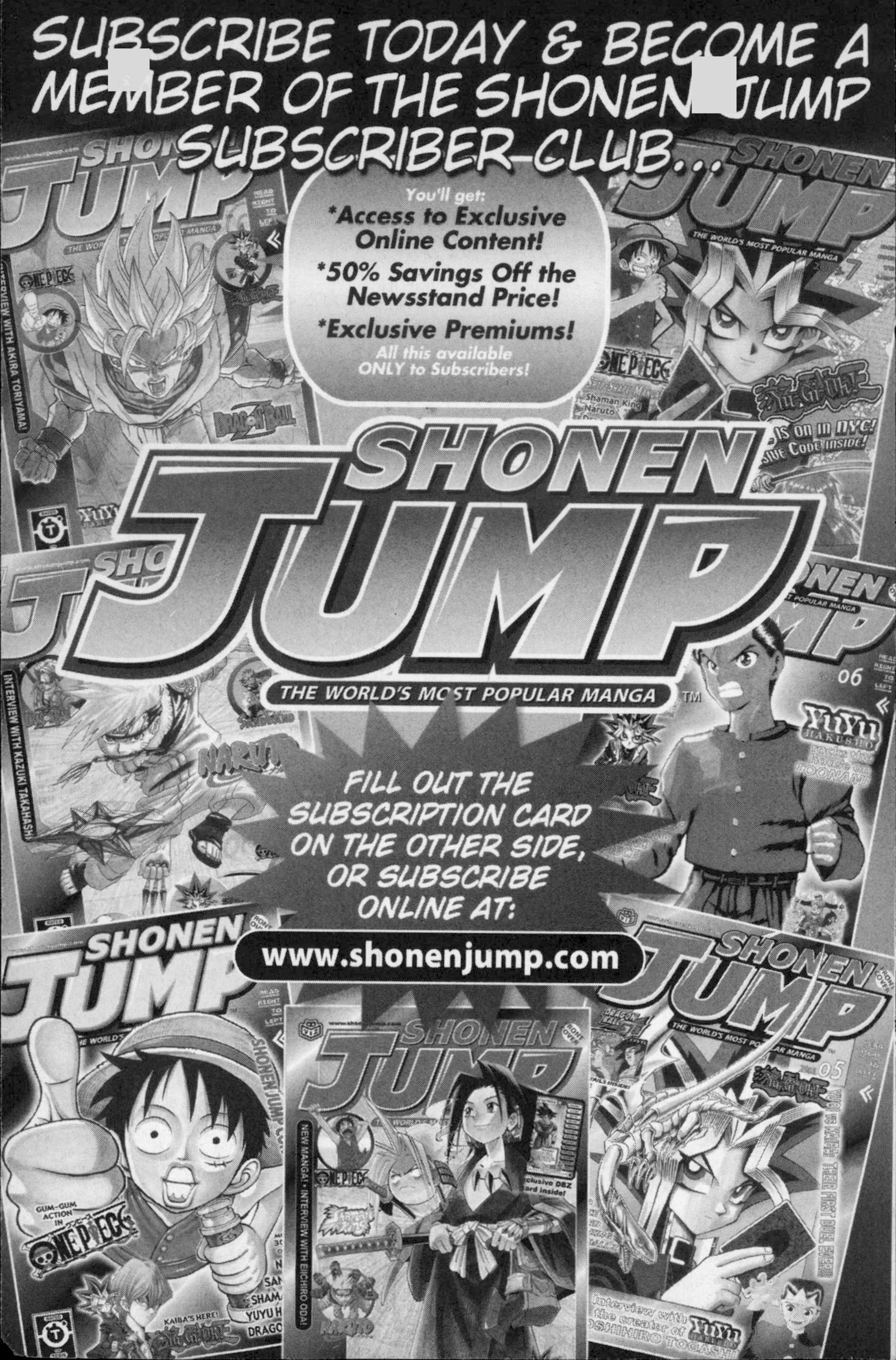
SUBSCRIBE TODAY & BECOME A MEMBER OF THE SHONEN JUMP SUBSCRIBER CLUB...
You'll get:
*Access to Exclusive Online Content!
*50% Savings Off the Newsstand Price!
*Exclusive Premiums!
All this available ONLY to Subscribers!
SHONEN JUMP
THE WORLD'S MOST POPULAR MANGA
FILL OUT THE SUBSCRIPTION CARD ON THE OTHER SIDE, OR SUBSCRIBE ONLINE AT:
www.shonenjump.com

Only
$29.95!

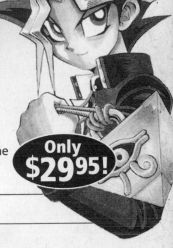